Crisis Stability and Nuclear War

Crisis Stability and Nuclear War

Edited by
Kurt Gottfried and
Bruce G. Blair

New York   Oxford
Oxford University Press
1988

Oxford University Press

Oxford   New York   Toronto
Delhi   Bombay   Calcutta   Madras   Karachi
Petaling Jaya   Singapore   Hong Kong   Tokyo
Nairobi   Dar es Salaam   Cape Town
Melbourne   Auckland

and associated companies in
Berlin   Ibadan

Copyright © 1988 by Oxford University Press, Inc.

Published by Oxford University Press, Inc.,
200 Madison Avenue, New York, New York 10016

Library of Congress Cataloging-in-Publication Data
Crisis stability and nuclear war / edited by Kurt Gottfried and Bruce
G. Blair.
p.   cm.   Bibliography: p.   Includes index.
ISBN 0-19-505146-7 (alk. paper).
ISBN 0-19-505147-5 (pbk.   : alk. paper)
1. Nuclear crisis stability.   I. Gottfried, Kurt.
II. Blair, Bruce G., 1947–   .
U263.C75 1988
355'.0217—dc 19   88-12552   CIP

9 8 7 6 5 4 3 2 1
Printed in the United States of America
on acid-free paper

Authors

Desmond Ball   Australian National University
Hans A. Bethe   Cornell University
Bruce G. Blair   The Brookings Institution
Paul Bracken   Yale University
Ashton B. Carter   Harvard University
Hillman Dickinson   Lieutenant General, U.S. Army (retired)
Richard L. Garwin   IBM Thomas J. Watson Research Center
Kurt Gottfried   Cornell University
David Holloway   Stanford University
Henry W. Kendall   Massachusetts Institute of Technology
Lloyd R. Leavitt, Jr.   Lieutenant General, U.S. Air Force (retired)
Richard Ned Lebow   Cornell University
Condoleezza Rice   Stanford University
Peter C. Stein   Cornell University
John D. Steinbruner   The Brookings Institution
Lucja U. Swiatkowski   The National Institute for Public Policy
Paul C. Tomb   Rear Admiral, U.S. Navy (retired)

Preface

The paths that might lead the superpowers from peacetime through crisis to nuclear war is the subject of this book. The study it summarizes strove, first, to construct a synoptic overview of this terra incognita by interweaving perspectives that draw on historical, military, political, organizational, psychological, and technological knowledge and experience, and second, to put forward concrete policy recommendations that could ameliorate the threats posed by crises involving nuclear-armed powers. These objectives led to the mix of scholars, military officers, and scientists that constitute the authorship of this book.

The study was conceived and initiated by Paul Bracken, Richard L. Garwin, Kurt Gottfried, and Henry W. Kendall. The American Academy of Arts and Sciences and the Cornell University Peace Studies Program offered to be the study's joint sponsors, provided seed support, and appointed Gottfried as project director and Garwin as associate director. Subsequently, the informal steering committee was joined by Bruce G. Blair and Richard Ned Lebow.

The authors first met for a week in June 1985 at the Academy's House in Cambridge, Massachusetts. They held a two-week workshop at Cornell the following August, and met for several days at the Academy in March 1986. In addition, through interviews and meetings, the authors were exposed to insights of individuals who had held positions of high responsibility in the U.S. government, and of persons with expertise complementary to that of the study's membership. In that connection, and on behalf of our co-authors, we gratefully acknowledge invaluable briefings from and conversations with President Jimmy Carter, McGeorge Bundy, Jonathan Dean, Noel Gayler, Irving Janis, Stephen M. Meyer, Scott D. Sagan, Brent Scowcroft, Walter Slocombe, Stansfield Turner, and Edward Warner. Furthermore, we convey our very special thanks for extensive discussions, wide-ranging advice, and generous help to Theodore Jarvis, Jr., Robert S. McNamara, William Y. Smith, and Charles A. Zraket. A condensed version of the manuscript was subjected to penetrating and constructive critiques by Spurgeon M. Keeny, Jr., and George Rathjens.

From its very inception this project had the enthusiastic support of Franklin A. Long, as well as the benefit of his sage advice and broad experience. In conducting our work, we have had the dedicated help of a group of talented research associates: Jeffrey Boutwell, Arthur Charo, Lori Esposito, Matthew Evangelista, Herbert Lin, Lisa Mages, and Peter Trubowitz. Much of the administrative responsibility was ably and diligently discharged by David Cohen, who also assisted extensively in research and drafting. Judith Reppy gave us generous advice and help in numerous ways. Ellen Culver provided secretarial support during the early phases of the study; Christine Hammon and John Oakley helped extensively with the preparation of the manuscript; and Steven Bedney, Jacqueline E. Hartt, and Jeffrey W. House at Oxford University Press greatly facilitated its publication. Throughout this long endeavor, we the editors have relied heavily on the advice and support of Sorel Gottfried and Monica M. Yin.

This study was funded by major grants from the Carnegie Corporation of New York and the Ford Foundation; additional support was provided by the John D. and Catherine T. MacArthur Foundation. A condensed version of this book, published and distributed in 1987, was made possible by a grant from the William and Flora Hewlett Foundation. We gratefully acknowledge all of this generous support.

The opinions expressed herein do not represent the position of the American Academy of Arts and Science, Cornell University, the funding organizations, or the reviewers. The undersigned, as editors, assume full responsibility for the contents of this book in their entirety. Our co-authors, while not necessarily supporting every detail, have expressed general agreement with the volume's substance and conclusions, and with its recommendations, except for the dissent on p. 315.

Ithaca NY   K.G.
Washington DC   B.G.B.
May 1988

Contents

Crisis Stability and Nuclear War

1
Introduction

Perhaps once in a generation, some chain of purposeful or inadvertent events could bring the United States and the Soviet Union within sight of war. As that danger mounted, each would feel compelled to enhance its combat readiness. Modern intelligence would quickly reveal those measures to the other, and thereby amplify its urge toward yet greater readiness. Such a process, stoked by misperceptions, malevolence, human frailty, and political turmoil, could produce a level of threat unlike any we have ever seen and ignite an armed conflict between the superpowers. While it is unlikely that nuclear weapons would be used initially, existing strategies and military postures imply that the risk of escalation to nuclear war would then be high. These dangers are the focus of this book.

The role that crisis could play as the precursor to a nuclear catastrophe impels us to analyze the nature of crisis, to identify major weaknesses in our means for coping with and containing crisis, and to suggest steps for strengthening those means. By contrast, the shape and size of the nuclear arsenals have dominated public debate, the decisions of governments, and arms control negotiations. If the risk of nuclear war is to be reduced, however, far more attention must also be paid to the ability of governments to stay in control of events in a crisis.

Whether or not such control could be maintained would depend on a multitude of factors; some are tangible and even quantifiable, such as the capabilities of technical intelligence or of military forces, while others, though intangible, may also be amenable to systematic assessment, such as the soundness of the policies that the confrontation would put to the test. But there will always be critical factors that defy prior analysis, especially the competence and idiosyncrasies of the leaders that happen to be in power, and how they will fare in the struggle of knowledge and understanding against

3

ignorance and misconception. The manner in which all of these ingredients would interact as events unfold would depend on the peculiarities of a crisis. An appreciation, therefore, of what governments, and their citizens, would face in crisis can only emerge from a synthesis of historical, military, political, organizational, psychological, and technical perspectives.

Human decisions, whether by intent or omission, create crises, and wars. Ultimate authority and responsibility for such decisions—for command—is held by civilian leaders in both superpowers despite the profound political differences between their two systems. To exercise that command, both states have vast diplomatic, military, and intelligence organizations—personnel, machines, and procedures that gather, analyze, and interpret information; reach and transmit decisions; and execute orders. The term for the military portion of this system is *command, control, communications, and intelligence,* or *C³I,* but we shall usually refer to it simply as *command.* Often, we draw no line between its military and civilian components, or its inanimate and human elements. While examining these facets of command, we frequently exploit history to illustrate that, in crisis, command must contend with forces and circumstances over which it holds an uncertain sway.

We have already used the term *crisis* repeatedly. But this is a word whose meaning has been transformed by the advent of nuclear-armed missiles that can destroy a distant opponent's heartland on demand. Today any conflict that had not yet engaged these strategic forces, even one in which tactical nuclear weapons had been used in support of conventional forces, would bear some resemblance to an intense but nonviolent pre-Hiroshima crisis because the transition to "total war" would still hang in the balance. Indeed, deterrence of strategic war is expected to be the supreme objective of both superpowers in the foreseeable future. In light of these remarks, the term *crisis stability* will be taken to mean the likelihood that governments, while pursuing conflicting policies that have enmeshed them in crisis, can reach accommodations that prevent the outbreak of armed conflict or, failing that, can avert escalation to strategic nuclear war.

There is widespread belief that strategic war is a remote contingency in comparison to lower-level confrontations between the United States and the Soviet Union. Even if that is granted, the capability to wage strategic war would loom as an ominous backdrop to any superpower crisis. In view of these perceptions, this book is divided into two parts: the strategic setting and crisis phenomena.

That the nuclear strategic setting has no historic precedent is known to everyone. Nevertheless, our image of incipient conflict continues to be shaped by the traumatic events that set off this century's two world wars: July 1914—the crisis nonpareil, and the surprise attacks by Germany on the Soviet Union and by Japan on Pearl Harbor in 1941. Furthermore, as we shall see, the catastrophes of 1941 have not only left a psychological imprint, but have also had a profound influence on the evolution of both superpowers' nuclear forces, command organizations, and intelligence services; both have devoted prodigious efforts to acquiring the means for prompt warning of attack and for swift and devastating retaliation. Although strategic war per se is beyond the scope of this book, the relative significance of various military options at the threshold of strategic war are of vital importance to crisis stability. We examine these options from a U.S. perspective and assess the vulnerability of the U.S. command system to strategic attack, describe the U.S. command-and-control improvement program as presently planned and put forward suggestions for further improvements to the strategic command system. We then turn to the Soviet Union's military doctrine, and to its strategic forces and their command.

As we shall see, the destructive capabilities of the strategic forces, their combat readiness, and the vulnerability of the forces and their commands to attack, combine to severely constrain the military options should deterrence of strategic war fail. These "objective" factors, and statements by the U.S. and Soviet governments, shall lead us to the following conclusion:

- A preemptive attack that seeks to destroy an opponent's strategic capabilities, or to "decapitate" its government, is not a rational strategy for either side under essentially all circumstances. Nevertheless, one cannot establish that preemption has been abandoned as a possible Soviet option.
- As for retaliation, both sides place considerable reliance on counterattacks that would launch intercontinental ballistic missiles (ICBMs) *while* the original attack is in progress, despite the many daunting drawbacks that such a strategy entails. The likelihood that, under present circumstances, command would collapse in the wake of a major attack, and that forces would suffer severe attrition, leads to this forbidding conclusion.
- Circumstances could thus arise in which the time available for decisions of unprecedented gravity would be reduced to the vanishing point and render the prospects for control ephemeral.

The second part of this book is devoted to the core of our subject—crisis behavior and phenomena at levels of conflict ranging from peacetime posturing to warfare that does *not* involve the strategic nuclear forces. Our fortunate ignorance about war between nuclear-armed states compels the analysis of such crises to be couched largely in abstractions. To provide a closer link between experience and what the future might hold than 1914 or 1941 can offer, we shall discuss four important post-Hiroshima crises: the Berlin Blockade of 1948, the outbreak of the Korean War and China's intervention, the Cuban Missile Crisis, and the Yom Kippur Crisis of 1973. These crises of the nuclear age, and the events of 1914 and 1941, illustrate dilemmas that chronically rear their heads when war threatens. In particular,

- Intelligence regarding an adversary's military measures is often sound, but the political intentions that impel them are usually difficult to decipher.
- Prudent preparations based on a pessimistic estimate of the adversary's

intent can be misread as preparations for attack, and provoke a preemptive strike; yet failure to take such precautions may also invite attack.

- Military organizations are so vast and complex that plans and operations must be prepared and exercised over long periods on the basis of assumed contingencies; should events fail to conform with those assumptions, the degree to which those plans can be promptly modified may be inadequate.
- An aggressive action taken because of an opponent's apparent intention not to resist may shatter his basic policy assumptions and cause him to resist.

The unique characteristics of the various geopolitical arenas in which crises are likely to occur are also central to an understanding of crisis and stability. In the European theater, the strategies, command structures, and forces of the North Atlantic Treaty Organization (NATO) and the Warsaw Pact, are interrelated, and we pay particular attention to the increasingly ominous alert postures that both sides could mount as a crisis intensifies. In the Middle East, we place special emphasis on the confrontation between Syria and Israel, and the dangers posed by locally owned chemical and nuclear weapons. In Europe the likelihood that a serious crisis will erupt is small, but once started it is inherently more dangerous than elsewhere because of the vital interest at stake and the close proximity of very large superpower forces. In contrast, the risk of crisis outbreak is relatively high in the Middle East, but prospects for containment are rather better than in Europe. The Middle East also offers the warning that wars involving minor nuclear powers allied to the superpowers may carry even greater risks to global security than direct confrontation between them. The international effort to impede nuclear proliferation should, therefore, be pursued with the utmost vigor.

The oceans and space merit separate treatment and special attention. Although hostile encounters at sea or in space are isolated from populations, and may appear to be relatively benign, these global arenas are actually a medium in which a crisis could quickly spread outward from a localized terrestrial origin. In peacetime the superpower navies, carrying many thousands of tactical nuclear weapons, are in continuous contact over widely dispersed regions, and perform reconnaissance in highly sensitive areas. The distinction between nuclear and conventional forces is especially murky under the sea. Naval activities during a crisis could therefore spread the confrontation and trigger escalation. In space, growing antisatellite capabilities could turn that arena into a medium for exceptionally swift crisis propagation and escalation. Once deployed, such weapons could even initiate a crisis.

There are also generic features in the flow of events that might carry a superpower crisis to armed conflict and onward to nuclear war. These include the enigmas that have faced decision makers in past crises—the assessment of a breaking crisis; domestic and alliance politics; the interpretation of intelligence; and the dilemmas posed by choices between diplomatic and military initiatives. To avert escalation to armed combat, the superpowers appear to have developed a tacit code of conduct in crisis. A breakdown of that code could initiate an interlocking sequence of escalating alerts, possibly stimulate public unrest and panic, and, as the crisis grows in complexity, force national leaders to restrict their attention to a shrinking subset of potentially crucial issues. Such dangers are especially acute in Europe, where a crisis could reach the intensity of imminent war in a matter of days.

Despite the many factors that could lead to a loss of political control, it is our view that conventional war would, in all likelihood, begin as a conscious act of national policy. Nevertheless, that act could be the final step in an inexorable chain of events created by rising combat readiness and a mounting fear of war. Or in an intense crisis, precipitous overreactions to acts of ambiguous origin or intent could lead to severe lapses of control. In a deeper sense, such paths would have led to conventional war by inadvertence. Once large-scale conventional combat begins, serious damage to the command systems of both sides should be expected to ensue, and that would erode their ability to exercise control. Should contingent authority to use tactical nuclear weapons have been granted to compensate for inadequate command endurance, nuclear escalation might then be inadvertently triggered through legitimate actions by local commanders on land or at sea. In Europe, further escalation to theater-range and intercontinental nuclear war could occur if the Soviets would adhere to their doctrine of swift escalation (or even preemption) should NATO use (or appear to be readying) its tactical nuclear forces, and on whether the United States or its allies launched nuclear attacks on targets in the Soviet Union.

That, in a nutshell, is the situation today. Despite the prodigious dangers to which we have alluded, and in some unknown measure because of them, there has been no serious crisis between the United States and the Soviet Union since the Cuban Missile Crisis in 1962, nor have hostilities ever broken out in any of their direct confrontations. This fortunate record has led some to the belief that the there exists a craft called crisis management, and that the superpowers have mastered it. We do not share this view. Indeed, we would attach a warning label to our product:

As the gravity of a crisis increases, past experience becomes progressively less relevant, comprehension of events more problematic, stress and fatigue on men, machines, organizations, and societies more severe, and control correspondingly less firm. Crisis "management," though indispensible, can only cope with crisis. The Cuban Missile Crisis, and other successfully "managed" crises, have been tame confrontations in that they only involved marginal interactions between the superpowers' armed forces. It would be reckless to assume that those experiences imply that crises are manageable to the degree of confidence required by the existence of nuclear weapons. Prudence unambiguously dictates that avoidance and deterrence of crisis by sound diplomacy combined with a robust though unprovocative defense posture is the first and foremost priority.

I
THE STRATEGIC SETTING

2

A Bird's-Eye View

STRATEGIC WAR: THEN AND NOW

One-hundred and fifty-six years separate the French Revolution from the atomic bombing of Hiroshima. During that time the spread of the Industrial Revolution and the evolution of the modern state allowed many nations to field vast armies equipped with the latest inventions in armaments, transport, and communications. Nevertheless, while the firepower and mobility of armed forces grew enormously between 1789 and 1945, the time required for a campaign with profound strategic objectives against a large territorial power did not change: whether it was Napoleon or Hitler who sought to defeat Russia, it was measured in months. Chemical explosives simply could not be delivered at a rate that could destroy more than a small fraction of a strong nation's resources in a shorter period. Even when long-range aircraft freed strategic warfare from the march of men, that time scale did not change, as the years of intensive bombing of Germany and Japan in World War II demonstrated.

In the 16 years following Hiroshima several interdependent technological revolutions transformed the meaning of the term *strategic warfare*. First came nuclear explosives that could destroy an essentially unlimited set of unprotected targets in one blow. That was followed by missiles that, in half an hour, could carry such explosives over the distance separating Wyoming from the Urals—a feat they can now perform with an accuracy that threatens even the most prodigiously reinforced target. Satellites carrying sophisticated sensors arrived at the same time. They now give an almost "real-time" pic-

This chapter has two purposes. First, it offers a shortcut to our discussion of crisis stability in Part II; second, it provides an overview of our findings regarding the strategic setting which will be examined in detail in Chapters 3–7.

ture of an adversary's military preparations of a quality that could not have been matched by World War II intelligence even if thousands of enemy officers had been spies. Such a flood of data could not have been assembled and digested without the electronic computer, which appeared during this same postwar period, and without which the other new technologies could not exist.

As a result, what a Napoleon or Hitler could not accomplish in many months could now, in principle, be done by one blow in less than an hour. But unless such a first strike were to "decapitate" the victim's command or to disarm him, he could, even if mortally wounded, retaliate with a counterblow that could devastate the attacker. Hence the strategic forces are so powerful, so swift, but also so crude, that their massive use would contravene von Clausewitz's dictum that "war is nothing but the continuation of politics by other means."

ARE THERE VALID LESSONS FROM PRENUCLEAR WARS?

Two devastating wars have been fought in this century. The ways in which they started have continued to haunt military and political leaders.

July 1914 revealed that the military forces, organizations, and plans that European powers had perfected during the course of the previous century could take on a life of their own and unleash events that could not be controlled. Many fear that July 1914 might be a paradigm for the first nuclear war because some of the imperatives and conundrums that led to war then are inherent to major armed confrontation.

Because the traumatic experiences of World War II are fresher in our collective memory, they may retain greater psychological relevance, even though they are widely regarded as being less germane to current circumstances. The United States and Soviet Union both entered the war as victims of highly effective surprise attacks. Pearl Harbor, although a debacle, was of relatively little strategic significance compared to the German invasion of Russia on June 22, 1941. Japan knew that the destruction of the Pacific Fleet could not eliminate America as a Pacific power, but she hoped that it would break America's will to wage the war that would be required to maintain the United States' prior strategic position. Hitler was more ambitious; he set out to eradicate the Soviet Union. Both Washington and Moscow had ample warning that war was likely, but neither was ready when the blow fell. The Pearl Harbor debacle itself was readily avoidable because nothing would have been risked had the fleet left port. Stalin faced a more trying predicament; he feared that by alerting Soviet forces he would provoke a war that he was not yet prepared to fight—a miscalculation that nearly allowed Hitler to gain his objective. It is understandable, therefore, why both superpowers fear surprise attack. The Soviet military, in particular, has devoted much attention to plans for averting a disaster like June 22, 1941, for among other things, the

German attack produced a catastrophic disruption of the entire Soviet command system.

Care must be taken not to draw misleading inferences from these pre-Hiroshima experiences. Nuclear weapons have created a context that is profoundly new. In 1914 all the continental powers harbored at least some influential elements that wanted war, millions were enthralled by romantic images of combat, and Germany had been prepared to go to war for some time should political circumstances become propitious. In World War II, Germany, and to a lesser degree Japan, had rulers that were willing to run the most egregious risks. Today, leaders on both sides, and virtually all segments of every society, understand that strategic conflict would be a disaster—anyone with romantic visions of nuclear skirmishing would be judged insane.

While nuclear explosives have quelled adventurism, modern technology has created a decision-making environment that could become extremely volatile. The interlocking and inexorable military plans that propelled the July 1914 crisis to disaster had a tempo that was glacial in comparison to the speed with which today's forces can be readied and used, and modern surveillance quickly reveals when an adversary embarks on military operations. Hence there is likely to be intense pressure to respond to an opponent's alert by an immediate increase in one's own military readiness.

Today's risk calculus is thus fundamentally new. The benefit of strategic surprise, which once reigned supreme, pales before the benefit of averting strategic nuclear war—unless there was certainty that such a war was unavoidable, as well as an expectation that damage to oneself could be significantly reduced by attacking first. Nevertheless, large-scale retaliation is the almost certain response to any attack, even one that, through surprise, had destroyed the apex of the victim's command. All of this compels caution. On the other hand, the speed with which the risks would have to be weighed might readily outstrip the abilities of any leadership group, and thereby lead to chaos.

THE EVOLUTION OF NUCLEAR FORCES

The growth of nucler forces has had three reasonably distinct phases: the early postwar years preceding the outbreak of the Korean War in 1950; from there to the mid-1960s; and the last two decades.

During the immediate postwar period, U.S. nuclear forces grew very slowly. In 1948, at the time of the first serious East–West confrontation in Berlin, the United States had 50 unassembled Nagasaki-type fission weapons that could only be carried by bombers based in New Mexico. The Berlin Blockade and the first Soviet fission bomb test in 1949 spurred the Truman administration to a number of seminal decisions, including the effort to develop a thermonuclear (hydrogen) bomb, the expansion of the stockpile of fission weapons, and the growth of the Strategic Air Command (SAC) for delivery of these weapons from bases that surrounded the Soviet Union.

Stalin had become aware of the potential significance of nuclear weapons as early as 1942, and committed appreciable resources to their development while the Nazis still held vast stretches of Russian territory.[1] The destruction of Hiroshima in 1945, which was perceived by the Kremlin as an implicit threat, stimulated a great expansion of the Soviet effort to develop nuclear weapons and long-range rockets. The Soviets had also begun work on thermonuclear weapons before the first American H-bomb test.

The invasion of South Korea by the communist North in 1950 brought Western apprehension concerning Soviet intentions to a head. In the following decade the Truman and Eisenhower administrations stationed thousands of tactical nuclear weapons in Europe, greatly expanded the SAC long-range bomber fleet until it numbered well over 2,000 in the late 1950s, and developed missiles of intercontinental range to be based on both land and on nuclear-powered submarines. In the 1960s silo-based Minutemen ICBMs and submarine-based Polaris submarine launched ballistic missles (SLBMs) were deployed in large numbers, while the bomber fleet was greatly reduced. The Soviets, on the other hand, did not invest heavily in long-range bombers until very recently, and went instead directly to land-based ballistic missiles, which were followed much later by a far-less capable fleet of ballistic missile submarines.

These features are still visible in today's strategic nuclear forces because they reflect certain deep geographic and political differences:

- The United States has commitments to its NATO allies that are difficult to meet with purely conventional forces since Western Europe occupies only one fringe of the Eurasian landmass controlled by the large armies of the Soviet Union and its satellites.
- The United States has long been a global power, with heavy reliance on sea lanes, ready access to the oceans, and air bases on several continents, while the Soviet Union is a continental power with limited access to the oceans—to blue water.
- The Soviets place much greater emphasis on continuous centralized control, which is relatively easy with groundbased forces, more difficult with bombers far afield, and tenuous with submarines that hide by never sending or acknowledging messages.

Force developments in the last two decades have been dominated by two features: the Soviets' attainment of strategic parity and the ceaseless refinement of weapons. Accuracy has reached the point where a few ballistic missile warheads can destroy virtually any single fixed target; multiple independently targeted reentry vehicles, (MIRVs) now allow one missile to threaten a set of targets with simultaneous destruction; to evade accurate targeting, mobile ICBMs are being deployed by the Soviet Union and developed by the United States; and cruise missiles, with an accuracy independent of range, and which

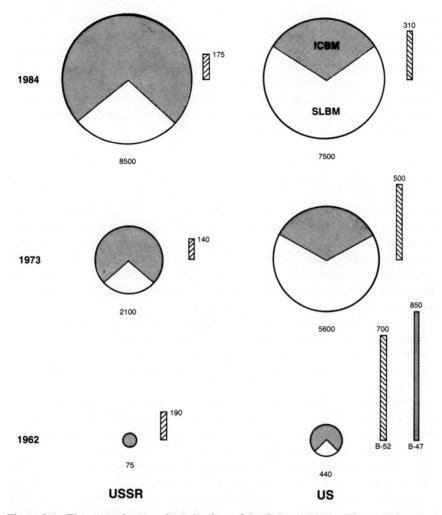

Figure 2.1. The strategic arsenals at the time of the Cuba and Yom Kippur Crises, and in 1985. Ballistic missile warheads (reentry vehicles, RVs) are shown as pie charts whose areas are proportional to the total numbers indicated. The bar charts show strategic aircraft, not the number of warheads they carry, because there are serious disagreements concerning Soviet bomb loadings in the literature.[2] This depiction conceals some important features: on average, Soviet ICBM RVs have much larger yields; the portion of the submarine fleets on alert at sea is much greater for the United States; both the readiness and armament (in particular, long-range highly accurate cruise missiles) of U.S. bombers are significantly better.

fly below radar surveillance, are being deployed on land, at sea, and on aircraft.

Another significant trend, impelled by the fear of surprise attack, is the steady increase in the portion of forces always ready for immediate use. But this urge to protect against surprise has also enhanced the ability to surprise.

The United States was the first to attain a high degree of strategic readiness—by the late 1950s SAC bombers could take off to evade attack and receive their orders en route; the subsequent deployment of the Minuteman force greatly increased peacetime readiness. The Soviets took longer to develop missiles that could be launched on short notice, but they too have had thousands of strategic warheads ready for launch on command for many years, and today the peacetime readiness of the two sides' strategic forces is quite comparable.

THE APEX OF COMMAND

By the mid-1960s the United States had acquired all of the essential human, procedural, and technical components of today's strategic command system. At its apex stands the National Command Authority (NCA), consisting of the president as commander-in-chief and the secretary of defense, or their duly constituted successors. The NCA is itself connected to the commanders of the nuclear forces by a highly streamlined chain-of-command. Only the NCA can authorize the firing of nuclear weapons.

Two legal mechanisms are available for the continuity of legitimate government under the most dire of circumstances. The first, *devolution,* is codified by a 1947 act of Congress that defines a sequence of successors should the president be killed or incapacitated. The second is called *predelegation.* It is the president's right to delegate authority, in this instance his command over nuclear forces in contingencies that cannot be fully anticipated, such as his death or his inability to communicate, so as to provide insurance against any attempt to decapitate the nation's body politic. Whether or not any president has made arrangements for predelegation is unknown.

Little is known about the upper reaches of the Soviet command structure, but some significant features are evident. The Soviet Union attaches great importance to the primacy of political control, even in wartime. This attitude is visible in Soviet military exercises, and was at one time reflected in an arrangement whereby the KGB had custody of nuclear warheads and kept them separate from the means of delivery. It is believed that the KGB continues to hold an essential role in the command and control of nuclear forces.

Most experts agree that in wartime the Soviet command organization would resemble the Soviet command of World War II. The peactime Defense Council, headed by the general secretary of the Communist Party, would become the State Committee on Defense (GKO), and would provide centralized direction of the entire war effort. The main command authority, however, including that over strategic forces, would rest with the *Stavka* (General Headquarters) of the Supreme High Command. This body would consist of a small group of the most senior military leaders, and be chaired by the general secretary in his capacity as supreme commander-in-chief of the armed forces. The General Staff would serve as the executive agent and operational staff of the *Stavka.* Although nothing is known about Soviet arrangements for assuring the continuity of government, arrangements akin to predelegation presumably exist.

The measures that each state has taken to protect its upper levels of command against nuclear attack display systematic differences that reflect their very different political cultures.

In peacetime, the U.S. leadership issues orders from the Pentagon to commanders stationed in vulnerable headquarters. The NCA and all major combat commands have alternate airborne command posts. The SAC airborne command post is always on station with a battle staff, while those of other major commands stand ready for takeoff on short notice. SAC's airborne system can send orders to Minuteman launch control centers, to bombers in flight, and to submerged submarines, and it can also fire Minutemen directly should the launch control centers be destroyed. Unarmed Minutemen that can broadcast orders to the strategic forces while in flight are one backup for the alternate airborne system.

While our understanding of the Soviet command infrastructure is fragmentary, it is known that the Soviets have constructed a large number of hardened command centers; some 75, of widely varying hardness, are in the capital. An antiballistic missile (ABM) installation, as well as extensive air defense, cover the Moscow region. More than 1,500 hardened shelters for well over 100,000 military personnel and civilian officials are scattered across the Soviet Union. In addition to its fixed wartime command centers, the Soviet military has alternate command posts on trains, trucks, and aircraft, but the latter have capabilities markedly inferior to the U.S. airborne command system.

In short, the Soviet Union has sought to protect its wartime command by constructing a redundant and robust physical system, but it appears to be reluctant to rely on human redundancy. In contrast, the United States has emphasized mobility and human redundancy. It has made no effort to protect an entire upper layer of government against direct nuclear attack—perhaps a reflection of confidence in the continuity of its political institutions despite frequent replacements of that layer. In particular, it is widely believed that the president would stay in the White House even if the threat of attack were high because knowledge of his evacuation, which might be difficult to conceal, could have grave repercussions at home and abroad. The whereabouts of the Kremlin leadership, on the other hand, are rarely known, especially to the Soviet public, so the leadership's evacuation in a crisis would run relatively few risks.

WARNING

Attack warning can come in differing forms and at various times. *Strategic warning* is the analysis of intelligence data from any and all sources leading to a determination that an attack will come, while *tactical warning* is the determination that an attack is actually underway. It is generally agreed that despite the prodigious technical advances in the ability to gather intelligence data, its political interpretation has remained what it always was: more an art than a science, with a record so mixed as to instill caution. Furthermore, the United States, on many occasions, has been unwilling to act on strategic warning.

The superpowers do not have identical attitudes toward warning. While these differences reflect their technical capabilities and their differing ability to peer into their opponent's doings, they also have historical and cultural roots. The Soviet Union appears to place greater emphasis on strategic, as opposed to tactical, warning than does the United States, although both nations assiduously seek to strengthen their ability to discern indications that contribute to warning of both kinds. To that end, both superpowers have made enormous investments in facilities for intercepting electronic messages, and for extracting information from that traffic. These signals intelligence organizations, in conjunction with satellite observations and human sources, share the mission of providing both tactical and strategic warning; however, the high state of readiness of strategic forces, even in peacetime, implies that the victim of a strategic attack might *not* have conclusive strategic warning.

Tactical warning of a missile attack on the United States would come from early warning satellites that can see rocket plumes shortly after launch from any point in the Soviet Union and from virtually all ocean areas. Approximately 10 minutes after the first warning, ground-based early warning radars surrounding the United States would detect warheads from ICBMs. In proper operation, the combination of these two sensing systems would provide independent, and therefore unambiguous, warning of an attack. It would not, however, provide an accurate picture of the size of the attack or of the intended targets. Soviet early warning and attack assessment are generally regarded as inferior to those of the United States. The Soviet Union has encountered persistent difficulties with its early warning satellites, and its radar network, although very extensive and growing, does not yet provide as good a coverage of potential ICBM and SLBM launch points as does the U.S. system. Like the United States, the Soviet Union would certainly ascertain that it was coming under attack, but it would have an even poorer understanding of the nature of the attack, with the exception, perhaps, of its magnitude.

STRATEGIC ALERTS

Changes in military readiness can have grave repercussions. The United States has long had a centrally coordinated alerting procedure, covering all nuclear and conventional forces, that seeks to ensure that changes in readiness will be coherent and deliberate acts of national policy taken in the light of prevailing political and military circumstances. It consists of five different alert levels, or defense conditions (DEFCONs), ranging from peacetime (DEFCON 5) to deployment for imminent combat (DEFCON 1). The system has a considerable degree of flexibility and allows the alert level to be tailored to local conditions; commanders may alter their own alert level, but they must notify their superiors should they do so. Finally, to provide for control over nuclear weapons in crisis and war, all U.S. nuclear weapons, except those at sea, can only be armed by a coded message received from higher authority.

Little is known about Soviet strategic alert procedures. Whereas the United States did raise the alert level of its strategic forces during the Cuban Missile Crisis of 1962 and the Middle East Crisis of 1973, the Soviet Union did not respond in kind in either case, nor, to our knowledge, has it held large-scale strategic alerts at any other time.

COMMAND VULNERABILITY

Soviet missile submarines near U.S. shores pose a grave threat to U.S. command, especially if the system is at its peacetime posture. In an attack in which land- and submarine-based missiles were launched simultaneously, warheads from SLBMs could impact Washington before radars had confirmed ICBM launches. Even before that, SLBM warheads could be detonated at high altitude in an effort to disrupt radio communications over wide areas. Severe requirements on the warning and decision elements of command stem from the SLBM threat to the command system. Indeed, rough estimates indicate that as few as several tens of deliberately targeted nuclear explosions might severely damage the current U.S. strategic command system at its peacetime alert level, possibly to an extent that could preclude coordinated retaliation. Were the system fully alerted, perhaps ten times as many weapons might be required for the same mission. Such an attack could not be "surgical"; it would result in widespread collateral damage to the United States.

The apex of Soviet command is rather less vulnerable to surprise attack. Moscow is further than Washington from the nearest potential missile launch points (submarines in the North Atlantic, and until the INF Treaty is in force, Pershing II missiles based in Germany). Furthermore, hard command posts exist in Moscow itself, so that a strike that sought to destroy the Soviet leadership, or to isolate it from its forces, would be virtually indistinguishable from an attack aimed at the destruction of Soviet society. Serious degradation of Soviet command would probably result even from more limited attacks. In particular, Soviet long-range communications, although very redundant, have significant vulnerabilities. But the most serious vulnerabiity of the Soviet command system is probably the emphasis on tight central control that characterizes all Soviet organizations.

The vulnerabilities of U.S. command should be appraised in the light of statements by senior spokesmen for all recent administrations that emphasize that arrangements are in place that would guarantee large-scale retaliation under all circumstances. Soviet spokesmen have also warned against attempts at decapitation and alluded to preparations for such a contingency.

STRATEGIC WAR PLANS

Weapons are impotent without an organization that can decide whether, when, and how they are to be employed. Those decisions can only be a selection from among a set of detailed plans that have already been incorporated into lengthy military training programs. Those plans, in turn, are based on military training programs. Those plans, in turn, are based on military doctrine—basic premises and objectives agreed to by the highest authorities.

War plans for all U.S. strategic forces, most notably the Single Integrated Operational Plan (SIOP), are prepared under guidelines set by the president, the National Security Council (NSC), the secretary of defense, and the Joint Chiefs of Staff (JCS). That ongoing task is carried out by an interservice staff under the SAC commander. These plans include a large number of options that range from small strikes against a highly restricted target set to massive attacks against a very comprehensive set of targets.

This wide choice, and terms such as *flexible response,* should not be taken to imply that combinations of options can readily be improvised to meet unforeseen contingencies, or that operational plans for strategic attacks can be modified in mid-stream. Once the decision is taken to exercise a particular SIOP option, the selected actions must run their course to the extent that enemy action permits.

CURRENT STRATEGIC OPTIONS

Deterrence of nuclear war is expected to remain the supreme military objective of both superpowers into the foreseeable future. Nevertheless, the possibility that deterrence might fail must be addressed. This raises the question of what the most likely military options would be at the brink of strategic nuclear war.

It has long been a U.S. objective to have the capacity to retaliate against any strategic assault on the basis of proper political and military attack assessment. But the vulnerabilities of the current command system imply that it is likely to be severely degraded, if not to have collapsed, in the wake of a major nuclear attack. The United States, therefore, must depend heavily on strategies that can use the command system while it is still substantially intact and before accurate attack assessment would be in hand. Given the limited endurance of command, forces withheld could no longer be used in a coordinated fashion. In consequence, U.S. retaliation to a major attack would be organized around a large SIOP option involving thousands of warheads. Responses that call for *escalation control,*—carefully calibrated retaliatory strikes following full attack assessment—are well beyond the capabilities of the U.S. command system, unless the Soviet attack were small and unambiguously structured to spare that system. Even with the command improvements now underway, escalation control would continue to depend on voluntary Soviet restraint.

In stark contrast to retaliation subsequent to a major attack is the option of a large preemptive strike in anticipation of such an attack. But as we have argued, with the arsenals now deployed the advantage of surprise is overshadowed by other considerations. Preemption would forfeit any chance that the catastrophe could be avoided because strategic warning could be erroneous, or the attack order might yet be revoked. Massive retaliation seems inevitable if either side preempts; in particular, both sides should recognize that a large preemptive attack is likely to trigger a prompt and massive launch by their adversary, thereby making a large-scale preemption an irrational option for either superpower.

Rationality, however, does not always prevail in human affairs. In particular, military writings and statements by senior Soviet officers have occasionally indicated that preemption based on strategic warning of a U.S. attack is a distinct possibility, and they have advocated such a posture in the light of June 22, 1941. But such statements were most prevalent in the era when the United States held overwhelming strategic superiority. At that time the Soviets could not have ridden out an attack, nor could their forces have been quickly readied for launch, which made preemption their only viable option. Claims that nuclear weapons had not revolutionized warfare, presumably intended to bolster morale, also appeared during that period.

Since the advent of strategic parity Soviet statements have become progressively more circumspect. The destructiveness of nuclear war has been emphasized both by political leaders and by senior military officers. Furthermore, Soviet forces are now at a much higher level of peacetime alert, possess improved if still inadequate early warning, and should be assumed to have a prompt launch capability comparable to that of the United States. For whatever reason, there has been a steady shift of emphasis away from preemption in Soviet military statements, which from a U.S. perspective, seems entirely reasonable because the case against preemption would appear to apply with equal force to both sides. Nevertheless, it cannot be established that preemption has been abandoned as a possible Soviet option.

The extreme hazards that attend preemption, and the punishment that would have to be borne if a major assault were to be absorbed before retaliation, imply that *prompt launch*,[3] which refers to counterattacks ranging from a launch *before* there are any enemy nuclear detonations, on the basis of unambiguous tactical warning that a major attack has been initiated, to a retaliatory launch that does not begin until there are such detonations,[4] has become, by default, a serious strategic option for *both* sides. Neither, it should be noted, has made a secret of that fact.

If both sides had full (even if unwarranted) confidence that they could execute a prompt launch, that should at least minimize the pressure to preempt. But prompt launch has many chilling drawbacks:

- The crushing tempo of decision and execution would restrict the political leaderships to an immediate, reflexive choice from among a handful of preselected options.

- The decision would be dependent on a tactical warning system that cannot provide an accurate picture of the attack in the time available.
- Execution would demand a very high level of human performance in an intricate organizational setting under unprecedented stress.
- In the case of the United States, the launch order might have to be formulated and transmitted to the forces in the face of precursor attacks on the command system by off-shore submarines.

To summarize, continuing technical innovation has resulted in two strategic forces whose fixed land-based components are vulnerable. That weakness, however, is overshadowed by the fragility of their command systems. As a result, a confrontation could create circumstances in which the time available to political leaders for decisions of immeasurable gravity could be reduced to the vanishing point.

THE COMMAND-AND-CONTROL IMPROVEMENT PROGRAM

The continuing C³I improvement program is intended to provide the United States with a significantly more capable strategic command system. The program's major objective is a communication network between the NCA and its alternates, the senior nuclear commanders, and the strategic forces, that would be reliable and secure even in the aftermath of a nuclear attack, including nuclear detonations along transmission paths. Contrary to a widespread impression, the program will *not* yield a system that would have the endurance required to conduct a "controlled" nuclear war *unless* the Soviet Union were to voluntarily limit its attacks on the U.S. strategic command system.

The program has the following essential components: the Ground Wave Emergency Network (GWEN), a constellation of Military Strategic and Tactical Relay (MILSTAR) communication satellites, and a variety of ground-mobile systems for command, communications, and read-out of data from early warning satellites, radars, and other sources.

GWEN is to provide for the dissemination of tactical warning, attack assessment, and Emergency Action Messages (EAMs) in the early phases of a nuclear attack, before there are detonations on U.S. soil, when the threat to communications would be from high-altitude bursts of warheads from off-shore submarines, jamming, and sabotage. The network is expected to be operational in 1989 with 127 sites, and will offer greater resistance against electromagnetic pulses (EMPs) generated by high-altitude nuclear detonations than do existing communications; the network is also designed to withstand disruption by sabotage or jamming. It is not intended to survive in the face of deliberate nuclear attack; the 127-site configuration could be disrupted with judicious targeting by some tens of warheads. Only a much larger network could survive deliberate attack.

The high-altitude MILSTAR satellite constellation will provide highly jam-resistant, encrypted, two-way communications for both voice and data even in the physical environment created by nuclear explosions.[5] In addition, MILSTAR will enhance the reliability of links between intelligence sources and users *(intelligence connectivity)*. In conjunction with mobile ground terminals, MILSTAR represents a substantial increment in capability and survivability.

Should antisatellite (ASAT) capabilities continue to evolve, MILSTAR could prove to be vulnerable, whether in the near future to *space mines* (small satellites carrying explosive devices that hound their potential quarry and destroy it on receipt of a radio message), or in the long run to lasers and other directed energy weapons. Verifiable treaties to limit ASAT capabilities can help MILSTAR to survive, but these must be supported with programs that could include increased hardening, evasion, and provisions for defense. With no guarantee that such an augmented program can stay ahead of the ASAT threat, supplementary growth paths must be considered for essential strategic communications.

After the committed improvements are completed in approximately 5 years, the command system should be able to perform its basic intelligence and communications functions up to the level of damage inflicted by a surprise attack of hundreds of nuclear explosions. If the system were at maximum alert before the attack, it should be able to survive a considerably larger attack, and endure for many hours longer than the present system. The primary NCA (in contrast to alternate NCAs) will remain vulnerable to one or a few nuclear explosions. These narrow technical assessments of vulnerability, naturally, do not capture the significance of direct attacks on command.

STABILITY AT THE STRATEGIC THRESHOLD

We have focused on those aspects of strategic warfare that impinge on crisis stability. For that reason we have examined whether a preemptive attack that seeks to destroy the opponent's strategic capability, or to decapitate his government, is a rational option.

We conclude that preemption is not a rational option for either side under essentially all circumstances. First, each side must assume that the other will have sufficient warning to allow it to execute a "prompt launch," that is, to launch on warning or under attack. Second, preemption would forfeit all chances of avoiding the catastrophe of strategic nuclear war. And third, rational planners on both sides should recognize that each government has, and can continue to have, arrangements that are sufficiently robust, secure, and efficacious to make massive retaliation a virtually certain response to any attempt at the destruction of the other's leadership. Nevertheless, one cannot establish that preemption has been abandoned as a possible Soviet option, even though recent Soviet writings and statements reflect recognition of the case against preemption. In particular, Soviet planners might expect that a decapitation attack would degrade retaliation by the United States.

As for retaliation to a strategic attack, prompt launch has become a serious option for both sides despite the many daunting drawbacks that such a strategy entails. The likelihood that, under present circumstances, command would collapse in the wake of a major attack and that forces would suffer severe attrition lead to this forbidding conclusion.

Stability at the brink of strategic nucler war would be enhanced were both superpowers confident that their command systems and forces could ride out an attack. The measures that are necessary to move both nations away from their current hair-trigger postures are clear:

- strengthening of command systems; and
- restructuring of the strategic forces to make them more survivable and less threatening to the adversary's forces, and above all to his command system.

Policies having these objectives would serve the interests of both sides. Measures toward those ends can be taken independently, as the Carter and, especially, the Reagan administrations have demonstrated with the command-and-control improvement program. Our capsule history, however, shows that the independent policies of the superpowers have not produced coherent motion in the desired direction. Strong pressures to enhance offensive capabilities have tended to dominate and have produced a net outcome that has exposed both sides to a growing threat. In the prevailing international climate, a combination of prudent independent policies and negotiated constraints offers the best hope for systematic movement toward greater stability.

NOTES

1. Holloway, pp. 15–20.

2. Current figures are from Collins. For 1962 and 1973, the figures are from the annual compilations of the International Institute of Strategic Studies. The intercontinental B-52s, largely based in the United States, are shown separately from medium range B-47s that were forward based.

3. Prompt launch, which is becoming an accepted part of the strategic lexicon, thus includes launch-on-warning and launch-under-attack.

4. By "ranging from" we allude to the possibility that the magnitude of the attack (as estimated from data provided by tactical warning sensors), and the number of nuclear detonations, could be parameters that determine the timing of launch. For example, detection of ICBM and SLBM launches by satellite-borne infrared sensors, observation of their subsequent flight by ground-based radars, and detonation at high altitude of one precursor RV from an SSBN, might suffice to trigger prompt launch. Whether that is launch-on-warning or launch-under-attack is a question of semantics.

5. The acronym stands for Military Strategic and Tactical Relay Satellite. As the name implies, these satellites are also intended for communications to nonstrategic forces having suitable receivers and transmitters. Current plans call for some 4,000 MILSTAR terminals for all three services.

3

Historical Prologue

The organizations and machines engaged in a severe nuclear crisis would be its tangible and partially quantifiable factors. For that reason they often dominate our thinking about superpower confrontations. Military organizations, however, are not automatons that can run amok on their own. The perceptions of leaders and populations propel the course of events, and their mindsets are shaped by what experience, history, and myth claim to say about war.

Since there has never been combat between nuclear-armed states, it is debatable whether the past has any relevance to what we now face. But the past is all we have to go on. Thus soldiers and statesmen are still haunted by the manner in which this century's two great wars began, and the past thereby influences the thoughts that lead to weapons, to military plans, and to decisions that could turn peace into war. It is therefore essential to have some appreciation for the historical roots that nourish our expectations about international conflict. This chapter describes some of these roots.

The phenomenon of peace shattering swiftly into all-out war is a recent development. Before the nineteenth century states needed lengthy preparations to launch a major campaign on land, and they could only channel a small portion of their manpower and resources into war. The raw material for crisis—readiness for total war on short notice in peacetime—is a child of the Enlightenment and the French Revolution. During the 125 years preceding 1914, the energies that gave birth to the modern state and the Industrial Revolution also created sophisticated military staffs, communications, and transportation so that armies could swell overnight by calling up reserves by the millions and send them quickly into battle. The nation-state thus became perenially ready for war, and in 1914 this vast enterprise gutted a generation.

The events of July 1914 had an intensity, pace and complexity that no other crisis has come close to matching. The July Crisis is widely viewed as being particularly germane to the dangers that we confront, for it revealed that the European powers' military plans could take on a life of their own and bring on a catastrophe that either undermined or liquidated all the adversaries of 1914. Indeed, during the Cuban Missile Crisis, President Kennedy feared that the world could be swept toward nuclear war in a similar torrent of "uncontrollable" events—he and members of his entourage had recently read *The Guns of August,* Barbara Tuchman's celebrated account of the beginnings of the Great War.[1] Many scholars have analyzed July 1914 with an eye to "lessons" for the nuclear age.[2] Some have argued that one or another cause dominated. The relative importance of the various pressures that then propelled the march to war is not really our concern, however, for no future conflagration will be ignited by that same mixture.

Both superpowers entered their last major war as victims of devastating surprise attacks: the German invasion of Russia on June 22, 1941, and the Japanese destruction of the Pacific Fleet in Pearl Harbor the following December 7. These traumatic setbacks influenced the subsequent development of the American and Soviet command systems, intelligence services, forces, and strategies. As one would expect, both states have sought to insure that they would not be caught by surprise again, but by pursuing that objective both have acquired military postures that instill great fear of surprise attack. The events surrounding June 22 and December 7, 1941, therefore, elucidate the origins of some striking features of current military organizations and strategies, and also illustrate in graphic terms some of the generic features of the outset of conflict.

THE CREATION OF PEACETIME READINESS FOR TOTAL WAR

Napoleon is the father of the agressive nation–state, ever ready to project enough force to threaten an unprepared adversary with quick defeat.[3] He achieved this by creating the first command system that allowed vast armies to move efficiently over large distances, and to rapidly initiate and then prosecute coordinated actions over a broad front.[4] His innovation was wholly organizational. The technology at Napoleon's disposal, whether in weapons, transport, or communications, was identical to that of his adversaries.

The key element in Napoleon's military organization was that his *Grand Armee* was divided into identical corps, each an army in miniature with its own general staff and units of all types, so that it could perform any function. This innovation gave the *Grand Armee* its devastating flexibility: the corps, while acting independently on the tactical level, worked in concert toward strategic objectives.

Napoleon's command organization had two complementary features. The first was a structured system for collecting information. A corp's general staff did not only flesh out and execute Napoleon's commands, but it also gathered data regarding its own corp's status and that of the enemy. This information went to Imperial Headquarters, where it was digested and collated with more specialized reports. Although the quill pen was then the only piece of office equipment, meticulous records were kept, even when headquarters was housed in tents during a rapidly moving campaign. The second feature was the "directed telescope," which elicited vital information that might not enter into the routinized reporting system, or rise through its filters. This "telescope" consisted of about a dozen roving officers who reported directly to Napoleon. Their duties ranged from reconnaissance to on-site assessment of French forces. The "telescope" thus sought to pierce the barriers that insulate the top levels of any large organization from the real world. This remarkable feature of Napoleonic command appears to have no true counterpart at the national level in modern defense organizations.

As a result of his innovations, "Napoleon was the first leader since Roman times able to dissolve the chaos and uncertainty of combat through organization."[5] He accomplished this by combining two seemingly incompatible concepts: highly centralized control over strategy and logistics on the one hand, and increasing independence as one descended his chain of command on the other. As a result, in its heyday Napoleon's army could adapt to changing circumstances at a pace "that present-day armies, for all their telecommunications equipment, can barely equal and certainly not improve on."[6]

The descendants of Napoleon's command organization are in clear evidence today, but his concentration of power in a single mind has never been repeated. The institution that recast the Napoleonic system into a form that did not require the existence of a Napoleon was the Prussian General Staff. The Staff was the first command organization to be fully manned in peacetime, and Prussia was the first modern state to systematically prepare for war regardless of the international climate. These ceaseless preparations, backed by large, well-trained and equipped reserves that could be mobilized and deployed with great speed, made the Prussian Army under Chief-of-Staff Moltke the preeminent fighting force on the Continent during the latter half of the nineteenth century. This raw power, coupled with Bismarck's brilliant political leadership, allowed Prussia to unify Germany under its crown in 1871. By the end of the century, all major powers, with the exception of Great Britain and the United States, had general staffs patterned to varying degrees after that of Prussia.

The Prussian General Staff's emphasis on continuing education and on the application of the scientific method to warfare led it to exploit the inventions and mass production techniques spewed forth by the Industrial Revolution. Most noteworthy was the combination of railway logistics and telegraph communications, which the Staff exploited with surpassing skill.[7]

The success of the German army led to the steady erosion of the primacy of politics, even though that had been a basic tenet of such founders of the General Staff as von Clausewitz. The heights to which the military rose can be seen in the Schlieffen Plan for the defeat of France by an invasion launched through Holland and Belgium. Conceived by Chief-of-Staff Schlieffen in the 1890s, it became Germany's fundamental strategic axiom, even though it wittingly ran the egregious risk of enmeshing Germany in a war not only with

France and Russia, but also the British Empire. The calculating combination of diplomacy and naked military power that had marked Bismarck's conduct of Prussia's foreign policy had given way to an adventurism unfettered by political constraints.

Naturally, Germany's militarization did not evolve in isolation. The other powers, especially France and Russia, also developed huge armies that were fueled by conscription,[8] transported by rail, linked to their commands by the best communications that their technology could offer, and governed by military doctrines and plans equally dedicated to the offensive.[9]

JULY 1914

On June 28, 1914, the heir to the Austro-Hungarian throne was assassinated by a Serbo-Croatian nationalist.[10] For almost 1 month few had any inkling that this incident would soon start a war that would send millions to their graves. But on July 23 Austria served a humiliating ultimatum on Serbia, and the pace of events accelerated mercilessly. On July 25 Austria broke diplomatic relations with Serbia even though it had accepted all but one of Austria's conditions. Russia, Serbia's ally, ordered a partial mobilization the next day, and on July 31 both Russia and Austria mobilized fully. On August 1 Germany declared war on Russia, and the arch-enemies France and Germany mobilized. Germany demanded free passage for her army through Belgium on August 2; that ultimatum expired the next morning and in the afternoon Germany and France declared war on each other. The next evening, August 4, Britain withdrew its ambassador from Berlin, and during that night Germany, in compliance with the Schlieffen Plan, launched its offensive through Belgium. Four years of slaughter had begun.

There are two general features of 1914 especially worth noting. The first is that the July crisis was exceedingly complex—far more so than the events that attended the outbreak of World War II. Thus, we shall depict the decisions that presaged Pearl Harbor by plotting the probability of war as a function of time, but an equally naive representation of 1914 would require a multidimensional piece of paper since there were not just two but five major actors. In a grave confrontation between the superpowers and their allies, a high degree of complexity is also to be anticipated, which is one reason why 1914 may offer a useful warning.

The second general feature arises from a central question regarding 1914: Did war break out by volition or inadvertently through loss of control? Most of the European powers quickly found themselves hurtling into a war that they had not wanted to risk, but the case of Germany is more complex.[11]

While it is true that the Kaiser and his chancellor hesitated on July 29, they were not teetering at the brink by happenstance:

Germa
[y's] . . . readiness to risk war for its own ends—either a local Balkan war fought by its ally in Vienna or a larger, continental-sized war in

which it, France, and Russia participated—now seems unshakably established. . . . By either one of these two wars the German government thought its interests would be served: at a minimum, a successful localized war— kept limited by Russia's backing off in fear—would in the German view probably break up the Franco-Russian alliance, shore up the tottering Austro-Hungarian empire, and clear the way in Central Europe for an eventual German breakthrough to successful *Weltpolitik*. On a more ambitious level, the German government was emphatically in a triumphant continental war. As for the world war that happened, German leaders did not consciously aim at it . . . What they hoped was that Britain would remain neutral or at least a nonbelligerent at the outset. Nonetheless, the possibility of British intervention was appreciated . . . [12]

The ambitious but rather amorphous *Weltpolitik* was a partially subconscious quest for world power that set Germany on a collision course with not only France and Russia, but also Great Britain. The army, led by Chief of Staff Moltke the Younger, was in the vanguard of this quest. He had long been committed to war "the sooner the better" because of the army's fear that Russia's industrialization was rapidly erasing Germany's military supremacy on the continent. In the prewar years, the influence of Moltke and other military leaders over the quixotic kaiser, who held ultimate power, became dominant.[13] Germany's policies, especially her naval buildup, stimulated reactions that German leaders interpreted as offensive—"they denied their own aggressive intentions and projected them instead upon the enemies of their own devising."[14] Furthermore, Germany was increasingly troubled by the centrifugal forces that threatened the survival of her only ally, the Hapsburg Empire. Hence the view gained hold among the ruling elite that Germany must take the initiative if it were not to be doomed to permanent second-class status, or, worse still, to political isolation on a hostile continent. Finally, in December, 1912, the kaiser and his advisers apparently concluded that war was inevitable,[15] and decided to risk a "preventive" war should propitious political circumstances arise. And in the Schlieffen Plan, Germany had, to use today's terminology, a strategy of preemption for that contingency.

This then is a second reason why 1914 was so complex. War did not break out by deliberate intent, as did World War II, nor through mere inadvertence. The latter is often the tacit assumption underlying studies of 1914 that seek lessons for our nuclear age, but such a depiction does not do justice to the nature of the July Crisis. In reality, the Great War began because political leaders lost control over a stream of events that was carried onward by a current that had been consciously channeled in the direction of war.

In addition to these general features, there are narrower facets of 1914 that recur in crisis and war. Among these are alliance commitments, the role of military plans and objectives, perceptions of political intent, and how these merged in decision making.

In 1914 two major alliances confronted each other: France and Russia on one hand, and Germany and Austria–Hungary on the other. Britain had rather ill-defined military commitments to France, and it was unclear under what circumstances they would be upheld. These alliances were embedded in a volatile scene: widespread social conflict and domestic political instability, enormous industrial growth in Germany and Russia, and a fierce competition for colonies.

The alliances, the facts of geography and demography, and the ethos of the military elites led all the continental powers to adopt military doctrines and plans that were zealously devoted to offensive operations.[16] The Schlieffen Plan sought to avoid simultaneous large-scale campaigns against France and Russia by exploiting Germany's ability to mobilize and deploy its forces in several days. Russia, because of its relative backwardness and huge size, could not do so in less than 3 to 4 weeks. The Plan, therefore, called for an all-out offensive through the Low Countries to enable the German army to outflank, envelope, and then shatter the French army within a month, followed immediately by rail transport of troops to reinforce the light forces that were to fend off the huge Russian army that would be assembling in the East. From a narrow military viewpoint, Schlieffen's plan was audacious but not entirely far-fetched. The German army came close to attaining the Plan's objectives even though Moltke did not have the nerve to adhere consistently to Schlieffen's draconian discipline in preparing and prosecuting the campaign.[17] On the other hand, as World War II would demonstrate, defeating the French army and winning a war in which France is allied to Britain and Russia are two quite different undertakings.

On both the Western and the Eastern fronts the offensive war plans made it imperative for Germany and her enemies to attain combat readiness *and* to begin operations as promptly as possible.[18] These pressures were mutually amplifying since an unmobilized state was highly vulnerable to a mobilized enemy. Response to an enemy's mobilization within a day or so was widely deemed to be essential. Furthermore, the mobilization plans were enormously complex—once engaged it was believed that they turned a state into a monstrous robot. As the Russian Chief of Mobilization explained,

> The whole plan of mobilization is worked out ahead in all its details. When the moment has been chosen, one only has to press the button, and the whole state begins to function automatically with the precision of a clock's mechanism. . . . The choice of the moment is influenced by a complex of varied political cause. But once the moment has been fixed, everything is settled; there is no going back; it determines mechanically the beginning of war.[19]

Not only were mobilizations irreversible "mechanisms" without the flexibility that statecraft requires, but

> European war plans in general and those of Germany in particular were based exclusively on military considerations. They . . . placed [priority] on winning any war that might occur, rather than deterring its occurrence. They were not particularly concerned with the specific political conditions

that might make war necessary or with how the mobilization plans themselves might make war more likely. More generally, the military plans were
devised without regard for the specific national political interests that
might be at stake.[20]

Under such circumstances it is hardly surprising that civilian leaders rarely
knew, let alone understood, their military's war plans. Indeed, military staffs
often took advantage of their leader's ignorance, exaggerated the inflexibility
of their mobilization and war plans, and abandoned planning for less ambitious alternatives in the years preceding 1914.[21]

July 1914 also illustrates a situation that recurs repeatedly: intelligence
about ongoing military activities was often quite good, but when it came to
deciphering the larger purposes that those activities were intended to serve
the opposite was the case. Thus, the contenders often had a sound picture of
their enemies' state of readiness,[22] secret mobilization activities were detected
within 6 to 18 hours, and there were responses within 1 or 2 days.[23] France
was also aware that Germany would strike first in her direction, and that Belgian neutrality would probably be violated en route.

In contrast to such tactical intelligence, however, assessments of the strategic goals and political intentions of other states were usually poor and sometimes abysmal. When the bulk of the German army swept through Belgium,
it took France (and England) by surprise. Some Russian leaders, and the
whole British government, did not understand that German mobilization was
tantamount to the outbreak of war because the Schlieffen Plan strove to meet
its awesome deadlines by knitting mobilization and the launch of the westward offensive into a single operation. At a deeper level, it is remarkable that
the Austrian and German governments hoped that by being aggressive they
could intimidate Russia and that leading figures in Berlin hoped that Great
Britain would stand idly by while German armies were occupying the entire
Atlantic coastline. It is also remarkable that the British government, until just
a few days before it decided that it too had to enter the war, hoped that it
could remain suspended "at a dangerous point half-way between isolation
and full-fledged alliance."[24] Never has so much hope killed so many.

That the alliances and military plans had created a tinderbox first became
evident in the East. Austria's uncompromising policy towards Serbia was
encouraged by Germany and personally endorsed by the kaiser. While the
Austro-Hungarian government deliberated, its "allies in Berlin were repeatedly urging the need for action and leaving their own willingness to risk war
in no doubt."[25] When the terms of the Austrian ultimatum were published on
July 25, Europe suddenly saw what might be at hand. The next move was up
to Russia. Her slow pace of mobilization placed her in an excruciating position: She had to begin the process well before Germany, but by doing so She
would legitimize a German decision to go to war. The Russian foreign minister sought to avoid this trap by a partial mobilization against Austria alone,
but the General Staff balked, preferring the abandonment of Serbia to a partial mobilization, which might not only produce disarray, but would leave

Russia highly vulnerable to Germany. "Convinced that inaction would result in humiliating loss of prestige . . . Russian decision makers felt they had no choice but to mobilize for war with Germany . . ."[26] Austria and Germany had failed to intimidate Russia. But thanks to French pressure for prompt Russian mobilization, and the inflexibility of the Russian General Staff,[27] Germany had at least maneuvered Russia into mobilizing first, thereby marshaling domestic support for going to war.

Russia did not offer an isolated example of military planning incompatible with political objectives, or of profound misunderstandings between civilian and military leaders. Many key decision makers had little comprehension of how the flow events was drowning options they may once have had: "Again and again during the last days of peace we have the impression that the politicians and diplomats were taking decisions about situations that had already changed without their knowing it."[28] Not only St. Petersburg, but also Berlin, made a futile attempt to stem the tide. At the last moment the kaiser wanted a partial mobilization against Russia so as not to provoke England,[29] but his General Staff claimed that it had no plan ready other than Schlieffen's, and Moltke, in an emotional outburst, warned the kaiser that improvisation would turn history's most magnificent military machine into a hungry mob.

In contrast to the hyperactivity of the continental powers, Great Britain was close to paralysis. Internal divisions still reflected Great Britain's historic aversion to continental alliances,[30] and the government, preoccupied by rebellion in Ireland, had an inadequate understanding of Germany's plans and objectives. Foreign Secretary Sir Edward Grey knew that Great Britain's strategic interest and political credibility required her to join in the defense of France, but he had too little confidence in the support of the Cabinet and Parliament to clearly enunciate a British position to either France or Germany as they rushed toward war. At last, as recognition of what was at stake grew, the government rallied around the somewhat symbolic principle that Great Britain would honor her guarantee of Belgium's neutrality, but by then Germany and France were already at war. Had England reached that conclusion *and* made its intentions evident to Berlin a few days earlier, Germany would have faced a clear-cut choice because the Schlieffen plan required the immediate capture of critical railway junctions in Belgium.[31] While the General Staff itself was certainly prepared to risk war against Great Britain, it is just possible that the German leadership as a whole might have lost its nerve had it known beyond any doubt that Germany would not only face France and Russia, but also the Royal Navy and the British Empire. Everyone, therefore, hung on Great Britain's decision, including Great Britain itself. German leaders either prayed or gambled that Great Britain would remain neutral. France hoped she would not but based her war plan on the assumption that France would fight alone. Once Germany struck, the fog lifted in London, and England dispatched its Expeditionary Force to France within 3 days.

These, then, were the ingredients that came to a boil in the cauldron of the July crisis: wishful thinking, reckless ambitions, grandiose military plans, a chasm between civilian and military leaders, high-risk alliance commitments, misconceived self-interests, and deeply flawed perceptions of other states' objectives and constraints. In retrospect, at least, it is not astonishing that this brew produced the most rapid sequence of catastrophic decisions of modern history.

JUNE 22, 1941: OPERATION BARBAROSSA

On June 22, 1941, Hitler launched Operation Barbarossa against the Soviet Union and caught the Red Army by surprise.[32] Within 2 weeks the *Wehrmacht* had occupied an area equivalent to three times the size of France. By the end of November several million Soviet troops had been killed or captured, and the Soviet state had lost control of the territory on which 45 percent of its population lived, and on which 47 percent of the grain and 60 percent of the country's coal, iron, steel, and aluminum were produced.[33] While these figures do not take account of the massive evacuation of people and industry to the East, they indicate the scale of Soviet setbacks in the opening months of the war.

Stalin had embarked on the forcible collectivization of agriculture and rapid industrialization in order to turn the Soviet Union into a great military–industrial power, and had justified his policies by pointing to the threat from the capitalist states. Once the Nazis came to power in 1933 the threat posed by Germany loomed large in Soviet thinking. Even after the Non-aggression Pact with Germany in 1939, and especially after Germany had defeated France and the Low Countries in 1940, Stalin believed that a German attack was inevitable. But he wanted to put it off as long as possible in order to make the Red Army ready and to build up stocks of arms and materiel. In February 1941 he remarked to General K. A. Meretskov, the deputy people's commissar of defense, that the Soviet Union could not stay out of the war until 1943, but might manage to do so until 1942.[34]

In the early months of 1941 Germany began to build up its forces along the Soviet border. Stalin received many warnings that Hitler was preparing to attack, but he suspected that these preparations were purposeful provocations.[35] He believed that Hitler would not attack until Great Britain either had been defeated or had concluded a peace treaty with Germany because he was impressed by Bismarck's view that Germany could never achieve victory if it fought on two fronts, and he thought that Hitler had drawn the same conclusion from World War I.[36] He refused to put the border forces on full alert, for fear that the Nazi leaders might use that as an excuse for attacking. On June 14 Marshal S. K. Timoshenko, the people's commissar of defense, and General G. K. Zhukov, the chief of the general staff, advocated that the forces in the frontier military districts be brought up to full combat readiness. Stalin's answer implied a fear that, as in 1914, mobilization might lead directly to war: "You are proposing to mobilize the country, raise troops now, and move them to the Western frontiers? But that is war! Do the two of you understand that or not?"[37] As a result, only partial and piecemeal measures were taken to increase the readiness of the Red Army in the days before the attack. On the evening of June 21 he once more refused to bring Soviet forces up to full combat readiness, lest this should provoke the war he was so anxious to avoid.[38]

Stalin apparently believed that a German attack would be preceded by an ultimatum and that this would provide time in which to bring the Red Army up to full readiness or to forestall the war by making political concessions.[39] The Soviet military compounded this misconception by assuming, despite the *Wehrmacht's* victories in the West, that Germany would not attempt a *blitzkrieg* against a state as powerful as the Soviet Union, and that the war would start with frontier battles before the main forces were engaged.[40]

Some commanders, however, did take steps to raise the combat readiness of their forces. On June 15, for example, the Baltic Military District took such a series of measures: ammunition was distributed, leaves were canceled, preparations were made to blow up bridges and plant mine fields, and the air defense forces and signals troops were ordered to full combat readiness. But these steps were still incomplete on June 22, and even the Baltic Military District refrained from actions such as building antitank obstacles and blowing up bridges on the Neman on the grounds that they might be provocative.[41]

The Naval Command, under the pretext of training, "hastened to increase the readiness of the fleets, demanded the acceleration of various measures for strengthening the defense of [naval] bases and at the same time feared a 'lowering of the boom' for displaying too much initiative."[42] In effect, this brought the fleets up to alert status No. 2 in the week before the German attack.[43] The order to go to combat alert (No. 1) was given by Marshal Timoshenko at about midnight on June 21.[44]

The German High Command completed the deployment of its forces along the Soviet frontier before the Soviet Union did, launched a full-scale attack without any prior ultimatum, and thereby seized the strategic initiative from the very outset.

Stalin's failure to anticipate the German attack illustrates two intimately related dangers. The first is failure to ready forces when one should—this was Stalin's mistake. The second is that one will provoke a conflict by taking such measures—this was Stalin's fear. His desire to avoid war with Germany conflicted with the need to ready the Red Army, and he knowingly resolved that dilemma by choosing what proved to be the wrong alternative.

Operation Barbarossa illustrated how an attacker can use surprise to disrupt a defense. The *Wehrmacht* could not strike directly at Moscow, but it made a special effort to destroy communications between Moscow and the forces at the front. Marshal I. T. Peresypkin, who was chief of signals during the war, wrote later that

in the first months of the war the enemy tried by various methods to disorganize or in some measure to destroy command and control of the Soviet Army. . . . As a result of massive enemy air raids there was great destruction and damage to the permanent overhead communications lines, which led to long interruptions in the work of wire communications and to serious breaches of command and control.[45]

Before attacking, the Germans had sent agents across the lines to cut communications lines, and the Red Army staffs, which were not well supplied with radios, found it extremely difficult to communicate with their forces in the first hours of the war.[46] The Soviet leaders in Moscow also had trouble in communicating with the front: on the evening of June 23, for example, they could not contact some of the military districts, and on June 29 they had no communication with the forces on the Western Front and could not tell what the situation there was.[47]

In the state of shock caused by the German attack Soviet leaders took some weeks to create an effective central command organization. On June 23 the *Stavka* (Headquarters) of the High Command was set up with Marshal Timoshenko as chairman, and Stalin, Molotov, General Zhukov, and three other military commanders as members. By the end of the first week of the war it became clear to Politburo members that an extraordinary body was needed to manage the war effort as a whole, and on June 30 the State Defense Committee was established with "all power in the state" in its hands. Stalin chaired this committee, which consisted of a small number of party and State leaders.[48] On July 10 he took over chairmanship of the *Stavka* as well, and on August 8 he assumed the title of supreme commander-in-chief; the *Stavka* was renamed the *Stavka* of the Supreme High Command *(Stavka-VGK)*.[49] This highly centralized system proved effective and flexible during the war: it enabled the Soviet Union to mobilize resources for the war effort and ensured the close coordination of military and political leadership.

Stalin subsequently played down the disasters of 1941, portraying the Red Army"s chaotic retreat as part of a plan of active defense, and describing "surprise" as only a "transitory factor" in war.[50] But the memory of June 22 was not to be erased—as one of the most traumatic events in Russian history it had indelibly impressed the grave danger of miscalculating the competing requirements of preparing for war and preventing war on Russian minds.

DECEMBER 7, 1941: PEARL HARBOR

The wreckage that Japan made of the Pacific Fleet while it was anchored at Pearl Harbor was a shocking setback for the United States,[51] but it did not have anything like the strategic impact of the German attack on the Soviet Union. Despite her remarkable military feats on December 7, Japan did not erase America's military power in the Pacific. Furthermore, Japan knew that it could not jeopardize the survival of the United States. Hitler, on the other hand, did not only conquer much of Russia's heartland, but he came within reach of destroying the Soviet state. Nevertheless, Pearl Harbor had an influence on the postwar reorganization of the U.S. defense establishment, and left an imprint on the American military–political psyche, that is quite comparable to the effect that Operation Barbarossa had on the Soviet Union.

Japan's expansion into China, Korea, and Manchuria during the years preceding Pearl Harbor, and its alliance with Nazi Germany, brought it into growing conflict with the United States and Great Britain. Through diplomacy, economic pressure, and aid to China, the Roosevelt administration sought to force Japan to relinquish its aims and its conquests in China. But American policy posed a greater threat to Japan's vital interests than Washington realized because, in Japan's eyes, her economic and geopolitical aspirations made control of the entire Western Pacific basin an imperative. Whereas "Stalin had erred by hypersensitivity to provocation when conciliation would not have deterred Hitler anyway, Roosevelt's error was the opposite—not fully recognizing how American steadfastness would provoke rather than deter the Japanese."[52]

United States–Japanese relations deteriorated further after Germany's capture of Holland and France, both of which had extensive colonies that Japan coveted, and turned sharply for the worse in July 1941 when the United States imposed an oil embargo that deprived the Japanese navy of its principal fuel supply, which faced Japanese with the agonizing choice of either abandoning its long-term objectives, or of going to war to acquire the oil fields in Dutch Indonesia.[53] Negotiations continued until the end of November, but the American government was keenly aware that the likelihood of war was growing. Although the Japanese achieved total surprise at Pearl Harbor, Washington had actually issued a war warning to its Pacific commanders *10 days* before the attack.

The warning was but one fruit of a remarkable achievement: William Friedman of the Signal Corps had deciphered Japan's diplomatic code in 1940. Messages between Tokyo and its embassies and consulates were then intercepted routinely. This traffic, given the codename MAGIC by the United States, provided a detailed picture of policy formation, requests for intelligence, and forthcoming diplomatic maneuvers. As a result, the United States already knew in July that Japan was under German pressure to enter the war, and that the Japanese government had formally decided that it would seek to establish hegemony over at least Southeast Asia and Indonesia "regardless of how the world situation may change."[54] This intelligence, and the decisions that culminated in Pearl Harbor are shown schematically in Figure 3.1.

Why was this penetration of the Japanese government not translated into effective warning? After the war Congress addressed this question to the tune of 39 volumes.[57] As with most major fiascoes, the failure to anticipate Pearl Harbor stemmed from many interacting factors, among which stupidity and duplicity were *not* significant.[58] On the other hand, flaws in the organization and capabilities of American intelligence, a haphazard information flow between military and political leaders in Washington, as well as between Washington and its widely dispersed forces, and widespread lack of collaboration between different branches of the military were all of capital importance. These weaknesses exacerbated the chronic difficulty of discerning the intentions and plans of a resourceful enemy.

While MAGIC showed that Japan was moving toward war, and U.S. military intelligence saw much evidence of combat preparations, there were hardly any signs that Japan would commence hostilities by attacking U.S. territory, let alone Pearl Harbor.[59] "Hard" intelligence thus supported the widely held assumption that Japan would attack some combination of Siberia, the British and Dutch colonies, and possibly remote U.S. bases. American leaders could not imagine that Japan would be so reckless as to challenge the United States frontally since that would engulf Japan in a struggle it could not hope to win.

Japanese intelligence knew that Japan could not sustain an all-out war against the United States, but these estimates were ignored by policymakers.[60] The latter viewed the American commitment to its European allies as being so firm that an attack on their colonies was tantamount to an attack on the United States.[61] The leadership, which considered Japan's goals in China and the Western Pacific to be nonnegotiable, therefore gambled that a devastating blow would impel a U.S. withdrawal to the Eastern Pacific. Bigotry and fanaticism were also in evidence; thus, leading Japanese thought that the "Americans, being merchants, would not continue for long with an unprofitable war,"[62] while the chief of military intelligence, in firing a colonel who presented a detailed report that concluded that the United States could out-produce Japan by a factor of 10, said that "a Japan–America war is necessary; it is no longer a question of victory or defeat."[63]

The American intelligence failure was also abetted by racial prejudice, which prevented Americans from imagining that Japan had the daring and virtuosity demanded for coordinated assaults on Pearl Harbor, the Philippines, and Southeast Asia.[64] In the last analysis, however, Japan was reckless, and was seen as such even by some senior officers planning the Pearl Harbor attack.[65]

In the absence of any suspicion that Pearl Harbor might be attacked it was difficult to discern in the massive intelligence traffic those few hints that pointed to such a possibility. In addition, Roosevelt and his aides were preoccupied with Europe, where war with Germany was looming. The difficulty of hearing a weak signal against a drumbeat was compounded by the astounding source of the signal: enormous precautions were taken to insure that Japan would not realize that the United States had MAGIC! Only Roosevelt, Chief-of-Staff George Marshall, and eight other senior officials had regular access to MAGIC. They were only shown messages individually, and were not allowed to keep copies or take notes; therefore, they could not ponder MAGIC's implications in a systematic manner. Nor did they know the distribution list; the Chiefs in Washington incorrectly assumed that commanders in Honolulu had full access to MAGIC. And Joseph Grew, the highly competent ambassador in Tokyo, who was the only senior official to have perceived—and warned—that Japan might take desperate actions, also did not see MAGIC.

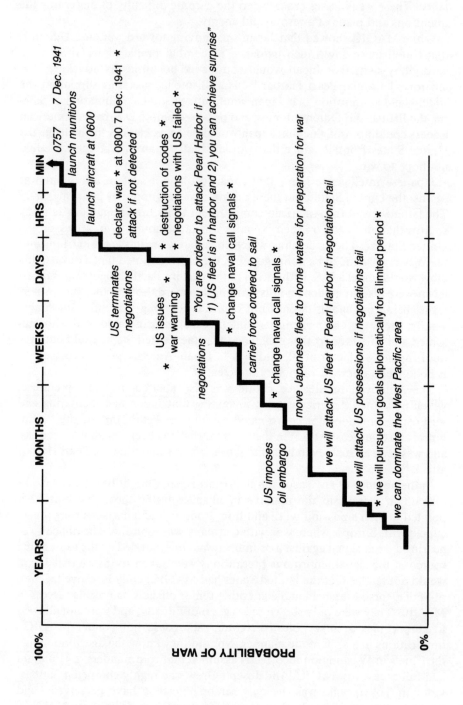

PROBABILITY OF WAR

100%

YEARS — MONTHS — WEEKS — DAYS — HRS — MIN

0%

0757   7 Dec. 1941

launch munitions

launch aircraft at 0600

declare war * at 0800 7 Dec. 1941
attack if not detected

* destruction of codes *
* negotiations with US failed *

US terminates
negotiations

* change naval call signals *

US issues
war warning   *

"You are ordered to attack Pearl Harbor if
1) US fleet is in harbor and 2) you can achieve surprise"

negotiations
*

carrier force ordered to sail

* change naval call signals *

* change naval call signals *

move Japanese fleet to home waters for preparation for war

we will attack US fleet at Pearl Harbor if negotiations fail

US imposes
oil embargo

we will attack US possessions if negotiations fail

* we will pursue our goals diplomatically for a limited period *

we can dominate the West Pacific area

This fragmentation was exacerbated by the absence of systematic intelligence estimates of Japan's objectives and plans. There was really no intelligence community. The intelligence services of the navy, army, and state department rarely cooperated, and there was no counterpart to the director of central intelligence. Within the military, intelligence had low status and was often ignored despite the brilliant code breaking, and other excellent work done in the Pacific.

The war warning of November 27 neither specified the type of alert to be taken nor explained the political context—Pearl Harbor was not listed among the likely targets. The response to the warning, therefore, varied widely. In the Philippines, General MacArthur promptly ordered his most valuable bombers south out of harm's way, but compliance was sluggish. In Honolulu the warning was ordered to mean that only sabotage and submarine attacks should be expected; no alert directed against other possible enemy actions was taken. While it is true that the reconnaissance required for tactical warning would have exacted a large toll on planes and crews, and reduced combat readiness for the war that was then expected, less costly precautions were also not taken. The bulk of the fleet continued to berth in Pearl Harbor on weekends, which is why the Japanese struck on Sunday, while a more prudent pattern of naval operations might have led to a cancellation of the attack (see Figure 3.1). Indeed, on December 7, Naval Intelligence in Washington thought the fleet would be at sea. This misunderstanding stemmed from the practice of leaving alert actions to the discretion of the combat commanders, who were not obliged to report their actions to Washington.

A succession of tragic failures scarred the days preceding December 7. First, MAGIC revealed that key Japanese embassies and consulates were to destroy their encryption machines, but the commanders in Hawaii ordered no change in combat readiness on learning this. An intercepted message to the Washington embassy then disclosed that the ambassador was to convey a note restating Japan's position at 1:00 PM that very day—a Sunday. Since diplo-

←

Figure 3.1. Japanese and American decisions leading to Pearl Harbor (adapted from Belden[55]). The vertical scale is a purely subjective representation of the probability of war, whereas the horizontal axis depicts the time at which events actually occurred. Japanese decisions *known* to the U.S. through decoded MAGIC messages are between asterisks, and American decisions that were *unknown* to Japan are set off in the same way.

Two aspects of the figure that should be noted, for they capture themes that recur at the threshold of conflict, are 1) to compensate for the quickening pace of events, the time scale becomes ever more compressed as the moment of attack is approached, and 2) MAGIC only contained information about the Japanese political decisions marked by asterisks; the United States was not privy to any of the Japanese military decisions that are shown. Finally, such phrases as "Japan decided" do not mean that "Japan" was a unitary decision maker; in reality, complex rivalries between its army, navy, and civilians were fought out as these "decisions" were reached.[56]

macy is not normally conducted on Sunday or timed with such precision, it was immediately recognized that this could be a declaration of war and that attacks might then occur at one or more unknown points. That proved to be correct: 1:00 PM in Washington was 8:00 AM in Hawaii, and the first bombs exploded on Pearl Harbor at 7:57. Intelligence officers, however, were unable to reach General Marshall for more than 2 hours, and his alert order to all major commands only went out 90 minutes before the attack. Normally it would have reached Honolulu in 30 minutes, but a breakdown in radio communications led to its arrival via bicycle messenger during the bombing.

This failure to convey strategic warning was followed by a total void in tactical warning. At 7:02 AM a novice radar operator spotted a mysterious plane north of Pearl Harbor, but his novice supervisor dismissed the sighting.

Even in retrospect, the inability to anticipate the attack against Pearl Harbor is understandable, but the failure to take precautions is not. That war was imminent was widely recognized in the U.S. government. MAGIC had revealed that the Japanese consulate was collecting detailed intelligence regarding Pearl Harbor.[66] United States intelligence knew that the Japanese Navy had changed its call signals twice in November, which was seen as ominous, and it had lost track of much of the Japanese Navy. Furthermore, the U.S. Navy had studied possible attacks against Hawaii, and concluded that Pearl Harbor was vulnerable to a dawn air raid "delivered as a complete surprise."[67] Short of sending the fleet to sea, the habit of having most ships in port on Sundays could have been broken on receipt of the war warning of November 27, if not before. Dawn reconnaissance flights, even though they would have interfered with other important activities, should at least have been *considered* at that point, but the commanders in Hawaii never even informed their subordinates responsible for reconnaissance that a war warning had been received. Still more striking, U.S. forces in the Philippines were promptly informed about the Pearl Harbor attack, but an air raid some *9 hours later* was unopposed and caught a large number of aircraft neatly arrayed on the ground.[68]

EPILOGUE

What lessons can be extracted from these tragedies? Only one can be stated with confidence: paradoxes and enigmas, not rules of thumb, characterize conflicts between modern states. After decades of analysis based on innumerable memoirs and vast repositories of official documents an aura of mystery continues to cling to the drama of July 1914. Phenomena as complex as "July 1914" ultimately frustrate analysis. Copious evidence and tenacious scholarship cannot establish how the flow of events would have been altered had even one important variable been changed (for example, the actions of the Russian government on the eve of war). It is therefore not astonishing that instigators of conflict usually fail to foresee the outcome of what they set in train. What is surprising, however, is that the notion persists that crises can be managed with a level of confidence commensurate with the risks that science has created.

Two linked paradoxes repeatedly appear at the outset of international conflicts:[69]

- Prudent defensive preparations based on a pessimistic assessment of an opponent's intentions can be misperceived as a signal of impending attack, and could provoke preemption. Failure to take such precautions, however, can invite an attack.
- Military organizations have become so complex that plans and operations must be prepared over long periods on the basis of assumed contingencies. Should events fail to conform to those assumptions, the degree to which these plans can be promptly modified may be woefully inadequate.

The mobilization plans of 1914 cut these Gordian knots by making combat readiness for an immediate offensive the overriding priority; in effect, they wished the dilemmas out of existence. In 1941, Stalin sought to deny Germany the pretext for attack that his predecessors had offered 27 years earlier. His reward for having "learned the lesson of 1914" was vast devastation. This should be read not as a plea for ignorance, but for caution. Analogies to prior circumstances, although often helpful, can miss the mark. They may suppress the most important variables in the actual situation, especially when those who glimpse the analogy have an image of reality distorted by fear or hope.

Our case histories from 1914 and 1941 demonstrate that even when intelligence concerning an adversary's military preparations is quite sound, the political intentions that impel those preparations are difficult to fathom. Indeed, a government may not know its own intentions until an adversary has acted. That was true of Great Britain in 1914, and of the United States at the outbreak of the Korean War. The wizardry of modern technology will not dispel this enigma.

The bitter experiences of 1941 have led both superpowers to devote great effort to correcting the systemic flaws that Pearl Harbor and June 22 revealed. These will be described in later chapters, and we mention just one example here: the United States now has a centralized system for the coordinated alerting of its forces around the globe that exploits not only modern telecommunications but also rigorous organizational routines that would almost certainly have averted the Pearl Harbor fiasco, even with the technology of 1941. Whether today's command systems are as capable in relation to the nuclear-armed missile as their 1941 predecessors were in the face of TNT dropped from slow-flying aircraft is, of course, quite another matter.

In addressing the failures of 1941, however, the two superpowers have recreated some of the dangers of 1914, but in a far more virulent form. Thus modern intelligence is likely to reveal changes of an adversary's combat readiness almost immediately, which could require—or be believed to require—response at too rapid a pace for political deliberations. As in 1914, today's political leaders are often unaware of the substance or implications of their nation's military plans, and given the speed of modern forces, even well-versed political leaders (and military commanders) could easily fail to comprehend a fast-moving crisis. But by far the most awesome analogy to 1914 would arise should the superpowers ever be in a situation where both of their ICBM forces were fully prepared to execute a prompt launch, for that could initiate a virtually automated chain of events that would make the interlocking mobilizations and offensives of 1914 look like child's play.

Such analogies, however, ignore the mood of 1914.[70] That mood nurtured the thrust toward war, and it has virtually no counterpart today. Before the advent of nuclear weapons there was widespread acceptance of war as a natural part of international life. In 1914, a considerable number of leaders believed that war was inevitable. In particular, Germany's leaders were convinced of this, but they were by no means alone. This attitude created an insidious and fatalistic acceptance of the coming of war in many minds. Furthermore, millions of men from all walks of life and in all the warring nations held romantic visions of war. Even working class reservists of Marxist persuasions answered the call to the colors without question. And there were powerful constituencies in all the continental states advocating belligerent foreign policies that openly risked war. In contrast, no significant body of opinion in any nuclear-armed state suffers from illusions concerning the consequences of nuclear war—anyone with a romantic image of nuclear combat would be judged insane.

This sober attitude poses a formidable barrier to war that did not exist in 1914. Furthermore, in both superpowers, despite the great differences in their political cultures, the supremacy of political control by civilians is deeply entrenched—since the death of Stalin no major power has been ruled by a clique as minuscule as those that took Germany into war in 1914 and 1939. Nevertheless, one attitude that played an essential role in starting both World Wars should give us pause. Germany's rulers risked war in 1914, and Japan's rulers went to war in 1941, because both perceived intolerable threats from enemies that their own policies had done so much to create. If the catastrophe of nuclear war is to be kept at bay, it is essential that the superpowers pursue foreign policies that make such perceptions as manifestly implausible as possible. To that end they should protect their separate interests by military forces and deployments whose defensive purpose is as evident as that purpose permits, and imbed these military postures in a diplomatic relationship that can defuse misperceptions of hostile intent.

NOTES

1. Barbara W. Tuchman, *The Guns of August* (New York: Dell, 1962).

2. Steven E. Miller, (ed.), *Military Strategy and the Origins of the First World War* (Princeton, N.J.: Princeton University, 1985), which reprints articles by Paul Kennedy, Michael Howard, Stephen Van Evera, Jack Snyder, and Richard Ned Lebow that first appeared in *International Security*. See further: Richard Ned Lebow, *Between War and*

Peace; Scott D. Sagan, "Allies, Offense, and Stability," *International Security* (1986), *11*:2, 151; Sean M. Lynn-Jones, "Detente and Deterrence: Anglo-German Relations, 1911-1914, ibid., (1986) *11*:2, 121; Richard Ned Lebow, "The Soviet Offensive in Europe: The Schlieffen Plan Revisited?," ibid., (1985); *9*:4, 52; Jack S. Levy, "Organizational Routines and the Causes of War," International Studies Quarterly (1986), *30*:2, 193; and Miles Kahler, "Rumors of War: 1914 Revisited," *Foreign Affairs* (1979-80), *58*:2, 278.

3. For the evolution of military forces and command in the period 1789-1914, see especially van Creveld, Chapters 2-4; William H. McNeill, *The Pursuit of Power* (Chicago: University of Chicago Press, 1982), Chapters 6-8; T. N. Dupuy, *A Genius for War: The German Army and General Staff, 1807-1945* (Englewood Cliffs, N.J.: Prentice-Hall, 1977); and Gordon A. Craig, *The Politics of the Prussian Army, 1640-1945* (Oxford: Oxford University Press, 1955). We have also drawn on an unpublished syllabus of Paul Bracken's ("Governance and Control of Security Organization," Yale University, Spring 1985).

4. van Creveld has aptly called the era before Napoleon "the Stone Age of Command," even though Roman armies through superior logistics and organization were able to perform some of the tasks of Napoleonic armies. In contrast, European military forces during the nearly two millennia that preceded 1789 were unable to pursue what we would now call strategic objectives.

5. Bracken, cf. note No. 3, p. 3.

6. van Creveld, p. 88.

7. McNeill, pp. 248-251.

8. Great Britain, however, did not have conscription until 1916.

9. Jack Snyder, *The Ideology of the Offensive* (Ithaca, N.Y.: Cornell University Press, 1984).

10. For a brief, authoritative summary of the origins of World War I, and an extensive bibliography, see Joll. The standard treatise is L. Albertini, *The Origins of the War of 1914,* 3 vols. (Oxford: Oxford University Press, 1957).

11. For references to the extensive literature on German decision making see Joll, p. 5, and Lebow, *Between War and Peace,* pp. 249-253.

12. Michael R. Gordon, "Domestic Conflict and the Origins of the First World War: The British and German Case," *Journal of Modern History* (1974), *46,* 191; pp. 194-195.

13. See especially Isabell V. Hull, *The Entourage of Kaiser Wilhelm II: 1888-1918* (Cambridge: Cambridge University Press, 1982), Chapter 9.

14. Ibid., p. 254.

15. Ibid., pp. 261-265; Joll, p. 202.

16. Jack Snyder, op. cit.

17. See B. H. Liddel Hart, *Encyclopedia Britannica* (Chicago: William Benton, 1965), Vol. 23, pp. 751-754.

18. For a good discussion of mobilization plans, see Levy, op. cit., pp. 195-203.

19. Quotation from Levy, op. cit., p. 196.

20. Ibid., p. 208.

21. See Snyder, op. cit.

22. See the detailed discussions of intelligence assessments before World War I of all the European powers in May, Chapters 1 through 8.

23. Van Evera, op. cit., p. 78.

24. Gordon, op. cit., p. 224.

25. Joll, p. 11.

26. Levy, op. cit., p. 201.

27. Snyder, op. cit., especially Chapter 7.

28. Joll, p. 80.

29. Levy, op. cit., p. 199.

30. For a detailed comparison of the British and German social and political environments and their influence on policymakers in 1914, see Gordon, op. cit.

31. On July 29 Grey warned Berlin that if Germany and France were to go to war, "the British government might possibly find itself impelled to take a rapid decision. In this case it would not do to stand aside. . . . " This induced the German chancellor to a frantic but futile 1-day attempt to reverse Austria's course on which Germany's prodding had set her. See Lebow, pp. 133–137.

32. This section on the invasion of Russia is taken from David Holloway and Condeleezza Rice, *Soviet Military Doctrine and its Implications for Crisis Management* (unpublished).

33. On the early setbacks and losses of territory see John Erickson, *The Road to Stalingrad* (New York: Harper and Row, 1975), pp. 136–222.

34. K. A. Meretskov, *Na sluzhbe narodu* (Moscow: Politizdat, 1968), p. 222.

35. A. I. Mikoian, "V pervye mesiatsy velikoi otechestvennoi voiny," *Novaia i noveishaia istoriia*, 1985, no. 6, pp. 95–96; S. P. Ivanov (ed.), *Nachal 'nyi period voiny* (Moscow: Voenizdat, 1974), pp. 209–213; Barton Whaley, *Codeword Barbarossa* (Cambridge, Mass.: MIT Press), 1973. Some of the intelligence was presented by the GRU (the Main Intelligence Directorate of the General Staff) as disinformation, because General Golikov, the Chief of the GRU, knew that Stalin was afraid of war with Germany. See G. K. Zhukov, *Vospominaniia i Razmyshleniia* (Moscow: Novosti, 1969), pp. 248–249.

36. See Mikoian, loc. cit., pp. 95–96.

37. Zhukov, op. cit., p. 249.

38. V. A. Anfilov, *Bessmertnyi podvig* (Moscow: Nauka, 1971), pp. 179–186; A. M. Nekrich, *1941, 22 iiunia* (Moscow: Nauka, 1965), esp. part 3. Even on the night of the 21st June he dismissed the warning given by a German deserter, who had crossed the lines in order to warn the Soviet Union of the impending German attack as an act of provocation arranged by the German military (See Mikoian, loc. cit., p. 96).

39. John Erickson, "Threat Identification and Strategic Appraisal by the Soviet Union, 1930–1941," in May, esp. pp. 417–422.

40. Ibid., Ivanov, op. cit., pp. 206–213.

41. Anfilov, op. cit., pp. 183–185.

42. Admiral N. G. Kuznetsov, People's Commissar of the Navy, "At Naval Headquarters," in Seweryn Bialer (ed.), *Stalin and His Generals. Soviet Military Memoirs of World War II* (Boulder: Westview Press, 1984), p. 191.

43. The Soviet Navy had three stages of alert at that time. Under alert No. 3 "the fleets continued their normal training and exercises, and shore leave was granted, but ships were kept fully fueled and no major repairs were undertaken"; under No. 2 "ships received all necessary munitions and stores; shore leaves were restricted; preparations were made so that ships could put out to sea on short notice; battle shifts were established for some guns"; while No. 1 "was the full combat alert, with ships under their own power and all crews manning battle stations." Bialer, ibid., pp. 193–194, p. 580.

44. Ibid., pp. 193–194.

45. I. T. Peresypkin, *Voennaia radiosvaiaz* (Moscow: Voenizdat, 1962), p. 155.

46. Zhukov, op. cit., p. 256.

47. Mikoian, loc. cit., pp. 97–98. Mikoian was a member of the Politburo at the time.

48. Mikoian, loc. cit., pp. 96–98 gives the best account of the setting up of the State Defense Committee. Zhukov notes that the appointment of Timoshenko as Commander-in-Chief on June 23 created difficulties because while Timoshenko was the formal commander-in-chief, Stalin was the real one. Zhukov, op. cit., p. 258.

49. *KPSS o Vooruzhennykh Silakh Sovetskogo Soiuza, Dokumenty 1917–1981* (Moscow: Voenizdat, 1981), pp. 303, 308.

50. See Matthew P. Gallagher, *The Soviet History of World War II. Myths, Memories and Realities* (New York: Frederick A. Praeger, 1963), pp. 10–13; Raymond L. Garthoff, *How Russia Makes War* (London: Allen and Unwin, 1954), p. 34.

51. We have drawn principally on Wohlstetter, and also on Michael A. Barnhart, "Japanese Intelligence Before the Second World War: Best Case Analysis," pp. 424–455, in May; and David Kahn, "United States Views of Germany and Japan in 1941," ibid., pp. 476–502. See in addition Ariel Levite, *Intelligence and Strategic Surprise* (New York: Columbia University Press, 1987).

52. Betts, *Surprise Attack*, p. 42.

53. For a study of the oil embargo and its implications from both a U.S. and Japanese perspective, see Scott D. Sagan, "The Origins of the Pacific War," *Journal of Interdisciplinary History* (1988), *18*:4, 893.

54. Wohlstetter, p. 346. The decision taken by the Japanese government was actually firmer—it would "carry out the above program no matter what obstacles may be encountered," but this was either not transmitted to the embassy in Washington, or not intercepted.

55. Thomas G. Belden, "Indications, Warning and Crisis Operations," *International Studies Quarterly* (1977), *21*:1, 181; fig. 3, p. 186.

56. See Barnhart, op. cit.

57. The classic analysis of this mountain of data, and of other sources, is that of Roberta Wohlstetter. What follows is largely, although not wholly, based on her findings.

58. One theme in the investigation concerned the suspicion that FDR had purposely withheld warning because he believed that the shock of an attack was necessary to bring the United States into the war against Hitler. Although the record shows that this suspicion is unfounded, it continues to linger in American folklore. What is true is that the Roosevelt administration was apprehensive that Japan would nibble away at the British colonies, which would make it difficult for the government to honor its obligations; furthermore, it was determined not to initiate hostilities, and had issued orders to the forces to that effect.

59. There is some debate on this point. Wohlstetter (p. 387) concludes that "we failed to anticipate Pearl Harbor not for want of relevant materials, but because of a plethora of irrelevant ones." Kahn (op. cit., pp. 500–501) disagrees: "Sufficient indication of an attack simply did not exist within the mass of American intelligence data. Not one intercept, not one datum of intelligence ever said anything about an attack on Pearl Harbor or any other possession. That there were many distractions is true but irrelevant; the most refined analysis cannot bring out what is not present. . . . The intelligence failure at Pearl Harbor was one not of analysis, but of collection."

60. Japan estimated that the United States had an industrial potential some eight times greater than its own, and its predictions of U.S. war materiel production proved to be more accurate than those of the United States; see Wohlstetter, p. 348, and Barnhart, op. cit., pp. 449–451.

61. Sagan (op. cit., p. 898) presents evidence that indicates that Japan greatly overestimated the American commitment to its European allies.

62. Barnhart, op. cit., p. 447.

63. Ibid., p. 452.

64. The Japanese planned and trained meticulously. Modifications of torpedoes were devised to allow their use in the supposedly too shallow waters of Pearl Harbor; studies of airplane performance to stretch their range beyond specifications were carried out; complex war games were staged; extraordinary security precautions were imposed, etc. These were essential to the surprise attained at both Pearl Harbor and in the Philippines.

65. The commander-in-chief of Japan's navy reluctantly supported war against the United States,but was totally committed to the attack on Pearl Harbor as the only hope of avoiding a drawn-out war. His chief planner came to the conclusion that the attack was too risky, but he was ignored. To the dismay of many members of the government, *all* large carriers were committed to the attack even though it was estimated that a large portion would be lost.

66. This intelligence, however, was masked by the knowledge that Japanese consulates at other ports were engaged in similar activities.

67. Wohlstetter, p. 23.

68. As another indication of racial attitudes, we note that MacArthur was so impressed with these attacks that he was convinced the Japanese must have used German pilots; see John Toland, *The Rising Sun: The Decline and Fall of the Japanese Empire, 1936-1945* (New York: Random House, 1970), pp. 58–59.

69. For extensive discussion of these paradoxes, see Jervis; and Jervis, Lebow and Stein.

70. See Joll, chapter 8; Gordon, op. cit., and references cited therein.

4

The Evolution of Western Nuclear Capabilities

NUCLEAR FORCES, COMMAND, AND DOCTRINE: 1945 TO 1960

Presidents Truman and Eisenhower largely cast the die that determined the role, size, and organization of today's nuclear forces.[1] The milestones were Truman's vast expansion of the nuclear weapons stockpile, followed by a series of seminal decisions by Eisenhower: transfer of peacetime civilian custody of nuclear weapons to the military; creation of a streamlined chain of command and a centrally coordinated war plan for all U.S. strategic forces; and the commitment to develop and deploy land- and submarine-based missiles of intercontinental range. That current U.S. strategic forces have some 11,000 widely dispersed nuclear warheads, of which more than 6,000 are ready for launch within minutes, can be traced back to these initiatives. Naturally, they were not taken in a geopolitical vacuum. Truman and Eisenhower had to contend with the Berlin Blockade in 1948, followed shortly thereafter by the Korean War (see Chapter 8). The commitments undertaken by these administrations, and the nuclear arsenals they led to, were dictated to a considerable degree by forecasts of Soviet capabilities, by assessments of Soviet intentions, and by the monetary and political cost of countering large Soviet conventional forces by convential means.[2]

Nuclear Forces

Demobilization of U.S. and allied armed forces after World War II left Western Europe vulnerable to the large, standing Soviet armies. As early as 1948, American planners had turned to "cheap" nuclear weapons to compensate for conventional weakness, although at that time the arsenal only held some 50 unassembled Nagasaki-type fission weapons that could only be carried by bombers based in New Mexico.[3] In 1949, following the Berlin Crisis, an even greater emphasis was put on nuclear weapons, and their manufacture was expanded significantly by Truman. After the outbreak of the Korean War in June 1950, which had raised the specter of communist aggression spreading to Europe,[4] Truman decided to station American combat troops permanently in Europe, appointed Eisenhower as the first Supreme Allied Commander-Europe (SACEUR) that September, and approved a second increase in the production of fissionable materials. As SACEUR, Eisenhower encouraged planning for a defense of Europe based on the thousands of nuclear weapons then on order.[5] The military sought custody over these weapons to ensure prompt dispatch against Soviet targets, particularly the airfields from which Soviet nuclear strikes might be launched. In September 1952, Truman reluctantly gave the Defense Department broad custodial responsibilities during peacetime.

It was President Eisenhower, however, who opened the floodgates for global dispersion of launch-ready nuclear weapons: The American stockpile grew from about 1,000 weapons in 1953 to nearly 18,000 by 1960. In contrast to Truman, Eisenhower regarded nuclear weapons as an integral part of American and allied defense when he entered the White House in January 1953. Within weeks of taking office he was considering the use of tactical nuclear weapons against targets in North Korea,[6] and, together with Secretary of State Dulles, advocated dropping the nuclear taboo. By May, Eisenhower had grown weary of the slow progress in negotiating a Korean truce and "had reached the point of being convinced that we have got to consider the atomic bomb as simply another weapon in our arsenal."[7] In 1953 Eisenhower endorsed the doctrine of "massive retaliation," which threatened all-out nuclear attack on the Soviet Union at the outset of hostilities. By the end of his second term, 82 percent of the U.S. nuclear stockpile, approximately 15,000 weapons, had been consigned to the military, although by that time he had come to recognize that a nuclear weapon was not "simply another weapon."[8]

Many thousands of these "tactical" weapons were intended for the European battlefield. They were to be stored in depots during peacetime, and therefore, were not to be immediately available. Many longer-range tactical weapons, however, were mated to delivery vehicles whose peacetime readiness allowed rapid employment.[9]

Thousands of nuclear weapons were also acquired by American strategic forces. Under the direction of General Curtis LeMay, the number of SAC long-range aircraft capable of nuclear delivery based in Europe and the United States grew from a few dozen to well over 2,000 during the 1950s. Equally impressive was the ever-growing readiness of these forces. At the time of the Berlin Blockade, nuclear bomber missions required several days of round-the-clock preparation, including more than 2 days just for bomb assembly. By 1957, SAC stood ready to launch the first wave of nuclear-armed combat aircraft against the Soviet Union within a few hours of receiving the order. Three years later one-third of its bomber fleet was ready for immediate take-off with some 1,400 nuclear bombs aboard. In 1962, during the Cuban Missile Crisis, SAC flew one-eighth of its B-52 bombers on airborne alert continuously for weeks.[10]

The Command System

In sharp contrast to weapons development and deployment, the command system underwent a slow and chaotic evolution without the semblance of a grand design. In one vital respect this evolution was doomed to be an uphill battle since the inherent destructiveness of nuclear weapons, and the advent of ICBMs, would soon render command facilities vulnerable to sudden and massive disruption.

President Eisenhower anticipated the difficulties ahead, and proposed a thorough overhaul of the command system to help ensure rapid reaction should the Soviets attack. To justify a streamlined chain of command from the president to the nuclear combatant commanders, particularly the SAC commander who directed America's long-range nuclear forces, Eisenhower told Congress that

> warning times are vanishing. There can be little confidence that we would surely know of an attack before it is launched. Speeds of flight are already such as to make timely reaction difficult and interpretation uncertain ... [existing command arrangements are] cumbersome and unreliable in time of peace and not usable in time of war.... The number of headquarters between the commander-in-chief and the commander of each unified command must be kept at the very minimum. Every additional level courts delay, confusion of authority, and diffusion of responsibility.[11]

A convinced Congress enacted the Defense Reorganization Act of 1958, which remains in force today. It defines the chain of combat command as running from the National Command Authority (NCA) (the president and the secretary of defense, or their duly constituted successors) through the Joint Chiefs of Staff (JCS) directly to the unified and specified commands[12] (See Figure 4.1).

The Eisenhower administration also instituted more coherent arrangements for increasing readiness in anticipation of war, and for coordinating wartime operations. In 1959 the JCS established five different levels of alert readiness. These so-called defense conditions, or DEFCONs, enable the NCA and the JCS to raise or lower force readiness in discrete stages with clear understandings of the basic military steps that each stage entails. The DEFCON system seeks to ensure that changes in readiness and operations will be deliberate acts of national policy, and that transitions between alert levels will be orderly and appropriately timed. The system does not, however, attempt to prescribe these operations in full detail, so that readiness within the various military commands can be adjusted to correspond to prevailing political and military circumstances.

By today's standard of worldwide communications via satellite, Eisenhow-

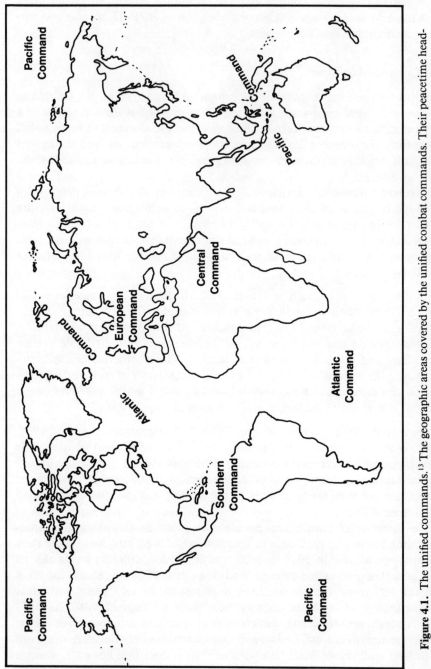

Figure 4.1. The unified commands.[13] The geographic areas covered by the unified combat commands. Their peacetime head-quarters are European at Stuttgart; Southern at Quarry Heights, Panama; Central, which grew out of the Rapid Deployment Force, at MacDill Air Force Base (AFB); Atlantic at Norfolk, VA; and Pacific at Honolulu.

er's chain of command depended on an unsophisticated technology: radio communications of lower reliability and much smaller data capacity linked Washington to its far-flung nuclear forces. Transoceanic telephone cables were not laid to Europe and Hawaii until 1956 and 1964, respectively. Even after they entered service, high frequency and troposcatter radio, which can be degraded by a variety of natural and nuclear phenomena, were the primary links to nuclear forces outside the continental United States.[14] And yet the nuclear arsenal, including a large portion of the SAC bomber fleet, was forward-deployed and thus dependent on these links.

Nuclear operations in Europe, including those of SAC, were coordinated from a JCS facility at High Wycombe, England, which was linked to what was later to become the National Military Command Center (NMCC) in the Pentagon, and to what is now the Alternate National Military Command Center (ANMCC) beneath a mountain at Fort Ritchie, Maryland, some 75 miles from Washington. The latter, built in 1953, provided (and still provides) the principal emergency relocation site for national officals and the JCS from which wartime nuclear operations would have been authorized and monitored.[15] SAC bombers in Europe were directed from SAC Headquarters in Omaha in coordination with the Pentagon or the Ft. Ritchie facility.[16] By the early 1960s, SAC could transmit voice commands to the globally dispersed bombers. This was the primary means of sending an Emergency Action Message (EAM), popularly known as the *go code,* to bombers already aloft following a "Positive Control Launch." The latter procedure enables the SAC commander to order his bomber fleet on ground alert to take off for survival, fly to turnaround points near Soviet territory, and return to base unless attack orders are received.

Doctrine: The First SIOP

In 1960 Eisenhower created new institutional means of producing master plans for attacking enemy targets with nuclear forces.[17] A new JCS organization, called the Joint Strategic Targeting Planning Staff (JSTPS), representing all nuclear combat commands, and headed by the SAC Commander, undertook to integrate all nuclear attack plans and to align them with national guidance issued by higher authorities. The JSTPS produced the first Single Integrated Operational Plan (SIOP) in 1960. Although tactical nuclear weapons were excluded from the SIOP, plans for their use were at least checked against the SIOP to ensure general compatibility and minimal conflict between target assignments. The SACEUR's nuclear war plans were similarly coordinated after NATO representatives joined JSTPS in 1963.

The creation of the SIOP reflected America's reliance on nuclear weapons. The SIOP, and the JCS nuclear guidance issued shortly before Eisenhower left office, reflected the president's view that in the event of war the initial strike must "be firmly laid on," and involve the integrated and simultaneous use of the bulk of the air force's and navy's nuclear weapons, with the objective of eliminating Soviet nuclear forces, and of inflicting severe damage on a large portion of Soviet military and urban-industrial targets.[18]

During the 1950s, the whole U.S. strategic posture was "primitive" by current standards. The strategic war plan had but one option—massive retaliation, to be ordered by a president who was basically limited to providing authorization to unleash the forces. The main responsibility of the JCS was to transmit his approval via an unsophisticated but reliable communications net to the nuclear commanders, who would prosecute the war in accordance with their plan. Beyond this initial involvement, the president and the JCS would almost be reduced to the role of spectators. But while the Eisenhower posture may have been primitive, and as lacking in political credibility as the Kennedy administration was to contend, it did have the virtue of having an internally consistent combination of forces, command technology, and doctrine.

NUCLEAR FORCES, COMMAND, AND DOCTRINE: 1960 TO THE PRESENT

The Evolution of Forces and Doctrine

The trend toward higher peacetime readiness has continued during the last 25 years, resulting in a four- to fivefold growth in the number of nuclear (and notably strategic) weapons maintained at close to peak readiness. This trend is principally due to large scale deployment of solid-fueled ICBMs, 85 percent of which are always available for almost instanteneous launch; the deployment of strategic missile-launching submarines (SSBNs), 55 percent of which operate at sea in peacetime; [19] the equipping of ICBM and SLBMs with multiple warheads; and the extended range of strategic delivery vehicles, particularly SLBMs, so that submarines now have much shorter transit times to launch areas, as well as reduced vulnerability. Strategic Air Command bombers also have yielded a net growth, although in their case the situation is more complex.[20] Furthermore, since 1979 a growing proportion of the SAC bombers carry air-launched cruise missiles (ALCM), which can be launched from outside Soviet airspace. The ALCM has a terrain-matching guidance system that gives it an accuracy that is superior to that of other strategic weapons.

An elaborate command infrastructure has been created for this arsenal. For many tasks it performs adequately—even superbly. Functional coherence in peacetime has been achieved, and progress toward effective command for conflicts below the level of large-scale strategic war has been considerable. Serious vulnerabilities and deficiencies, however, have continued to plague U.S. command because the United States now faces a far more capable adversary, and the command system is now expected to implement a more demanding war plan.

The Kennedy administration initiated the doctrinal move away from massive retaliation. The last Eisenhower strategic war plan, SIOP-62, was presented to President Kennedy in a briefing by JCS Chairman General Lyman

Lemnitzer that has recently been declassified.[21] Two types of flexibility were incorporated into the plan: execution could either be in retaliation or by preemption, and targets in any or all satellite states could be withheld. All preplanned attack options called for strikes by the entire available U.S. strategic force against an "optimum-mix" of military and industrial targets spread across the Soviet Union. The briefing warned that while "it would be possible to order that no direct attacks be made on cities . . . it must be clearly understood that any decision to execute only a portion of the entire plan would involve acceptance of certain grave risks"[22] because "the ability to defeat the enemy must not be lost by the introduction into the SIOP of an excessive number of options which would contribute to confusion and lower our assurance of success under the most adverse circumstances." At the time the United States enjoyed an enormous degree of superiority over the Soviet Union:[23] more than 1,500 weapons were normally on alert, versus some 200 Soviet weapons in all of which only a very small portion could be kept on day-to-day alert. Nevertheless, Gen. Lemnitzer was very cautious regarding the prospects for preemption: "under any circumstances—even a preemptive attack—it would be expected that some portion of the Soviet long-range nuclear force would strike the United States."

Kennedy's advisers were highly dissatisfied with the plan. Before the JCS briefing McGeorge Bundy, Kennedy's National security adviser, had already warned that "the current war plan is dangerously rigid . . . In essence, [it] calls for shooting off everything we have in one shot, and so is constructed to make any more flexible course very difficult."[24] Massive retaliation was therefore supplanted by a new employment strategy, *flexible response*, which envisaged tailored responses to a nuclear attacks.[25] The goal was not only to control escalation and thereby limit damage to the United States, but also to make the threat of nuclear retaliation more credible by providing a wider range of options than an all-out strike.

Flexible response, as opposed to massive retaliation, requires a command system that can perform many more tasks during and following an enemy attack: It must discern not only the initiation but also the details of the attack; calibrate a proportionate response; issue targeting instructions to the released forces; assess the effectiveness of the counterattack; redirect operations during conflict; manage withheld forces; and, if necessary, ensure control over nuclear operations through repeated exchanges. To achieve these objectives, a president would need a military organization that would permit controlled and selective response, as well as negotiating pauses. As these were to be strictly presidential prerogatives, the president's role would be greatly enlarged—the president would not only decide whether to employ strategic forces, but also which option to exercise. By implication, the president would be involved in assessing attacks and weighing the response in the light of unfolding events, and his responsibilities would extend to follow-on nuclear strikes, negotiations, and war termination.

The command structure inherited from the Eisenhower administration could not begin to accommodate these ambitions. To assert political control over details of nuclear operations in wartime, command would have had to be far more survivable and better linked to national decision makers. To ensure civilian control, safeguards against unintended employment of nuclear weapons had to be strengthened. Kennedy's secretary of defense, Robert McNamara, identified these problems early on and took steps to alleviate them. Less vulnerable national command centers, including an air- and ship-based alternate command post, were deployed, along with hardened communications. All were merged into a National Military Command System (NMCS) designed to bring nuclear operations under the strict control of national policy officials.

Elaborate safeguards—human, procedural, and physical—were also created to prevent nuclear war from starting as a consequence of human or machine error, false alarms, or willful acts. The Defense Department instituted the screening of individuals with access to nuclear weapons, imposed a "two-man rule" to eliminate access by a single individual, and began a program for installing electromechanical locks, called Permissive Action Links (PALs), on nuclear weapons, especially those consigned to the NATO allies.[26] A weapon equipped with a PAL cannot be armed unless it is first unlocked by a combination known only to higher authorities, who must transmit a message containing the unlock codes down to the user. For many years all U.S. strategic and nonstrategic nuclear weapons, except for those operated by the navy (including the SLBM force), have been outfitted with PALs.

In 1967 the U.S. and its NATO allies formally adopted the strategy of flexible response.[27] The prior policy, in which NATO's conventional forces were to act as a "trip-wire" that would set off a massive nuclear counterattack, was replaced by a posture in which the conventional forces were promoted to the mission of repelling a conventional attack on their own, with tactical nuclear forces serving as a back-up should that defense fail, while U.S. strategic forces would stand ready as weapons of last resort. During the mid-1970s, flexible response also became the official U.S. doctrine for deterring strategic attack, although it has been de facto policy since the early 1960s when the ability to "withhold" weapons intended for certain target sets, such as urban-industrial areas, was introduced into the nuclear war plan. The objective of recent administrations has been to enhance the credibility of deterrence by developing forces, plans, and command infrastructures that would allow retaliation to be carried out in stages, so that if strategic deterrence should fail, it could do so gradually, rather than suddenly and entirely. As we shall see, the present command system is too vulnerable to support this strategy unless the Soviet Union were to adhere to a policy of restraint in attacking the U.S. command system, and the ongoing improvement program will not alter that situation.

The Command System in the 1960s

The introduction of Soviet ICBMs during the early 1960s led SAC to erect an elaborate airborne command network to back up its increasingly vulnerable fixed command facilities. Beginning in 1961, SAC flew an alternate command post, nicknamed "Looking Glass," on continuous airborne alert. By rotating a fleet of EC-135 aircraft, SAC kept a general officer and a battle staff aloft at all times, ready to assume control should the underground command center near Omaha be destroyed. Other EC-135 aircraft were maintained on 15-minute ground alert both to augment Looking Glass and to serve in a radio relay network.[28] To employ Minutemen, the command aircraft could send radio messages to the underground launch centers. Special aircraft flying nearby could also launch missiles directly should the manned launch centers be destroyed. Certain command aircraft also carried low frequency radios and 2-mile long trailing wire antennas for long-range communication that would be relatively immune to radio interference caused by nuclear bursts. This created links to naval strategic forces, bomber bases, and Minuteman launch control centers. The primary survivable link to the far-flung bomber forces was High Frequency radio from the airborne command posts.

During the 1960s the command infrastructure had to be extended out to sea to support the newly christened Polaris SSBN force. For sending launch order to submerged submarines, the navy constructed a handful of globally dispersed very low frequency (VLF) radio towers. Radio waves having such frequencies penetrate several feet of sea water and allow receipt of messages on board a submarine with an unexposed antenna cable, or by towing a buoy controlled to ride below the surface. Backup VLF was supplied by specially outfitted aircraft called TACAMO, which was able to reel out a wire antenna that would trail 5 miles beneath the aircraft in order to send VLF signals. By the end of the 1960s, one of these aircraft was usually aloft over the Atlantic, with another typically on ground alert in the Pacific. Communication links between TACAMOs and SAC's airborne command system were also established during this period. Beginning in 1965, the navy also deployed alternate airborne command posts on ground alert for the commander-in-chief, Pacific (CINCPAC), whose headquarters in Hawaii had become vulnerable to nuclear missile attack. Similar alternate command posts were assigned to the Atlantic Command in 1973. It should be noted that nuclear forces in Europe were also being built up during this period.

The National Military Command System formed the highest layer of this command infrastructure. Created in 1962, the NMCS's protection was seen as an urgent priority from the outset, and the most important step to that end, the deployment of an airborne command post for the NCA, took place that year. This was provided by EC-135 aircraft on ground alert near Washington. These aircraft were given the official designation of National Emergency Airborne Command Post (NEACP, pronounced "Kneecap"). It provided the most survivable of the national level command centers then in operation, with the others being the NMCC in the Pentagon, the ANMCC at Ft. Ritchie, and a cruiser deployed off the East Coast from 1962 until 1969. Given its relative invulnerability, NEACP would have played a pivotal role in the national control of nuclear forces during a nuclear attack during the 1960s.

The basic structure of the American nuclear command system was complete by the late 1960s. Its coherence and partial survivability stemmed from the deployment of a survivable airborne command network, the rationalization and integration of planning, the imposition of elaborate safeguards to prevent unauthorized firing of nuclear weapons, the establishment of the DEFCON system for alerting forces, and the creation of a global command infrastructure. Subsequent efforts to incorporate new technologies and reduce command vulnerability were needed in the light of emerging threats—for instance, the first patrols of Soviet SSBNs off U.S. coasts, which cut Soviet missile flight times in half, began in 1969. These endeavors have received an increasing emphasis in recent years. Nevertheless, they will leave the basic architecture of the command edifice built during the 1960s intact.

Evolution of Command Technology Since 1970

The 1970s and 1980s marked a new era in command sophistication. The space program and the computer revolution created unprecedented capabilities for surveillance, communications, and automatic data processing. American security institutions have acquired the ability to closely monitor a wide range of Soviet military operations promptly and nearly continuously, [29] as well as to quickly adjust U.S. military operations in the light of events. Surveillance was transformed by improved electronic intelligence and by powerful airborne and space-based electrooptical imaging systems. A vast improvement in the coverage and in the timeliness of missile attack warning arrived in the early 1970s. Satellites were placed in stationary (geosynchronous) orbit 22,000 miles above the equator where their infrared sensors would reliably detect the fiery plumes of Soviet ICBMs and SLBMs shortly after missile ignition. Within one minute after lift-off, this satellite early warning network would flash the alarm to all major command centers. A comprehensive net of ground-based radars, which has undergone continuous upgrading, (see Figure 4.2) would subsequently detect and track the warheads disgorged by these missiles. This observation by two *independent* sensors is referred to as *dual phenomenology,* a term that fails to convey the fact that the combined system actually provides a large body of data that must, within instrumental errors, conform to an internally consistent pattern (e.g., appropriate time intervals between launch and radar detection, tracks heading in plausible directions, etc.). While this system—and indeed any such system—is bound to register false alarms, the likelihood that a false alarm would survive human scrutiny and trigger a military response beyond a rise in the alert level is considered to be very remote.[30] In the midst of a severe crisis, however, when fear of a strategic attack is heightened, and if there is a substantial reliance on prompt retaliation, the risk that a false alarm would be accepted as real may be appreciable.

Communications have also been revolutionized. Although enormous traffic still flows over terrestrial lines, undersea cable, and atmospheric radio, satellites carry a heavy load of long-haul communications and would perform many critical functions in wartime. First- and second-generation communication satellites interconnect the national military command posts, including NEACP, the major fixed military headquarters, many of the early warning and intelligence sensors, and American embassies. The navy's satellite network links naval command posts with every deployed ship and TACAMO aircraft. The air force transponders on various host satellites connect senior military commanders, and their alternate airborne command posts, to NEACP, SAC bombers, Minuteman launch control centers, land- and sea-based theater nuclear forces, and TACAMO aircraft. Also, NATO has its own dedicated satellites. Satellites, therefore, provide a means of direct, global, virtually instantaneous communications with every significant nuclear force element. They would be extensively used during a crisis to regulate force readiness and during wartime to disseminate orders.

Computerization of the command system has been slower than might be expected, but that does not diminish its impact. Among the notable applications are computerized fusion of intelligence/warning indicators; computer-based communications networks for distribution of raw and processed intelligence data; and interlocking standardized computers for transfer, storage, and display of the voluminous data on force status.

THE PRELUDE TO WAR

We have now depicted what military men might call "the nuclear order of battle"—the list of arms that could be thrown into a fray, as well as the command system that would strive to marshal all those resources in pursuit of military objectives. But that only gives a static picture of what could suddenly become a swiftly changing scene. To comprehend crisis behavior one must envision what nuclear forces and their commands are likely to do in anticipation of impending chaos.

Political, Strategic, and Tactical Warning

A major attack that involves forces beyond alert ballistic missiles cannot be launched without engaging in significant departures from normal peacetime behavior that are difficult to hide and disguise in their entirety. Recognition of such behavior constitutes strategic warning. To be precise, we shall call *strategic warning* the prediction of an impending attack on the basis of any and all sources of intelligence, such as the detection of ominous troop movements, intercepted messages, peculiar leadership behavior, etc. In contrast, *tactical warning* is the detection of the actual attack before combat is joined.

Prolonged political strife usually precedes the outbreak of war. In most instances, rising diplomatic tensions have provided political warning that war might be imminent. Throughout the twentieth century, and only with rare exceptions, the intelligence services of the major powers have been able to offer strategic warning. Nevertheless, two of the century's most devastating attacks, the bombing of Pearl Harbor and the Nazi invasion of Russia, caught their victims by surprise even though Washington and Moscow had acquired ominous evidence that war could be at hand. As we have already seen in Chapter 3, today's DEFCON system, even with 1941 communications, would probably have translated Washington's knowledge of Japan's intentions into effective precautionary measures, but even microelectronics and satellites would probably not have helped Stalin because he committed an understandable error in political judgment.

Today the superpowers possess intelligence gathering systems of great power and sophistication that allow them to monitor each other constantly. That would seem to say that warning of a major attack is virtually certain; however, several entries stand on the other side of the ledger. First, there is no discernable improvement in human ability to assess political warning. Were Bismarck to reappear, he could surely assume masterful leadership of any diplomatic service, but the intelligence officers on Moltke's General Staff could not begin to understand the tools that would be put at their disposal. Second, to compound this problem, there is the unprecedented circumstance of two great powers with vast forces confronting each other for decades on end, so that useful warning must discern departures from a military configuration that other ages would have construed as ominous strategic warning. Finally, the American and Soviet strategic organizations have been designed to cope with sudden attack, and for that very reason large portions of their forces are always ready to strike on the shortest of notice. This vicious circle could create circumstances in which strategic warning of a missile attack would be short, or perhaps even non-existent.

To protect against the failure of strategic warning indicators, two options are available. The first option is prompt launch—counterattacks ranging from a launch before there are any enemy nuclear detonations, on the basis of unambiguous tactical warning that a major attack has been initiated, to a retaliatory launch that does not begin until there are such detonations. Here "ranging from" alludes to the possibility that the magnitude of the attack (as estimated from data provided by tactical warning sensors), and the number of nuclear detonations, could be parameters that determine the timing of launch. For example, detection of ICBM and SLBM launches by satellite-borne infrared sensors, observation of their subsequent flight by ground-based radars, and detonation at high altitude of one precursor submarine-launched warhead, might suffice to trigger prompt launch. Whether that is launch-on-warning or launch-under-attack is a question of semantics. The second option is the protection of the strategic command system and forces so that an attack can be ridden out. Both superpowers have sought to protect their forces and command facilities by fortification ("hardening"), by hiding under the sea, or by mobility, as with the airborne command posts; however, as will be discussed later, there is good reason to believe that both rely on prompt launch to a considerable degree.

The nuclear command apparatus is far more vulnerable to surprise attack than the strategic forces themselves. timely alerting, especially of key military and civilian commanders, is of vital importance; legitimate authorization and successful implementation of the SIOP would be at stake, although even a massive surprise attack could not eliminate the ability to retaliate. Furthermore, a surgical surprise attack that seeks to decapitate an unalerted U.S. government and incapacitate large surviving forces could not be undertaken with confidence, and should be recognized as running immeasurable risks given the consequences of failure. To significantly enhance peacetime protection against decapitation, several hours of strategic warning are needed for basic emergency measures, such as the evacuation of key leaders. The generation of nearly full wartime C^3I capability and protection would require many additional hours.

The upper range of these warning times—hours—is interminable in comparison to what is, at least in principle, required to order, launch, and deliver a ballistic missile attack. Such an attack "out-of-the-blue" is considered to be very improbable, however. In all likelihood, serious consideration of nuclear conflict would only come into play in a severe crisis, probably only after conventional hostilities had already begun, and by then the command system and its nuclear forces would already be at heightened alert.[31] How political decision making would be expected to perform under such circumstances is then the crucial question.

Political and strategic warning can come in many forms, as a sampling of recent historical cases illustrates.[32] Primary intelligence concerning the clandestine emplacement of Soviet missiles in Cuba in 1962 included shipping surveillance, reports from agents in Cuba, and, most importantly, photos by U-2 reconnaissance planes. On the other hand, it appears likely that American preparations for the blockade of Cuba were not apprehended by Soviet intelligence. In 1968, Soviet maneuvers near the Czech border were detected by optical surveillance and communications intercepts, but the actual invasion escaped detection by normal NATO monitoring methods; press dispatches alerted key U.S. military commanders in Europe, while President Johnson was informed by the Soviet ambassador.[33]

Response to Warning: Decision Machinery and Process

Existing U.S. government organizations responsible for coping with crises will be described in Chapter 11, but as they are central to our subject, we will provide a thumbnail sketch here, emphasizing the components directly involved with strategic forces.

The oldest and highest body with responsibility for advising the president during international crises is the NSC, whose statutory members are the president, vice president, secretary of state, and secretary of defense, with the JCS chairman and the director of central intelligence (DCI) as statutory advisors. The NSC staff, which has consisted of several scores of professionals in recent administrations, is directed by the president's assistant for national security affairs, colloquially known as the national security advisor.[34]

During a crisis, the president can either rely on the NSC, or form an ad hoc group. Thus President Kennedy formed a hand-picked team called the *executive committee* (ExComm) at the outbreak of the Cuban Missle Crisis some days before convening the NSC. In subsequent administrations the NSC has also been supplemented by high-level groups. For example, President Nixon established the Washington Special Actions Group (WSAG) headed by Secretary of State Henry Kissinger. We shall examine the performance of ExComm and WSAG in Chapter 8.

In addition to the White House, the various executive departments have crisis management organizations. Within the Defense Department, the JCS is the locus of crisis management. Although crisis-action teams form at all major military command centers around the world when strategic warning indicators light up, or at local command centers in the case of isolated incidents, the JCS exert primary control over military operations in a major crisis. The JCS formally recognizes three degrees of crisis and organizes itself accordingly. Situations that fall into the highest category of severity, such as escalating tension in Europe, would trigger *emergency operating procedures,* (EOP), which can be implemented by JCS or at the request of higher authority. Normally, formation of the EOP organization at the Pentagon should take about 4 hours. That step would resonate not only within the military command structure but throughout the entire security apparatus, and would institute government-wide emergency procedures. If war appeared to be imminent, the EOP would be implemented at the ANMCC, and would probably coincide with implementation of the Joint Emergency Evacuation Plan, which relocates military and civilian leaders and staff to the ANMCC and other emergency sites.

Once these emergency procedures are in effect, the JCS would meet on an urgent basis to assist the NCA. Depending on circumstances, the JCS and the NCA would confer in the Pentagon, at Ft. Ritchie, on board NEACP, or via telephone; the president is always linked to the NMCC wherever he may be, and he always has an airborne command post as his disposal.

The agenda for these conferences is, in principle, set by decisions at the highest level. In practice, however, the political and military context of the crisis would have a large impact on the very nature of that agenda. The EOP establishes filters at several layers to ensure that only the most critical issues require NCA/JCS decision. A very intense and complex confrontation, especially one that had led to outbreak of hostilities, would therefore produce a decision-making context very different from that of the worst post-1945 crisis, when President Kennedy was personally engaged in even quite minor matters. Under such circumstances only the weightiest of military decisions are likely to be made at the presidential level. Time-sensitive military operations would be managed by the JCS organization. One item in this intricate web deserves special mention: the issuing of nuclear attack orders. Only the NCA (or its duly constituted successor) can authorize nuclear weapons employment. Once the NCA has made its decisions, the Pentagon command center and its backups, including NEACP, have dedicated communications to disseminate the required EAM to all nuclear combat commands.[35]

While these two key groups—the Joint Chiefs and the president's ExComm—are being alerted and assembled, allied governments also gear up to deal with the crisis. Heads of state may consult directly over dedicated communication networks such as ACE HIGH, and their embassy staffs perform related functions.[36] Should Europe be directly involved, the situation center at NATO headquarters would become a hub of information-sharing and coordination.

Military Alert Options

The response of the governments obviously would depend on the nature of the crisis. Increasing the alert readiness of military forces is one option. Orders moving U.S. forces to a higher alert level, or DEFCON, are normally issued by the Joint Chiefs. Normal peacetime readiness for all U.S. forces, except for SAC, is called DEFCON 5; SAC readiness is normally a notch higher, at DEFCON 4. Crisis alerts could place the forces at progressively higher levels of readiness: DEFCON 3—units at heightened readiness to await further orders; DEFCON 2—ready for combat; or DEFCON 1—deployed for imminent combat.

The United States has declared global nuclear alerts three times since the inception of the DEFCON system.[37] During the Cuban Crisis of 1962, the alert status was raised to DEFCON 3, with the exception of SAC, which moved to DEFCON 2, whereas the European Command was kept below DEFCON 3 but above its peacetime status. In the Yom Kippur Crisis of 1973 a rather attentuated global DEFCON 3 alert was called. None of these provoked a reciprocal alert by the Soviet Union; indeed, to our knowledge the Soviets have never raised the alert level of their nuclear forces for the purpose of political "signaling."

A similar mechanism governs NATO readiness, known as the NATO alert condition, or LERTCON, system. The three formal rungs above the normal peacetime status are designated LERTCON 3 (simple alert), LERTCON 2 (reinforced alert), and LERTCON 1 (general alert).

In addition to these global and NATO-wide alerting procedures, there is also an extensive distribution of alert authority throughout the American military establishment. Combat commanders are ultimately accountable for troop safety and for maintaining the capability to accomplish their assigned missions, and must decide themselves what alert measures are necessary. To that end, individual commands have their own alerting procedures but they are coordinated with the JCS DEFCON system.[38] Furthermore, changes in alert level set by JCS are widely construed as instructions on what steps to take at a minimum. Additional measures deemed prudent by subordinate echelons may be taken at their discretion. In unusual circumstances, even individual weapon commanders could order steps normally not taken until the formal declaration of a new DEFCON posture. Naturally, such discretionary authority is not a license, and abuse thereof could lead to disciplinary action.[39] Commanders may also appeal to higher authority to revoke any order that in their view overreacts to the actual threat. Field commanders can act, therefore, as a buffer to moderate certain excesses that an untempered alerting system might produce.[40]

Another important feature of the alerting system is its flexibility in permitting operations to be tailored to the requirements of a particular situation. Provisions exist to alert units selectively.[41] Detailed checklists also allow specific commands or even individual units to be exempted from universal alerts, or to specify actions not to be taken.[42]

In a serious crisis, central authorities could not micromanage alerts; however, national political and military leaders could only consider the most critical alert items. Lower levels of command would be responsible for inescapably elaborate alert operations and the detailed instructions they require.

STRATEGIC OPERATIONS IN WARTIME

Nuclear forces must not only be managed in crisis, but also in wartime. Scenarios and military contingency plans for dealing with them must be constructed. While a good deal is publicly known about the technical and organizational parts of the nuclear infrastructure, the opposite is true of operations plans.

Conventional War

Conventional war would involve nuclear forces in many ways. The great majority of forces designed to deliver tactical nuclear weapons can also deliver conventional munitions. Such *dual-capable* forces may be assigned non-nuclear missions, and deployed to areas where conventional battles may be fought. This mingling of nuclear and nonnuclear weaponry is especially pronounced in Western Europe, where some two thousand nuclear warheads for short-range delivery systems stand ready just behind the intra-German border.

In a large conventional war the NATO command infrastructure could be severely disrupted by jamming, sabotage, antisatellite warfare, and direct attack. Should that occur, command of nuclear forces in the theater would also be severely impaired, and even the worldwide strategic command systems would suffer some degradation.

Nuclear War

Should the Soviets strike first with a massive nuclear attack, the United States and NATO would lose their primary command facilities and communications. They would then fall back on emergency mobile command posts, especially aircraft, to direct regional and intercontinental nuclear forces. Back-up communications links between mobile command posts and deployed forces would be tenuous, and could result in the isolation of large portions of the force.

Although the U.S. strategic command system would suffer significant collateral damage during a regional nuclear war, it would remain largely intact until struck by Soviet strategic forces. Early warning satellites would observe launches of Soviet missiles against Western Europe and Navstar satellites would detect nuclear detonations in the NATO theater. As a result, Washington would probably have a considerably clearer and more comprehensive picture of the situation than that available to European governments.

The major attack options available to strategic forces in the event of war are best classified in accordance to their timing: preemption, prompt launch, and retaliation subsequent to an attack. Putting aside the question of their plausibility, it is instructive to examine how these options would be carried out with the *current* U.S. command system, and to what extent the U.S. command-and-control improvement program will enhance the feasibility of prompt launch and retaliation.

First, and solely for the sake of clarity, we describe the steps entailed were the United States to initiate strategic warfare. The president's decision would be translated into a launch order by the NMCC in the Pentagon or by one of its alternates. The order is a short message giving the targeting option to be implemented, its timing, and codes establishing the validity of the order. As the message is read aloud over a dedicated telephone system that connects national headquarters to subordinate nuclear units, many individual commanders would write it down, verify its authenticity, and proceed to implement it. Others would receive the message via radio relay sites.

Crews in the 100 underground launch-control centers at the six Minuteman bases would hear that message as it is read. Repetitions of the order would also be received over a variety of redundant links. After verifying the legitimizing codes, the crews would begin their launch checklists culminating in a synchronized turn of the launch keys that fire the missiles. Prior to key turn, the crews must send the targeting instructions to their missiles. They must also have received special codes that unlock the PALs. Without these so-called enabling codes, the crews cannot transmit the commands that arm the weapons, and the missiles cannot launch. Under normal circumstances, all launch procedures could be completed within a few minutes. Less time would be needed had crews already been alerted to expect launch orders.

Bomber crews would receive the order from their wing command posts. Like the Minuteman launch crews, staff in these posts would copy the voice message as it is transmitted by telephone from the Pentagon. They would then relay the message by local radio transmitters to the bombers being prepared for take-off. Once airborne, the bombers would listen for follow-on instructions from the base radio towers and from the SAC high frequency radio net used for long-distance communications. Bombers would also monitor satellite and other radio frequencies.

Ballistic missile submarines monitor the VLF signals sent from navy shore stations in Maine and Washington state. These high-power radio transmitters can reach virtually the entire SSBN force patrolling in the Atlantic and Pacific as long as the submarines are trailing an antenna at or just below the surface. Staff at remote locations, such as Atlantic Command headquarters in Virginia, can operate the shore stations and transmit the message.

The demand on the command system would be vastly greater should the Soviet Union initiate strategic conflict. The performance of strategic command, therefore, must be assessed against the conditions likely to be created by a massive Soviet first strike.

It is commonly assumed that Soviet command would minimize warning by simultaneously firing ICBMs and SLBMs. The ICBM warheads would begin to land about 25 minutes after lift-off. For missiles launched near the U.S. coasts, the time between SLBM breakwater and impact could be less than 10 minutes. Warheads on SLBMs could also be used to produce environmental disturbances in an attempt to disrupt U.S. strategic communications before any warheads actually hit U.S. targets. Ionizing radiation from high-altitude bursts could create electromagnetic pulses, auroral effects, radio and radar blackout, and magnetic disturbances over areas as large as major portions of the continental United States. Such environmental phenomena can impair or disrupt the emission, propagation, and reception of the electromagnetic waves that are to detect incoming warheads, and which would carry communications traffic.

Early warning satellites would provide the earliest indication of a missile attack.[43] Their infrared sensors would detect the fiery plumes of ICBM and SLBM boosters during their first few minutes of powered flight into space. Reports on the size of the attack would be received immediately at the Pentagon, Ft. Ritchie, SAC headquarters, and North American Air Defense Command (NORAD) headquarters in Colorado. Rearward communications from the satellite ground stations to these major facilities are routed over satellites, undersea cable, and terrestrial communications within the United States. Radars scanning toward all potential launch sites in the Soviet Union (see Figure 4.2) would confirm an ICBM attack within about 10 minutes after launch and report to NORAD. Other radars on the perimeter of the continental United States would confirm SLBM launches, and report to all four major command posts. Fine-grained assessment of the nature of the attack leading to a prompt identification of targets is not possible using the present sensor network.

Several minutes after launch of the attack, tactical warning would be flashed from the major command centers to all nuclear units; this would trigger extensive precautionary reactions at hundreds of locations. Bomber and command aircraft crews would scramble to their planes and stand by for take-off orders to avoid destruction on the ground. Command aircraft on ground alert, such as NEACP, would probably be sent aloft immediately. Minuteman launch crews would unlock their safes containing launch codes and keys, insert the keys into launch switches, and strap themselves into their chairs to brace for the expected shock waves.

The NORAD commander and the NMCC senior duty personnel are

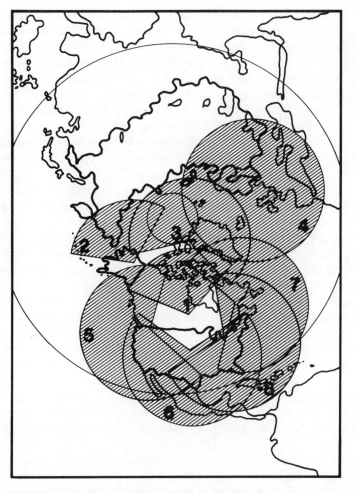

Figure 4.2. Ballistic missile warning radar coverage. This figure shows the areas covered at 1,000 km altitude by the phased-array radars.[44] Fan No. 1 is the radar in North Dakota that was originally part of the dismantled Safeguard ABM system. Fans 2 to 4 are the Ballistic Missile Early Warning System (BMEWS) radars respectively at Clear, AK; Thule, Greenland; and Fylingdale, U.K. Fans 5 to 8 are, respectively, the PAVE PAWS radars at Beale AFB, CA; Goodfellow AFB, TX; Cape Cod AFB, MA; and Robins AFB, GA.

responsible for inhibiting the alert momentum if it is a false alarm, and for accelerating it if it is a confirmed attack. They are expected to reach a definitive judgment in a matter of a few minutes. If possible, this judgment would be based on a combination of various preexisting strategic warning indicators, tactical warning of the attack from at least two distinct and independent sensors (such as detectors on infrared satellites and ground-based radars), and confirming reports from human operators of the sensors.

Assume for a moment that the NORAD commander has decided that the United States is under attack. Senior commanders would then take some immediate precautionary decisions, such as the protective launch of the SAC bomber force. The president, senior military advisors (including the NORAD and SAC commanders), and other policy officials would convene in emergency telecommunications Threat Assessment and Missile Attack Conferences to consider whether to retaliate and, if so, against what targets. The timing of retaliation would also be an essential consideration. A prompt launch of the Minuteman force to prevent its destruction by incoming ICBM warheads would require an almost instantaneous decision by the president. A quick decision would also facilitate delivery of the launch order to the other legs of the triad. The earlier approval is granted, the better are the chances of finding the command system still intact to transmit the order. Much of the network described in the U.S. initiation scenario should be available for use in a prompt-launch mode. Even under the best of circumstances, however, launch-on-warning or launch-under-attack would permit the president only a few minutes for deliberation, and the information available would not provide a clear picture of the attack.

Furthermore, the attack might be specifically designed to prevent prompt launch. To that end the Soviets could attempt to disrupt communications, at the very outset by jamming and perhaps sabotage, followed a scant few minutes later by producing the environmental disturbances described earlier, and some minutes thereafter by physical destruction of vital command elements. It is not unduly pessimistic, therefore, to suppose that telephone links used for the missile attack conference among U.S. decision makers and for sending orders to the forces would experience outages, or that the Pentagon and Ft. Ritchie would be destroyed by SLBMs with flight times of less than 10 minutes.

Under these conditions, prompt launch would depend on the back-up command networks that constitute the Post Attack Command and Control System (PACCS), which is shown schematically in Figure 4.3. Its ability to implement such a launch is limited in comparison to the primary ground-based command system.

The back-up networks are principally airborne: NEACP, SAC's Looking Glass, SAC airborne launch control centers, SAC communications relay aircraft, commander-in-chief, Atlantic (CINCLANT), and CINCPAC airborne command posts, and TACAMO submarine communications relay aircraft. Only Looking Glass and the TACAMO aircraft are airborne at all times. The others are normally kept on ground alert, so the establishment of a complete network would depend on whether or not aircraft had been destroyed on the ground. Some aircraft could be sent aloft in a crisis, with the others at heightened readiness for take-off. Calculations suggest[45] that although these measures would greatly mitigate vulnerability, they cannot guarantee that command aircraft on ground alert, particularly those located near the coasts, could avoid destruction by SLBMs. A combination of short missile flight

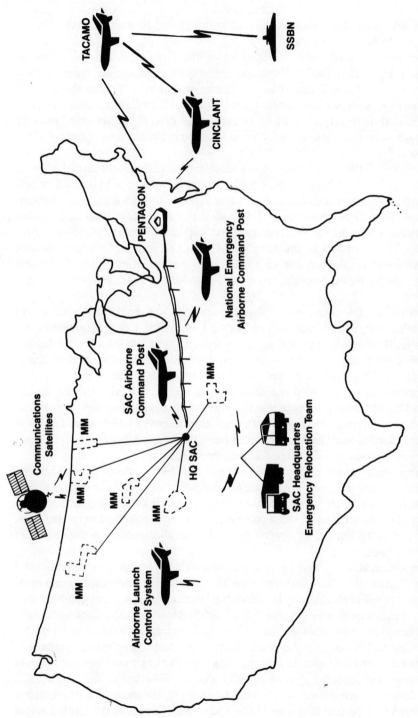

Figure 4.3. The Post Attack Command and Control System (PACCS). This figure depicts many (but not all) essential elements of this system; the areas marked MM designate Minuteman bases. The systems to be provided by the command improvement program, which will be discussed in Chapter 6 are not shown.

times, and early disruption of the communications used to order the aircraft aloft, could be lethal to them.

Aircraft that had safely escaped from their bases would thereafter be exposed to EMPs, radioactive dust clouds, and turbulence from nuclear explosions. Airborne launch control centers, which must fly near the Minuteman missile fields, would be particularly vulnerable to these collateral nuclear effects. Although airplanes in flight cannot be directly attacked by existing strategic weapons, these indirect hazards could elminate some portion of the network.[46]

In short, if the attack were to disrupt the peacetime command system, transmission of the launch order to the strategic forces would depend largely on airborne communications. The most reliable link in a nuclear environment is ultra-high frequency (UHF) radio, but it has the disadvantage that the transmitter and the receiver must be within each other's line of sight.[47] Transmittal of orders to the navy's TACAMO aircraft in such a postattack environment are not reliable with existing communications capabilities, and long-range VLF communications from TACAMO to submarines are also not assured.

Minuteman crews can also receive launch orders from aircraft flying within 200 miles of their underground centers via UHF radio. Every Minuteman silo has a UHF receiver that will accept a launch "vote" from airborne launch control centers in lieu of the "vote" from manned underground centers. Some silos also hold Minutemen that carry communications equipment instead of nuclear weapons, and will record messages inserted by airborne or underground launch crews. After taping the voice message, the missiles can be fired on lofted trajectories to broadcast the launch order over UHF radio. Far-flung strategic forces, such as bombers that have flown great distances away from their home bases, would listen for these messages.

Many other means of communications exist. Most aircraft in the airborne command network, and most strategic forces, are equipped for satellite communications, as well as with conventional radio links in various frequency bands. The endurance of the airborne systems as a coherent network, however, would be limited to several hours in the aftermath of a major Soviet nuclear attack.

The vulnerabilities and operating characteristics of the diverse command posts, communications, and forces are too complex to allow any simple measure of overall performance. In Chapter 6 we shall offer a crude estimate that indicates that as few as several tens of deliberately targeted nuclear detonations could severely damage the current U.S. command system in its peacetime alert status and that this might thereby preclude coordinated retaliation. The same exercise indicates that perhaps ten times as many weapons would be required should the system be fully alerted. Whether or not one assigns confidence to such a narrow technical assessment, the multitude of identified problems tend to cast strong doubt on the current ability of the United States to prosecute a coordinated strategic campaign in the wake of an attack on the command system. There is, therefore, a considerable likelihood that retaliation would not accomplish a significant fraction of the objectives embodied in the SIOP option that had been selected. From a Soviet perspective, on the other hand, that probability should not offer much comfort given the damage that would ensue from a large if incomplete retaliatory strike.

The United States has for some years pursued an extensive effort to strengthen its command system. A principal objective of the program is to provide reliable and secure communications in the environment created by nuclear explosions. In addition, the program will provide ground-mobile command posts as a complement to the airborne back-up facilities, and ground-mobile back-up terminals for read-outs from early-warning satellites and other warning sensors. Taken together, these should yield a command system that, in its peacetime state of readiness, would be roughly as sturdy as the current system when fully alerted, but would have much stronger communications capabilities under all circumstances and a greater capability to execute a prompt launch. The viability of U.S. strategic operations will therefore be considerably strengthened once these improvements are in place.

BRITISH AND FRENCH STRATEGIC NUCLEAR FORCES

Since the 1950s, both Great Britain and France have fielded nuclear forces[48] that, from their perspective, have strategic capabilities because they have sufficient range to reach high-value targets in the Soviet Union—in particular, Moscow. The numbers of weapons and the variety of delivery systems possessed by the British and French do not, of course, approach the magnitude of the superpowers' arsenals. Nevertheless, British and French forces are certainly powerful enough to provide a considerable deterrent that is independent of U.S. nuclear forces. In the coming years, the size of both nation's strategic arsenals are expected to increase markedly. Great Britain's inventory of strategic warheads is planned to more than quintuple to about 500 by the mid-1990s, while that of France will undergo a comparable growth to more than 600 warheads during the same period.[49] These expansions, when combined with the removal of the superpowers' theater-range nuclear weapons in accordance with the INF Treaty, imply that the British and French nuclear forces will acquire a considerably greater significance than they have today. As a result, in an intense crisis NATO decision making and interalliance bargaining could even be more intractable than they would be under present conditions.

Despite a common motivation for developing a nuclear capability, the route each nation has followed in developing that arsenal, as well as the arsenals themselves, are quite different. Great Britain has maintained its unique relationship with the United States over the years in which it relies on the United States for testing and training, and also for a target list that is coordinated with the SIOP by the Joint Strategic Target Planning Staff at SAC headquarters. While Great Britain retains the right to use its weapons in any way it sees fit should its supreme interests be threatened, it is expected that if British weapons are to be used, it will occur only in the context of a larger United States/NATO operation.

The entire British strategic nuclear force is currently carried on four "Resolution" class nuclear-powered submarines. Each is outfitted with 16 SLBMs having a range of 4,600 km carrying two recently developed British "Chevaline" 200 KT warheads along with "penetration aids" for overcoming the Moscow "Galosh" ABM system. One or two of these submarines, which are usually under NATO command, are on patrol at all times. In the early- to mid-1990s Great Britain will begin receiving American-made intercontinental Trident II SLBMs with the D-5 warhead that will be installed in four new British-built SSBNs. These SSBNs, with 16 D-5 missiles per boat and eight MIRVed warheads per missile, will replace the currently deployed submarines.

The British command infrastructure has some important elements in common with that of the United States and NATO. The large phased-array BMEW radar at Fylingdales is operated by the Royal Air Force, but is also an integral part of the U.S. early warning system. Several ground terminals for NATO communication satellites are located on British soil. Great Britain also operates VLF transmitters suitable for communication with submerged SSBNs. Finally, Great Britain has built a number of wartime command posts for civilian and military leaders.

Unlike Great Britain, France has pursued its nuclear program independently of the United States. The French strategic nuclear force is more diversified than is Great Britain's. It is composed of bombers, intermediate range ballistic missiles, and submarines. France has approximately 22 aging Mirage IV bombers with an unrefuelled range of 3,200 km that carry one or two 70 KT gravity bombs. In the very near future, 18 Mirage IVs will be refitted to carry a modern air-to-surface nuclear-armed medium range missile. Complementing the bomber fleet are 18 silo-based "S3" missiles with a range of 3,500 km, each with one 1-MT warhead. The French have also devoted some effort to developing a ground-mobile missile.

In common with the British, the cornerstone of the French strategic nuclear force is the SSBN. Currently, the French have five "Redoubtable" class and one "Inflexible" class SSBNs. Each Redoubtable carries 16 SLBMs with a range of 3,000 km and one 1-MT warhead per missile. The Inflexible carries 16 SLBMs, each with 4 to 6 independently targetted 150 KT warheads. Three French submarines are on patrol at all times, with a fourth one ready to go to sea on very short notice. In the early 1990s, the Redoubtable class submarines will be outfitted with the newer MIRVed SLBM, and a seventh SSBN with similar, although perhaps slightly enhanced, capabilities to the Inflexible will be commissioned.

The greater diversity of French forces allow somewhat more flexibility in the targeting plans, especially in terms of "withholds," but the French, like the British, subscribe primarily to a countercity employment doctrine. The relatively small numbers of weapons and their inaccuracy dictates countervalue rather than counterforce targeting.

France's command system is not integrated with that of the United States or of NATO. While rather little concerning this system is available in the open literature, it is known that France has early warning and missile tracking radars, VLF communications facilities for its SSBN force, and wartime command posts.

EPILOGUE

The nuclear forces of the Western alliance have evolved into an exceedingly complex system. Within the U.S. government alone, the nuclear control structures encompass physical, procedural, and organizational arrangements involving many agencies beyond the Department of Defense. The very existence of NATO necessitates other layers of command: those operated by NATO as such, which are strongly intermingled with the separate national systems belonging to the allies; bodies for formal consultation between them; and the supreme if intangible command system of traditional diplomacy. Control over nuclear operations in a crisis would involve this entire web of organizations.

NOTES

1. David Alan Rosenberg, "The Origins of Overkill," *International Security* (1983), 7:4, 3; "U.S. Nuclear War Planning 1945–1960," in Ball & Richelson, pp. 35–56; "Reality and Responsibility: Power and Process in the Making of U.S. Nuclear Strategy 1945–1968," *Journal of Strategic Studies* (1986), 9:1, 35.

2. The basic foreign policy document of the 1950s, NSC-68, was drafted by Paul Nitze 2 months *before* the invasion of South Korea. It called for a rapid expansion of nuclear capabilities, but also argued for stronger conventional forces to reduce reliance on nuclear weapons. See *Foreign Relations of the United States, 1950,* Vol. I, pp. 235–292; and Samuel F. Wells, Jr. "Sounding the Tocsin: NSC-68 and the Soviet Threat", *International Security* (1979), 4:2, 116.

3. The first American nuclear war plan (Halfmoon, 1948) called for nuclear attack at the onset of hostilities with the Soviet Union. In 1950, "Shakedown," gave first priority, in case of war, to destroying the incipient Soviet nuclear capability revealed by the first Soviet bomb test in August 1949. Regarding U.S. capabilities in 1948, see Rosenberg, in Ball and Richelson, pp. 38–39.

4. In August 1950, The National Security Council (NSC 73/4) concluded that the invasion of South Korea could be the initial phase of a Soviet plan for world war.

5. By the end of 1950, U.S. medium-range bombers in Europe were triple the number a year before, substantially reducing the time required to implement the planned nuclear offensive against the Soviet Union. Atomic bomb components also had been shipped overseas; locations included Great Britain, a Pacific base, and two carriers stationed in the Mediterranean. The military took custody of several complete atomic bombs in early 1951; Korea was their probable destination. Several months later, Truman approved a third increase in fissionable material production, auguring a dramatic accumulation of nuclear weapons.

6. In February 1953, Eisenhower identified Kaesong as "a good target for this type of weapon." A month later, he expressed the view that the use of tactical atomic weapons would be worth the political cost if it meant victory in Korea.

7. "Memorandum of Discussion at the 143rd. Meeting of the NSC, May 6, 1953," in Department of State, *Foreign Relations of the United States 1952-54*, Vol. 15, Korea, Pt. 1, p. 977.

8. See Rosenberg, (1983) loc. cit., p. 8.

9. These included land- and carrier-based aircraft, and various types of missiles stationed in Europe and Turkey. By 1960 U.S. and allied regional forces could deliver about 800 nuclear warheads. A small but significant fraction of this force operated in peacetime at a high level of readiness. They, along with nonalert weapons, were fully integrated into operational plans for the defense of Western Europe. Furthermore, a portion of SAC's long-range bomber force was forward-deployed at NATO bases. For the evolution of the NATO nuclear stockpile, see M. Leitenberg, in Frank Barnaby, ed., *Tactical Nuclear Weapons: European Perspectives* (London: Taylor and Francis, 1978); and *Report of the Special Committee on Nuclear Weapons in the Atlantic Alliance*, U.S. Senate, Committee on Foreign Relations, 98th Cong., 2nd session (USGPO, 1985).

10. For SAC operations during the Missile Crisis, see p. 194.

11. U.S. President, *Public Papers of the Presidents, 1958* (Washington: USGPO, 1959), pp. 275, 280–281.

12. For a detailed discussion of the U.S. command organization, see *Defense Organization: The Need for Change,* Staff Report to the Committee on Armed Services, U.S. Senate, 99th Cong., 1st Session, October 16, 1985; Chapters 2–5.

13. *Defense Organization: The Need for Change, op. cit.,* pp. 288–296.

14. For an explanation of these and other communications technologies, see Chapter 6.

15. A second center in Hawaii served SAC forces there, in Guam and the Philippines.

16. Emergency messages from Omaha were to reach all the way to SAC bases in Libya, Morocco, Cypress, and Turkey via troposcatter extensions of the European network. Once airborne, the bombers would have received further instructions via a worldwide network of high frequency radio transmitters.

17. Before this time the separate commands drew up target lists and planned missions quite independently. Despite JCS oversight and coordination, target coverage remained far below the theoretical optimum, and lethal interference between attacking forces would probably have been considerable. For a discussion of the technical and bureaucratic factors that entered into the lengthy, elaborate, and contentious process that culminated in the JSTPS and the first SIOP, see Rosenberg, in Ball and Richelson, pp. 50–56.

18. Documentation concerning the creation of the first SIOP, and associated guidelines, is contained in the declassified papers of General Andrew Goodpaster and Admiral Arleigh Burke, and in the Navy's declassified Operational Archives, as cited by Rosenberg (1983), *loc. cit.,* pp. 4–8, 64–67. See also George B. Kistiakowski, *A Scientist at the White House: The Private Diary of President Eisenhower's Special Assistant for Science and Technology* (Cambridge, Mass.: Harvard University Press, 1975).

19. Half of the at-sea SLBM force is fully alert and capable of being fired in 15 minutes; the other half could be launched within a matter of hours.

20. Increased loading for bombers, from a few weapons per bomber in 1960 to more

than 10 apiece today has been offset by the reduced size of the SAC fleet, and declining ground alert rates, from a high of 50 percent ground alert during the mid-1960s to a low of 30 percent today.

21. "SIOP-62 Briefing, September 13, 1961," *International Security* (1987), *12:*1, 41.

22. This quotation, and those that follow in this paragraph, are from pp. 50 and 51 of the preceding document.

23. Scott D. Sagan, "SIOP-62: The Nuclear War Plan Briefing to President Kennedy," *International Security* (1987), *12:*1, 22. Regarding Soviet readiness in 1961, see Chapter 8.

24. Ibid., p. 23.

25. The Kennedy administration (especially Secretary of Defense Robert McNamaral), is usually associated with the principle of deterrence based on *assured destruction,* which stated that a credible threat to destroy a large portion of Soviet population and industry in retaliation to Soviet nuclear attack was sufficient to deter that attack. But this principle was actually not the basis for employment strategy during the administration, even though it was the basis for nuclear force acquisition. Contrary to the impression that its war plans emphasized the targeting of cities in 1962, the Kennedy administration created the first SIOP containing preplanned options to withhold forces aimed at Soviet cities. (See Desmond Ball, in Ball and Richelson, pp. 62–65; David Alan Rosenberg, "U.S. Nuclear Strategy: Theory vs. Practice," *Bulletin of Atomic Scientists,* March 1987, pp. 20–26.)

26. Peter Stein and Peter Feaver, *Assuring Control of Nuclear Weapons: The Evolution of Permissive Action Links,* Center for Science and International Affairs, Harvard University, Occasional Paper No. 2 (Lantham, MD: University Press of America, 1987).

27. See Legge, pp. 5–10.

28. Backup long-range communications to bombers was provided by unarmed Minutemen equipped to broadcast orders following launch.

29. See John C. Toomay, "Warning and Assessment Sensors" in *MNO.*

30. U.S. Senate, Committee on Armed Sevices, *Recent False Alerts from the Nation's Missile Attack Warning System,* 96th Congress, 2nd Session, October 9, 1980.

31. At first sight an inconsistency seems to exist between the relative states of readiness of various categories of U.S. and NATO nuclear weapons, and the expected sequence of their use. It is widely assumed that battlefield nuclear weapons would be the first to be used, followed by theater, and lastly by strategic weapons. In terms of normal alert readiness, however, the order is reversed. Strategic forces are widely dispersed, largely invulnerable, and primed for immediate use. Theater nuclear forces are partially dispersed, largely vulnerable, and combat ready in relatively small numbers. Ground-based battlefield weapons are stockpiled at a few dozen storage depots, highly vulnerable, and require days to be dispersed and otherwise prepared for actual combat. The lower readiness of ground-based NATO battlefield and theater nuclear forces, however, is consistent with their envisioned use as weapons of last resort should conventional defeat loom. A war on that scale implies weeks or months of preparation and warning, which would allow all categories of nuclear weapons to achieve a high state of combat readiness, at least in principal. There are, however, important political constraints on the readying of tactical nuclear forces; see Chapter 9.

32. Two minor affairs illustrate the mechanisms for crisis notification. The 1975 seizure of the U.S. merchantman *Mayaguez* by Cambodian forces became known because the ship's radio appeal was passed to the U.S. Embassy in Jakarta, which

relayed it to Washington. The message reached the NMCC, the White House Situation Room, and the State Department about 2 hours after the call for help; President Ford heard about the seizure 2 hours later from Lt. Gen. Scowcroft.

In 1976, an Army forward operations center in Seoul filed the initial report on the killing of two army officials by North Korean soldiers during a tree-cutting incident in the Demilitarized Zone; that report went directly to the NMCC only minutes after the lethal skirmish. The NMCC promptly activated an interagency network to inform other govenment departments.

33. See Betts, *Surprise Attack,* pp. 81–86.

34. See also *The Tower Commission Report* (New York: Times Books, 1987), pp. 6–13.

35. Currently the two principle circuits for EAM dissemination are the JCS Alerting Network, which is a nonsecure (unencrypted) voice channel, and the Improved Emergency Action Message Automatic Transmission System, which is a secure teletype link.

36. United States embassies are linked to Washington by the Diplomatic Telecommunications Network, which relies heavily on satellies.

37. The third occasion was a misconceived military exercise ordered by Secretary of Defense Gates during an Eisenhower–Khruschev summit.

38. For example, should the commander-in-chief, SAC (CINCSAC) independently place his forces on higher alert, SAC checklists would instruct units to perform the appropriate SAC procedures and then to perform any unaccomplished procedures on the DEFCON checklist.

39. The authority of military commanders to take additional steps can be traced back to a Joint Chief's guidance issued in 1959. According to declassified JCS documents (JCS 977405 and JCS 1968/84, Record Group 218, Records of the U.S.J.C.S., National Archives, Washington, D.C.), this guidance (JCS SM-833-59, August 25, 1959) allowed the unified and specified commanders "to establish at any time their own DEFCON appropriate to circumstances . . . based upon their own estimate of the situation." The guidance does direct these commanders "to consult with the Joint Chiefs of Staff prior to assuming either DEFCON 1 or 2 because of the possible effects that such actions might have on public opinion and world events." For specific illustrations of discretionary alert authority, see Scott D. Sagan, 'Nuclear Alerts and Crisis Management," *International Security* (1985) 9:4, 113; p. 135.

40. Thus Gen. Lauris Norstad, who was SACEUR during the Cuban Crisis, greatly attentuated the DEFCON 3 alert order for European Command because of his concern for alliance sensitivities; "The Air Force Response to the Cuban Crisis," USAF Historical Division Liason Office, Headquarters USAF.

41. For example, only one airborne division in the United States and two airborne battalions in West Germany were alerted during the 1970 civil war in Jordan.

42. For instance, when NATO forces moved into "military vigilance" in response to the Soviet invasion of Czechoslovakia, European Command expressly forbade the U.S. Seventh Army from preparing armored cavalry to move toward the border. After the JCS issued DEFCON 3 orders during the 1973 Yom Kippur Crisis, they immediately rescinded certain items on that checklist.

43. Two early warning satellites in geosynchronous orbits can see the entire Eurasian landmass, and almost all Soviet SSBN patrol areas. The remaining patrol areas in the Arctic are covered by various radars, and this capability will be enhanced when the phased array radars in Greenland and the U.K. are completed (see Fig. 4.2). The Navstar satellites in the Global Positioning System carry gamma ray detectors that promptly determine the yield and location of nuclear detonations anywhere on the

globe; see H. V. Argo, "Satellite Verification of Arms Control Agreements," Los Alamos National Laboratory, 1984.

44. John C. Toomay, op. cit., pp. 311–312.

45. Blair, pp: 148–155.

46. In principal, maneuvering reentry vehicles in combination with space-based radar surveillance could be used to target command aircraft.

47. Thus for aircraft flying at an altitude of 30,000 feet, the distance between them cannot exceed about 400 miles. For that reason, most of the aircraft in the airborne command network fly in a compact formation to maintain UHF communications (see Blair, pp. 194 & 197). SAC bombers that traverse the resulting UHF envelope on the initial leg of their flight toward enemy territory would therefore be able to receive attack instructions over UHF radio. But a significant fraction of the bombers do not come within range due to their designated flight corridors, and those that do pass out of range very quickly. Several hours after take-off, the bomber force would have flown beyond the effective communications range of UHF radio transmissions from command aircraft. However, extensions of the UHF links are possible by relaying messages among tankers and bombers. (UHF satellite would also augment this network, but with lower reliability.)

48. For more detailed information see International Institute of Strategic Studies, *The Military Balance 1987–1988* (London: IISS, 1987); John Prados, Joel S. Wit, and Michael J. Zagurek, Jr. "The Strategic Nuclear Forces of Britain and France," *Scientific American* (August 1986) Vol. 225, pp. 33–41; Lawrence Freedman, "British Nuclear Targeting," pp. 109–126 and David Yost, "French Nuclear Targeting," pp. 126–156, in Ball and Richelson; William M. Arkin and Richard W. Fieldhouse, *Nuclear Battlefields: Global Links in the Arms Race* (Cambridge, MA: Ballinger, 1985); Eric J. Grove, "Allied Nuclear Forces Complicate Negotiations," *Bulletin of the Atomic Scientists* (June/July 1986) Vol. 42, pp. 18–23.

49. Prados et al., op. cit.

5

American Strategic Options

In the preceding chapter we encountered a seemingly unending array of concrete objects—warheads, radars, submarines, airborne command posts, satellites, etc., as well as vast organizations responsible for their management and use in peacetime, crisis, and war. In contrast, discussions of how the strategic forces might actually be used are inevitably couched in a language of inhuman abstraction because of our fortunate dearth of experience with nuclear warfare.[1] In particular, the military operations that might be attempted in a strategic war are usually examined in a manner that ignores the events that had led to that war. Surely that is naive. Nevertheless, the options available to a strategic planner are circumscribed less by the particulars of many situations than they are by such constant factors as the speed and destructive power of nuclear-armed missiles, the vulnerability of command structures, and certain broad features of the foreign policies and political systems of the United States and the Soviet Union.

There is, therefore, some merit in context-free descriptions of the principal options that would face the U.S. government should the use of the strategic forces be at hand and in delineating those facets of U.S. policy, law, and administrative arrangements that pertain to strategic command in wartime. This chapter will be devoted to these matters. What is known about Soviet attitudes and doctrines regarding strategic warfare will be discussed in Chapter 7.

NATIONAL POLICY

In a severe crisis, as in war, a nation's long-standing fundamental policies are bound to have a large bearing on its behavior. it is therefore appropriate to summarize certain widely accepted axioms that underlie United States national policy.

That policy emanates from a combination of history, principles, laws, and procedures. It is formulated and interpreted by the three branches of the federal government in interaction with public opinion via a volatile process involving the media and a wide variety of groups and constituencies. National policy provides the underpinning for actions undertaken by the federal government in the execution of its responsibilities. For the most part national policy in the United States is known (or at least knowable) by the public and is subject to open debate and scrutiny. For that reason, national policy in a democracy is endowed with an aura of legitimacy that is both a support for and a constraint on the national leadership, whether or not that policy can withstand close scrutiny by academics or other "experts."

The basic elements of U.S. national policy were generally adopted soon after World War II. Naturally, they have undergone modifications since then, and continue to do so. Although each political party often professes somewhat different variations of particular policies, by and large both parties, especially when in control of the White House, have maintained support for the following nonexclusive list of propositions: (1) The United States is a recognized superpower and intends to maintain that status into the indefinite future. (2) Soviet interests are often inimical to those of the United States, and the spread of Soviet influence in areas of the world that are important to the U.S. from a political, economic, geographic, or military viewpoint will be resisted. (3) The United States has formed various alignments with nations having similar or compatible objectives. These alignments are viewed as essential to maintaining peace and to attaining U.S. national objectives. (4) The United States will maintain strong military forces, both conventional and nuclear, that are commensurate with its worldwide commitments and responsibilities. To a large extent, the sizes of these forces are set by U.S. interpretations of Soviet capabilities and intentions. (5) The United States is deeply concerned by subversion or coercion of legitimate governments by the Soviet Union, its allies, and surrogates. The response to such threats will depend on the circumstances and the degree of U.S. interest. (6) The fundamental foreign policy objective of the United States is peace, and stable relationships with other nations. On the other hand, the United States will use whatever military force is necessary to preserve itself and honor its international commitments.

During the four decades that have passed since the United States began to adopt these policies there has been a gradual transition from American nuclear monopoly to approximate nuclear parity with the Soviet Union. Both the United States and the Soviet Union have apparently come to the firm conclusion that the consequences of nuclear war are so catastrophic that the penalty for fighting a nuclear war far outweighs any conceivable advantage that might be gained from it. This mutual understanding underlies the strategy of nuclear deterrence.

It may be claimed that deterrence has been successful since there has been neither conventional nor nuclear war between the superpowers.[2] But it has also become apparent that deterrence is neither static nor absolute. It has not been static because military technology has evolved rapidly since Hiroshima. Intercontinental ballistic missiles, nuclear-powered submarines with SLBMs, MIRVs, cruise missiles, yield and accuracy gains, and stealth technology, have all multiplied the threat posed by offensive forces. In the absence of negotiated constraints, that trend is bound to continue. During the same period, both sides have increased the number of weapons in their nuclear inventories, and they have adopted various strategies that would govern the use of these forces should deterrence ever fail.

Nuclear weapons have made today's great powers much more cautious than their predecessors. Nevertheless, deterrence is certainly not absolute because neither side can ignore the possibility, however remote, that unforeseen events could lead to nuclear war. This becomes apparent as soon as one asks what, precisely, nuclear deterrence is intended to deter: Conventional aggression? Or only nuclear attack?

Consider, first, nuclear deterrence of conventional war. That this is a perplexing issue is demonstrated by the evolution of NATO nuclear doctrine (to be discussed in Chapter 9).[3] In the 1950s, NATO sought to deter all forms of attack by the threat of rapid and massive nuclear retaliation. During the Kennedy and Johnson administrations, growing concern that nuclear escalation would be difficult to avoid in the European theater led NATO to adopt the flexible response doctrine in 1967. In this doctrine nuclear weapons were seen as "a weapon of last resort, if conventional defense failed."[4] With the arrival of strategic parity, the credibility of nuclear deterrence against conventional attack has been brought further into question. Some prominent figures have concluded[5] that NATO cannot continue to rely on nuclear deterrence of conventional attack; they advocate that NATO should strengthen its conventional forces and then adopt a "No-First Use" policy, according to which nuclear weapons are never to be used except in retaliation to nuclear attack. At this time, however, the prevailing view[6] in influential quarters on both sides of the Atlantic appears to be that No-First-Use would increase the risk of a conventional Soviet attack, which would then be likely to escalate to nuclear warfare no matter what NATO declaratory doctrine might say. In short, those who would retain flexible response argue that by confining nuclear weapons to nuclear deterrence one would, in the last analysis, be increasing the risk of nuclear war.

This debate within a sophisticated and highly experienced community illustrates that nuclear deterrence of conventional war is hardly an absolute or static conception. As we shall see in Chapter 7, the Soviets also have begun to voice doubts concerning the advisability of initiating nuclear conflict in a conventional war.

Finally, we come to deterrence of attack by strategic nuclear forces. Given the deep and long-standing distrust between the two societies, neither the Soviet Union nor the United States is likely to reduce its strategic forces below the level it deems necessary to deter a strategic attack. In a crisis or conflict, nuclear deterrence should be expected to prevail as long as neither side has an incentive to use its nuclear forces to strike first, provided that control over the forces can be maintained. Hence maintenance of stability under the stress of crisis is of prime importance. In the strategic context, this requires a credible deterrent and an adequately sturdy command system. That credibility depends on the assessment by a potential attacker that the capacity and the will to use those forces exist.

The issue of national will must be approached cautiously. Despite all assertions to the contrary, some doubt must always exist regarding any nation's willingness to sacrifice lives and treasure in the pursuit of national policy. Vietnam is at least one case where the national will of the United States became a more important factor than the ability of its military forces to fight to a successful conclusion. The Vietnam experience is still a significant factor in any contemplated military intervention in Central America. Heavy loss of life by the Marines in Lebanon dampened whatever public support that existed for intervention in the Middle East. These and other examples illustrate that national will must be carefully considered as an important facet in any confrontation that has a potential for armed conflict, especially if it is likely to be prolonged.

The long-term consequences of failing to honor international commitments cannot be fully appraised in advance. Nevertheless, one can reasonably conclude that one important reason why a nation aligns itself with the United States is that it has calculated that the commitments made to it by the United States will be honored. Indeed, the U.S. record in this regard is generally good, and in the two World Wars the United States even assumed commitments for which it had no prior obligations. If the United States were to renege on a major commitment, however, there is strong reason to presume that significant changes in geopolitical relationships are likely to ensue.

No nation, however, has been confronted with the situation that the superpowers face today. No one can know what effect stress would have on individuals responsible for coping with future nuclear crises. Nor can the public mood be forecast in any meaningful way. Furthermore, the time has long passed when the United States clearly dominated the Soviet Union in terms of nuclear capability. In fact, surviving key players in the Cuban Missile Crisis hold differing views as to whether the United States could have mounted a conventional attack on Soviet forces in Cuba without running an unacceptable risk of a Soviet response that might eventually have terminated in nuclear war, even though the United States then had a far more powerful strategic arsenal than did the Soviet Union. The advent of rough parity has raised doubts whether the United States would be willing to risk attack on its people in support of its foreign commitment, which inevitably weakens the confidence of U.S. allies in Europe and elsewhere.

Thus deterrence presents a paradox. On one hand, the Soviet Union and the United States appear to share a deep respect for the unacceptable level of damage that would occur in their own societies should a major nuclear exchange occur. That would say that deterrence of nuclear war between the superpowers is strong. On the other hand, deterring conventional war by threatening the use of nuclear weapons seems less credible, especially in areas where the use of nuclear weapons (Central Europe, in particular) would be difficult to constrain. In short, while it is clear that United States nuclear forces deter nuclear attack and reinforce caution in Soviet behavior, it is obscure to what extent the nuclear forces support other facets of U.S. national policy, and how that ambiguity would influence the flow of events in a crisis.

THE CONTINUITY OF GOVERNMENT UNDER NUCLEAR ATTACK[7]

Nuclear weapons borne by intercontinental missiles give little warning of an attack that could obliterate an entire government in minutes. This reality has placed an enormous burden on the Constitution and the president. Measures that would have shocked the Framers have had to be devised to maximize the likelihood that legitimate government would be maintained, and that a nuclear counterstrike could be executed. Procedures must always be in place that allow rapid decisions under the most dire of circumstances—decisions that could have the most far-reaching and long-lasting effects on the nation. These measures and procedures are referred to by the terms *devolution, delegation,* and *predelegation.*

As defined by the Constitution, the president of the United States holds a position that combines three distinct roles: head of state, chief executive officer of the government, and commander-in-chief. Delegation and predelegation relate solely to his function as commander-in-chief. In this role the president commands the nation's armed forces in conflicts with other nations (it being understood that only Congress has the de jure, as compared to the de facto, power to declare war). *Delegation* can be defined as the process by which nuclear release authority is specifically granted by the president to one or more individuals to make immediate decisions regarding the use of nuclear weapons. *Predelegation* is the process by which nuclear release authority is specifically granted by the president to be exercised in conformity with understood constraints on occasions whose nature cannot be fully anticipated, but in which the president is either dead, disabled, or unable to communicate with the relevant parties. It is important to recognize that predelegation is *not* the same thing as authorizing the arming and firing of nuclear weapons. Predelegation is insurance against a decapitating strike that could leave the United States unable to respond; its objective is to provide for continuity of legitimate control over nuclear weapons.

Devolution is the process by which the president's death or incapacity causes the president's entire constitutional authority to be assumed by the most senior surviving person on the statutory succession list[8] as defined by the 1947 Presidential Succession Act; that person is then president and thereby holds nuclear release authority.

The problem of maintaining continuity in decision making concerning nuclear weapon release is, first and foremost, the problem of protecting the president and others on the statutory succession list. In recent years the U.S. Government has begun to address this matter more seriously. Effort has concentrated on measures to protect the vice president, and to provide him with the advisory staff, survivable command posts, and communication facilities that would be needed to fulfill the responsibilities of the presidency in the event of a nuclear war in which the president is killed or totally isolated. This is an appropriate emphasis in view of the unquestioned legitimacy of vice-presidential succession. Of equal importance, the vice president can participate actively in planning for such contingencies in normal times, and it is feasible to protect him in time of crisis without causing public alarm or escalating the crisis, whereas evacuation of the president could have such consequences. Apparently, Vice Presidents Mondale and Bush have been involved in these preparations, which, when completed, should raise confidence in the functioning of the succession process if a crisis were to erupt into nuclear war.

There is, of course, no assurance that the vice president would survive or remain connected with the military chain of command, particularly in the event of a nuclear surprise attack. Plans should therefore be made to protect and prepare others on the statutory succession list. It would be prudent to keep at least one *well-briefed* successor out of the Washington area at all times during a crisis. Should a crisis become severe, the vice president should be evacuated, as should other successors with backgrounds that are as appropriate as possible for national leadership in the aftermath of a nuclear attack.

The president, or his successor, may legally delegate nuclear release authority to any individual. This decision involves a legal and universally acknowledged prerogative of the president (delegation in general) with respect to an action (nuclear release) that only the president is empowered to perform. Depending on the president's assessment of the military situation, he may delegate the authority to decide whether, when, where, and how to employ nuclear weapons to achieve national military or political objectives. For instance, in the event of a full-scale conventional war in Europe, the president could grant general or selective nuclear release authority to military commanders who are prosecuting the campaign. Or he might direct the secretary of defense and the JCS chairman to assume responsibility for approving or denying nulcear release requests by combat commanders. Delegation arrangements of this sort may be established at any time—in peacetime or in the midst of a national emergency.

Predelegation usually refers to a contingent delegation of nuclear release authority, where the contingency of concern is the death, disability, or unavailability of the president. Predelegation thus covers the unpredictable circumstances envisioned by the 1947 Presidental Succession Act, such as assassination, heart attack, nuclear decapitation, and the like, but permits decision-making authority to diverge from the statutory succession path in accordance with presidential preference as specified in advance.

There are numerous reasons why predelegation might be preferred to devolution. Reliance on the statutory line of succession risks putting authority into the hands of an individual who is woefully unprepared to exercise it, and who is only loosely tied into the surviving military command system. Whatever the legality of that authority, the individual's competence could be called into serious question, and undermine his or her de facto legitimacy.

Many of the civilian and military policy officials with foreign and national security responsibilities who are not legally entitled to succeed to the presidency may be far better qualified to exercise nuclear authority than those on the statutory succession list, although they may be quite ill-suited to direct the reconstitution of the government and the nation, a primary responsibility of national leadership during and after a nuclear attack. A president would be well-advised to consider drawing on his power of delegation to insure that, in the event of his death or disability, release authority would pass to the most qualified individuals—those who possess suitable backgrounds and understand the president's own perspective on the employment of nuclear weapons. If the president does choose to predelegate, he has the opportunity and responsibility to provide specific guidelines to the parties affected. It is especially important for the expeditious and orderly transfer of authority that he identify what rules of delegation apply if the president's chosen designee is also killed or incapacitated.

The detailed arrangements for the continuity of government are highly classified, and speculation concerning such matters is outside our purview. Rather, in later chapters we shall describe the technical, organizational, and human aspects of the command system, including the various command posts at which the president and other key commanders and officials would be stationed to direct nuclear operations.

STRATEGIC OPTIONS

Broadly speaking, strategic nuclear options may be distinguished by their timing and their intended targets.[9] Official discussions of strategic targeting reveal that the United States has developed military plans ranging from very small "limited nuclear options" to very massive "major attack options." Limited nuclear options, as their name suggests, are designed to serve a specific, limited military purpose. They might also serve a political purpose by demonstrating "resolve" to a far greater degree than is likely to be attained with presidential pronouncements, conventional weapons, or a nuclear "shot across the bow." Major attack options, on the other hand, embody a nation's most comprehensive military objectives. Between these extremes lie intermediate options that withhold forces aimed at certain target categories. One class of targets that merit special mention is the opponent's national leadership. The choice between attacking and sparing the enemy's national command authority poses a dilemma: attacking might be the most promising way of blunting the opponent's own attack, but if it were to succeed a negotiated cease-fire would become virtually impossible.

An attack could be mounted before, during or after the opponent attacks. These basic options are referred to, respectively, as *preemption, launch-on-*

warning or *launch-under-attack,* and *retaliation subsequent to attack.* We shall examine them in some detail because of their fundamental importance to the questions of crisis stability, nuclear restraint, and the failure of deterrence.

Preemption

Preemption is the initiation of nuclear attack when strategic warning indicates that the enemy is preparing to launch a strike. Preemption thus presupposes an assessment by one or both sides that deterrence has failed. Any evaluation of the penalties and payoffs of preemption must first come to grips with the problem of determining whether an enemy strike is truly inevitable. The prevailing Western view is that only tactical warning resolves this uncertainty. Very marginal credence is given to the view that any other form of intelligence would be sufficiently "hard" to be compelling.

That tactical warning is inherently less ambiguous and more reliable than strategic warning is not necessarily true. For example, a combination of reports from agents that the Soviet leadership had suddenly left the Kremlin, along with satellite data showing Soviet SSBNs leaving port in strength, and unusually intense signal traffic to various elements of the Soviet strategic forces, would constitute strong warning, albeit strategic. In contrast, a missile attack that happens to coincide with a malfunctioning of a critical warning sensor or a related data processing facility, or which came amidst electronic warfare, might elicit an ambiguous and uncertain tactical warning signal.

Although strategic warning could strongly suggest that the probability of attack is very high, the possibility would remain that the attack could be averted. While the United Sates has no actual experience with strategic warning of nuclear attack, Americans who have served in positions of very high responsibility in the military and the executive branch testify to their conviction that such a circumstance would only intensify negotiations to defuse the crisis, and that, as a crisis deepens, the more desperate would be the effort to find a way out. They aver that our pre-Hiroshima experience with preemption, when surprise often provided a decisive advantage, has little relevance today since even a modest nuclear counterattack would cause destruction on a scale unknown to history.

A deep reluctance to concede the inevitability of nuclear war under even the most threatening circumstances should not be denigrated as psychological "denial." It would reflect the urge to delay an action that would bring disaster. Still, the possibility exists that the adversary might irrevocably commit to a nuclear attack, that this commitment would be ascertained, and that responsible and rational leaders would have to consider the advantages and disadvantages of preemption. The relative advantages of preemption versus prevention of nuclear war would then be moot. The relevant choices would be preemption, prompt launch, or retaliation subsequent to the attack, and the question would be whether preemption is the most advantageous of these alternatives. (Prompt launch subsumes launch-on-warning and launch-under-attack.)

Assuming that it was decided that a Soviet attack against the United States was imminent and irreversible by any and all diplomatic means, including direct contact with the Kremlin, other factors must be weighed before the United States would preempt. First, what would be the nature of the Soviet attack? Would it be limited to military targets? If so, would U.S. preemption cause the Soviets to alter their attack by launching a larger strike against both military and civilian targets in the United States? Although these questions cannot be answered with certainty, the Soviets would probably have much less incentive to limit their retaliation once they detected a large U.S. preemptive attack, whatever the intended targets of U.S. weapons might be.[10]

Another factor concerns the military advantage that could be gained by preemption. Soviet and U.S. forces are asymmetrical. The preponderance of Soviet capability lies in its ICBM force; the United States distributes its strategic capability over the triad of ICBMs, SLBM-carrying submarines, and bombers. Assuming the Soviets are able to launch their missiles on warning (as would be more likely if they have been readied to attack the United States), the results of a U.S. preemptive damage-limiting (or counterforce) attack against Soviet land- and sea-based strategic forces would be minimal. Indeed, as already mentioned, U.S. preemption could trigger a massive firing of Soviet ICBMs, and damage to the United States would be extreme. There seems to be no appreciable distinction, therefore, between the net destruction of Soviet strategic forces following a U.S. preemptive attack as compared to a prompt launch by the United States in retaliation, assuming the Soviets were also prepared to execute a prompt launch. Moreover, a U.S. preemptive attack could result in an unrestrained Soviet response against American society.

Although it seems likely that both sides could carry out a prompt launch, neither side can have absolute confidence in its own, or in its opponent's, ability to execute such a launch. In the absence of a Soviet prompt-launch capability, a U.S. preemptive attack focused on Soviet ICBMs would probably reduce U.S. fatalities, although not appreciably if the bulk of the Soviet SLBM force were to survive and attack U.S. cities.

In short, although U.S. preemption is conceivable, it would not be a rational option under virtually any circumstance for a variety of reasons:

- Strategic warning of an imminent nuclear attack could be mistaken and preemption would therefore foreclose any opportunity to avoid the disaster of nuclear war.
- Nuclear retaliation by the Soviet Union seems inevitable if the United States preempts.
- Soviet retaliation would probably be unrestrained once a massive U.S. preemptive attack was detected.
- Since prudence dictates the assumption that the Soviets have a prompt-

launch capability, there is probably no appreciable difference between the effectiveness of U.S. preemption and a prompt retaliatory launch.

Prompt Launch

Longstanding vulnerabilities in the U.S. command system, together with the more recent growth of the Soviet ICBM threat to the Minuteman force have created very strong disincentives to absorb the brunt of a Soviet nuclear attack before retaliating. As we have just argued, preemption is not a rational option. Almost by default, therefore, the United States has been forced to seriously consider the option of a prompt launch of its strategic forces.

The term prompt launch incorporates launch-on-warning (LOW) and launch-under-attack (LUA). The latter, LUA, could be defined as a special case of LOW where the tactical warning required to authorize launch included some specified number of enemy nuclear detonations, some or all of which might be high-altitude EMP bursts.

There are many obvious and serious drawbacks to prompt launch. First and foremost, it places tremendous time constraints on the decision process.[11] In the few minutes available from launch detection to missile detonation, the attack would have to be assessed and an appropriate response determined. Furthermore, a decision to launch would have to be transmitted and received by the strategic forces. They, in turn, would have to execute their launch instructions. Of these elements in the decision process, the most significant is the nontechnical component, alluded to by the antiseptic phrase "an appropriate response." Given the pace of events, this choice would have to follow a drill-like pattern: attack assessment, however imperfect, would place the enemy's launch in one of a small set of predefined categories. A few U.S. attack options would correspond to each of these categories. All that could be left to the nation's leadership, at this most fateful moment in human history, would be an immediate selection from this handful of alternatives.

A second drawback relates to weaknesses of the command system itself. Some observers[12] believe that there are major uncertainties concerning the system's performance, even in the period preceding ICBM impacts, resulting (1) in particular, from the vulnerability of the NCA and of national command centers to missiles with short flight times launched by nearby Soviet submarines, and (2) from the vulnerability to disruption of primary communications used for the decision conference between the NCA and senior military advisors, and for the dissemination of the EAM to the forces.

A third drawback is the dependence on a tactical warning system that has identifiable deficiencies. At present the system has a severely limited ability to promptly characterize and assess an attack. Consequently, while there would probably be high confidence that the United States is under attack, there would be but low confidence as to the nature of the attack. Sensor design deficiencies, equipment malfunctions, undetected bugs in computer software, maintenance problems, vulnerability to sabotage or conventional weapon attacks, and psychological stress on personnel responsible for reaching definitive judgments within a very few minutes could combine to diminish significantly the confidence that the tactical warning system must provide. In addition, the present system has a poor capability to detect low-flying cruise missiles that could be aimed at Washington as the precursor to a large scale attack.

A fourth drawback is the acute tension between the opposing requirements of launching on true warning and not launching on false warning. There is an obvious potential for friction as priorities shift from absolute avoidance of any release of nuclear weapons to absolute certainty that the attack ordered will be executed immediately. The military and scientific communities have devoted a substantial effort to minimizing this complex problem. Nevertheless, it should be recognized that execution of a prompt launch would require a complex combination of men and machines to perform an intricate set of tasks under extreme time pressure and inordinate psychological stress, which might reveal failure modes that peacetime exercises would not disclose.

Other drawbacks to prompt launch stem from physical phenomena. For example, ICBMs might have to pass through a barrage of high altitude nuclear explosions over each ICBM base that could damage missiles as they fly out from their launch points.[13]

Despite this impressive list of drawbacks, it seems increasingly evident that the United States is being pushed into some dependence on prompt launch because the alternatives of preemption and rideout are even worse in important respects. This trend can be discerned from Congressional testimony by senior Department of Defense officials and military commanders. At one time, prompt launch was described as an option that existed to strengthen deterrence, but such statements were habitually accompanied by the admonition that this tactic had very undesirable features.[14] In this decade testimony has stated that the technical capability for prompt launch has appreciably improved.[15] More significantly, in recent times senior commanders have said that while it would be desirable[16] "to provide the National Command Authority with the flexibility to ride out at least some portion of an attack," that[17] "as a practical matter we have been unable to attain that," while[18] "we have been able to keep up with the capability to launch on warning."

While the U.S. leadership may harbor some doubts concerning the ability to execute a prompt launch, from the perspective of a cautious Soviet planner that U.S. capability is probably very credible. The advantage of this perception to the United States is that it reduces the appeal of preemption to the Soviets. If conservative Soviet calculations discount the vulnerability of the U.S. command system because a U.S. prompt launch appears credible, then reliance on this strategy does have its advantages. It reinforces the credibility of the U.S. threat to retaliate, and would also bolster the Soviet perception of stability since prompt launch concedes the nuclear first strike to the Soviets. The ongoing effort to improve the U.S. command system will improve the prompt-launch capability whether or not the enhancement of that capability is an explicit aim of modernization.

Retaliation Subsequent to Attack

For decades the U.S. government has sought to enforce deterrence by deploying strategic forces that could retaliate to any attack in a deliberate manner, and that would under all circumstances have the capacity to respond with a level of destruction that would make it irrational to mount a strategic attack on the United States. The composition of U.S. forces has long reflected this fundamental objective in that some 75 percent of the strategic warheads are on submarines and bombers,[19] both of which are ideally suited to retaliation. In more recent times various administrations have also sought forces and doctrines that would allow retaliation at a level commensurate with an attack, and that might therefore inhibit escalation.

On the other hand, reliance on retaliation subsequent to attack requires a command system that can survive that attack to the degree necessary for a response. If that response is to be carefully matched to the prevailing military and political circumstances, the demands on command are even more severe, especially if the command system is also to facilitate a negotiated end to hostilities. As we shall see in the next chapter, the existing strategic command system cannot meet those requirements unless the Soviets deliberately sought to spare U.S. command.

It is essential to distinguish between retaliation that would be "deliberate" as compared to "uncoordinated." There is every reason to believe that there would be retaliation as the result of any attempt at nuclear decapitation. For two decades senior administration spokesmen have stated that provisions designed to assure retaliation under the most dire of circumstances exist. Indeed, an attempt at decapitation could trigger a response that was not centrally coordinated—one that would actually result in the "assured destruction" of Soviet society—in contrast to the less apocalyptic retaliatory options that are likely to receive serious consideration in a "deliberate" centrally coordinated response following full assessment of an attack.

Let us then focus on such *deliberate* retaliation, which we define as implementation, following approval by the president or other duly constituted authorities, of the SIOP after the brunt of a Soviet nuclear attack has been absorbed.[20] While the SIOP contains a large set of preplanned options, the term flexible response should not be taken to mean that retaliation would be some melange improvised from the SIOP "menu" as the conflict progresses. Once an option is selected, execution of the complex military operations that it calls for will unfold as planned insofar as enemy action permits.

We assume that the attack would involve the simultaneous launch at H-hour of missiles by components of all Soviet strategic forces. Impact times for SLBMs could range from as little as $H + 7$ minutes for those from submarines off U.S. coasts[21] to $H + 30$ minutes for those in Soviet home waters, with the largest portion of the force arriving at $H + 10$ to $H + 15$ minutes from submarines in their normal patrol zones in the Atlantic and Pacific. As previously discussed, a small number of SLBMs might be able to interfere with U.S. communications prior to the onset of blast damage from SLBMs fused for atmospheric and ground detonation. Impact times for ICBMs would range from H + 25 to H + 40 minutes. Long-range bombers would arrive much later (approximately H + 15 hours). The brunt of the attack would thus be received during the first half hour or so after H-hour.

Unless the attack had been carefully designed to avoid the U.S. command system, and that intent was quickly recognized, retaliation would have to be ordered in the immediate wake of the assault. Under these circumstances, damage suffered by command facilities during the first half hour would have been so severe that retaliation would depend largely on an airborne command network whose coherent endurance could not be confidently expected to exceed a few hours. Central control over strategic forces would thereafter be so tenuous that withheld strategic forces, strategic reserve forces, and bombers that had completed their missions and returned to the continental United States in 1 to 3 days could find themselves disconnected from central command.

For two reasons retaliation would probably be organized around a large option in the SIOP, involving thousands of nuclear warheads. First, the current U.S. assessment system is incapable of accurately depicting the character of an attack by Soviet forces. Furthermore, much of that system would probably cease to function by H+30 minutes, and perhaps before that. Decision makers might obtain a fairly reliable estimate of the size of the initial salvo, but neither the full magnitude of the attack nor the exact weapon aim points would be known. Too much would be at stake to give the attacker the benefit of the doubt. Second, due to the limited endurance of the backup command network, decision makers could not expect to employ withheld forces in a coordinated fashion. In all likelihood, the selection of a small SIOP option would mean that all other strategic options would be relinquished forever. This consideration would thus encourage selection of a major attack option.

American deterrence strategy is consistent with the circumstances and limited choices just described. This strategy is based on maintaining a credible threat of prompt nuclear retaliation against a comprehensive enemy target base. Although many hold the view that a strategy based on a more graduated set of responses would strengthen deterrence because it may be more credible, the cornerstone of past and present policy is the capability to inflict swift and severe damage in retaliation to nuclear attack. Few dispute the judgment that the specter of retaliation based on a major attack option—the largest of which would devastate Soviet cities and industry—powerfully deters a Soviet first strike. But in any event, the U.S. command system is not sturdy enough to support strategies that seek to coerce the Soviet Union to refrain from escalation. Even after completion of the committed improvement program, escalation control and command endurance could not be maintained unless the Soviet Union were to restrict its attacks on the U.S. command system.

SUMMARY

The fragility of command in the face of attack by today's strategic forces implies that the options available to the strategic planner are severely circumscribed. They can be divided into three categories:

1. Preemption: a first strike launched on the basis of convincing strategic warning.
2. Prompt launch: a retaliatory strike, launched on the basis of firm tactical attack warning, but initiated while the enemy's attack is underway— possibly even before there are enemy nuclear detonations.
3. Retaliation subsequent to attack, with the option chosen in the light of proper assessment of the initial attack.

We have concluded that preemption is not a rational option. In contrast to prenuclear war, the benefit of strategic surprise that preemption offers is overshadowed by the fact that it would extinguish whatever hope there might be that the warning was erroneous, or that the disaster could still be averted. Furthermore, preemption is likely to trigger a massive prompt launch by the adversary; in consequence, preemption is unlikely to limit damage.

While retaliation following rideout is generally accepted as the most desirable option, adoption of that strategy runs the risk that the command system may not have sufficient coherence following a direct attack on itself to execute a coordinated counterattack. For that reason, considerable reliance is being placed in prompt counterattacks that would launch ICBMs while the original attack is still in progress, despite the fact that this option is burdened by a long list of chilling drawbacks.

NOTES

1. For a comprehensive survey, see L. Freedman, *The Evolution of Nuclear Strategy* (New York: St. Martin's Press, 1983).
2. See J. L. Gaddis, "The Long Peace: Elements of Stability in the Postwar International System," *International Security,* (1986), *10*:4, 99.
3. For a brief history of NATO policy concerning nuclear weapons, see David N. Schwartz in *Alliance Security: NATO and the No-First Use Question* (Washington, DC: Brookings, 1983), John D. Steinbruner and Leon V. Sigal, editors, and references cited therein.
4. The official flexible response policy document, MC 14/3, is still classified. This particular formulation is taken from Robert S. McNamara, who served as secretary of defense at the time; see *Blundering into Disaster* (New York: Pantheon Books, 1986), pp. 23–25.
5. McGeorge Bundy, George F. Kennan, Robert S. McNamara and Gerard Smith, "Nuclear Weapons and the Atlantic Alliance," *Foreign Affairs,* (1982) 60, 753; Robert S. McNamara, loc. cit.
6. See, for example, Karl Kaiser, Georg Laber, Alois Mertes, and Franz-Josef

Schulze, "Nuclear Weapons and the Preservation of Peace: A German Response to No First Use," *Foreign Affairs* (1982) 60, 1157. An extensive discussion of these issues can be found in "Alliance Security: NATO and the No-First-Use Question," loc. lit.

7. See also P. Bracken in *MNO,* Chapter 10.

8. The order of succession is the vice president, the Speaker of the House, and the president pro tempore of the Senate, followed by the Cabinet secretaries in the order in which their departments were created: state, treasury, defense, justice, interior, agriculture, commerce, labor, health and human services, housing and urban development, transportation, energy, and education.

9. For descriptions and analysis of what is publicy known about the strategic war plans of the United States, Soviet Union, France, and Great Britain, see *Strategic Nuclear Targeting* (Ithaca: Cornell Univesity Press, 1986), edited by Desmond Ball and Jeffrey Richelson, and cited henceforth as *SNT.*

10. As pointed out by Ball (*SNT,* p. 21), whereas Minutemen are based in a quite circumscribed region well-removed from major U.S. industrial and population centers, Soviet ICBM fields are spread across vast reaches of the Soviet Union, with some bases near Moscow and a considerable concentration in heavily populated areas west of the Urals. Hence Soviet attack assessment would be hard-put to distinguigh a counterforce strike from one aimed at industrial targets. Targeting of the Soviet leadership poses the same issue in spades. Even in wartime, the Soviet leadership would be located in or near urban centers, especially Moscow. As Colin Gray notes a "knock out blow against the control structure, leaving the Soviet society essentially untouched is simply not feasible, even with new technologies for very precise weapons delivery." ("Soviet Strategic Vulnerabilities," *Air Force Magazine,* March, 1979.)

11. John D. Steinbruner, "Launch Under Attack," *Scientific American,* January 1984.

12. See, in particular, Blair, Chapters 6 and 7.

13. This tactic, called *X-ray pin-down,* exploits the vulnerability of ICBM booster skins to X-rays. A rather modest sequence of high-altitude bursts in the megaton-range over each Minuteman field would suffice to suppress launch. In theory, at least, such a barrage could be laid down by off-shore submarines during the last 15 minutes of flight of attacking ICBMs, thereby compressing greatly the time available for launch-on-warning.

14. For example, in 1977 Secretary of Defense Harold Brown testified that "the question is, would [we] launch land-based missiles before explosions of nuclear weapons on the U.S.? . . . I think that is something that should be considered only with the greatest caution . . . I think that it is not our doctrine to do so—neither is it our doctrine that under no circumstances would we ever do so." *Department of Defense Appropriation Hearings for 1978,* Subcommittee on the Department of Defense, Committee on Appropriations, U.S. House of Representatives, 95th Congress, 1st Session, pp. 154–155. For a similar statement by CINCSAC Gen. Richard H. Ellis, see Subcommittee on Strategic and Theater Nuclear Forces, Committee on Armed Services, U.S. Senate, February 18, 1981, p. 3834.

15. Under Secretary of Defense for Research and Engineering William Perry has testified that "we have always had a launch-under-attack option for the President: the recent changes have, we believe, removed significant impediments to exercising the option." (*Department of Defense Authorization for Appropriations for FY1981,* Committee on Armed Services, U.S. Senate, 96th Congress, 2nd Session, p. 636.) CINCSAC Gen. B. L. Davis has said that since 1981 "we have a far better capability of executing

all three legs of the triad under an attack." (Subcommittee on Strategic and Theater Nuclear Forces, Committee on Armed Services, U.S. Senate, March 6, 1985.)

16. Gen. Robert Herres, CINCNORAD, *Our Nation's Nuclear Warning System: Will It Work If We Need It?* Committee on Government Operations, U.S. House of Representatives, 99th Congress, 1st Session, September 26, 1985, p. 72.

17. Gen. B. L. Davis, *MX Missile Basing and Related Issues,* Committee on Armed Services, U.S. Senate, 98th Congress, 1st Session, (April 18, 20, 21, 22, 26; May 3, 1983).

18. Gen. Robert Herres, loc. cit.

19. Bombers have no role in preemption. On the other hand, submarines could, in principle, be an important element in a preemptive attack because of the short flight times from off-shore SSBNs. Currently deployed U.S. SLBMs do not have the yield or accuracy for attacks on hardened C^3 facilities or silos. With the deployment of the highly accurate D5 SLBM, however, this character of the U.S. submarine force will change. Naturally, all the severe drawbacks to preemption discussed previously would still hold.

20. See *SNT;* and Desmond Ball, "Targeting for Strategic Deterrence," *Adelphi Paper No. 185* (London: International Institute for Strategic Studies, 1983).

21. These would probably be the lead elements in a decapitation attack. Sea-launched cruise missiles are another possibility.

6

U.S. Command Improvements and
Command Vulnerability

In essence, the United States still relies on the strategic command system erected during the 1960s and 1970s, but as we have seen, this system suffers from a number of serious weaknesses. Among these we emphasized the vulnerability of vital communications even before any warheads impact directly on U.S. targets, as well as the system's heavy reliance on a relatively small number of limited-endurance aircraft as command posts and radio relays.

The Carter administration recognized the seriousness of these flaws in the U.S. strategic posture, and initiated a program to redress them. In October 1981 the Reagan administration announced that these command-and-control improvements would have the highest priority in the strategic budget. While that level of commitment has not been fully maintained, there nevertheless has been steady progress toward a command system that will provide for secure command, control, and communications in the period just prior to and immediately following an attack, and one that will be considerably more robust at its peacetime posture than the current system. Contrary to a widespread impression, however, the improved system will not have the endurance required to conduct "controlled" or "protracted" nuclear war unless the Soviets were to spare U.S. command, and structured their attacks to make that intention immediately evident.

This chapter will focus on the committed improvement program,[1] assess its impact on command vulnerability, and offer suggestions for further command improvements designed to enhance crisis stability and to facilitate war termination should deterrence fail. The reader should note that this chapter is rather more technical than the remainder of this book, and that the summary in Chapter 2 may satisfy the needs of many readers. Those who wish to acquire some understanding of the physical principles underlying the communications techniques to be discussed should consult the Appendix.[2]

THE COMMITTED COMMAND-AND-CONTROL IMPROVEMENT PROGRAM

The primary objective of the command modernization program is a reliable communication network among the National Command Authority (NCA) and its alternates, the unified and specified nuclear commands, and the strategic forces. To achieve that goal, the system must provide survivable command facilities, and voice and data links of sufficient endurance and security, to allow command to perform its most vital functions in the face a wide variety of threats during the opening phase of a strategic war.

The program has the following major components: The Ground Wave Emergency Network (GWEN); a constellation of new MILSTAR communications satellites; ground-mobile command posts and mobile read-out terminals for early warning satellites; replacement of the TACAMO fleet by aircraft that are EMP-hardened and refuelable in flight; EMP hardening of other command and relay aircraft, and of fixed peacetime command posts; completion of the phased array radar network for early warning of ICBM and SLBM attack; Over-the-Horizon Backscatter radars for detection of cruise missiles and aircraft;[3] the Nuclear Detection System on Navstar satellites that will determine the location and yield of nuclear detonation; preattack communications to deeply submerged submarines; low frequency (LF) receivers for bombers; and an upgrade of existing space-based early warning sensors.

GWEN is a ground-based communication network designed to operate in the very earliest phase of a nuclear attack—*before* there are detonations on U.S. soil when the threat to communications would stem from sabotage, jamming, and EMP generated by high-altitude bursts of nuclear warheads from nearby submarines. Each node in the GWEN network consists of a 300-ft antenna tower equipped with a transmitter and receiver operating at a frequency somewhat lower than broadcast AM radio. The system uses a technique called packet-switching,[4] which assures transmission between two nodes in the network even when other nodes are destroyed, whether by nuclear attack or sabotage. The current GWEN program calls for 127 sites to be operational in 1989.

MILSTAR stands for Military Strategic and Tactical Relay Satellite. As the name implies, these are new communication satellites for strategic and other forces. The plans for the MILSTAR system call for a combination of satellites in high and low inclination synchronous orbits with some 4,000 terminals for users ranging from the NCA through major command centers and the strategic forces (Minuteman launch control centers, bombers, SSBNs) down to command posts for combat units in all services.

MILSTAR will provide survivable, enduring, and highly jam-resistant and encrypted two-way communications both for data and voice communication, even if the signal to and from the satellite must pass through upper atmosphere regions that have recently been exposed to nuclear explosions. These features of MILSTAR are achieved by operating at Extremely High Frequency (EHF) where the wave length is smaller than 1 cm. This short wavelength provides two further advantages:[5] antennas can be small and highly portable, and signals can be emitted into a very narrow cone so that interception is only possible near the line joining the transmitter and receiver.[6]

It is appropriate at this point to mention an important shortcoming of the improvement program. At this time, there is no means for a timely, reliable, secure, and high-fidelity voice missile attack conference between the NCA and the nuclear commands. MILSTAR will eventually provide such a capability even under postattack circumstances. A preliminary capability is now provided by a MILSTAR EHF package on a recent navy fleet communications satellite (FLTSAT-COM), and a second is planned.

Ground-mobile units are another important component of the modernization program. Mobile Ground Terminals[7] (MGTs) will serve as relays to airborne and ground-mobile command posts as well as down-links and ground control stations for early warning satellites. They will, therefore, be backups for the two fixed stations in Australia and Colorado. An MGT with its accompanying communications van is relatively small and correspondingly covert. Other mobile facilities will be developed for critical commands such as SAC and NORAD. A ground-mobile facility to serve an alternate NCA would be desirable as an alternate to the airborne command posts.[8]

The new system for preattack communications to deeply submerged ballistic missile submarines (SSBNs) exploits the fact that Extremely Low Frequency (ELF) radio waves penetrate to great depths (see the Appendix). On the other hand, the ELF transmitting antenna could not survive a direct nuclear attack, and its very low data rate (about one bit per minute) would probably not permit it to disseminate a useful message in the interval between NORAD's determination that an attack was underway and missile impact.[9] Nevertheless, the termination of its broadcast would tell the SSBNs that something was amiss and they could then take steps to receive signals at frequencies that do not penetrate to such great depths.

The command improvement program, launched with bipartisan support and a massive commitment of resources, is now in midstream. The degree to which it will achieve its stated objectives is still unclear for there are signs that competition from other military programs is mounting. Should this result in significant reductions in the scope of the improvements, the amelioration in command vulnerability originally envisaged will not be realized.

COMMAND VULNERABILITY

Given the complexity of the command organization, the spectrum of potential threats that it faces, the protective steps that can be taken in response to warning, the multitude of ineluctable mysteries concerning the performance of humans, weapons, hardware, and software in nuclear combat, and the unpredictable failure modes that bedevil complex technological systems that are not under nuclear attack, it is obvious that there can be no reliable, quantitative measure of command vulnerability. Any estimate of the number of detonations required to attain some given level of disruption for some specified period necessarily involves an assumed scenario for the attack, the prior alert level, and the response to warning. It thereby entails not only the performance of the physical system, but also that of its human component under circumstances and levels of stress never before encountered. Moreover, information not in the public domain, or even unknown to one or both of the adversaries, could well be of critical importance.

The crude estimates that will be given should be viewed, therefore, as averages over a statistical distribution comprised of a wide range of outcomes.[10] In view of all these imponderables, qualitative statements that give relative— not absolute—measures of vulnerability are more meaningful. Of these, one comparison has rather general, although not universal, validity: *Command systems are inherently more fragile than the forces they serve.*

Current Vulnerability

The peacetime disposition of command elements, and their existing communications, have already been described; together, they constitute the system that would have to cope with a "bolt out-of-the-blue"—that is, an attack not preceded by strategic warning. As we saw earlier, it is widely believed that an attack that emerges from a severe crisis is a far more likely occurrence. In that case the command system would be at a rather high alert status, such as DEFCON 2. Nevertheless, even in that circumstance the likelihood of a surprise attack depends to an unknown extent on the potential attacker's estimate of the performance of the victim's command system. If the latter is perceived to be "soft" and readily degradable under severe stress, it might encourage a surprise attack. The opposite perception, a "rugged" command system, would tend to discourage surprise attack.

When in its peacetime configuration, the airborne segment of the current command system would have to assume a wartime posture with great alacrity on receipt of tactical warning if major portions were not to be caught on the ground by an optimally timed SLBM attack. These SLBMs could also promptly destroy national command centers in and near Washington, Pacific and Atlantic command headquarters, the two ground stations for early warning satellite read-out, the missile warning radars, and most of the transmitters for communications with SSBNs, while high-altitude burst might interfere with the order to launch the command aircraft. Depending on their location, other critical nodes in the ground-based communication network could be targeted by SLBMs or ICBMs. In a worst-case scenario, with sluggish response to tactical warning, an attack comprising perhaps as few as some tens of judiciously targeted, accurate, and fully reliable warheads could disrupt the current command system at its peacetime posture to a point where it could seriously jeopardize a coordinated retaliatory attack. *The critical factor is seen to be response to tactical warning, a variable that is not under the attacker's control.*

The word *cooordinated* is essential here. The U.S. government has often stated that provisions are always in place that guarantee large-scale retaliation under the most dire of circumstances. Given the vast forces (primarily those at sea) that would survive any attack on command, the possibility of predelegated contingency arrangements, the possible existence of high-level command elements and communication links of which the attacker has no knowledge, and the multitude of communication channels that are likely to survive or that could be established, these official statements should be taken at face value by a potential attacker.

United States command and forces would be much less vulnerable if a crisis had caused the alert level to be raised to, say, DEFCON 2. While the president would be likely to remain in Washington, and thereby render the primary NCA highly vulnerable, one or more alternate NCAs (ANCAs) would presumably be at remote locations. One of these ANCAs is likely to be the NEACP airborne command post. Furthermore, the Post Attack Command and Control System (PACCS), which relies primarily on the SAC Looking Glass and various other command and relay aircraft, and the navy TACAMOs, would be partially airborne, with remaining elements on heightened strip alert. NORAD would have formed an austere emergency backup facility. Other critical but vulnerable commands, especially Pacific, Atlantic, and European, would be likely to have airborne command posts aloft. Nearly all SSBNs would be at sea; bombers and tankers would be dispersed, on heightened strip alert, and perhaps partially airborne, as they were during the Cuban Crisis; and the ICBM chain-of-command would be ready for the most expeditious execution of orders.

With the system the United States now has, many links within the alerted command system, and between forces and command, could be degraded or interrupted by environmental disturbances created by nuclear explosions, not to mention destruction by direct attack. Many communication channels between command aircraft, satellites, and force elements at frequencies currently in use could not reliably transmit signals through regions that recently had been exposed to the effects of nuclear detonations. The attacker might seek to maintain such conditions until the endurance of in-flight bombers awaiting orders to proceed to their targets was exhausted or for the duration of sorties by TACAMOs aloft at the time of attack. Those objectives would require attack on a large number of airfields and a succession of high-altitude bursts. In addition to the fixed ground nodes targeted in the peacetime scenario, attack against the alerted system would presumably also target a larger variety of ground entry points linking the airborne system to land lines.

An attack that sought to sever the alerted U.S. command system from its forces, therefore, would have to be significantly larger and of a longer duration than in the peacetime example—at least an order of magnitude (i.e., about 10 times) more warheads would have to be expended. Widespread collateral damage and heavy civilian casualties across large portions of the continental United States would accompany such an attack. For that and other reasons, the consequences of such a command attack would be subject to even greater uncertainty than in the peacetime alert scenario. A prudent estimation of the risk taken by the attacker should again be dominated by those critical factors over which he has no control. The most important factor would be whether the United States would have decided *beforehand* to retaliate immediately on receipt of tactical warning of such a large attack. Note that the attacker increases this risk by augmenting the size of his attack in seeking a higher level of confidence in his ability to destroy the command system.

Vulnerability of the Improved Command System

The question then arises as to how this assessment of vulnerability would change on the assumptions that the committed command improvements are in place *and* that the Soviet offensive threat is essentially unchanged. Both of these assumptions may be overly optimistic. For example, deployments of submarine-based cruise missiles exploiting stealth technology could seriously diminish the efficacy of the tactical warning system, maneuvering reentry vehicles guided by spaced-based radar could threaten mobile command posts, and ASAT weapons are of sufficient concern to merit a detailed discussion of their own. Should cutbacks in the improvement program result in significantly less capable systems than those described earlier, they would also raise the rough vulnerability estimates that follow by amounts that would depend on the specific nature of the shortfalls. As we shall see, MILSTAR satellites are especially critical to improved command performance; a curtailment of the MILSTAR survivability program, therefore, could have a serious negative impact should the Soviet Union acquire high altitude ASATs.

The possibility that communications could be disrupted in the interval between the detection of launches by early warning satellites and the first impact of SLBMs on vital targets will be partially eliminated by GWEN. During this crucial period this radio network will be able to disseminate essential orders and preattack information: tactical warning, initial attack assessment, orders for a Positive Control Launch of SAC bombers, and other EAMs. On the other hand, GWEN is not expected to survive the actual nuclear attack since the currently committed network could be disrupted by some tens of warheads.

Even though GWEN should be expected to collapse shortly after warheads begin to land, it would have increased the likelihood that command and relay aircraft previously on strip alert should have survived. In addition, the new MGTs and ground-mobile command centers (GMCCs) will reduce dependency on the airborne command system. And in the environment created by a nuclear attack the MILSTAR system should provide secure high-quality communications between new and current command elements and the forces.

The impact on the command system's capability, therefore, is not simply the sum of contributions from the separate components of the improvement program: these components reinforce each other, but they also enhance the capability of older elements that will continue in service. Communications will be much less vulnerable to jamming, sabotage, environmental disturbances from high-altitude bursts, and nuclear explosions on paths through which radio signals must propagate. The "connectivity" of the entire system during and in the wake of an attack will therefore be greatly strengthened. For example, links between intelligence sensors (such as those on satellites that detect missile launches or nuclear explosions) and users (such as NORAD) will be much more difficult to sever. The endurance of the improved system would still be limited in the face of sustained attack, but it should survive for many hours beyond the point where the current system would collapse. Of perhaps even greater significance, the ability to launch-on-warning or under a small attack will be significantly enhanced. The threshold for prompt launch, defined by the size of the detected attack and/or the number of enemy nuclear detonations, might thus be raised because ambiguities about the size of the attack and its objectives would be reduced; assuming, of course, that execution of such a launch were actually to be the response in certain contingencies.

Roughly speaking, the improved system will be about as difficult to disrupt at its peacetime status as the current system would be when on alert. For that reason, the command system—as compared to the forces—will be less dependent on prompt response to tactical attack warning. The upgraded system, were it on alert, would have both an airborne and a ground-mobile command network, knit together with MILSTAR communications, and with little dependence on vulnerable fixed elements. To gravely disrupt the improved system were it alerted, therefore, would require an attack considerably larger than what would be needed today under similar circumstances. Such an attack would require hundreds of detonations, and inevitably inflict damage on U.S. society of proportions that dwarf historical experience. Hence, the risk that such a command attack will provoke a prompt launch by the United States would be higher than today because

- The improved U.S. command system will be more capable of executing such a launch whether it is at its peacetime posture or on alert.
- The greater level of impending destruction would heighten the incentive to retaliate.
- The endurance of the improved system, while surpassing that of today, would still be too short-lived to provide full confidence that the attack could be absorbed and still allow coordinated retaliation following thorough attack assessment.

The Antisatellite Threat to Strategic Command

The preceding discussion has tacitly assumed that the space-based command elements would not be exposed to significant threats. This is a dubious assumption: U.S. and Soviet research on ASAT weapons and space-based ballistic missile defense technologies is creating new means for attacking satellites. It is necessary, therefore, to evaluate the impact of ASAT on the vulnerability of the future command system.

The vulnerability of a satellite depends crucially on its orbital characteristics. A low-orbit (LEO) satellite could be attacked with rockets launched from the ground in as little as a matter of 1 minute if it is within range, and on much larger portions of its orbital path by ASATs launched from aircraft or based in orbit. Ground-based and airborne ASAT interceptors have already been tested by both superpowers. The tested prototypes and their offspring are of little concern to us here because they are not designed to reach satellites crucial to U.S. strategic command, which are all in geosynchronous (GEO) or other high orbits.[11]

Attacks on a high-altitude target with a rocket launched from the ground or low altitude are conceivable, but the time required to reach the target is measured in hours, and would give tactical warning long before launch of the missile that actually constituted the strategic strike. That is, if ASAT operations are to abet a strategic strike they would have to destroy or disable high-orbit targets in a matter of a minute or so.[12] Two means to that end can be envisaged: (1) attack from prepositioned nearby satellites, which would, in principle, be feasible with techniques currently available, or (2) attack from a distant point, whether on the ground or in LEO, with a directed energy weapon (DEW) that travels at or near the speed of light. The latter is not feasible now, but could be a consequence of research on ballistic missile defense.[13]

The term *space mine* will be used for any satellite that accompanies a potential quarry and can unleash some means of destruction on receipt of a radio command. A high-altitude space mine should, like its target, have a mission lifetime measured in years. It must keep within range of its potential victim, which will be maneuvering for its own reasons and perhaps for evasion. Thus, there is a premium on minimizing the dead weight of the space mine in order to maximize its maneuverability and lifetime. The mine, therefore, might carry a nuclear weapon, even though that would violate the Outer Space Treaty, since that would give it the largest kill radius for a given weight. The radiation from the nuclear explosion would produce an instantaneous incapacitating surge in the electronics of a quite distant spacecraft[14] and inflict more serious damage at a closer range. The most likely light-weight nonnuclear kill mechanism would be detonation into a pellet or shrapnel burst directed toward the target.

A space mine can be overt or covert. The likelihood of detection diminishes as the size of the mine decreases and its kill radius increases. This might be counted as a second significant advantage to a nuclear device; on the other hand, that must be weighed against serious political consequences should evidence of a treaty violation emerge from an accident during or after launch, or from direct observation by an orbiting surveillance instrument.

According to Nicholas Johnson, a leading authority on Soviet space systems,[15] "covert deployment of a geosynchronous space mine is considered relatively easy [because] today hundreds of 'spent' rocket bodies and 'dead' payloads drift around the geosynchronous ring. Any could be used as a disguise for a space mine. A space mine could also be launched under the guise of a communications satellite which 'failed' to stabilize at the announced location."[16] Furthermore, Johnson points out that "a very small maneuver at the time of conjunction with the target satellite can stop the drift of the space mine, leaving it near its target." Since a portion of the MILSTAR constellation will not be in geosynchronous orbits, MILSTAR will be considerably less vulnerable to covert space mines than the current communications and early warning satellites in GEO.

How the space mine threat to U.S. strategic satellites will evolve is likely to depend on both technical and political developments. Once MILSTAR becomes operational, the utility of a space mine attack confined to GEO targets would decrease sharply: it could only deprive the United States of information regarding Soviet missile launches from early warning satellites. Indeed, such an ASAT attack could increase the likelihood of a prompt launch ordered through the unharmed U.S. communication system because the sudden loss of contact with the early warning satellites might be interpreted as tactical warning of a massive missile attack. Once MILSTAR is deployed, an effective ASAT precursor to a strategic attack would therefore require space mines in MILSTAR orbits where covert deployment may be difficult—perhaps intolerably so if enough resources were to be devoted to space surveillance.

That still leaves the possibility of overt deployment of space mines against the MILSTAR constellation. This would not be an implausible scenario if diplomatic efforts to regulate military space activities, especially those associated with ballistic missile defense (BMD), had collapsed. MILSTAR reportedly has considerable maneuverability, and is hardened against nuclear radiation, but we are not in a position to say whether these or other capabilities suffice to protect it against the space mine threat that could evolve should the political climate be adverse during its lifetime, which is supposed to extend into the next century. Given the key role that MILSTAR is intended to play, the rather small number of satellites in the MILSTAR constellation, and the possibility that sophisticated weapons will actually be deployed in space, it would be prudent to have backups for MILSTAR.

We now turn to the threat to high altitude spacecraft from DEWs. The beam weapons that are likely to be available in the next decade are not expected to be sufficiently powerful to meet the requirements for ASAT attacks against high-altitude targets; the same cannot be said for LEO targets. That does not mean that lasers could not disrupt or incapacitate the infrared sensors on early warning satellites before then, but the hazards of such an attack have already been noted.

Should DEW techniques sufficiently potent for boost phase BMD become available, however, they could pose a threat to existing and future strategic satellites. At this time the BMD scheme with the greatest high-altitude ASAT potential appears to be a ground-based laser sufficiently powerful to destroy boosters with the aid of high-altitude mirrors.[17] Such a system could incinerate any other object at the mirrors' altitudes that did not have near-perfect reflectivity.[18] Indeed, a laser-mirror configuration that did not reach the performance level required for the boost phase BMD mission could readily be a proficient high altitude ASAT; whether either side would go to these lengths solely for an ASAT capability is, of course, another matter.

Since many U.S. military satellites are designed to be in service for about one decade, during which time the threats they face could grow significantly, they should have the capability to automatically broadcast diagnostic data should they come under attack. On-board instruments, for example, could determine whether the spacecraft is being irradiated by a particle beam, or overheated by a laser. In particular, early warning satellites should have the capability to broadcast a signal confirming their destruction so that their disappearance would not merely constitute ambiguous tactical warning.

FURTHER TECHNICAL IMPROVEMENTS FOR STRATEGIC COMMAND

Technical improvements of the U.S. command system can be envisaged that address significant weaknesses not touched or only partially cured by the government's committed program. For that purpose, it is useful to rank the problems faced by command according to the level of perceived threat and physical destruction in terms of four sets of circumstances. The first covers *low-intensity crises,* unaccompanied by warfare, when the threat of a strategic attack on U.S. command would be estimated as being remote. The second concerns *intense crises,* which would probably be accompanied by warfare that may even have involved tactical nuclear weapons, when the threat of a strategic attack would be judged to be appreciable. The third is a *strategic confrontation* between the superpowers in which a strategic exchange appears to be imminent or already underway. And the fourth is the *postattack* command environment, in which the peacetime infrastructure and unevacuated personnel would have been largely destroyed.

In low-intensity crises American leaders must ponder their decisions in the turbulent environment of an open peacetime society, which can be a serious handicap in a confrontation with the Soviet Union or other potential adversaries. This problem could be overcome by a secure high-quality teleconferencing network for confidential consultations between geographically separated officials.

To provide reassurance in more serious crises, the president is likely to remain in Washington, even if the threat of attack is judged to be appreciable. Precautions must therefore be taken to preserve the NCA. Several broad options are available, of which two seem more feasible than the others. The first is to deploy one or more ANCAs as a crisis intensifies. The United States has adopted this option as a practical way to insure that there is a surviving NCA if the president is killed in an attack on Washington (or elsewhere). This mode of protection can be strengthened further by providing the ANCAs with better communications to the forces and to the primary NCA, with more enduring mobile command posts, and with better backup communications.

The second option would be to build a super-hardened underground com-

mand center in or near Washington. Such a facility would contribute significantly to crisis stability. Unfortunately, a hardened presidential command
center in Washington itself carries heavy political liabilities, and has been
rejected in the past. The feasibility of such a facility in the proximity of the
capital should therefore be considered.

Our suggested improvements for postattack command network have two
objectives: first, to provide sturdier communications between the ANCA and
the forces, and second, to create a hot line linking the superpowers that could
survive a strategic exchange. The former are intended to strengthen deterrence—to reduce the risk that what we have antiseptically called "the postattack environment" will ever be experienced. The latter would provide the
minimum essential means for negotiating a cease-fire should deterrence have
collapsed, a requirement that the existing hot line does not meet should a
nuclear exchange have destroyed either capital.

The following suggestions have been selected from a longer list by such
criteria as urgency, technical feasibility, and compatibility with installed and
forthcoming systems. While we have made no cost estimates, a rough idea of
likely cost has influenced the selection. Many, if not all, of these suggestions
have been considered at one time or another by the government. A few are
currently under consideration. In our view these suggestions merit serious
consideration (or reconsideration) by the government at this time.

Secure Crisis Conferencing

Close interaction in a relatively secluded environment among senior officials
and their staffs is essential to sound decision making during a crisis. On the
other hand, the U.S. government is scattered about Washington, and senior
officials would therefore be forced to traverse the city to converge for crisis
meetings—usually at the White House or the Old Executive Office Building.
Although such movements were kept secret for nearly a week during the
Cuban Missile Crisis, this could probably not be repeated unless wartime
measures, such as censorship and curfews, were in force.

Knowledge that high-level meetings were occurring could be valuable intelligence in a low-intensity crisis, and would arouse media attention and create
pressures on the U.S. government from many quarters. In addition, the
senior officials involved in national security decisions have other pressing
day-to-day responsibilities. The full cost of gathering such persons at the
White House, therefore, can be high, while the cost incurred by delays in
travel, or of not meeting, could be enormous.

This problem could be mitigated by a secure audiovisual teleconferencing
network that would link key participants in crisis deliberations. Security and
high fidelity for both picture and sound would be provided by digitizing and
then by encrypting all signals for wide-band transmission by fiberoptic or
microwave links in the Washington area.[19]

Most high-level executives are not yet accustomed to teleconferencing;[20]

strong antipathy has been encountered because the intimacy of face-to-face meeting is lacking. In the context of crisis management, however, the advantages of immediate and secure consultations should outweigh such objections to teleconferencing. This observation is supported by operational experience with a voice-only conferencing network—the National Operations and Intelligence Watch Officers Net connecting CIA, DIA, NSA, State, JCS, and the White House Situation Room.[21] Although 10 months were needed to overcome "cultural differences" among different user communities, this network is now a very important tool and has been used as much as four times per hour during low-intensity crises.

The potential advantages of secure teleconferencing will only be realized if a convenient high-quality system is installed. The offices, and probably the homes, of likely participants should be in the two-way network. This would encourage day-to-day use, familiarize users with the medium, and lead to the evolution and adaptation of the facilities and procedures to the individuals involved. Even under ideal conditions, however, teleconferencing should not be envisaged as a substitute for face-to-face meetings, but rather as a complement to them.

We have so-far focused on low-intensity crises, when it may be more a matter of discretion whether a physical meeting is necessary. But the ability to "meet" while having to be separated could be very useful in a more intense crisis. In such circumstances the Washington-based high-fidelity network could be expanded to provide somewhat lower picture quality (i.e., narrower bandwidth) secure teleconferencing via satellite between command centers in Washington and key command centers such as the ANMCC, Air Force One, SAC, NORAD, and command posts for the ANCA, such as NEACP. This capability could serve a number of purposes. Above all, it would allow the ANCA, while deployed at a remote location, to be party to the briefings and deliberations that preceded the events that could suddenly transform the ANCA into the primary NCA. (Such a facility would also allow key officials who are not at their normal posts to participate in less momentous "meetings.") For all these functions, high quality secure voice communications must be assured.

Finally, we consider the transition from the pre- to the postattack environments that would be brought about by a missile attack. A Missile Attack Conference between the NCA, the JCS chairman, the SAC and NORAD commanders, and other key advisers to the president (in particular, the secretaries of defense and state) must be convened immediately after confirmation of tactical warning of a missile attack. A reliable, dedicated standby network providing secure voice communications is needed for this purpose. MILSTAR will eventually provide such a capability even in the face of nuclear attack. In the meantime, however, a less sophisticated network that could perform these functions in a preattack environment is urgently needed and could be provided by a fleet of unmanned aircraft. For this purpose, some capability can also be provided by the MILSTAR packages now on Fleet Satellite Communications.

The Postattack Command-and-Control System

The PACCS would be fully alerted in an intense crisis prior to attack. The apex of command would still be the primary NCA, whether or not Washington had been evacuated, but one or more ANCAs would be deployed. Even after the committed command-and-control improvement program is complete, PACCS will continue to rely heavily on a small number of critical facilities, such as airborne command posts and high-value satellites. Furthermore, should the president remain in Washington the primary NCA would be as highly vulnerable as it is today. There are, however, several possibilities to consider for reducing these vulnerabilities.

The Alternate NCA: Role and Requirements. From discussions with individuals who have borne high responsibilities, it is our judgment that the president is likely to remain a visible presence in Washington regardless of the threat, and that in an intense crisis the vice president would be at a remote location as the head of an ANCA. This arrangement would serve the dual purpose of providing reassurance to the American public, and possibly to the Soviet Union, that the U.S. government assumes that the crisis will not explode into strategic war, while securing the safety of the legitimate successor to the president should that confidence have been misplaced.

The ANCA must have a team of senior decision makers, adequate staff, and logistical support in a command post that is survivable and enduring, and which can remain in contact with the primary NCA without divulging the ANCA's position. Ideally, covert access to this command post should be available.

The communications requirements of the ANCA are more demanding than those of the NCA. Not only must they connect these two vital command elements prior to an attack, but they must be able to link the ANCA to the military command system, and in particular the strategic forces, following an attack. While all communications must be secure against jamming and interception, pre- and postattack requirements differ in other respects. Preattack communications should have high-fidelity, preferably for both audio and video, so that all participants in decision making, *including* the ANCA, have a psychological sense of "presence." Fortunately, preattack communications can assume that most (if not all) facilities are fully operational. In contrast, postattack communications will, of necessity, be much more austere: they need only transmit information encoded as low-fidelity voice or as data (bit streams);[22] they must be as invulnerable as possible but they need not be continuous. Above all, they must function in the electromagnetic environment created by nuclear bursts in space and the atmosphere, which could reduce the possible communication options sharply and unpredictably. Thus adaptive high frequency (HF) is one possible technique because it can seek out pathways that avoid portions of the ionosphere disrupted by nuclear explosions.[23]

Short Takeoff and Landing Airborne Command Posts. As we have seen, the relatively small number of postattack command posts are now largely on aircraft; soon these will be augmented by ground-mobile facilities. The risk that a ground-based facility, even though mobile, could be discovered and attacked is probably greater than that for aircraft that may frequently move or remain airborne for extended periods. Airborne command posts for the NCA and its alternates, therefore, will remain essential.

The major disadvantages of most current airborne command posts are that they lack endurance, are not hardened, and require long runways. For example, the EC-135 fleet can stay aloft for about 10 hours without air refueling. The E-4 aircraft used for NEACAP have much more endurance (24 hours without air refueling), but are also tied to long runways. These limitations could be greatly reduced if STOL aircraft were used as airborne command posts. Instead of a few hundred available airfields, they would have thousands from which to operate. This, in turn, would relax their dependency upon air refueling and greatly reduce the overall logistics problem created by sustained operations. When such factors are taken into account, the use of STOL aircraft for PACCS and NEACP operations could both simplify and strengthen these vital functions.

The aircraft currently used in the PACCS fleet require runways approximately 10,000 feet long, of which there are only 232 in the continental United States. In contrast, a STOL command post based on the four-engined C-17 airframe could use 3,000-ft long airstrips, of which there are about 3,700 in all, with nearly 1,400 in the central and Great Lake states where there would be maximum time for takeoff between SLBM breakwater and impact.[24] The C-17 could carry the same useful payload as the current NEACP, with enough fuel for a flight time of about 5 hours and a range between stops of about 2,700 miles.[25] To take off in as little as 3,000 ft would require rocket assistance from strap-on boosters.

A STOL command post must be able to disperse on tactical warning of SLBM launch, which would be received 60 seconds after breakwater. Since the flight crew should be aboard continuously, and staff quartered alongside, an interval of perhaps 60 seconds between warning and takeoff, or 120 seconds following SLBM launch, may be attainable under optimum conditions. The probability of survival grows as the square of the flyout distance, so rocket boosters should also be used to accelerate the STOL airplane promptly to its 400-MPH maximum sea-level cruising speed.

Rough estimates show that a STOL command post with this performance would have a very high probability of evading an SLBM attack if the warheads were launched in the most fuel-efficient manner (i.e., along "minimum energy trajectories"), taking about 15 minutes from breakwater to impact on a midwestern target. This time could be halved by use of untested "depressed trajectories," in which the warheads travel more rapidly at lower altitudes. In that case the chance that a barrage attack would destroy the command post becomes appreciable.[26] Normal peacetime deployment practice by the Soviet

SSBN fleet, however, would probably not support a barrage attack, unless all other major targets were ignored. Nevertheless, this does illustrate that a ban on the testing of depressed-trajectory ballistic missiles would make a valuable contribution to the survivability of command and to overall stability.

A Deep Underground Command Center (DUCC). A survivable command post for the NCA with direct and covert access to the White House, or in the vicinity of the capital for the ANCA, would have some major advantages over distant and mobile command centers. A DUCC connected to the White House would allow the NCA to enhance its survivability with little or no political cost during a crisis. Proximity would minimize the time required to relocate the NCA on receipt of tactical warning—a few minutes should suffice. As a result, virtually the only nuclear threat to the survival of the NCA would be from a clandestine bomb detonated before missile launch. Indeed, the Soviet leadership appears to have such facilities, although we do not know to what extent they could endure *and* communicate if attacked.[27]

On the other hand, a hard command center in the capital also faces severe technical problems and political hurdles. The former concern any fixed command center's endurance and ability to remain in contact with the outside world following attack. As we shall see, these technical problems are solvable in principle, especially if the requirement that the DUCC should continue to function during a massive and prolonged attack is relaxed because the more modest requirement that the primary NCA or its first alternate would always be operational during the early phase of a nuclear attack should be adequate. By far the most serious drawback to a hard command center inside the capital is political. Construction of a DUCC in Washington is bound to produce public alarm and opposition on several grounds, including the concern that the capital could come under much heavier attack because of the DUCC.

For these reasons consideration should be given to the construction of a DUCC at an appropriate location in the vicinity of Washington, such as Ft. Ritchie in Maryland. If the threat of nuclear attack was deemed to be significant, the vice president and other senior civilian and military leaders could quickly move to the DUCC without the political penalty that an evacuation of the president would incur. By use of the teleconferencing system already described, this ANCA could remain in continuous high-fidelity contact with the primary NCA in Washington. Such an arrangement would evade the political hurdles faced by a DUCC in the capital, and would have a number of significant advantages over the present system, in which the ANCA must use a mobile command center. Of necessity, a mobile center is rather austere and can only accommodate a limited staff, which could be a serious handicap in a prolonged crisis. Furthermore, mobile posts are not readily accessible, and their survival requires concealment, which cannot be assured because such centers have distinctive features.

A DUCC would have to be located at depths greater than those usually considered for missile basing because the missile force need only attain statistical survivability, while the one and only DUCC must survive. As depths of 300 to 2,500 ft have been considered for missile basing, a DUCC should be buried as deeply as 5,000 to 10,000 ft.[28]

Communications from deep underground present great technical difficulties; self-sufficiency is also a must, but presents no profound problems.[29] Nuclear weapons used to attack the DUCC would produce large craters and destroy communications facilities at or near the surface above the DUCC. Nearby cabling not within craters might also be vulnerable to ground shear. Radio communications[30] would therefore have to leave and enter a DUCC from a redundant and spatially dispersed set of exit/entry ports so that some links would survive even a barrage attack.[31]

Postattack Communications and Intelligence. At present postattack communications within the United States would rely heavily on the radio relay aircraft in the PACCS fleet. For this purpose remotely piloted vehicles (RPVs) could offer a number of significant advantages over manned aircraft: they impose a much lighter burden on personnel, and they have longer flight endurance. On the other hand, it remains to be demonstrated that RPVs can attain the reliability and safety required for operation in air space that must be shared with civilian aircraft. Should such a level of performance become possible at reasonable cost, it would be feasible to deploy a portion of the backup command network in peacetime.[32] Furthermore, a larger portion of the backup network could also be deployed in a prolonged crisis than is possible with today's manned system. Consideration should therefore be given to supplementing or replacing the manned network with unmanned drones.

At altitudes of 50,000 to 60,000 ft, a single RPV could communicate with points on the ground out to a few hundred miles, and to twice that distance to a platform at equal altitude. Three RPVs could link NORAD, SAC, NEACP, ANMCC, NMCC, and perhaps even the PAVE PAWS radars and Atlantic Command. Ten to 12 could provide UHF coverage over virtually the entire continental United States. The system could also provide secure voice conferencing between the NCA, NMCS, SAC, and NORAD, especially during threat assessment and missile attack conferences.

We now turn to communications with SSBNs patrolling on alert, when they are always in a receive-only mode via VLF radio. Electromagnetic waves in the VLF range penetrate sea water to a depth of a few meters. Depending on the SSBN's speed, signals are received via a buoyant antenna cable towed on the surface, or a towed buoy that controls its depth appropriately. Neither the towed buoy nor the floating cable create a significant vulnerability, but it may be useful to eliminate the cable entirely since its use does force certain operational restrictions related to speed and depth on the SSBN. New approaches appear to be feasible for this purpose. Visible light in the blue portion of the spectrum (having a wavelength of about 5,000 Å) penetrates seawater to depths of approximately 100 m; this is comparable to those at which submarines attain covertness with high probability. Thus, it is technically feasible for a satellite or airplane carrying a modulated laser to communicate with an optical receiver mounted on a submarine's hull.[33]

In designing the laser link, the possibility of cloud cover must be considered, as should the chance that the highly directional laser beam could reveal the submarine's location. Cloud cover would spread the beam and elongate a short pulse, thereby reducing the light intensity and the inherent data rate. When these effects are taken into account, a one-watt laser could communicate at 10 kilobaud with a submarine at a depth of about 100 m, and at 10 times that rate in clear weather. To preclude location of a particular submarine, the beam would have to be swept across the vessel's entire patrol area, which would reduce the data rate by a factor of about 1,000. If communications with the entire SSBN fleet were necessary, 3 million km^2 of ocean would have to be scanned. Each submarine near the surface could then receive at an effective rate of 0.3 bits/second. This would suffice to transmit a 100-bit message in 10 seconds by a 30-watt laser to submarines at depths where the light attenuation is 100-fold.[34]

Lasers could also be used to communicate with attack submarine (SSN). This would be useful for several reasons. The missions of an attack submarine, in contrast to those of an SSBN, do not require it to remain near the surface where it can listen to VLF. Hence an SSN is normally out of contact with higher authority, which could have serious consequences in a fast-paced crisis, especially with the deployment of nuclear-armed cruise missiles on SSNs. The laser technique could also link a carrier group to its SSN escorts. Since the carrier should have an early-warning (E-2) aircraft up at all times, a laser on the aircraft would allow communication with SSNs over an area exceeding 10,000 square miles. Light from a ship-mounted laser scattered from the air or from clouds into the water could also be used for this purpose.

Surface ships are not presently part of the Minimum Essential Emergency Communications Network (MEECN), although they are expected to relay EAMs and other high-priority traffic. With little operational or logistical overhead, they could be an important backup to TACAMO in communications to the SSBN force if they were to carry an untethered balloon-borne package capable of receiving HF and VHF and converting it to VLF signals. The balloon launcher should be designed to require minimal human intervention since crew training would inevitably have low priority.[35]

Thus far we have concerned ourselves with communications, not with what is to be communicated. The information that would reach the NCA following a nuclear attack is likely to be limited in scope, which could contribute to the NCA's inability to make informed decisions. In particular, attack assessment may be very sketchy despite the dramatic increase in precision and timeliness of data on the location and yield of nuclear explosions that will be provided with the deployment of the Integrated Operation Nuclear Detonation Detection System (IONDS) aboard Navstar satellites. The Navstar platforms have multiple missions, however, which would create an incentive for ASAT attack.

Therefore, a system that would provide independent information on the survival or destruction of assets critical to the United States (such as the NCA, other command centers, missile fields, airfields, and so on) would be an important complement to the IONDS. Such a system should probably be ground-based and could employ a combination of seismic, thermal, optical, or EMP sensors to detect nuclear explosions at or near the ground. Information emerging from these sensors might be distributed into many different encrypted "bulletin boards" for interrogation by authorized parties. Such a system would be useful to the NCA in situation assessment, and also for the operation of bombers and airborne command posts, which should avoid radiation-contaminated airspace. More importantly, it could be crucial in deciding when to transfer authority to an ANCA should the primary NCA be destroyed, and in providing a data base for the ANCA.

Finally, we turn from hardware to software. In times of exceptional stress message traffic chronically overwhelms the capacity of communication networks.[36] This is then compounded by the sending of multiple copies over various routes when no acknowledgment is in hand. A large fraction of U.S. military communications are presently transmitted by satellite. In normal peacetime operations their capacity is probably adequate to insure that transmitted messages are received; however, the antijam capabilities of current communication satellites are not adequate to insure sufficient bandwidth for all messages should jamming occur. While this impediment will be eased by the advent of MILSTAR, if history is any guide the demand for communication capacity will always keep ahead of supply.[37] It is important, therefore, to adopt a protocol in which acknowledgment of high-priority messages is routinely and automatically acknowledged, with the acknowledgment having a higher priority than the corresponding (and longer) message.

Reconstitution of Postattack C³I

Since a strategic attack will inevitably lead to disruption or destruction of some, if not all, essential command facilities, an ability to reconstitute communication links is of great importance.

In view of the vulnerability of small constellations of high-value satellites, as exemplified by MILSTAR, serious consideration should be given to a backup system. The Defense Advanced Research Project Agency (DARPA) is now studying large constellations composed of redundant and low-value satellites. A large constellation in many orbits, with each carrying a burst radio relay at EHF would provide survivable high-bandwidth communications on a worldwide basis.[38] The cost of an individual satellite could be kept down by sacrificing reliability since the system, like GWEN, is designed to tolerate multiple node failure. Another system concept would use a few operating satellites with many dark spares and suitable decoys so that a surviving dark satellite could assume the job of a destroyed satellite.[39] A careful trade-off and cost comparison is needed to decide between proliferation and survivable system designs for the optimum approach to this vital problem.

A Strategic Mail Box

The destruction caused by a strategic attack is likely to isolate many surviving forces and command elements. Communication links could be difficult to re-establish since receiver and transmitter might not be able to operate simultaneously, as required by conventional radio, although this is not required by postal services. For that reasons it would be desirable to provide an automated message handling facility—a Strategic Mail Box.

MILSTAR satellites are the obvious candidates for this role. The Mail Box could be accessed at various levels of security by authorized users, ranging from the NCA to SSBN and bomber commanders. The NCA could place a continually updated attack and damage assessment up to the time of its own destruction, as well as recommendations and orders, on this mail system. The data from the NDS, and the backup to it suggested previously, should be stored in the Mail Box. Surviving command and forces (especially the SSBNs at sea) could access as well as contribute to a common pool of information. Messages could be made available to selected groups of recipients, at the discretion of the sender.

The facility could be especially important for SSBNs because their communications are generally regarded as the most tenuous of all strategic links. We are not in a position to comment on the concerns that have been raised in some quarters as to what would transpire if a strategic attack had prevented the NCA from disseminating *any* EAM to the SSBN force, nor on whether that is even a realistic contingency. Nevertheless, it is certainly conceivable that the SSBN force might find its assets scattered and isolated in the postattack period. Each remaining SSBN would have to consider itself a potential target; it would most likely maintain radio silence and refrain from communicating with either higher authorities or other SSBNs. Coordination would therefore be difficult. Deterrence is strengthened to the extent that there is an increased certainty that adequate retaliation would follow even if an attack were so heavy that it would destroy all communication links to the SSBN force. The Strategic Mail Box could allow otherwise isolated SSBN commanders to act in a coherent fashion toward some common goal, whether it be for retaliation or in negotiations toward a cease-fire.

A Survivable Hot Line

The current Hot Line links the national command authorities in Washington and Moscow via commercial telecommunications satellites. During wartime such satellites are likely to be used for military purposes, thus creating an incentive for attack. The currently installed backup cable link could also be destroyed unintentionally in attacks on other targets. Furthermore, the satellite link is served by a single ground station in each nation's capital. If the NCA has shifted to an alternate command post, direct Hot Line communication is not possible. Should strategic war have commenced, the terminals could well be destroyed.

Survivable links are urgently needed for the Hot Line. Two proposals appear to have promise: (1) a dedicated geosynchronous satellite and (2) an HF ground-based radio system as a backup to the satellite.

A satellite whose *sole* purpose was to provide communications between the two national command authorities would be effectively invulnerable because neither side would have any incentive to attack it. The satellite should be in geosynchronous orbit, using narrow bandwidth EHF transmission. Teletype-speed communications at this frequency would require only those modest bandwidths that would be available during an unpredictable nuclear environment. Equally important, small portable receiver–transmitter stations can be used for EHF communications and located on a variety of command posts.

In a nuclear environment, many HF channels are likely to be blocked, but many others should remain open. The problem in using the HF band to communicate is that the usable channels will not be known in advance. An HF communication system that avoids this problem at the expense of a reduction in bandwidth, while still sufficient for teletype-speed communications, is one that employs the entire HF band, using one channel after another, according to a protocol known to the other side. Such a system would transmit its message successfully through at least one channel. Encryption of appropriate messages would prevent unauthorized parties from simply recording messages and retransmitting them. Since this system would employ rather simple radio equipment, it avoids the difficulty of either side needing to transfer its own sophisticated equipment used for communicating in a nuclear environment to the other. Finally, since the equipment can be small, terminals can be dispersed easily over many platforms.

APPENDIX: TECHNICAL ASPECTS OF
STRATEGIC COMMUNICATIONS

Communications[40] among early warning sensors, the NCA, and strategic forces must be timely, secure, and error-free even in the face of effects created by nuclear explosions. This requirement is easily stated, but exceedingly difficult to meet at best. Indeed, as we have seen earlier, the United States has devoted a great and ongoing effort in pursuit of what often has proved to be an elusive objective. We will now take a brief look at the technical aspects of strategic communications, placing a particular emphasis on radio communications in normal and nuclear-disturbed environments.[41]

Strategic communications are transmitted over a redundant set of pathways that exploit portions of the electromagnetic spectrum ranging from extremely low radio frequencies to visible light as well as hard-wired telephone circuits. Radio is likely to remain the predominant communication mode because of the relative ease with which signals can be generated and detected, even when the receiver and/or transmitter are in rapid motion. Furthermore, radio signals can travel long distances over a broad range of frequencies despite the curvature of the earth. For these reasons, we shall largely ignore communications other than radio in this discussion, focusing instead on such properties as range, information capacity, and vulnerability to nuclear disruption. These properties vary with frequency, so a particular communication band is usually appropriate only for a subset of strategic missions.

Radio Waves: Frequency, Bandwidth, and Data Rate

Radio waves are periodic variations of electric and magnetic fields that propagate with the speed of light c, which is 300,000 km/second in space or in the atmosphere. The distance between crests is called the *wavelength,* and the number of times per second that the electric field reaches its maximum value is called the *frequency.* The frequency is measured in hertz (Hz). Wavelength and frequency are inversely proportional: wavelength = c/frequency. Thus, a wavelength of 300 m corresponds to a frequency of 1 million Hz (1 MHz). Henceforth, we shall use abbreviations such as M for both frequency and wavelength:

giga (G) billion	10^9
mega (M) million	10^6
kilo (k) thousand	10^3
milli (m) thousandth	10^{-3}
micro (μ) millionth	10^{-6}
nano (n) billionth	10^{-9}

The portion of the spectrum referred to as "radio" is somewhat arbitrary; we shall use the term for frequencies ranging from tens of hertz to the very far infrared (IR), or roughly 1,000 GHz. Figure 6.1 shows the portion of the electromagnetic spectrum relevant to strategic communications and summarizes other related information.

The rate at which information that can be transmitted is an essential characteristic of any means of communication. A radio wave that constantly operates at a fixed frequency and intensity cannot transmit any information. If it is to carry information it must be "modulated," as in Morse code, where the message is conveyed by a combination of short and long interruptions of a single frequency wave.[42] A more relevant example is FM radio, where the frequency varies (or is modulated) about some "carrier," or average frequency.

The range of frequencies occupied by a modulated carrier wave is called the *bandwidth.* In a noiseless and distortion-free binary mode (like Morse code), a bandwidth of B hertz can easily transmit $2B$ bits/second, where one *bit* is defined as the choice of a binary digit (e.g., 0 or 1). Six bits are required to encode a letter from the alphabet, and the average word in English has seven letters, or some 40 bits. Consequently, a standard teletype operating at 66 words/minute requires a bandwidth of about 25 Hz.

The bandwidth that can be attained rises with the carrier frequency.[43] With sufficient transmitter power, a high-bandwidth link can support multiple

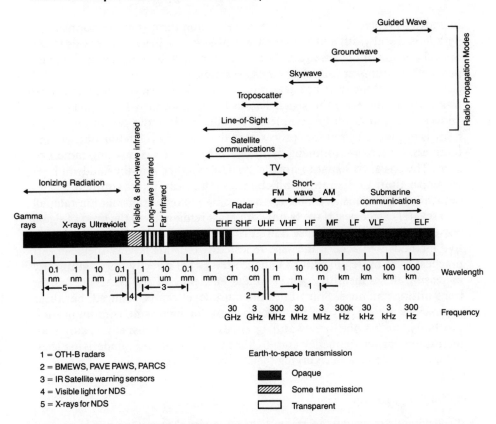

1 = OTH-B radars
2 = BMEWS, PAVE PAWS, PARCS
3 = IR Satellite warning sensors
4 = Visible light for NDS
5 = X-rays for NDS

Earth-to-space transmission

Opaque
Some transmission
Transparent

Figure 6.1. The electromagnetic spectrum, showing frequencies relevant to communications, early warning and attack assessment, and to natural and nuclear phenomena that can disturb signal propagation. The figure indicates whether signals can pass through the atmosphere ("Earth-to-space transmission"); the frequency bands exploited by radar and infrared (IR) early warning sensors (enumerated from 1 to 3); by nuclear explosion detectors (NDS); the frequencies of radiation above those of visible light, which can ionize the atmosphere and thereby alter its propagation characteristics; and the principal propagation modes of radio signals. It should be noted that of the frequencies that cannot pass through the atmosphere, those below HF are reflected, and, therefore, permit communications between points on or near the earth's surface not within each others' line-of-sight (LOS), whereas those above SHF are absorbed. (Adapted from Toomay, op. cit., p. 284, and Carter, op. cit., p. 232.)

channels of a smaller bandwidth, a single high-data-rate channel, or a single low-data-rate channel with protection against jamming. For example, a system with a bandwidth of 10 kHz could (in the absence of noise) carry 400 simultaneous teletype channels, or three voice channels. Television quality video transmission is more demanding, requiring bandwidths in excess of about 4 MHz, with even larger bandwidths needed for the data streams from space-based early warning sensors. The development of fiberoptic cable is intended to replace lower frequency transmission through bulky copper wire with large bandwidth and low-loss transmission at carrier frequencies in the optical portion of the spectrum. For permanent installations it will also compete with multitower microwave relay systems.

Bandwidth alone does not determine the rate at which information can be transmitted; however, the signal has to be distinguished from background "noise" that can never be completely eliminated. In radio communications, noise is produced by random processes at the atomic level in transmitters and receivers, by the environment, as in lightning, and by competing radio systems. The so-called signal-to-noise ratio S/N together with the bandwidth set the upper limit to the rate at which information can be transmitted.[44] Consequently, the means available for increasing the data transmission rate fall into several categories. If the bandwidth must remain fixed, the ratio of signal power at the receiver-to-noise power, S/N, must be raised. The most primitive method is to send a message repeatedly, but this is very inefficient. If practical, it is more efficient to enhance the signal directly, for example, by increasing the transmitter power or the efficiency of the receiving and/or transmitting antennas. Sometimes the noise level can be reduced, but these approaches are of very limited effectiveness for increasing communication capability, unless the bandwidth is enlarged,[45] which usually requires an increase in carrier frequency and, by that token, a different underlying technology for creating and receiving the signal.

Radio Propagation

Electromagnetic waves can travel between a signal generator and a receiver along an artificial guiding structure, such as a coaxial or fiberoptic cable, or by propagating through the atmosphere and/or empty space. The former include what is often referred to as "landlines," undersea telephone cables, etc. In view of the obvious limitations of such static transmission links for widely dispersed and mobile forces, especially in wartime, these will not be discussed here.

The earth's curvature severely restricts line-of-sight (LOS) communications: from the top of a 100-ft tower, or an aircraft at 35,000 ft, points on the horizon are at a distance of 20 km and 375 km, respectively. Two such aircraft could therefore only have LOS communications over distances ranging up to the separation of Omaha from Chicago or Washington from Detroit.

In empty space, radio waves of all frequencies can provide LOS links, but if points that are not within sight of each other are to communicate, they must use waves that can by some means overcome the obstacle posed by the earth. The most obvious is provided by satellites, which allow communication between two arbitrarily distant points on or near the earth through a succession of LOS links. In effect, the satellites act like mirrors that bounce the radio wave around the curve of the earth, although they actually carry transponders and antennas that enormously amplify the signal and redirect it before sending it onward. The earth and its normal atmosphere can also reflect and guide radio waves to link distant points, but, in contrast to LOS, that is not possible at all frequencies. Even when it is possible the range and reliability of such links vary markedly with frequency.

A variety of physical mechanisms in the earth's surface and atmosphere can influence electromagnetic waves and cause them to travel beyond the horizon or to be strongly absorbed. The earth's surface, and especially its oceans, form a reasonably good electrical conductor over a broad frequency range. Furthermore, the sun's ultraviolet light *ionizes* the upper atmosphere; that is, it separates electrons from molecules, and these free electrons thereby create a high-altitude region, called the *ionosphere,* which acts like an electrical conductor over a broad band of frequency. Acting separately or together, the atmosphere (especially the ionosphere) and the earth's surface can then reflect and channel radio waves so that they do not merely propagate outward into space. Such waves, therefore, can provide *over-the-horizon* (OTH) communication links, as depicted in Figure 6.2.

The various OTH propagation modes are conventionally classified as *guided* waves, *ground* waves, and *sky* (or *ionospheric*) waves; their frequency regimes are shown in Figure 6.1. At sufficiently low frequencies (up to several kilohertz), where the wavelength is comparable to the altitude of the ionosphere, waves are trapped in the waveguide formed by the space between the earth's surface and the ionosphere. Such waves, therefore, are called guided waves; absorption is small and worldwide transmission is possible. In the

Figure 6.2. The influence of the earth and the atmosphere on radio propagation.[46] The ionosphere is actually composed of several fairly distinct layers that differ in the density of free electrons. Consequently, they differ in their ability to reflect, bend, transmit, and absorb electromagnetic waves of various frequencies.

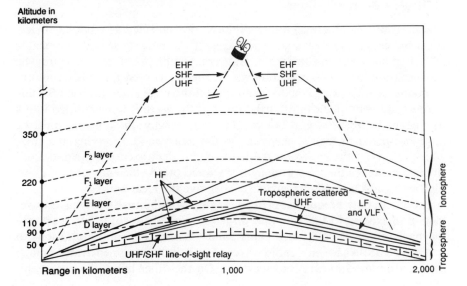

next higher frequency regime, the waves tend to "hug" the earth's surface; these are called ground waves—absorption by the surface is high and propagation is limited to several hundred kilometers. At yet higher frequencies waves are reflected at various altitudes from the ionosphere; these are called sky waves, and they can reach a receiver at distances of thousands of kilometers. At still higher frequencies turbulence in the troposphere, which is comprised of the ionosphere's lowest layers, suffices to scatter such a radio beam slightly, so that a region of the troposphere can be used as a high-altitude reflector and thereby permit OTH "troposcatter" communications. At frequencies above about 10 GHz or wavelengths below 3 cm, the atmosphere does not scatter significantly, and only LOS communications is possible.

Since these OTH communication links rely on the environment, they can also be influenced by natural and artificial changes in the environment. The transmission of ground waves is improved if the ground is moist, and even more so if the link crosses saltwater. The influence of the ionosphere on radio waves is largely determined by the electrons set free by the sun's light, and that influence therefore varies with time of day, season, sunspot activity, and so forth. One consequence of such effects is familiar to all: AM radio broadcasts at night are often heard at distances far beyond their normal daytime range.[47] Finally, nuclear explosions can drastically alter the electron density, thereby altering propagation characteristics dramatically.

The frequency of a radio wave may not select a single propagation mode, although it usually determines the most efficient mode available; the signal may also propagate with reduced intensity in a subsidiary mode.[48] In this connection, the characteristics of the transmitter—in particular, the geometry and orientation of the antenna—are important.[49] Such matters must be considered in assessing communications security.

Strategic Communications

The transmitting antenna converts information encoded as modulated electrical currents into electromagnetic waves. It will only do so with reasonable efficiency if its dimensions are at least comparable to the wavelength. The wavelength of a 100-Hz signal, however, such as is used for SSBN communications, is 3,000 km. For that reason even the huge antennas used for this purpose are very inefficient. Furthermore, if the wave is to be emitted into a well-defined direction, and not roughly isotropically, the antenna must be large compared to the wavelength. On the other hand, receiving antennas, which reconvert the electromagnetic wave into electric currents, can be considerably smaller than a wavelength since reception efficiency need only be high enough to bring the received signal above the local noise.

Extremely Low Frequencies (ELF) ranging from 30 to 300 Hz have wavelengths in excess of 1,000 km; they propagate globally as guided waves by the mechanism already discussed. This band[50] is used for communications to submerged SSBNs because radio waves of such frequencies penetrate as much as a few hundred meters into seawater. On the other hand, the pitiful efficiency attained even with a 50-mile long antenna implies that the data rate is exceedingly low—in the range of bits per minute.

Very Low Frequencies (VLF), from 3 to 30 kHz, propagate by a combination of guided and ground wave modes. Reception is possible up to a range of about 10,000 km at a depth of several meters in seawater. For that reason VLF is the primary mode of communications to alert SSBNs.

Low Frequencies (LF), from 30 to 300 kHz, propagate as a ground wave, and are not vulnerable to ionospheric disruption by high-altitude nuclear bursts. The GWEN network operates in the LF.

Medium Frequencies (MF), from 300 kHz to 3 MHz, include broadcast AM radio, but are not presently important for strategic communications.

High Frequencies (HF), from 3 to 30 MHz, have long played an important role in military (and amateur) long-distance communications. It propagates via sky-wave reflection to distances ranging from about 900 to 9,000 km by up to three hops between the earth and the ionosphere. At HF the available bandwidth suffices to support multiple voice conversations; only relatively small, low-power transmitters are required; both transmitting and receiving antennas can be fairly small since the wavelength ranges from 10 to 100 m; and the technology for generating and detecting the signal is inexpensive. Together with satellites, HF provides the principal means of communications for dispersed forces.

Nevertheless, HF also suffers from serious disadvantages. Its widespread use implies that interference from other users is likely. Furthermore, it is subject to interception, and the location of even a mobile HF transmitter can be found by direction-finding devices. Above all, HF transmission is sensitive to ionospheric conditions, and can be severely degraded by sunspot activity, auroral effects, and the like.[51] By that token, HF is particularly vulnerable to disruption by nuclear bursts whether by design or as a collateral effect. This phenomenon is called *blackout,* and, as will be discussed later, it is expected to vary unpredictably with the frequency and path of the signal.

To a considerable degree, ionospheric variations can be overcome by *adaptive* HF, wherein a microprocessor automatically varies the frequency until a two-way connection through the ionosphere is established to a designated receiver. At that point communications begins; if it is subsequently severed, the search is started again, and repeated until the message is completed. Adaptive HF can maintain connectivity during considerable fluctuations in the ionosphere, but not in the face of severe disruption. Another new HF technique is to spread the signal across a broad band, so that different frequencies will travel along various paths and arrive at the receiver at different times, where a microprocessor reassembles the message. These sophisticated HF techniques have led to a resurgence of interest in HF as a backup to satellite communications.

Very High Frequencies (VHF), from 30 to 300 MHz, constitute the lowest frequency LOS band. VHF is used for civilian television and FM radio, and in military short-range ground-to-ground, ground-to-air, and air-to-air communications.[52]

Ultra and Super High Frequencies (UHF and SHF), from 300 MHz to 30 GHz, correspond to wavelengths of from 1 m to 1 cm. These frequencies are largely unaffected by the atmosphere unless it has been disrupted by nuclear explosions. Only LOS communications are practical.[53] Enormous data rates can be attained even with transmitters that radiate considerably less power than a household light bulb, and very small (and therefore easily portable) antennas can form a wave that is highly collimated and significantly vulnerable to interception only by a hostile receiver situated on the LOS. The PACCS airborne relay network uses UHF, as do airborne command posts and the transmitters on the Minutemen consigned to the Emergency Rocket Communications System (ERCS). Both UHF and SHF are used by currently deployed military communications satellites. Despite its high intrinsic data capacity, UHF has a severely restricted capability for voice conferencing in comparison to the number of potential users. On the whole, the UHF bandwidth is divided into a large number of two-way teletype circuits.

Extremely High Frequencies (EHF), from 30 to 300 GHz, have wavelengths ranging from 1 cm to 1 mm. The technology to generate signals at such frequencies is relatively new, and will be used by MILSTAR satellites to provide protection against jamming, interception, and nuclear effects while maintaining the high data rates already available at UHF and SHF under less demanding circumstances.

Communications at frequencies above SHF must contend with the fact that the atmosphere absorbs most of such frequencies (see Figure 6.1). There are some windows in the infrared and visible portions of the spectrum, as we know from everyday life, and these could be used for laser communication links between points below the atmosphere and in orbit above it; however, these windows can be closed by fog, rain, and so forth. Hence lasers are presently envisaged for only two communications purposes: to submerged submarines in the blue portion of the visible and for cross-links between satellites where the signal travels unmolested in vacuum. Ultrahigh data rate communications in the visible has also become available with the advent of fiberoptic cable that can "channel" light over long distances. Such cabling can be spread on the ocean floor to acoustic transponders, which convert the message encoded on the light wave into sound waves that propagate efficiently for distances of several kilometers in water and would thereby provide communications to submerged submarines.

Communication Vulnerabilities

Aside from direct physical destruction, communications can be disrupted by jamming and by a variety of electromagnetic phenomena created by nuclear explosions.

Jamming is achieved when a hostile transmitter swamps a signal with noise or makes it unintelligible by some other means. Susceptibility to jamming is a function of the signal's strength and bandwidth, the modulation technique that encodes the message, and the characteristics and locations of the transmitting and receiving antennas. Thus, a highly directional receiving antenna can only be jammed by a hostile transmitter on the LOS, while any receiver becomes more vulnerable to jamming as its distance from the friendly transmitter increases since the power reaching it falls off as the square of the range.

Antijamming techniques can be passive or active. Passive techniques are exemplified by the use of highly directional LOS communications. Active methods exploit the techniques of communications engineering. Thus, a signal can be disguised by making it appear like noise by spreading it in a pseudorandom fashion across a large bandwidth ("spread-spectrum" broadcast) or by transmitting and receiving it over a narrow but constantly changing frequency band ("frequency hopping"). If carried far enough, such techniques can compel the jammer to rely on brute force; that is, to broadcast high-power signals across the entire bandwidth available to his adversary. Since the available bandwidth rises with frequency, so does the power required for brute force jamming. For that reason SHF and EHF communications are less vulnerable to this form of electronic warfare.

Nuclear effects[54] arising from nuclear explosions can have a profound effect on radio communications. Bursts above or within the ionosphere drastically increase the free electron density and affect propagation across the entire radio band from ELF to SHF because the ionosphere's ability to reflect and absorb electromagnetic waves of various frequencies is sensitive to that density. Furthermore, these electrons can produce secondary electromagnetic effects that can create widespread disturbances of communications. Surface bursts can also disrupt LOS and ionospheric communications as radioactive debris and particulates are lofted upward by the fireballs.

A thermonuclear explosion radiates an intense flux of gamma rays—ultrashort wavelength electromagnetic waves with sufficient energy to eject high-velocity electrons from air molecules. These electrons in turn radiate electromagnetic waves and knock out other electrons. If the nuclear detonation is above the atmosphere, its gamma rays thereby initiate an avalanche of processes that result in a pulse of electromagnetic radiation covering a very extensive area—a *high altitude electromagnetic pulse* (HEMP). The frequencies contained in the pulse extend from ELF to VHF, and in addition, low frequency "magnetohydrodynamic" (MHD) effects are also generated.

A single burst at an altitude of 300 km can produce an EMP covering much of the United States with a pulse of electrical fields reaching strengths of order 25,000 V/m with a rise time more than 1,000 times faster than that of a lightning bolt. Surface bursts can produce even more intense EMP effects, but only locally over distances of some tens of kilometers. These properties of EMP make it difficult to protect sensitive electronics, particularly microchips, from disruption or permanent damage. Even buried cables are vulnerable to low frequency EMP and MHD effects. Nevertheless, shielding against EMP is possible, but it requires proper design, costly construction, and careful testing because realistic simulation of EMP is difficult to attain given the remarkable characteristics of the effect.[55] Most critical links in U.S. strategic communications, ranging from underground cabling at ICBM bases to the electronics aboard command aircraft, are now hardened against EMP.

Aside from EMP effects, nuclear explosions can cause other types of disruption to communications and to radar. As already mentioned, the detonation itself releases ionizing radiation; furthermore, surface bursts loft radioactive debris that also emits such radiation over prolonged periods. The electrons thus freed will alter the propagation of radio waves in a complicated manner that depends on the yield and altitude of the explosion, the elapsed time since the explosion,[56] and the frequency and altitude of the wave itself. Thus megaton-range surface bursts, and bursts in the kiloton range above about 100 km, will produce blackout. Conventional HF is especially vulnerable to blackout for periods that can last many hours; higher frequencies are progressively less sensitive, with terrestrial UHF disruption persisting only for some seconds, while terrestrial SHF and EHF are essentially unaffected. The low frequencies used for SSBN communications (VLF and ELF) are not subject to blackout.

While blackout is not a serious problem for the frequencies use in satellite communications, such signals can be degraded by fluctuations in the electron density induced by nuclear explosions. This *scintillation* effect is similar to the familiar shimmering and blinking of stars, which are due to atmospheric density fluctuations. Scintillation can seriously disturb UHF radio communications to or from satellites over large regions and continue for hours. The effect decreases with frequency, however, and for that reason MILSTAR uses EHF in contrast to the lower frequencies of current satellite links.

X-rays and gamma rays from nuclear detonations in space can induce damaging electrical currents on the metallic skin of a satellite, and on-board electronics are vulnerable to damage or disruption from this "system-generated EMP" effect (SGEMP). In addition, neutrons and gamma rays can penetrate the skin and damage electronics directly. In space these are long-range effects and their intensity is limited only by the $1/R^2$ fall-off. Important space assets, like MILSTAR, can be hardened to some extent against such nuclear effects.[57]

NOTES

1. For a description of the program, see U.S. Congress, House, Committee on Appropriation Hearings, *Department of Defense Appropriations for 1987,* 99th Cong., 2nd Session, Part 3, pp. 427–686. A useful survey is provided by James W. Canan, "Steady Progress in Strategic C³I," *Air Force Magazine* (1987), *17*:6.

2. More detailed treatment of specific systems and technologies can be found in the following chapters of Carter, Steinbruner, and Zraket, *MNO:* Ashton B. Carter, "Communications Technologies and Vulnerabilities," pp. 217–281; John C. Toomay, "Warning and Assessment Sensors," pp. 282–321; Albert E. Babbitt, "Command Centers," pp. 322–351; and Paul B. Stares, "Nuclear Operations and Antisatellites," pp. 679–703.

3. Toomay, op. cit., pp. 288–291.

4. This technique breaks a message up into packets, and then transmits each

packet along a multitude of paths through the network. The message is then reassembled at its destination. Temporary jamming of the entire system simply delays slightly this automatic process. To sever connectivity between two given nodes a number of other nodes must be destroyed; this number obviously depends on the size and complexity of the network. In GWEN not all nodes can enter and retrieve data, however, so the committed system is more vulnerable than it could be.

5. There are some disadvantages, however. In particular, EHF suffers considerably from atmospheric attenuation, and is disturbed by rainfall.

6. This is one aspect of what is called Low Probability of Intercept (LPI) communications.

7. An MGT will be accompanied by a communication van that will link it to communication satellites (*Department of Defense Authorization for Appropriations for FY1983,* Senate Hearings, pt. 7, pp. 4618, 4699, 4701).

8. Such a facility would be a quite-substantial convoy if it would have to transport, house, and maintain advisory personnel, a battle staff, and personnel responsible for security and other support functions. The size and activity level associated with such a convoy would make it susceptible to detection by various forms of enemy intelligence, and for that reason austerity should be an important design consideration.

9. Carter, op. cit, pp. 235–236.

10. See also Ashton B. Carter, "Assessing Command Vulnerability," pp. 555–610, in *MNO.*

11. Recall that current U.S. early warning and communication satellites are at geosynchronous altitudes of 36,000 km, and that the Navstar satellites responsible for navigation data and nuclear explosion detection are in semisynchronous orbits at about 20,000 km. Soviet satellites performing the same missions are either in geosynchronous orbit, or in highly elliptical "Molniya" orbits that dip to low altitudes near the South Pole but are above geosynchronous altitudes in the northern hemisphere. In principle, therefore, Soviet satellites could be attacked by low-altitude ASATs based at southern latitudes. To our knowledge the United States has no plans for deploying the ASAT it is currently developing in this manner.

12. Here we pass over the possibility that "slow" ASAT techniques could in principle be used to destroy high-orbit satellites (e.g., for communications and navigation) in a prestrategic phase of the conflict.

13. Here and elsewhere we base our projection of DEW capabilities on The American Physical Society Study Group, "Science and Technology of Directed Energy Weapons," *Reviews of Modern Physics,* 59:3, Part II (1987); cited as *APS* henceforth.

14. This is called a *system generated electromagnetic pulse.* The range at which such a device could incapacitate a satellite depends on the yield of the explosion and the extent to which the circuitry had been "hardened." See Blair, p. 206.

15. Nicholas L. Johnson, "Threats to the Strategic Defense Initiative: The Feasibility of Space Mines," *The C³I Handbook* (Palo Alto, CA: EW Communication, 1987), pp. 165–170. This article also discusses problems associated with deploying nuclear devices in space in defiance of the Outer Space Treaty, and argues that deployment in orbits below about 700 km would be unlikely to evade detection since such space objects will reenter the atmosphere and disintegrate in an unacceptably short time.

16. This alludes to the international agreement that assigns locations in GEO to communication satellites.

17. Another exotic BMD candidate that could have an ASAT capability against GEO targets is the x-ray laser. Weighing perhaps no more than 1 ton, it would be powered (and then destroyed) by a specially designed nuclear explosive a few feet

away. This device could be lofted out of the atmosphere by a high-acceleration rocket such as the Soviets now deploy in their BMD system surrounding Moscow. The blow from the x-ray beam might be sufficiently potent to damage the skin of a GEO satellite. A neutral particle-beam accelerator based in LEO, which might be deployed as part of a BMD system for the purpose of discriminating reentry vehicles from decoys in midcourse, or less plausibly as a weapon, could be powerful enough to damage electronics on a high-altitude satellite, but the threshold for damage could be raised by a factor of order 100 by the use of gallium arsenide semiconductors or other new techniques.

18. Indeed, one of the problems faced by this BMD scheme is to devise mirrors that can withstand the heating produced by the minute portion of the incident light that is not reflected (see *APS,* Section 5.5).

19. Required video bandwidths are of order 1.5 megabaud with frame subtraction and compression techniques, and higher otherwise.

20. Information for this paragraph comes from discussion with Gail Herb, WGBH Productions, and an article by Joe Bracatelli, "The Problem with Teleconferencing," January 1985.

21. Thomas G. Belden, "Uses of Teleconferencing in Crisis and Warning Situations," in *Telecommunications Technology, Networking and Libraries,* National Bureau of Standards, Special Publication 610, 1981, Nancy Knight (editor).

22. Bandwidths of a few kilohertz would suffice.

23. Antijamming techniques that spread the signal over many frequencies are less suitable since nuclear effects are frequency-dependent and could impede reassembly of the message at the receiver.

24. FAA Statistical Handbook of Aviation: 1983.

25. *Jane's All the World's Aircraft:* 1984–85; p. 456.

26. These statements are illustrated by the following estimates for STOL survival probabilities. All warheads are taken as 1 MT, the aircraft hardness is assumed to be 1 psi, and the indicated percentages are assumed reliabilities, where 60 percent and 40 percent are merely suggested discounts for untested depressed (DT) as compared to minimum energy trajectories (MET). The other assumptions are that rocket-assisted take-off starts 150 seconds after SLBM breakwater, and attains a peak sea-level cruising speed of 400 MPH in 30 seconds.

Survival Probabilities

	Reliability of strike			
Warheads in attack	MET 85%	DT 85%	DT 60%	DT 40%
1	0.99	0.89	0.92	0.95
4	0.94	0.62	0.72	0.81
10	0.86	0.31	0.43	0.60
16	0.79	0.15	0.26	0.44
32	0.62	0.02	0.07	0.19

27. Desmond Ball, "The Soviet Strategic C³I System," *The C³I Handbook* (Palo Alto, CA: EW Communications, 1986); pp. 207–208.

28. The geology beneath Washington appears to be well-suited to a DUCC; the porous rock near the surface would attenuate the shock wave produced by a nuclear explosion, and the crystalline rock underneath would provide structural strength for

the DUCC. The crystalline formations extend to a depth of at least a few thousand feet. (John Reed and Stephen Obermeier, "The Geology Beneath Washington DC: The Foundations of a Nation's Capitol," *Reviews in Engineering Geology,* Geological Society of America, 1982, pp. 1–24.) Conversations with U.S. Geological Survey staff have revealed that the actual depth of crystalline rock is unknown, but that they have no reason to believe that other types of rock appear with increasing depth. Within 200 ft of the surface the formations are mostly sedimentary. We have not looked into the geology in areas outside Washington (such as Ft. Ritchie) where it may be appropriate to locate a DUCC for the alternate NCA.

Gene Sevin notes that a 100-MT surface burst would create a 7250 psi overpressure no deeper than about 3,500 ft in porous rock; thus, a DUCC hardened to 15,000 psi and twice as deep should be survivable even under repeated attacks. (*Design and Construction of Deep Underground Basing Facilities for Strategic Missiles,* Vol. 2, April 1982; p. 21. Available from National Technical Information Service: PB82-261819.)

29. Maintenance of air quality and disposal of waste products, especially waste heat, would be essential, and could require the existence of underground aquifers, although it may be feasible to use a prechambered reservoir of water for this purpose. (See Sevin, op. cit.)

30. It is also possible that the DUCC could communicate using electromagnetic radiation in the ELF range. Because of attenuation in the rock this technique would only provide a data rate of some 30–60 bits/second—a slow teletype rate, but not negligible. The signal would be relayed to and from the DUCC system by radio relay equipment in surface microsilos that would need no communication wells. Long-endurance communication relay platforms (such as RPVs) could receive these signals and translate them to any desired frequency. Acoustic signals sent through the surrounding rock might also serve as a means of communication, but our estimates indicate that the attainable data rate is too low.

31. This could be provided by several dozen cabling channels radiating horizontally outward from the DUCC, then rising vertically to the surface at a distance of about 10 miles, and pierced by vertical wells to form an array of surface ports with a spacing that would prevent a single warhead from destroying more than one port. Technology for drilling oil wells horizontally could be adapted for this purpose. Each surface port would have a microsilo housing a variety of receivers, and some fraction could be equipped to transmit to MILSTAR and the PACCS aircraft. Antenna vulnerability could be addressed by adapting submarine MILSTAR links which would be "popped up" upon destruction of the previous antenna. However, since these microsilos would be vulnerable, proliferation in large numbers would be required. (MF radio links, along the lines once proposed for the MX multiple shelter basing mode, would also be possible at smaller cost for larger proliferation.)

32. A rough idea of the RPV's potential can be gained from the Teledyne Ryan SPIRIT drone, which cruises at 50,000 ft for 80 hours carrying a payload of 300 lbs, and whose procurement and operating costs are said to be $2M and $300 per hour, respectively. The RPV should be capable of highly autonomous operations. For that purpose it should have two engines, a landing system similar to that used on the space shuttle, and both inertial and electronic navigation systems. Its payload would consist of a UHF radio and antenna protected against EMP, and at little additional cost a data recorder in which encrypted message could be dropped (a mailbox). (Keith Mordoff, "Teledyne Ryan Focuses R&D Effort on New RPV's," *Av. Week & Space Tech.,* June 24, 1985, pp. 89–91.)

33. Another scheme would use a free-swimming "fish" that keeps station at a depth

of a few meters in the vicinity of the patrolling submarine. [For greater detail, see Richard L. Garwin, *Fish Ragu (Fish, Radio-Receiving and Generally Useful),* SRI International, Technical Note JSN-81-64, August 1981.] The SSBN would have several fish powered by rechargeable batteries, which would carry a VLF radio receiver, and relay the signal to the SSBN below acoustically; by operating in the megahertz range the acoustic signal would be absorbed sufficiently to prevent detection at a range of 1 km. If a very large bandwidth is required, a fiberoptic link could be used. If VLF reception were lost, the fish could be ordered to approach the surface to project a small satellite dish for only a second or so to receive 10 kbits or more of satellite transmission scheduled at that time. Under unusual circumstances, a fish could transmit a message to higher authorities via satellite; to maximize covertness, spread-spectrum and highly directional EHF or SHF transmission could be used. In addition to providing a communication capability, the fish could also be used by the submarine for remote monitoring of its own noise and magnetic field, and to provide a long baseline for range determination on passive sonar targets.

34. The effective transmission rate could be raised significantly without endangering the submarine by equipping it with an optical receiver mounted on a buoy towed well below the surface, or on the fish described previously.

35. Another supplement to postattack communications could perhaps be provided by Meteor-Burst Communications (MBCs), which would exploit naturally occurring (and frequent) meteors that leave ionized trails in the upper atmosphere. HF signals can be bounced from these trails without steady ionospheric disturbances. The existence of message paths is statistically assured over time, but cannot be guaranteed at any specific time; the trails are long and provide point-to-point communication, *not* broadcast to a number of users simultaneously. MBCs are feasible over distances of several hundred miles with a low-data rate—several tens of seconds to transmit reliably a very short message of a few hundred bits. It is, however, unsettled whether high-altitude nuclear bursts would disrupt MBC.

36. See the interview with Lt. Gen. Clarence E. McKnight, Jr., director of C^3 systems, JCS, (Richard Halloran, "Military's Message System Is Overloaded, Officers Say," *The New York Times,* November 25, 1985).

37. See van Creveld, chapters 7 and 8.

38. "DARPA Considering Packet Switched Multisatellite Network," *Defense Electronics,* August 1985, p. 27. Recall that packet switching is already used in GWEN; see Note 4.

39. In this connection see Richard L. Garwin, "Launch Under Attack to Address Minuteman Vulnerability?," *International Security* (1979/80) 4:3, 117.

40. This appendix is an abbreviation of an unpublished manuscript by Arthur Charo.

41. More detailed treatments can be found in Ashton B. Carter, "Communications Technologies and Vulnerabilities", *MNO,* pp. 217–281; John C. Toomay, "Warning and Assessment Sensors", *MNO,* pp. 282–321; *The C^{3}I Handbook* (Palo Alto, CA: EW Communications, 1986); and in references cited therein. See also Ashton B. Carter and Theodore A. Postol in "Command, Control and Communications," *MX Missile Basing* (U.S. Congress, Office of Technology Assessment, OTA-ISC-140, September 1981). For a detailed discussion of the theory of information transmission, see George Kennedy, *Electronic Communication Systems,* 3rd. edition, (New York: McGraw-Hill, 1985).

42. The widely used modern version is called pulsed-code modulation, or PCM.

43. In principle, attainable bandwidth is proportional to carrier frequency, but this

theoretical limit requires sources that are phase-coherent over the bandwidth. In practice, data rates are at most 1 Gbit/second, and far below the theoretical limit set by the carrier frequency. The CO_2 laser, for example, which operates in the infrared at 30,000 GHz, transmits data at a rate in the 1-GHz range, or a factor of 10,000 below the theoretical optimum.

44. If R is the signal-to-noise ratio, the channel capacity in bits/second is given by $B\log_2(1 + R)$.

45. The signal energy S is proportional to the number K of repetitions, while the noise, if it is random, only rises as the square-root of K, and therefore S/N also grows in proportion to $K^{1/2}$. Hence a 10-fold increase in signal-to-noise requires 100 repetitions. Furthermore, as the preceding note indicates, a channel's data capacity only grows logarithmically with S/N, whereas it is proportional to the bandwidth.

46. Source: Carter and Postol, op. cit., p. 299, and Carter, op. cit., p. 234.

47. AM operates at MF, which is completely absorbed in the D-layer during daytime. At night the electron density in the D-layer falls drastically, and it becomes transparent to MF waves, which can then reach the E-layer whose residual night-time ionization suffices to reflect the waves back to earth; see Figure 6.2.

48. For example, for each frequency and ionospheric condition there is a maximum angle with respect to the horizon above which the wave will not be reflected by the ionosphere but be "lost" into space. Furthermore, even if the angle is such that most of the wave is reflected, enough energy may be transmitted through the ionosphere to provide a detectable signal to a satellite.

49. Thus on-station TACAMO aircraft fly in tight circles so as to keep their several-mile long trailing-wire antennas in a nearly vertical position because this is an efficient way of producing a guided VLF wave.

50. Voice frequencies, by convention defined in radio communications as the band from 300 Hz to 3 kHz, also contribute to SSBN communications (see Figure 6.1).

51. OTH radars for early warning against air attack use HF, but ionospheric effects prevent their use in a northerly direction, and they must therefore be supplemented by LOS radars.

52. HF and VHF is also used in Meteor Burst Communications; see note 35.

53. UHF can be used for OTH communications because it is weakly reflected from boundary layers and turbulence in the troposphere (see Figure 6.2) and associated discussion). This troposcatter mode was used extensively before the advent of satellite communications.

54. Samuel Glasstone and Philip J. Dolan, *The Effects of Nuclear Weapons,* 3rd. edition, (Washington DC: U.S. Departments of Defense and Energy, 1977).

55. J. R. Pierce et. al., *Evaluation of Methodologies for Estimating Vulnerability to Electromagnetic Pulse Effects,* (Washington DC: National Academy Press, 1984).

56. Insofar as radio propagation is concerned, the disturbance disappears when the electrons and ions recombine to a level that is dictated by the frequency in question—a million times lower for 3 MHz than for 3 GHz. The time required to attain a given degree of recombination also depends on the atmospheric density and the rate at which the decaying radioactive debris continues to produce new electrons, that is, on the yield and height of the explosion, and the altitude of the signal path.

57. For instance, the goal stated by SDIO is the ability to withstand nuclear effects emanating from a 1 MT burst at 80 km.

7

The Evolution of Soviet Forces, Strategy, and Command*

Soviet leaders have repeatedly emphasized that it would be tantamount to suicide to start a nuclear war.[1] Mutual deterrence, however, does not make nuclear war impossible. The danger remains that a large-scale nuclear war could start inadvertently in an intense crisis, or by escalation out of a conventional war, or as an unforeseen combination of these. For these reasons crisis management has become a central issue in the United States, but the standard Soviet response to this Western interest has been to say that what is needed is crisis avoidance, not recipes for brinkmanship masquerading under another name. There is much sense in this view. Nevertheless, this demeanor does not mean that the Soviet Union has given no thought to the danger that a crisis might lead to nuclear war, only that Soviet categories for thinking about such matters differ from those employed in the United States. This chapter will examine Soviet approaches to military doctrine and crisis management from several perspectives in the hope that this will yield an understanding of Soviet attitudes to the tension that can arise between the "requirements for prudent crisis management" and the "requirements of conventional military strategy."[2]

Four specific questions throw light on the Soviet understanding of this crucial problem:

1. How has history affected Soviet leaders' views of this issue?

---

*This chapter is largely identical to *Soviet Military Doctrine and Its Implications For Crisis Management* (unpublished) by David Holloway and Condoleezza Rice. Unless indicated otherwise, detailed documentation regarding the technical aspects of the Soviet strategic command infrastructure can be found in Desmond Ball, "Soviet C³I," *The C³I Handbook* (Palo Alto, CA: EW Communications, 1986), pp. 206–216.

2. What kinds of options has the Soviet Union acquired for use in a crisis with the United States?
3. What is the Soviet command and control system for nuclear forces, and can it cope with acute crises?
4. What can we learn from Soviet arms control policy and crisis behavior about the Soviet approach to crisis management?

The central dilemma of crisis management raises a more general question about Soviet military doctrine. This doctrine consists of two elements: a sociopolitical side, which concerns itself with the political context in which wars might start and the political goals for which military force might be used; and a military–technical side, which attends to the question of how to fight wars and how to prepare for them. The political side of Soviet doctrine claims to be profoundly defensive, and to have as one of its primary goals the prevention of nuclear war. The military–technical side, on the other hand, focuses on the preparations for waging and winning wars, and stresses that the offensive is the primary form of military operation.[3] The sociopolitical side is supposed to be the dominant element in doctrine. But how do the Soviet leaders reconcile these two aspects of their doctrine? Are these two sides in fact reconciled, or is there a tension between them? And if there is, how do the Soviet leaders deal with it, and what are its implications for Soviet crisis behavior?[4]

THE KHRUSHCHEV YEARS

After Stalin's death his failure to anticipate Hitler's attack and to ready the Red Army in good time became one of the main indictments in Khrushchev's anti-Stalin campaign. In his "secret speech" to the Twentieth Party Congress in 1956 Khrushchev bitterly denounced Stalin's policy in 1941 and his overall conduct of the war. Stalin's failure to heed warnings, and the disasters that followed, pointed to the importance of not being caught by surprise again.[5] Soviet generals and historians also began to strip away the tissue of myths and lies with which Stalin had surrounded the events of 1941. The Red Army's disastrous retreat was no longer portrayed as a strategy of active defense, and surprise was rescued from the secondary position to which Stalin had relegated it. This effort to set the historical record straight had considerable bearing on current policy.[6] Nuclear weapons began to enter the Soviet operational inventory in 1953 or 1954, and their impact on the conduct of war now became the object of intense study.[7] As Hitler demonstrated in 1941, surprise could confer major advantages on an attacker, and Soviet military theorists believed that the advantages of surprise would be even greater in the nuclear age. They argued that the best method of foiling a surprise attack was to launch a preemptive strike that would break up the enemy attack before it could get off the ground.[8]

In January 1960, just 1 month after the Strategic Rocket Forces (SRF) had been established as a separate service, Khrushchev outlined Soviet military doctrine. If there were a world war, he said, it would begin with missile strikes deep into the enemy interior, and end with the victory of socialism.[9] In 1962 Marshal V. D. Sokolovskii, who had been chief of the General Staff from 1952 to 1960, put forward a strategy for waging the kind of war that Khrushchev had described. Sokolovskii argued that the initial period of the war might be decisive, and that the main problem was to master "methods of reliably repulsing a surprise nuclear attack, and also methods of frustrating the aggressive plans of the enemy, by means of a timely shattering blow against him."[10]

It may seem strange that Soviet strategy gave an important role to preemption at a time when Soviet nuclear forces were greatly inferior to those of the United States. But preemption was central precisely because the Soviet Union could not be sure that it would be able to retaliate against the United States in the event of an American first strike. If the Soviet Union did not strike first it might find itself disarmed. Before 1956 the Soviet Union had only a very limited capacity to deliver nuclear weapons against the United States, while the United States had had forward-based nuclear delivery systems around the periphery of the Soviet Union since the early 1950s. In 1956 the Soviet Union began to acquire a modest intercontinental bomber force, but in the late 1950s the United States still enjoyed an overwhelming nuclear superiority.[11]

The Soviet position actually worsened in the early 1960s. The United States, which had begun to deploy reconnaissance satellites, now knew where the small Soviet ICBM and long-range bomber forces were based, and possessed missiles and bombers that could destroy the Soviet systems. Soviet SLBMs, moreover, had a very short range, could only be fired from the surface, and the SSBNs themselves were vulnerable to U.S. antisubmarine warfare.[12] Marshal N. V. Ogarkov, while he was chief of the General Staff, wrote that in the early 1960s the United States could have counted "to some extent" on a disarming first strike, and there is good reason to believe his assessment.[13] Indeed, a detailed comparison of the superpowers' arsenals for mid-1961 based on official U.S. government sources shows that the U.S. strategic forces disposed of 1,530 weapons that could be launched on tactical warning (and 3,267 after some 14 hours of preparation), whereas the Soviet strategic forces were estimated to contain 10 to 25 ICBMs, 200 bombers, and "about 78" submarine-launched ballistic and cruise missiles, none of which were kept routinely on alert in peacetime.[14] The Soviet Union could probably have devastated Western Europe in retaliation to any U.S. attack, and even inflicted serious damage on U.S. society,[15] but that might have been small consolation to Soviet leaders who may not have been sure that the threat to do this would deter the United States from attacking the Soviet Union under all circumstances.

Although preemption occupied a central place in Soviet strategy, Soviet strategic forces were not kept on a high state of alert: before the mid-1960s no land-based missiles or bombers were deployed with warheads or bombs on board. When the Soviet armed forces first acquired nuclear bombs for operational use in 1953 or 1954, custody of the weapons remained with the KGB, which controlled and guarded nuclear weapons stockpiles, and was responsible for their transportation.[16] If the Soviet Union were to preempt it would need strategic warning of an impending attack in order to ready its forces and launch them in time. But the very act of readying the forces—a process that would take some hours and might be observed—could invite American preemption, while failure to put the forces on alert would leave them vulnerable to a disarming strike.

This dilemma was sharpened by Khrushchev's strenuous efforts to exploit the fear of nuclear war to achieve his political goals. He once told President Nasser of Egypt that "I think that the people with the strongest nerves will be the winners. That is the most important consideration in the power struggle of our time. The people with weak nerves will go to the wall."[17] From the Suez crisis of 1956 to the Cuban Missile Crisis in 1962 he "rattled" his rockets in an effort to intimidate the Western powers into making political concessions. His actions helped to precipitate two of the most serious crises of the nuclear age—the Berlin crisis of 1961 and the Cuban Missile Crisis of 1962.

Khrushchev was well aware of the destructive potential of nuclear weapons.[18] It was precisely this potential that made him regard them as powerful instruments of diplomacy. But his recognition that nuclear war would be devastating also constrained Khrushchev, for he was careful not to threaten the use of nuclear weapons when there was a serious chance that he might have to carry out his threat, and he apparently never raised the alert status of Soviet nuclear forces—even during the Cuban Missile Crisis.[19]

There are three possible explanations for Khrushchev's decision not to alert his nuclear forces during the Missile Crisis. The first is that the crisis was not regarded in Moscow as serious enough. But this is not plausible: the actions taken by the United States, Khrushchev's letters to Kennedy, and the ultimate withdrawal of the missiles from Cuba all indicate otherwise.[20] The second is that the Soviets "might have been unable for technical reasons to hold their forces on alert for more than a short period of time, and therefore might have been reluctant to place their forces on alert unless they were certain a war was coming."[21] A third, and perhaps more plausible, reason why the forces were not alerted during the crisis is that fueling the missiles, moving bombs and warheads from stores, and loading them on bombers and mating them to launchers might have invited a preemptive strike before the Soviet forces had been generated.[22] It was a major failing of Khrushchev's missile diplomacy that his forces were vulnerable, and that raising their readiness might prove dangerously provocative.

Just as his condemnation of Stalin's policy of 1941 betrayed no recognition of the complexities that might arise in trying to foretell or forestall a surprise attack, so Khrushchev displayed no doubts about his own ability to make Soviet forces ready and launch them in good time should the need arise. He accused Stalin of criminal negligence in failing to anticipate the German attack, but seems to have been confident that he himself would make no similar misjudgment. Khrushchev's confidence ultimately proved to be misplaced, for although he did not involve the Soviet Union in war with the United States, he did precipitate crises in which he was faced with a perilous choice between passivity and adventurism.

Khrushchev's missile diplomacy has not received the same detailed analysis in the Soviet literature as the events of 1941. Serious studies of the Berlin crisis of 1961 or of the Cuban Missile Crisis have been conspicuous by their absence from the public Soviet discussion of Soviet–American relations, though that is now changing (see Chapter 8). Nevertheless, it has long been evident from the veiled criticism of Khrushchev that appeared in the press after his fall from power in October 1964,[23] and especially from the changed behavior of the new Soviet leaders, that his successors learned from his failures. A principal lesson they drew from the Missile Crisis was pithily expressed by V. V. Kuznetsov, first deputy minister of foreign affairs, to an American diplomat: "You Americans will never be able to do this to us again."[24]

THE SEARCH FOR OPTIONS

Khrushchev had committed the solecism of power in commanding the ends but not willing the means. During the decade following his ouster, Soviet leaders sought to rectify this by bringing policy, doctrine, and capabilities more into line.

The Attainment of Parity: Preemption and Retaliation

In 1965 or 1966 the Soviet Union began to deploy its third generation of ICBMs. These missiles had storable liquid fuel (the SS-9 and SS-11) or solid fuel (the SS-13), which allowed them to be kept at a high state of readiness. Furthermore, they were more accurate than their predecessors, and they were housed in hardened silos. In particular, the SS-9 had hard-target kill capability because its warhead had the enormous yield of 20 to 25 MT; 288 SS-9s were deployed by 1970, and were apparently intended to neutralize the U.S. Minuteman force by destroying their 100 hardened launch-control centers.[25] With the deployment of these new ICBMs, the Soviet Union finally acquired a capacity to launch a preemptive strike against strategic forces based in the United States, in contrast to the preceding era when Soviet preemption could hardly have affected America's strategic capabilities.

More importantly, the new ICBM force provided the Soviet Union with an assured retaliatory capability.[26] Because they were housed in silos, these systems were less vulnerable to a disarming strike. The ICBM force grew rapidly, from 224 in 1965 to 1,527 by the time of the SALT Agreements in 1972, and essentially eliminated the danger of a disarming first strike by the United States. The Soviet ability to retaliate was further augmented by the deployment of the Yankee-class SSBNs, each of which carried 16 SS-N-6 SLBMs with a range of 2,400 km that could be launched while submerged. Thirty-four of these submarines were built between 1967 and 1974. At the opening of the SALT negotiations in 1969 the Soviet delegation declared that "even in the event that one of the sides was the first to be subjected to attack, it would undoubtedly retain the ability to inflict a retaliatory blow of destructive force."[27]

The attainment of strategic parity is portrayed by Soviet historians as a major turning-point in the Soviet–American strategic relationship: the new Program of the Communist Party adopted in 1986 declares that it was an achievement of historic significance for socialism. Parity is a vague concept, but at its root it signifies a relationship in which each side is vulnerable to a devastating retaliatory strike by the other.[28]

Prompt Launch

Soviet planners were not content, however, with the two options of preemption and retaliation after attack. As the new generation of ICBMs was deployed, the Soviet military began to express increasing interest in prompt launch.[29] In 1967 Engineer-Colonel A. Tatarchenko argued for the automation of command and control "from the lowest tactical levels to the highest strategic level of leadership." During the 30-minute flight time of strategic missiles, he wrote, "it is necessary not only to assess the situation, take a decision and give the appropriate commands, but to do this quickly enough so that the troops will have time to carry out the command they receive."[30]

Two years later Marshal N. I. Krylov, commander-in-chief of the Strategic Rocket Forces, provided a more authoritative statement of the Soviet interest in prompt launch when he wrote in the restricted-circulation *Voennaya Mysl'* that now, with the deployment

> of launchers and missiles which are completely ready for operation, as well as systems for detecting enemy missile launches and other types of reconnaissance, an aggressor is no longer able suddenly to destroy the missiles before their launch on the territory of the country against which the aggression is committed. They will have time during the flight of the missiles of the aggressor to leave their launchers and inflict a retaliatory strike against the enemy.[31]

In 1970 the Soviet delegation at SALT I referred to the possibility that, in view of the continuous improvement of early-warning systems, ICBM silos might be empty by the time an enemy strike reached them. The American delegation provided an official disavowal of the concept of launch-on-warning by the secretary of defense, with further criticism of the idea as potentially dangerous for automatic escalation, or even for starting a war by accident. The Soviet side refused to make a similar declaration, however, and a senior military figure on the delegation said that such issues went beyond SALT and should not be discussed with civilians.[32]

A prompt-launch policy requires that tactical warning provide, at a minimum, sufficient time to launch the missiles. In the late 1960s the Soviet Union began to hold a small proportion—about 20 to 25 percent—of its ICBM force on day-to-day alert, with warheads mated.[33] The early warning radars of that era (dubbed Hen House by U.S. intelligence) would have given the Soviet leaders no more than 15 minutes warning of ICBM impact.[34] Even if Soviet ICBMs could have been launched in a few minutes, it would have been a very close race between launch and detonation of incoming warheads. If the Soviet Union did in fact have a prompt launch posture in the late 1960s it must have been a very rudimentary capability.[35] It should be noted, however, that the United States faced the same problem until 1971 when it deployed its first early warning satellite, which could give warning of Soviet launches shortly after liftoff.[36]

By the end of the 1960s the Soviet Union had enhanced its strategic options. It had attained a capacity to launch a preemptive strike against U.S. strategic forces by acquiring more accurate ICBMs with larger-yield warheads. It now had an assured retaliatory capability and was on the way toward acquiring a prompt-launch capability. As a result of these shifts in the strategic balance, preemption was no longer the only option available to the Soviet leaders. If the Soviet Union did not preempt, it could still retaliate in the event of an American attack; such an attack was made less likely by the Soviet ability to retaliate.[37]

The evolution of Soviet strategic capabilities did not end after the attainment of parity with the deployment of its large silo-based ICBM force. As silos have become increasingly vulnerable, it has developed and is deploying mobile ICBMs.[38] The Soviet Union has also deployed a large SSBN fleet, although only 10 to 15 percent is at sea at any given time. By increasing the range of its SLBMs it has greatly expanded the ocean areas in which the SSBNs could be on station, and thereby complicated the antisubmarine warfare mission for the United States. These long-range SLBMs have also allowed the Soviet Navy to establish "bastions" for its SSBN fleet in the Sea of Okhotsk and the Barents Sea from which it could strike targets in the United States.

By diversifying its strategic forces the Soviet Union has increased its retaliatory capability. As we shall see, it has also taken steps to ensure that its command system could survive an attack and order a retaliatory strike. As proof that retaliation would be assured. Soviet military leaders have also pointed to their ability to launch their forces promptly.[39] Marshall Ustinov hinted at this when he said that "with the modern state of detection systems, and of the combat readiness of the Soviet Union's strategic nuclear weapons there will be no disarming strike by the U.S.A. on the socialist countries."[40]

The Third Stage of the Revolution in Military Affairs

The Soviet Union now possesses a range of military options that places immense demands on command: Leaders must be certain that nuclear weapons are used neither too early nor too late, and must make decisions quickly on the basis of information that may be imperfect; they must also assume that their own command system would be a high priority target for enemy nuclear strikes, just as the Soviet military have consistently listed enemy command as one of the chief targets for Soviet nuclear forces.[41]

The Soviet Union has made determined efforts to provide itself with a command system that could execute its military options despite these daunting problems posed by the advent of nuclear weapons and ballistic missiles.[42] Special exercises were conducted that showed that "the basic elements of a control system (the control points and the communications system) become priority targets for enemy nuclear strikes."[43] Efforts were made to ensure the survivability of command by establishing redundant command posts and communications systems. Computers and new communications equipment were introduced to increase command capability. Steps were taken to increase the reliability of communications systems, and "measures were adopted to ensure the rapid restoration of disrupted control after enemy nuclear strikes."[44]

Soviet military theorists, who like to categorize things, began to write in the mid-1960s of a third, "cybernetic" stage in the "contemporary revolution in military affairs."[45] The first two stages had been marked by the development of nuclear weapons and ballistic missiles, respectively; now "automated troop control systems" would be needed to handle the information required for command decisions.[46] The most important requirements for a command system, according to one recent study, are stability, high efficiency, quality, and secrecy.[47] These are defined as:

1. *Stability.* The ability to function in a complex and changing situation, with heavy enemy action against the command system.
2. *High efficiency.* The ability to complete tasks in a timely manner in preparing an operation, to react to changes in the combat environment, and to influence the course of the operation with the aim of achieving the operational mission.
3. *Quality.* The ability to make effective use of forces, which often comes into conflict with the need for timely decisions.
4. *Secrecy.* "The ability to keep secret from the enemy the position, state and functioning of all elements of the control system . . . "[48]

The Soviet Union has tried, with some success, to meet these requirements in organizing its command system.

Institutional Arrangements for Strategic Command

In 1962 Marshal Sokolovskii outlined the preferred form of command organization for a nuclear war, on the basis of the Soviet experience in World War II. Leadership would be exercised through a body armed with the same powers as the State Defense Committee (GKO), and this would be headed by the first secretary of the Central Committee and the head of government (Khrushchev then held both posts), who would function as supreme commander-in-chief. Direct leadership of the armed forces would be exercised by the *Stavka* of the Supreme High Command, under the chairmanship of the supreme commander-in-chief. The General Staff would be the main operational organ of the *Stavka VGK*.[49] It is not clear, however, whether the peacetime basis for such an organization actually existed when Sokolovskii wrote because the State Defense Committee and the *Stavka* had been disbanded at the end of the war.[50]

There is every reason to believe that a *Stavka* of the Supreme High Command exists today in some form, ready to go over to a war footing.[51] If historical precedent is a guide—and it is certainly treated as such in Soviet writings—the *Stavka* would be chaired by the general secretary in his role as supreme commander-in-chief, and would have the minister of defense and some of his deputies as its members. The Soviet command system consists of two structures. The first is responsible for administration procurement, equipping, and training—activities that are needed in both peacetime and war. It is headed by the Defense Council, which oversees the work of the Ministry of Defense and the Service Chiefs who report to the Chief of the General Staff.[52] The second structure, with the Supreme High Command (in effect the *Stavka*) would be responsible for wartime operations. It would have command authority that it would exercise by passing orders through the General Staff to the various commanders in the theaters of military operations (TVDs), as well as to the Strategic Rocket Forces, and to that portion of the Continental Air Defense (PVO) responsible for the Moscow region (including, in particular, the Galosh ABM system). Given the apparent existence of skip echelon communications, the General Staff can presumably also pass orders to "Front" commanders. These institutional arrangements are schematized in Figure 7.1.

The figure does not show one important feature, however: The KGB maintains political oversight on the military, may have a significant role in the nuclear chain of command, and may control some of the communication links between the *Stavka* and the armed forces.

The Soviet leaders have made a particular effort to provide continuity of command in the event of war. The first Soviet air-defense missiles were deployed around Moscow in the 1950s, and the first Soviet ABM defenses were deployed there in the 1960s. The ABM system around Moscow is now being upgraded, while more than half of the sites for the new SA-10 air defense missile are located near Moscow. This emphasis on the capital suggests that defense of the command authorities is a high priority of Soviet policy.[54]

The Soviet Union has also devoted large resources to passive protection of its leadership. There are underground command posts near Moscow,[55] and shelters with special communications for Party and government officials throughout the country. There are hundreds of such facilities of widely varying hardness, and they are believed to be able to accommodate more than 175,000 key personnel. In addition to this remarkably large system of fixed command posts, the Soviet Union also has some mobile command facilities. There is a small fleet of airborne command posts that are regularly used during exercises and crises, but these do not have capabilities comparable to their American counterparts. There are also train- and shipborne command posts.

Soviet leaders have claimed that decapitation of its highly redundant command system would be impossible. The most authoritative statement came from Defense Minister D. F. Ustinov in 1982:

> The aggressor will not escape an all-destructive answering strike. Whoever invents a "faultless recipe" for the conduct of a victorious nuclear war, and calculates, to put it figuratively, on "decapitating" the enemy by one knockout blow, will pass sentence on himself. It is appropriate to recall once more the stern warning of Comrade L. I. Brezhnev, that "only he who has decided to commit suicide can start a nuclear war in the hope of emerging victorious from it. No matter what might the attacker possesses, no matter what method of unleashing nuclear war he chooses, he will not achieve his goals. Retribution will inevitably follow."[56]

In December 1983 Marshal Ogarkov asserted that a disarming first strike was impossible because both sides now had large stocks of nuclear weapons, many and various basing systems, and redundant command systems: "retaliation will follow in all cases."[57]

There is no evidence that the Soviet Union has arrangements for predelegation of launch authority, although it may well have. In this connection, the description of the status of strategic forces on day-to-day alert may be of relevance. These are said to be on "combat duty" *(boevoe dezhurstvo)*, whose official definition is:[58]

> The presence *(prebyvanie)* of specially chosen forces and means in full combat readiness for the execution of tasks that arise suddenly or the conduct of military operations. It is implemented in peacetime and in wartime. *Forces and weapons on duty act according to the commands (signals) of senior commanders, but in cases where delays cannot be tolerated—by the decision of the commanders of the units and subunits on duty.* (Emphasis added)

This definition points to the possibility of predelegation, but it should be noted that combat duty is a term applied not only to nuclear missiles. Besides, predelegation—even in the heat of a severe crisis—would seem to go against the Soviet desire to retain very tight political control over its nuclear weapons. The very considerable effort that the Soviet Union has made to provide protection for its leadership might suggest a reluctance to predelegate. Nevertheless, it is conceivable that the Soviet Union has been forced to this by the exigencies of ensuring retaliation.

The Soviet Union has tried to create a redundant command system that could continue to function even if some elements were destroyed. Nevertheless, there is a tension in Soviet command between centralization and redun-

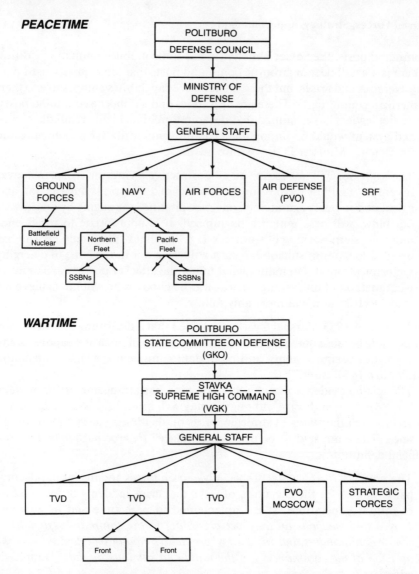

Figure 7.1. The Soviet chain of command. The upper and lower halves depict the peacetime and wartime systems, respectively. The Defense Council, composed largely of Politburo members and chaired by the general secretary, is an official state body; it is responsible for all aspects of defense policy, but it is unclear whether it can make decisions or only advises the Politburo. The minister of defense, whether a member of the Politburo or not, sits on the Defense Council and presides over the governing body of his ministry. The latter coordinates peacetime activities, such as training and readiness. The General Staff is responsible for strategic planning and supervises military operations.

In wartime, the Defense Council would be expanded to become the State Committee of Defense (the counterpart of the GKO in World War II), and be responsible for unified direction of the entire war effort. The supreme military command authority would be held by the *Stavka* (or General Headquarters) of the Supreme High Command, a body consisting of the chief of the general staff, the minister of defense, the other first dancy, and it is not clear how well this has been resolved. Khrushchev put the problem clearly in his memoirs:

> I know the means of communication which have been created and are being created in each state. But, listen, this command post could surely become blind, and those who would command from there could be buried in it.[59]

The Soviet Union may have built many hardened command posts and redundant communications links, but if command authority is as centralized as it appears to be, the Soviet leaders could not be certain that the Supreme High Command would survive intact. On the other hand, the Soviet Union has constructed so many alternative hardened command posts that the United States could not be sure of destroying them all in any attack. This uncertainty should be a powerful deterrent to an American attempt at decapitation.[60]

The Command Infrastructure

In the 1970s the Soviet Union built three over-the-horizon (OTH) radars, two of which (at Kiev and Komsomol'sk-na-Amure) could give 30-minutes' warning time of U.S. ICBM launches; the third radar, near Nikolaev, is directed at Chinese missile fields. In 1976 the Soviet Union began to deploy infrared telescope-carrying satellites,[61] which detect booster plumes and can determine more precisely than OTH radars the general area from which a U.S. ICBM strike is launched. The network of Hen House radars and large phased-array radars (LPARs) would confirm the warnings from the satellites and OTH radars, and assess the size of the attack.[62] It appears that a number of new LPARs, to provide more complete early warning coverage, are now under construction (see Figure 7.2).

The Soviet early-warning system, however, has serious defects. The OTH radars are susceptible to blinding by nuclear explosions and to naturally occurring auroral interference, the satellites have had serious failures and do

---

deputy ministers of defense, the chief of the main political directorate, and the commanders-in-chief of the five services shown in the peacetime structure.[53] The general secretary would chair both the GKO and the *Stavka* in his capacities as chief executive and supreme commander-in-chief, respectively. The General Staff would be the operational staff and executive agent of the *Stavka*. For the sake of simplicity the scheme only shows three TVDs; the actual number is uncertain.

The reader may find it helpful to note that there is an analogy between the Soviet and U.S. military chains of command. For the U.S. system the line of authority for the administrative and budgetary functions runs from the president through the secretary of defense and the service secretaries, whereas in the combat chain of command the NCA passes orders through the JCS to the unified and specified commands. The TVD commanders, therefore, are the counterparts of the U.S. unified commanders-in-chief.

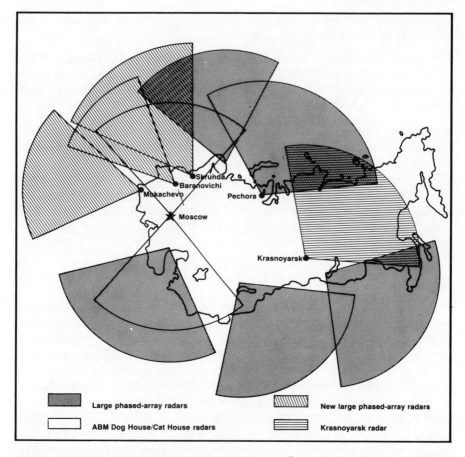

Figure 7.2. Soviet early warning and tracking radars.[63] The fans show the coverage of existing and forthcoming large phased-array BMEWs radars, and of the "Dog House/Cat House" warhead-tracking radars in the Moscow region that form a part of the capital's ballistic missile defenses. The radar at Krasnoyarsk is also an LPAR facility apparently intended as a BMEW radar even though its interior location would constitute a violation of the ABM Treaty once it becomes operational. The Soviets have claimed that it is intended for space-tracking, not as a BMEW radar, and have halted its construction.

not yet provide full coverage, and the Hen House radars and LPARs are vulnerable to blinding by nuclear effects and to jamming. Moreover, the early-warning system is poorly equipped to assess the nature of a strategic strike, and, therefore, is not ideally suited to a launch-on-warning posture because it cannot assess precisely the threat to its own forces from an enemy strike. The launch-detection systems cannot determine precise launch coordinates, nor can they assess the scale, nature, or purpose of an attack; the Hen House and LPAR systems have a limited capability to distinguish between warheads, decoys, and booster fragments.[64] The Soviet Union would nevertheless have close to 30 minutes warning of an ICBM attack, which is much longer than the time required to launch the fourth-generation ICBMs (the SS-17s, 18s, and 19s).[65] Prompt launch would still not be an easy option to implement, but it is much more feasible than it was in the late 1960s, when tactical warning would have been no more than 15 minutes. Besides, more than 90 percent of the new systems are on day-to-day alert, so most ICBMs would be available for prompt launch.[66]

On the other hand, the Soviet Union does not yet have an effective system for detecting SLBM launches. Neither the OTH radars nor the launch-detection satellites provide adequate coverage of the U.S. SSBN deployment areas. Consequently the warning of an SLBM attack might have to be provided by the Hen House/LPAR network. The new and highly accurate American D5 SLBM, which will carry 10 MIRVs, will pose a threat to hardened missile silos and command installations when it is deployed in the 1990s. It will be particularly important for the Soviet Union to be able to detect the launch of the D5 and to increase its warning of an SLBM attack if it is to maintain a prompt-launch capability.

Turning to communications, the Soviet Union has a highly redundant network that relies on a wide range of technologies from land lines to satellites. Because of the long distances that must be connected and the forbidding terrain, there is relatively heavy reliance on radio and on satellite relays. More than 60 satellites in low, elliptical *(Molniya)*, and geosynchronous orbits are deployed. For communication to submerged submarines, the Soviets have a considerable number of VLF radio transmitters, 11 of which have an output in excess of 500 kW for world-wide communications.

An American official has said that "the Soviets have the best command-and-control one can imagine."[67] This is an exaggeration, for important elements of the Soviet system—the launch-detection and navigation satellites, the early-warning radars, and the airborne command posts—are less capable than their American counterparts; however, the Soviet Union has made a far more serious effort than has the United States to protect its top military and political leaders, which could pay large dividends in wartime. This striking difference, however, is inherent to the nature of the two societies. The very construction of shelters for the top layer of government is not a viable option in a society where that activity would become widely known and elicit both fear and resentment. Laying that aside, covert evacuation of a sizeable leadership corps may be feasible in the Soviet Union, but not in the United States. In short, there is a deep internal consistency to the manner in which these two political cultures have sought to protect their leaderships.

Current Strategic Options and Capabilities

Although it now has an assured retaliatory force and some prompt-launch capability, the Soviet Union has not abandoned the search for a preemptive option. In the 1970s it deployed MIRVed ICBMs with a greatly increased hard-target-kill capability. The SS-18 and SS-19 ICBMs pose a serious threat to U.S. ICBM silos and command installations, and their deployment has created serious problems for U.S. military policy. The Soviet Union would require strategic warning of an impending attack in order to launch a preemptive strike. To that end the Soviet Union makes a major effort to monitor the military activities of its potential enemies, and maintains the most extensive signals intelligence capabilities in the world.[68] These are designed to intercept diplomatic messages, military communications, and telephone conversations, and thereby to provide evidence about the intentions of foreign governments. The Soviet Union also maintains extensive espionage networks in Western countries, and these might be able to provide information about military preparations and political intentions.[69]

The Soviet intelligence effort does not necessarily reflect a lack of interest in tactical warning, or a willingness to rely primarily on strategic warning. The deficiencies in the early-warning system are not due to a lack of interest or investment, but to technological failure. Moreover, in a crisis there would not be a sharp distinction between the utility of strategic and tactical warning. Strategic intelligence, for example, could provide the basis for putting forces on prompt-launch status and for raising the alert status of the early-warning system. On the other hand, it might be impossible to tell whether the adversary's military measures in a crisis were merely precautions or attempts to apply pressure, rather than indications of an intention to attack. It is unlikely, therefore, that intelligence would provide a firm basis for a decision to preempt.

Soviet military historians have been giving more attention to German efforts to deceive the Soviet Union in 1941, and have portrayed the problem of discerning German intentions as more complex than Khrushchev acknowledged.[70] If these writings are a guide, preemption is now regarded as more problematic than it was in the 1950s and early 1960s. Colonel-General M. A. Gareev, deputy chief of the General Staff, has written that Sokolovskii's recommendation that most of the measures for strategic deployment (concealment, mobilization, concentration, and deployment of forces) be completed before the outbreak of war is correct in a theoretical sense, but "does not take account of all the complexity of solving the task, and reminds one of the demand of one fire chief that his brigade arrive at the fire an hour before it starts."[71]

The main reason that preemption has lost its central role in Soviet military strategy, however, is not that preemption per se is difficult, but that the strategic relationship has changed since the early 1960s. The Soviet Union now has other options, and this must ease the pressure to preempt. Soviet leaders, both political and military, recognize that the danger of an American strike has been reduced by the growth of Soviet strategic forces.[72] In a more general sense the importance of strategic nuclear preemption has been diminished by the changing Soviet views of nuclear war. Marshal Ustinov, the defense minister, put the point concisely in 1982 when he explained the Soviet commitment not to be the first to use nuclear weapons: "The Soviet Union is not counting on victory in a nuclear war. An understanding of the impossibility of gaining the upper hand in such a conflict is also an argument in favor of rejecting the first use of nuclear weapons."[73]

The Conventional Option

The growth of Soviet strategic forces has also had an important impact on Soviet doctrine regarding the relationship between nuclear weapons and conventional warfare. Khrushchev had declared that a war with the United States would start with nuclear-missile strikes deep into the enemy interior, but after his fall from power this insistence on a single pattern was abandoned. The Soviet Union began to take seriously the possibility that war might begin with a conventional phase. The change in doctrine came in response to NATO's adoption of the doctrine of flexible response, which had been forced on NATO by the Soviet acquisition of an assured retaliatory capability because the United States could no longer use its strategic forces with impunity to defend Western Europe. Since the mid-1960s the Soviet Union has sought to develop balanced forces that could cope with the contingencies of conventional war and limited nuclear war in different theaters. The implication of this effort in the context of a European crisis will be explored later.

The increasing emphasis on the conventional option has enhanced the importance that Soviet doctrine has traditionally placed on offensive operations, on surprise and initiative, and even on preemption, and this could have serious implications in a crisis. If, for example, conventional attacks are to be carried out against NATO nuclear forces, the Soviet Union cannot wait too long for fear that NATO might disperse its nuclear weapons. Hence there would be pressure on the political leaders to use military force early in a crisis. Moreover, Soviet strategy assigns a high priority to the destruction of NATO's command system, and this threat would put pressure on NATO to disperse its nuclear weapons early in a crisis; however, this in turn would impel the Warsaw Pact to increase its own nuclear readiness as a precaution. Thus, the effort to prevent nuclear war could be overwhelmed by a spiral of increasingly provocative alerts and counteralerts.

STRATEGIC STABILITY AND CRISIS BEHAVIOR

Arms Control and the Prevention of Nuclear War

Soviet leaders have been aware that nuclear war might not start only as the result of a deliberate attack, but also by accident or through misunderstanding. In its opening statement at SALT I the Soviet delegation said that

In the Soviet Union view, mutual deterrence did not entirely preclude nuclear war. Each side has its own understanding and interpretation of the numerous factors and complex interactions of the evolving military political situation. This could lead to major miscalculations. The strategic situation by no means excluded the risk of nuclear conflict arising from unauthorized use of nuclear missiles from a provocation on the part of some third power possessing nuclear weapons.[74]

The Soviet Union has tried to use arms control to reduce the likelihood of inadvertent nuclear war. The Hot Line Agreement of 1963, the Accident Measures Agreement of 1971, the Incidents at Sea Agreement of 1972, and the confidence-building measures that have resulted from the Helsinki process, in particular the Stockholm Agreement constraining military exercises, reveal concern about the possibility of accidental or inadvertent war. At the Geneva summit meeting in November 1985, President Ronald Reagan and General Secretary Mikhail Gorbachev agreed to study centers to reduce nuclear risk.[75] In September 1987 the two nations agreed to set up such centers in Moscow and Washington.[76]

The Basic Principles of Relations between the Soviet Union and the United States (1972) and the Agreement on the Prevention of Nuclear War (1973) reflected a joint desire to reduce the risk of nuclear war.[77] The former committed the two sides to conduct their relations on the basis of peaceful coexistence and mutual restraint, and to seek to resolve their disputes by peaceful means. In the latter the two powers agreed to act "in such a manner as to prevent the development of situations capable of causing a dangerous exacerbation of their relations, as to avoid military confrontations, and as to exclude the outbreak of nuclear war between them and between either of the Parties and other countries." These two agreements, however, are couched in very general terms and flawed by internal inconsistencies; nor did they lead to any operational or institutional arrangements for avoiding crises.[78] The words in the agreements, however, do bear witness to the recognition by the two superpowers that they need to conduct their rivalry in such a way as to avoid crises.

The Soviet Union revealed anxieties of a more specific kind at SALT I by making it clear in the negotiations on the Agreement on the Prevention of Nuclear War that one of its main concerns was the possibility that a third state might launch a nuclear strike in order to provoke war between the superpowers. It was clearly China rather than Great Britain or France that gave the Soviet leaders anxiety. They were deeply suspicious of Chinese motives, and evidently feared that the Chinese leaders, who, they believed, did not appreciate the real significance of nuclear weapons, might try to provoke a Soviet–American war that would leave China as the *tertius gaudens*.[79]

At SALT I the Soviet Union tried to get American agreement to joint action in the event of a third country's using nuclear weapons to provoke a Soviet–American war. The United States rejected this proposal on the grounds that such an agreement would harm U.S. relations not only with China, but also with U.S. allies in NATO. The Prevention of Nuclear War Agreement may have given the Soviet Union something of what it wanted, but it was evidently not enough because in 1974 General Secretary Leonid Brezhnev brought up the idea of a Soviet–American treaty whereby each country would come to the aid of the other if either country or one of its allies were attacked. President Richard Nixon did not find this idea appealing: "this . . . smacks of condominium in the most blatant sense," he wrote in his diary.[80] Brezhnev returned to the idea of such a treaty at the Vienna summit in 1979, but with no success.[81]

Although earlier arms control negotiations had indicated that the Soviet Union was concerned about the possibility that crisis might lead to war, it was only in the 1980s that Soviet specialists began to discuss the concept of stability, which has long played a central role in American analyses of the risks of war. In the SALT II Agreement of 1979 the Soviet Union committed itself, along with the United States, to "consider other steps to ensure and enhance strategic stability." In line with this commitment the Soviet Union advanced proposals at the strategic arms reduction talks (START) that it said were aimed at preventing crises and building confidence:

> Ban the flights of heavy bombers and the cruising of aircraft carriers of one side in agreed zones adjacent to the territory of the other side; notify each other in advance about the mass take-off of heavy bombers and forward-based aircraft; establish for missile-carrying submarines zones in which any antisubmarine activities by the other side would be banned.[82]

Little progress was made on these proposals before START was ended by the Soviet withdrawal from the talks in November 1983, and there are no reports of further negotiations on these issues since the nuclear and space talks began in 1985, even though one purpose of those talks, as agreed by Secretary of State George Shultz and Foreign Minister Andrei Gromyko in January 1985, is to "enhance strategic stability."[83] In a commentary on START General N. Petrov said in January 1983:

> The thesis on the destabilizing properties of ground missiles is false; at the same time it represents an attempt to artificially acquire some kind of theoretical reason for supporting the American proposals. *From the military viewpoint, stability is primarily endangered by those systems which are most effective in destroying the defense warning system, command posts, and staffs and their communications, but which do not have sufficiently reliable communications with headquarters—this fact enhances the probability of their being used without approval and which require special operational measures which can aggravate tension (for example, the take-off of heavy bombers).* According to these indexes, the most destabilizing means are the ballistic missiles deployed on submarines; heavy bombers armed with stealth technology; long-range cruise missiles; and the Pershing II missiles deployed in forward positions.[84] (Emphasis added.)

This commentary was self-serving inasmuch as it supported the Soviet position at START, and listed types of systems on which the United States relies more heavily than does the Soviet Union. It may also provide some clues to Soviet thinking about stability. It suggests that weapons systems are destabilizing insofar as they pose a threat to the other side's early warning and command systems, and are themselves under inadequate command and control.

A similar argument is put forward from the Soviet Academy of Sciences.[85] Among the military–technical factors that they claim lower strategic stability, there are three that touch directly on command and control. The first is a reduction in the flight-time of systems with hard-target kill capability (for example, by the deployment of the Pershing II): this is destabilizing because it "reduces to a minimum the time for the political leadership to take a decision about a retaliatory strike." Second, stealth technology and unpredictable flight trajectories by maneuvering reentry vehicles are also destabilizing, they argue, because they can undermine the other side's early-warning capability. Third, SSBNs are destabilizing because they may have difficulty in maintaining reliable two-way communication with command centers, and this increases the danger of unsanctioned launch.

The Soviet Union has not always abided by these principles, however. It has deployed dual-capable systems and missiles that are designed to destroy hardened targets, such as ICBM silos and command-and-control installations. Moreover, Khrushchev's emplacement of missiles in Cuba in 1962 certainly would have shortened U.S. warning time, while communications between Moscow and the missile bases could hardly have been reliable. Further, the stationing of Yankee-class SSBNs off the east coast of the United States threatens U.S. bomber bases and, more importantly, Washington, with a strike with very little warning time.[86]

Nevertheless, these two Soviet attempts to devise criteria for defining destabilizing systems do reflect Soviet preoccupations. They show concern about the vulnerability of early warning and command systems, particularly about efforts to hinder the implementation of a prompt-launch policy. The Soviet Union, however, has not embraced the American concept of crisis stability. From Soviet doctrine and force structure it is clear that the most important element in the Soviet concept of stability is the ability to maintain tight command and control over nuclear forces. This may be one reason why the Soviet Union has invested more heavily in ICBMs than in SLBMs and bombers, and why so small a portion of the SSBN fleet is out of port at any given time. It may also explain why the Soviet Union has given so much attention to the redundancy and survivability of its command structure.

Crisis Behavior and Nuclear Alerts

As far as we know, the Soviet Union has never raised the alert status of its nuclear forces during a crisis. Khrushchev, who tried to exploit nuclear threats for political purposes, did not do so for reasons we have already explored. He may have been sure of his own ability to make use of nuclear threats, but his actual behavior showed a clear awareness of the danger that military moves could push a crisis into war. After the Cuban Missile Crisis Soviet diplomacy became more circumspect, no doubt because Khrushchev's policy of threats had proved both ineffective and dangerous. Brezhnev and his colleagues avoided making explicit nuclear threats against the United States, although they did make veiled threats against China in 1969.[87] Rather than inducing the Soviet leaders to take greater risks, the acquisition of an assured retaliatory capability by the Soviet Union seems to have given them confidence that they could expand their power and influence without engaging in dangerously provocative moves.

Even during the Middle East War of 1973, when the United States raised the status of its strategic forces to DEFCON 3, the Soviet Union did not raise the alert level of its nuclear forces. The explanation we have given for Soviet inaction during the Cuban missile crisis does not seem appropriate here, for both the general context and the immediate issues were very different. The Soviet Union had an assured retaliatory capability in 1973, and had some of its forces on day-to-day alert (and perhaps even on prompt-launch alert). The U.S. alert may have headed off a unilateral Soviet military intervention on behalf of Egypt, but it is not clear that it did in fact do so because the United States also put pressure on Israel to accept the cease-fire with Egypt, thereby giving the Soviet Union what it sought (and what the United States had already agreed to). In conversations with Arab leaders, Brezhnev later claimed to have been astonished by the American alert, and to have thought that it resulted from a desire to dramatize the crisis.[88] The absence of a Soviet alert in 1973 can thus be interpreted in one of two ways: (1) as an indication that the Soviet Union did not take the U.S. alert very seriously, or (2) as a sign that it was afraid of being drawn into a dangerous spiral of alerts and counteralerts.

Past experience, however, is not necessarily a guide to future actions. The Soviet Union and the United States have not experienced an intense crisis, threatening the vital interests of either side, since the advent of strategic parity. In an intense crisis readiness to wage war would be a more urgent priority than in peacetime. If preemption is seen by the Soviet High Command as the most effective strategic option from a military point of view, then there might be growing pressure in a crisis, if not to carry out a preemptive strike, at least to ready the forces for one. Even if preemption is not regarded as a realistic strategy, there may be pressure to reduce the vulnerability of the strategic forces by moving SSBNs out of port and raising the alert status of the bombers. Such nuclear alerts, even if undertaken for reasons of prudence, could in Soviet eyes become "so provocative and dangerous that the alert order is tantamount to a declaration of war . . . alerts may directly lead to war, through accident or inadvertence—or through compelling an opponent to preempt merely to protect himself."[89] It should be noted, however, that the Soviet Union has a high proportion of its warheads on land-based ICBMs that are assumed to be in a high state of readiness, and this should decrease the pressure to alert strategic forces in a crisis. The situation has changed markedly since the Cuban Missile Crisis when it would have taken a significant time to ready Soviet ICBMs—an action that might have provoked American preemption.

It has also been suggested that as their command technology improves, the

Soviet leaders may start to follow the United States in using nuclear alerts to send political signals during crises; otherwise, their nuclear forces will have no value in a crisis.[90] It is not evident that Soviet leaders will do this, however, for Soviet political and military commentators have argued that the Soviet Union, by attaining strategic parity, has deprived the United States of the ability to use its nuclear forces for political purposes, and they see this as a major gain.[91] This suggests that the Soviet Union will not feel impelled to use nuclear threats in crises; however, if the Soviet Union finds that, contrary to expectation, the United States does continue to use nuclear alerts for political purposes during crises, it may feel impelled—for reasons of military preparedness more than for political effect—to do likewise, and a dangerous competition in alerting could ensue.

SOVIET ATTITUDES REGARDING CRISIS STABILITY

Although crisis stability and crisis management do not figure in the Soviet literature on war and peace, many of the issues raised by Western analysts under the rubric of crisis management have also been studied in the Soviet Union. This is clear from our attempt to answer the four questions posed in the introduction to this chapter.

First, Soviet studies of 1941 show a clear awareness of the tension that can arise between the political effort to prevent war and the military measures that need to be taken in case war should come.[92] Although there are no comparable studies of international crises in the postwar years, it is evident that Khrushchev's attempts to exploit nuclear threats for political purposes left its mark on Soviet thinking.[93] His missile diplomacy showed the dangers, and ultimately also the ineffectiveness, of threatening to use nuclear forces when the forces at hand provided only a choice between military defeat and political capitulation. The Soviet leaders seem to have drawn the conclusion not only that nuclear threats needed to be backed by adequate forces, but that nuclear diplomacy, in the form of direct threats to use nuclear weapons, was either counterproductive or dangerous. In any event, when they acquired substantial forces they became circumspect in exploiting them for political purposes.

Second, in building up their strategic nuclear forces the Soviet leaders have taken pains to acquire a variety of options for the outbreak of war. The search for options suggests that they have been by no means sure that they could implement a strategy of preemption, even if that were their preferred military option. By giving themselves strategic options they have sought not only to increase their room for maneuver in a crisis, but also, and more importantly, to increase their ability to deter a nuclear attack. There is no good way to start a nuclear war, however, and the appreciation that nuclear war would have catastrophic consequences for both sides, coupled with the belief that Soviet nuclear forces could deter NATO from resorting to nuclear weapons, has apparently led the Soviet High Command to place increasing emphasis on the conventional option in its military policy.

Third, the Soviet Union has given consistent attention to the command and control of its nuclear forces. The advent of nuclear weapons and ballistic missiles opened up new opportunities for attacking enemy command installations, and Soviet military strategy has always given a high priority to such targets; however, nuclear weapons also created new threats to Soviet command. The Soviet Union has made great efforts to protect the Supreme High Command in time of war, and thereby to maintain the capacity to wage war. It has tried to create a command system that would enable it to carry out its strategic options.

Fourth, the Soviet Union has shown in arms control negotiations that it is concerned about the possibility of accidental or inadvertent nuclear war. Its behavior in crises has shown an awareness of the need to exercise military force in a circumspect way. The growth of Soviet military power has not induced the Soviet leaders to take greater risks in pursuing their political objectives.

These conclusions point to a clear understanding on the part of Soviet leaders of the danger that crisis might lead to war, and of the tension between military precautions and the requirements of political prudence. In spite of their concern about accidental or inadvertent war, Soviet leaders—political and military—have (as far as we can tell) seen the causes of war primarily in the East–West political conflict. Clausewitz's axiom that war is a continuation of politics by violent means is much quoted by Soviet military writers, and one of the chief meanings they give to it is that the causes of war have to be sought in the political context, not merely in the balance of arms on either side. The dominant Soviet view is that war would grow out of a political crisis, but the military balance has affected the Soviet assessment of how a crisis would move to war. In the 1950s and early 1960s, when the United States enjoyed strategic superiority, Soviet military doctrine held that war would begin with strategic nuclear strikes. As Soviet strategic forces grew, Soviet military doctrine moved to the position that a war would open with a conventional phase, and then to the view that it might remain conventional.

Most Soviet military writers warn against leaving military measures until too late. Marshal Zhukov asserted that the military could have done more in 1941 to convince Stalin of the inevitability of war and the need to take urgent measures.[94] It is not inconceivable that some commanders, remembering 1941, might take unauthorized action to raise the readiness of their forces if they believed the political leaders were blind to the danger of war; however, the primacy of politics is a cardinal rule in Party–military relations. Colonel-General Gareev, deputy chief of the General Staff, has noted that

> timely strategic deployment of the Armed Forces before the beginning of war, in spite of its advantages in a purely military connection, is not always possible to achieve for military–political reasons. Mobilization, not to

mention the whole complex of measures for strategic deployment, has always been considered tantamount to a state of war, and turning back from it to a peaceful position is very difficult to do. If war in general is political through and through, then on the eve of war and at the beginning of war its political aspects can be expected to prevail.[95]

Despite this primacy of politics, there are several aspects of Soviet military organization and doctrine that could, in an intense and complex crisis, contribute to a breakdown of efforts to prevent nuclear war.

First, while Stalin and Khrushchev exercised very tight control over relatively small nuclear forces, new problems have arisen as Soviet nuclear forces grew and military doctrine was revised to embrace a range of options, some of which impose immense strains on command. As a result, the Soviet command system has become increasingly complex, and this complexity may have entailed some loss of central control over nuclear forces. It is not clear, for example, how the Soviet Union has reconciled centralized control with flexible arrangements for command in the theater. Thus, Marshal Ustinov explained in 1982 that the Soviet Union's pledge not to be the first to use nuclear weapons means that

> in preparing the Armed Forces even more attention will now be devoted to the tasks of preventing military conflict from becoming nuclear. . . . Every specialist who knows even a little about military questions understands that [by this] an even stricter framework will be imposed in the training of troops and staffs, in determining the composition of armaments, in organizing even stricter control to exclude the unsanctioned launch of nuclear weapons, from tactical to strategic.[96]

This points to the need for tight control over nuclear weapons, but we do not know what measures, if any, have been taken to that end since the no-first-use pledge was made.

Second, Soviet leaders have publicly rejected the idea that either the United States or the Soviet Union could decapitate the other. Soviet leaders have been at pains to present their country as strong and invulnerable, and to prevent any U.S. president from sharing Hitler's illusion that the Soviet state could be smashed at one blow. They have made considerable efforts to protect the leadership in the event of war. There is no evidence that the Soviet military believes that a strike against the U.S. command system alone would prevent retaliation. At the same time, the Soviet Union has acquired forces with a large hard-target kill capability, and the military have made it clear that they assign high priority to attacking the enemy's command system.

Third, even though they have a range of options, the Soviet leaders still face difficult choices that bear very closely on the possibility of inadvertent war. Prompt launch may be less dangerous than preemption, but prompt launch also has grave problems: Soviet leaders would still need to decide what counts as sufficient warning to take a decision to launch. As former Under Secretary of Defense William Perry has written,

> Many of the actions that reduce our likelihood of false alarm increase the likelihood that we will fail to launch when we should, and vice versa. . . . [R]eliability of our alerting system depends not only on what kind of equipment we have and how much redundancy is built in, it also depends on a political decision: whether it is more important to reduce the risk of false alarm or to reduce the risk of failing to launch.[97]

We have found no Soviet discussion of these choices, or of the technical risks in a prompt-launch policy, even though presumably they must be taken into account in designing the early warning and command systems. Soviet specialists on command and control recognize that the pressure to make a quick decision makes it more difficult to take a good decision. Altukhov, for example, writes that "in actual practice it happens that in the execution of many measures speed and quality come into contradiction," but does not draw any conclusions from this.[98] More recently, since the Chernobyl accident, Soviet political leaders have acknowledged the fallibility of technical systems. Thus, Anatolii Dobrynin has stressed that

> the present arms race is creating a completely new situation—it is inexorably shortening the time for taking decisions, is increasingly handing them over to machines, to technology, and thereby depriving statesmen of the right to judgement, discussion, reflection. Yet technology, even when tested many times—as the destruction of the Challenger spaceship, the explosions of the Titan and Delta rockets, the accident at the atomic power station at Chernobyl, and many other similar events testify—fails once in a while. But "once in a while" in a certain situation can mean "once and for all." Is it acceptable to take such a risk?[99]

Similar sentiments have been voiced by Gorbachev. Whether these concerns have affected strategic policy is unknown.

A fourth troubling element in Soviet military doctrine is the current interest in the conventional option. If Soviet leaders believed that a conflict could be kept conventional, they might be tempted to launch a conventional offensive in a crisis; however, a major conventional conflict would surely create enormous pressures for nuclear escalation. In this sense, the conventional option, although less dangerous than the nuclear option, does carry its own dangers. It is therefore noteworthy that the Soviet Union has begun to investigate nonprovocative or defensive defense. In May 1987 the members of the Warsaw Pact issued a statement in which they stressed the defensive nature of their military doctrine, and called for the reduction of armed forces and conventional arms to a level "at which neither side, in ensuring its own defense, would have the means for a surprise attack on the other side, for mounting offensive operations at all."[100] It is too early to say whether this emphasis on defensive defense will affect Soviet force posture. But under Gorbachev the Soviet Union has already shown that it is willing to take practical steps to reduce the danger of crisis instability, for example, through confidence building measures such as those adopted in the 1986 Stockholm Agreement.

These four elements bring us back to the question raised at the outset about the tension between the political and the military–technical facets of Soviet doctrine, which can create a severe dilemma in crisis because there may then be inherent incompatibilities between the requirements of military strategy and those of political prudence. In the 1960s and 1970s the Soviet Union tried to address this problem with a range of military options, but could not dispose of the dilemma. Gorbachev, however, has emphasized that security is becoming increasingly a political matter, that it cannot be assured by military–technical means alone, and that in the context of Soviet–American relations security can only be mutual—if one side feels insecure both will feel insecure.[101] The Warsaw Pact's statement on military doctrine indicates that more serious attention is being paid to the relationship between the two elements of military doctrine. In commenting on that statement, three Soviet specialists have written that "the defensive character of doctrine presupposes a corresponding strategy and operational forms."[102] The flexibility that Gorbachev has shown already in arms control policy (for example, by accepting intrusive inspection in the Stockholm Agreement and the INF Treaty), along with a growing interest in stability and the discussion of the relationship between the two elements of doctrine, suggest that this is a good time for pursuing cooperative measures to enhance stability and reduce the risk of nuclear war.

NOTES

1. In its opening statement at SALT in 1969 the Soviet delegation declared that "it would be tantamount to suicide for the ones who decided to start war." (Gerard Smith, *Doubletalk. The Story of Salt I,* New York: Doubleday, 1980, p. 83.) In October 1981 President Reagan commented at a press conference that "the Soviet Union have made it very plain among themselves they believe [a nuclear war] is winnable." (*New York Times,* October 2, 1981, p. A26) In response General Secretary Brezhnev said that to start a nuclear war in the expectation of victory would be tantamount to suicide. (*Pravda,* October 20, 1981). In September 1983 Marshal N. V. Ogarkov, then chief of the General Staff, wrote that "in contemporary conditions only suicides can wager on a first nuclear strike." (*Krasnaia Zvezda,* September 23, 1983). Gorbachev has been more explicit in stating that there would be no victors in a nuclear war. See, for example, the joint U.S.–Soviet statement after the Geneva summit, *Washington Post,* November 22, 1985.

2. Alexander L. George, "Crisis Management: The Interaction of Military and Political Considerations," *Survival* (Sept.–Oct. 1984), p. 223.

3. For recent statements of doctrine see the entries on military doctrine and mil-

itary strategy in *Voennyi Entsiklopedicheskii Slovar'* (Moscow: Voenizdat, 1983), pp. 240, 711–712; and also Marshal N. V. Ogarkov, *Istoriia uchit bditel'nost'* (Moscow: Voenizdat, 1985), pp. 72–81. For a discussion of this distinction in the prewar period see Condoleezza Rice, "The Making of Soviet Strategy," in Peter Paret (ed.), *Makers of Modern Strategy* (Princeton: Princeton U.P., 1986), pp. 648–676. For the nuclear period see Holloway, pp. 31–35.

4. Henry Kissinger saw both of these elements in Brezhnev's personality. In one and the same conversation Brezhnev switched from hinting at a preemptive strike against China to a disquisition on peace as the noblest goal. "Which was the real Brezhnev?," writes Kissinger, "The leader who spoke so threateningly of China or the old man who recited his devotion to peace? Probably both were genuine." Henry A. Kissinger, *Years of Upheaval* (Boston: Little Brown & Co., 1982), pp. 233–234.

5. Khrushchev explained to the Egyptian journalist Mohammed Heikal that

> We must never be taken by surprise again, as we were when Hitler invaded us. Do you know what happened to Stalin then? When he heard the news of Germany's invasion he went to his bedroom, and locked himself in. The next day he summoned us and said, "Comrades, the state which Lenin built is finished!" This hit us like a thunderbolt.

Although this seems to be a typical piece of Khrushchevian hyperbole, it is evident that Stalin was shaken by the attack. Mohammed Heikal, *Sphinx and Commissar: The Rise and Fall of Soviet Influence in the Arab World* (London: Collins and Sons, 1978), p. 127.

6. Matthew P. Gallagher, *The Soviet History of World War II. Myths, Memories and Realities* (New York: Frederick A. Praeger, 1963), pp. 131–133. Herbert S. Dinerstein, *War and the Soviet Union* (New York: Frederick A. Praeger, 1962), pp. 194–195.

7. Holloway, pp. 34–39.

8. Gallagher, op. cit., ch. 2; Dinerstein, op. cit., pp. 189–211; Raymond L. Garthoff, *Soviet Strategy in the Nuclear Age* (London: Stevens and Sons, 1958), pp. 84–87.

9. *Pravda,* January 15, 1960.

10. V. D. Sokolovskii (ed.) *Voennaia Strategiia* (Moscow: Voenizdat, 1962), pp. 238–239.

11. Between 1956 and 1960 some 150 to 200 intercontinental bombers (Bisons and Bears) entered service. Both of these aircraft suffered from serious deficiencies. The Bison did not have the range to make return sorties, while the Bear was a turboprop bomber, and its slow speed made it vulnerable to air defenses. In the early 1950s the United States had a few strategic bombers in Europe and the Far East, but the number of forward-based systems capable of striking the Soviet Union had grown to more than 400 by 1955. At that time the Soviet Union had just over 300 medium-range nuclear systems, and no intercontinental systems, while the United States had 1,300 intercontinental bombers. In 1960 the Soviet Union had 145 intercontinental bombers and four ICBMs; it also had 200 medium/intermediate range ballistic missiles (M/IRBMs) and several hundred nuclear-capable medium-range bombers. In contrast, the United States and its NATO allies had almost 800 medium-range missiles and bombers, while the United States had 1,735 intercontinental bombers, 12 ICBMs and 32 SLBMs. [Robert P. Berman and John C. Baker, *Soviet Strategic Forces* (Washington D.C.: The Brookings Institution, 1982), pp. 42–43.]

12. Robert Weinland concludes that in the early 1960s the United States "was rapidly acquiring—in fact, probably already possessed—the capability to *disarm* the Soviet strategic strike force." He points out that in January 1962 the Soviet Union had

fewer than 100 ICBMs deployed at soft sites (in fact the Soviet Union probably had far fewer than 100 ICBMs [see p. 128]). Weinland notes that during the Cuban Missile Crisis (see Chapter 8), Soviet diesel-powered attack submarines escorted the merchant ships carrying missiles and military equipment to Cuba, but U.S. antisubmarine warfare (ASW) forces detected, localized, and surfaced each of those submarines, and would presumably have been able to do the same to the Soviet missile-carrying submarines. The Soviet Union did have a force of 200 intercontinental bombers, but these were not kept on alert, and would have been vulnerable to attack by the far larger and more capable U.S. arsenal. This situation, if anything, had worsened by January 1963, in view of the rate at which the U.S. force was growing. The Soviet Union took some naval measures (including the initiation of patrols of SLBM submarines in the Atlantic in 1964) to ensure retaliation, but the overall relationship probably did not change until the third generation of ICBMs began to enter service in 1965 or 1966. See Robert G. Weinland, "The Evolution of Soviet Requirements for Naval Forces: Solving the Problems of the Early 1960s," *Survival* (Jan./Feb. 1984), no. 1, pp. 16–25.

13. *Krasnaia Zvezda,* September 23, 1983, p. 2. This agrees with the view of Robert McNamara, secretary of defense at the time (see interview with Robert Scheer, *Los Angeles Times,* April 4, 1982).

14. Scott D. Sagan, "SIOP-62: The Nuclear War Plan Briefing to President Kennedy," *International Security* (1987) *12*:1, 22.

15. Despite its large margin of superiority, the U.S. military was not confident that the United States would escape damage even if the U.S. were to preempt; see Sagan, op. cit., pp. 30–32, 50.

16. John Barron, *KGB* (New York: Reader's Digest Press, 1974), p. 10; Oleg Penkovsky, *The Penkovsky Papers* (London: Fontana Books, 1965), p. 217.

17. Mohammed Heikal, op. cit., pp. 97–98. This was in 1958, and recalls Stalin's comment that "atomic bombs are meant to frighten those with weak nerves"; *Pravda,* September 25, 1946.

18. When he became first secretary of the Central Committee in September 1953 he received a briefing on nuclear weapons. Eleven years later he told Heikal that

> When I was appointed First Secretary of the Central Committee and learned all the facts about nuclear power I couldn't sleep for several days. Then I became convinced that we could never possibly use these weapons, and when I realized that I was able to sleep again. But all the same we must be prepared. Our understanding is not sufficient answer to the arrogance of the imperialists.

Heikal, op. cit., p. 129.

19. After the crisis Khrushchev claimed that the Soviet government had ordered "the whole army of the Soviet Union and above all the Soviet intercontinental and strategic rocket forces, the anti-air missile defense and fighter aviation of the PVO [Air Defense Forces], strategic aviation and the Navy" into a state of full combat readiness. "Our submarine fleet, including the atomic [fleet]," he said, "occupied its appointed positions" (*Pravda,* December 13, 1962, p. 1; see also *Pravda,* October 24, 1962). U.S. intelligence, however, did not detect any notable increase in the alert status of Soviet strategic forces; see Marc Trachtenberg, "The Influence of Nuclear Weapons in the Cuban Missile Crisis," *International Security* (Summer 1985), 10:157.

20. For the letter to Kennedy, see p. 184. In the same letter Khrushchev uses the image of suicide to describe what would be involved in a nuclear attack: "We are of sound mind and understand perfectly well that if we attack you, you will respond in the same way. But you too will receive the same that you hurl against us. And I think

that you also understand this. . . . Only lunatics or suicides, who themselves want to perish and to destroy the whole world before they die, could do this." Kennedy, p. 87.

21. Trachtenberg, loc. cit., p. 158.

22. Trachtenberg quotes Carl Kaysen, who was a deputy to Kennedy's Assistant for National Security Affairs, McGeorge Bundy: "Should sufficient warning of preparations for a Soviet strike or actual launching of one be available, U.S. missiles could be launched against Soviet missile sites and airfields, thus limiting to an extent depending on warning time the damage the Soviet strike would inflict." This was written in 1968, but the argument would apply *a fortiori* to 1962. The provocative nature of a decision to put strategic forces on full alert would be especially clear if both sides knew that the forces could not be held in that condition for long. Ibid., p. 160.

23. In February 1965 Marshal Zakharov, the chief of the General Staff, wrote that "with the appearance of nuclear-missile weapons, cybernetics, electronics and computers, a subjective approach to military problems, hare-brained planning and superficiality [code-words for Khrushchev's policies] may be very expensive and may cause irreparable harm." Zakharov also noted that "there can be no place for workers who, in trying to give weight to their superficial and primitive judgments, resort to referring to the so-called 'iron logic of military thinking' and 'strategic far-sightedness,' sometimes even of someone who has no direct connection with military strategy." (*Krasnaia Zvezda,* February 4, 1965.)

24. Charles E. Bohlen, *Witness to History 1929–1969* (New York: Norton, 1973), pp. 495–496.

25. William T. Lee, "Soviet Nuclear Targeting Strategy," pp. 84–108 in Ball and Richelson, esp. p. 97. See also Berman and Baker, op. cit., p. 53.

26. We use this term rather than "assured destruction capability" because the latter carries connotations of destroying population, which, as far as we can tell, would not be the primary goal of Soviet targeting doctrine, even in a retaliatory strike. See also Lee, op. cit., pp. 89–91.

27. Smith, op. cit., p. 83. In 1973 Major-General M. Cherednichenko, one of Marshal Sokolovskii's closest collaborators, wrote that the Soviet Union had "acquired the capability of delivering a devastating nuclear response to an aggressor in any and all circumstances, even under conditions of a sneak nuclear attack, and of inflicting on the aggressor a critical level of damage. An unusual situation has developed: an aggressor who would initiate nuclear war would irrevocably be subjected to a devastating return nuclear strike by the other side. It proved unrealistic for an aggressor to count on victory in such a war, in view of the enormous risk for the aggressor's own continued existence." M. Cherednichenko, "Military Strategy and Military Technology," *Voyennaya Mysl'* (1973), no. 4, FPD 0043, November 12, 1973, p. 53.

28. On the importance of attaining parity see, for example, Aleksei Arbatov, *Voenno-strategicheskii paritet i politika SShA* (Moscow: Politizdat, 1984), esp. pp. 3–6. S. A. Tiushkevich, a leading military philosopher, has written that "the essence of strategic equilibrium consists of the fact that the side that is subjected to attack has modern military equipment and is constantly ready to use it in case of necessity, and thus the aggressor is not allowed to escape a retaliatory blow"; see his *Voina i sovremennost'* (Moscow: Nauka, 1986), pp. 118–119.

29. We use prompt launch here to cover both launch-on-warning and launch-under-attack. Circumlocutions are used in the Soviet literature, rather than a single term of art.

30. A. Tatarchenko, 'Metodologicheskie voprosy upravleniia voiskami' *Kommunist Vooruzhennykh Sil* (1967), no. 8, p. 49.

31. N. I. Krylov, "The Nuclear Missile Shield of the Soviet State," *Voennaya Mysl'* 1967, no. 11, FDP 0157/68, p. 20; quoted by Raymond L. Garthoff, 'Mutual Deterrence and Strategic Arms Limitation in Soviet Policy,' *International Security* (Summer 1978), p. 128.

32. Garthoff, loc. cit., pp. 130–131.

33. Walter Pincus, in "Debut of Soviet Missiles Could Color U.S., NATO Politics," *Washington Post* (June 26, 1981), mentions a figure of 25 percent. According to one Western report, the launch control silos have two junior officers from the Strategic Forces, whose responsibility it is to launch the missile, and two KGB officers, who have the separate function of arming the warhead. This system would be a logical continuation of the earlier arrangement whereby the KGB had custody of the warheads and kept them separate from the launchers. It is likely that the KGB still controls the communications networks for strategic command and control. [Andrew Cockburn, *The Threat. Inside the Soviet Military Machine* (New York: Vintage Books, 1984), p. 298.] It may well have been in the late 1960s that the Soviet Union introduced special locks on its missiles to prevent unauthorized launch. The most complete account of Soviet command and control for nuclear operations is Stephen M. Meyer, "Soviet Nuclear Operations," in *MNO*.

34. No reliable public data are available on the time needed to launch SS-9s, SS-11s and SS-13s: estimates range from a few minutes to 1 hour. But there is no reason to suppose it would have been more than the few minutes needed to launch the American Titan II.

35. It would probably have involved "launching blind," since the Hen House radars are extremely vulnerable to jamming or to blinding by high-altitude nuclear explosions. The Soviet leaders might have had to take the view that blinding or jamming of their radars was sufficient evidence of an attack. It is possible, even probable, that Soviet statements about prompt launch in the late 1960s indicated intention rather than practice, or were an attempt to deter the United States, particularly U.S. preemption, by creating uncertainty about the Soviet posture.

36. See p. 56; also Blair, pp. 141–144.

37. Marshal Krylov, loc. cit., p. 20, writes that "even in the most unfavorable circumstance, if a portion of missiles is unable to be launched before the strike of missiles of the aggressor, as a result of the high degree of protection of the launchers from nuclear explosions, these missiles will be preserved and will carry out the combat missions assigned to them."

38. *Soviet Military Power 1986* (Washington: USGPO, 1986), pp. 26–28.

39. A *Pravda* article about a launch control center reported that "each officer here knows the time in which a Pershing-2 or Minuteman-3 would reach his very specific silo, the so-called flight time." One officer told the reporter that "we know precisely the flight time to our positions. And during that time we have to carry out our combat task. And if necessary, we will carry it out." A. Gorokhov, "Za pul'tami strategicheskikh," *Pravda* (May 29, 1985), p. 6.

40. *Pravda,* July 12, 1982. Marshal Tolubko, commander-in-chief of the Strategic Rocket Forces from 1969 to 1985, has said that his forces had "two combined tasks—to deprive any aggressor of the opportunity to catch us unawares and to be in constant readiness to execute the set tasks at any time. This order of service makes it possible to bring the entire powerful complex of forces and means into operation instantaneously. No scheming or subterfuge of a military–technical nature can give the imperialist aggressors the slightest hope of a disarming strike." (*Pravda,* November 19, 1984)

41. Sokolovskii writes that nuclear weapons makes it possible to inflict massive losses on the enemy's armed forces, to destroy the material-technical base of his war effort, and to destroy state and military control. V. D. Sokolovskii, *Voennaia strategiia,* 2nd ed. (Moscow: Voenizdat, 1963), p. 239. Notra Trulock III, in "Weapons of Mass Destruction in Soviet Military Strategy," unpublished ms., 1984, quotes some lecture materials from the Voroshilov General Staff Academy to the effect that in a general nuclear war "the roads, industries, electric power stations and military targets would be destroyed, the government and military command and control would be disrupted . . . ," pp. 64, 75.

42. The Russian term for command and control is "troop control" *(upravlenie voiskami).* The Soviet Military Encyclopedia, *Voennyi Entsiklopedicheskii Slovar'* (Moscow: Voenizdat, 1983), p. 766, defines this as: "the activity of commanders . . . staffs, political organs, services and other control organs in maintaining the combat readiness and fighting ability of troops (forces), in preparing operations and combat actions and in directing them in carrying out assigned missions." The basic requirements of troop control are: continuity, firmness, flexibility, and quickness of reaction to changes in the situation. This is a somewhat broader category than command and control, but the two concepts do overlap to a considerable degree.

43. Col. Gen. P. K. Altukhov (ed.), *Osnovy teorii upravleniia voiskami* (Moscow: Voenizdat, 1984), p. 9.

44. Ibid.

45. This literature is devoted, by and large, to the general criteria for designing an effective system, rather than to the analysis of specific systems. Much of it deals with command at the level of Front or division, but some of it is also applicable to the strategic and theater levels.

46. For a discussion of the early literature on military cybernetics see David Holloway, *Management, Technology and the Soviet Military Establishment,* Adelphi Paper no. 76 (London: Institute for Strategic Studies, 1971), pp. 16–26.; automated is not the same as automatic.

47. Altukhov, op. cit., p. 200.

48. Ibid., p. 214.

49. V. D. Sokolovskii, *Voennaia strategiia,* 2nd ed. (Moscow: Voenizdat, 1963), pp. 473–475.

50. Khrushchev apparently had the supreme authority for the use of nuclear weapons since becoming first secretary of the Central Committee in September 1953. When Brezhnev succeeded Khrushchev in October 1964 he also assumed the title of chairman of the Defense Council, but we do not know when the Council was set up. [See the entry on Brezhnev in *Voennyi Entsiklopedicheskii Slovar'* (Moscow: Voenizdat, 1983), p. 100.] The existence of the Defense Council, and Brezhnev's chairmanship of it, were made public only in May 1976. The precise membership of the Council remains a matter for speculation, but it appears to comprise a small group of Politburo members, including the defense minister; the chief of the General Staff may be a member too. Soviet discussions of the Defense Council suggest that in time of war it would function—with expanded powers and perhaps with expanded membership—in the way in which the GKO did in the war with Germany. [Ellen Jones, *Red Army and Society* (Boston: Allen and Unwin, 1985), pp. 6–10; see also the entry in *Voennyi Entsiklopedicheskii Slovar'* (Moscow: Voenizdat, 1983), p. 684.]

51. *Soviet Military Power 1986* (Washington D.C.: USGPO, 1986), pp. 18–19. The importance of the central command organization for the successful conduct of war was underlined in two important articles published in 1966 and 1967, which stressed the

need for a collegial approach in which both political and military leaders would have a place. Major-General V. Zemskov noted in *Krasnaia Zvezda* that nuclear war would increase the role of the political leadership, because "modern weapons are such that the political [authorities] cannot let them escape its control" (January 5, 1967). General Lomov wrote in *Military Thought* that "the experience of the past convincingly shows the necessity for political and strategic war direction unified in a single supreme military–political organ" ("Some Questions of Leadership in Modern War, *Voennaya Mysl'* [January 1966], pp. 23–40). Both generals emphasized the importance of having such institutions ready in peacetime, before war started. Altukhov (ed.), op. cit., p. 200, stresses the importance for all levels of the command system (from the strategic to the tactical) of being ready at any moment for combat.

52. The commander-in-chief of the Strategic Rocket Forces, Chief Marshal of Artillery V. Tolubko, told a reporter from *Pravda* that combat readiness "is the ability at any moment to deliver a retaliatory destructive blow on the order of the Supreme High Command"; A. Gorokhov, "Za pul'tami strategicheskikh," *Pravda* (May 29, 1985), p. 6. During the war with Germany orders of the *Stavka* had to be signed by both the supreme commander-in-chief and the chief of the General Staff. See *KPSS o Vooruzhennykh Silakh Sovetskogo Soiuza* (Moscow: Voenizdat, 1981), p. 308.

53. Concerning the composition of *Stavka,* see *Soviet Military Power,* p. 19.

54. *Soviet Military Power 1985,* pp. 47, 50.

55. As already stated, unless otherwise indicated, technical information is from Desmond Ball, "The Soviet Strategic C³I System," op. cit.

56. *Pravda,* July 12, 1982.

57. *Pravda,* December 6, 1983.

58. *The Soviet Military Encyclopedia,* 1983, op. cit., p. 87.

59. Transcript of Khrushchev's tape-recorded memoirs, Harriman Institute, Columbia University, p. 1289. Our thanks to Matthew Evangelista for this reference.

60. This is especially the case if the United States wishes to destroy other targets too; see in particular Desmond Ball, *Targeting for Strategic Deterrence,* Adelphi Paper no. 185 (London: International Institute for Strategic Studies, 1983), p. 26.

61. They are deployed in highly elliptical orbits with perigees of about 600 km and apogees of about 40,000 km. A constellation of nine operational satellites is needed to provide constant coverage of U.S. ICBM fields. Deployment of these satellites began in 1976, but they have had a very high failure rate, either failing to reach their proper orbit or breaking up after reaching their station. It was only in 1981 that the Soviet Union managed to deploy three such satellites simultaneously, and it still has not deployed a full constellation. See Nicholas Johnson, "Soviets in Space—A New Threat?," in *The International Countermeasures Handbook,* 12th ed. (Palo Alto: EW Publications, 1987), p. 46.

62. Writing in *Voennaya Mysl'* in 1969, Colonel A. B. Krasnov cited American military experts to the effect that "the idea is to neutralize the shortcomings inherent in each [radar] through combined development and application of these devices, achieving a high level of effectiveness and viability of the EW system as a whole." ("The Early Warning System: Means and Prospects of Development," *Voennaya Mysl'* [1969], 4, p. 86.) The Soviet Union has followed this principle.

63. *Soviet Military Power 1987* (Washington: USGPO, 1987), p. 48. In addition to these BMEWs, the Soviets also have an older generation of mechanically steered (so-called Hen House) radars; see *Soviet Military Power 1986* (Washington: USGPO, 1986), p. 43.

64. The ABM radars around Moscow would provide accurate attack assessment

for the capital's vicinity, but too late for any purpose other than the guidance of the high-acceleration ABM interceptors.

65. According to Daniel Ford, *The Button* (New York: Simon and Schuster, 1985), p. 45, these ICBMs can be launched within 4 to 8 minutes. Chief Marshal of Artillery V. Tolubko, command-in-chief of the Strategic Rocket Forces said in April 1985 that "there is more to a rocket weapon than the rocket itself. It is a complex of the most complicated equipment and systems, which ensure that the missiles are ready for immediate firing. . . . In recent years the combat readiness of the Rocket Forces has increased immeasurably. If in the period when they were being formed it took many hours to prepare a rocket for firing, now it takes just seconds." (*Krasnaya Zvezda,* April 25, 1985.)

66. The low alert levels of Soviet strategic forces in the 1960s and 1970s have been explained in various ways, perhaps the most common having been that the Soviet Union does not really fear a surprise attack, and expects adequate strategic warning. The recent increase in readiness levels suggests, however, that technological factors were the key constraint: Perhaps it was not the expectation of strategic warning that made high alert rates unnecessary, but rather the technological deficiencies that made high alert rates impossible and strategic warning crucial. See the discussion in Joseph J. Kruzel, "Military Alerts and Diplomatic Signals," in Ellen P. Stern (ed.) *The Limits of Military Intervention* (Beverly Hills: Sage Publications, 1977), pp. 87–89.

67. Former Secretary of the Navy J. William Middendorf, cited by Ball, loc. cit., p. 215.

68. It has built several hundred ground stations for signals intelligence, and deploys intelligence systems on submarines, surface ships, aircraft, satellites, and other platforms. See Desmond Ball, "Soviet Signals Intelligence," *The International Countermeasures Handbook,* 12th ed. (Palo Alto: EW Publications, 1987), pp. 73–89.

69. Jeffrey T. Richelson, *Sword and Shield: The Soviet Intelligence and Security Apparatus* (Cambridge, MA: Ballinger, 1986); and Laqueur, Chapt. 8.

70. Ivanov, op. cit., pp. 212–213.

71. M. A. Gareev, *Frunze—voennyi teoretik* (Moscow: Voenizdat, 1985), pp. 241–242.

72. As one commentator has put it, "He who shoots first, dies second. This is how the matter stands, and the Americans realize it." A Bovin in *New Times* (September 8, 1986), p. 32.

73. *Pravda,* July 12, 1982.

74. Smith, op. cit., p. 83.

75. Text of the Joint U.S.–Soviet Statement, *Washington Post* (November 22, 1985). For a recent Soviet discussion see M. A. Mil'shtein, "Ob ugroze sluchainnogo vozniknoveniia iadernoi voiny," *SShA,* October 1986, pp. 3–13. This, however, contains no information about Soviet arrangements to prevent accidental war, and only describes the Soviet view of problems with the U.S. command system.

76. For the text of the agreement, see *Arms Control Today* (1987), *17*:8, 28.

77. For complete texts, see *Arms Control and Disarmament Agreements,* U.S. Arms Control and Disarmament Agency (Washington: USGPO, 1982).

78. See Alexander L. George, *Managing U.S.-Soviet Rivalry. Problems of Crisis Prevention* (Boulder, CO: Westview Press, 1983), pp. 107–116.

79. Smith, op. cit., pp. 139–144, writes about the Soviet aims at SALT.

80. Richard Nixon, *The Memoirs of R.N.* (New York: Grosset and Dunlap, 1978), p. 1030.

81. Jimmy Carter, *Keeping Faith* (New York: Bantam Books, 1982), p. 258.

82. *Pravda*, January 2, 1983.

83. Joint Statement, Geneva, January 8th, 1985, *Department of State Bulletin* (March 1985), p. 30. See V. V. Zhurkin, "O strategicheskoi stabil'nosti", *SShA* (1986), no. 1, pp. 12–25.

84. Quoted by Douglas Hart in "Soviet Approaches to Crisis Management: The Military Dimension," *Survival* (1984), 5, pp. 220–221. N. Petrov is probably a pseudonym.

85. A. Vasilyev, "Stability—Or Nevertheless Destabilization," unpublished paper, 1984.

86. The deployment of submarines close to the United States coast was announced by the Soviet Union in 1983 in retaliation for NATO's deployment of GLCMs and Pershing IIs in Europe, but in fact Yankees had begun to patrol the Western Atlantic by the early 1970s. Bracken, p. 35.

87. In addition to veiled threats, there is also evidence that the use of nuclear weapons against China was considered during the 1969 border clashes; see Betts, *Nuclear Blackmail,* pp. 79–81.

88. Garthoff, p. 381.

89. Bracken, p. 242.

90. Paul Bracken, "The Study of Crisis Management," unpublished ms. (1985), pp. 24–25.

91. See, for example, V. Zhurkin and E. Primakov (eds.) *Mezhdunarodnye konflikty* (Moscow: Mezhdunarodnye otnosheniia, 1972), pp. 22–26, 215–217.

92. We have been able to do no more than refer briefly to some of the connections that exist between the historiography of 1941 and the preoccupations of Soviet policy since 1945. These connections deserve systematic analysis.

93. One of Khrushchev's advisers, Fiodor Burlatskii, later wrote a dramatised account of the deliberations in the White House during the Cuban Missile Crisis, which became a play, "The Burden of Decision," first staged in Moscow in 1986. The play points to dangers of precipitate military action during a crisis, and to the need for compromise to prevent war. F. Burlatskii, "Chernaia subbota," *Literaturnaia gazeta* (November 23, 1983), pp. 9–10.

94. G. K. Zhukov, *Vospominaniia i Razmyshleniia* (Moscow: Novosti, 1969), p. 247.

95. Gareev, op. cit., p. 242.

96. *Pravda,* July 12, 1982.

97. William Perry, "Measures to Reduce the Risk of Nuclear War" in John W. Lewis and Coit D. Blacker (eds.) *Next Steps in the Creation of an Accidental Nuclear War Prevention Center* (Stanford: Center for International Security and Arms Control, 1983), pp. 20–21.

98. Altukhov, op. cit., p. 210.

99. 'Za bez"iadernyi mir, navstrechu XXI veku', *Kommunist* (1986), no. 9, June, p. 19.

100. "O voennoi doktrine gosudarstv-uchastnikov Varshavskogo Dogovora", *Pravda,* May 30, 1987.

101. In his report to the 27th Congress of the Communist Party of the Soviet Union, April 1986.

102. Arbatov, Vasil'iev and Kokoshin, loc. cit., part 1, p. 12.

II
CRISIS STABILITY

Humanity has had very little experience with crises that carried a significant risk of imminent nuclear war. Nor have there been any confrontations that involved more than marginal interactions between the superpowers' enormously complex and powerful military forces. Given this fortunate lack of firm knowledge, the question of whether and how a crisis might lead to nuclear war lies at the "heart of darkness," and can only be addressed by uncertain inferences drawn from a variety of complementary approaches.

The first is historical. This approach was a major theme in our depiction of the strategic setting within which crises of the future would occur, and more explicitly, in our accounts of events surrounding the outbreak of the first and second world wars. In the next chapter this theme will be continued in depth by focusing on four post-Hiroshima confrontations: the Berlin Blockade, the early phases of the Korean War, the 1973 Yom Kippur Crisis, and, above all, the Cuban Missile Crisis.

These wars and crises underscore a truth already evident in Antiquity: conflict chronically entails crucial elements that cannot be anticipated, that remain implausible even in the noonday of hindsight, and that may never yield to a convincing explanation. Nevertheless, the dangers that we face today can only be reckoned by peering into the future. As we are not possessed by prophetic visions, we adopt an approach akin to that of a cautious insurance actuary. In that spirit we shall examine the multitude of intertwined factors that could play a significant role in future crises. The examination will be divided into two parts, although the boundary between them is not clearcut. First, we shall present an analysis of a variety of tangible and reasonably "objective" factors, especially the military organizations and their alerts operations in the various geopolitical arenas where there is an appreciable risk of confrontation between the superpowers. Intangible and "subjective" features, such as human and organizational performance under stress, political cohesion, and the often incompatible requirements of diplomacy and military readiness will then be explored. Our analysis will culminate with an examination, necessarily speculative, of the fundamental issue—escalation to nuclear conflict.

The risk that ongoing competition between the superpowers could lead to crisis and then to war is ultimately governed by politics, not technology. Nevertheless, technology can create new military capabilities that could exacerbate a crisis. Furthermore, technology can also provide new capabilities that could enhance stability if they were to be embedded in an appropriate political framework. To that end, we shall advocate arms control agreements that contribute to crisis stability by placing restrictions on technological developments inimical to stability, or that impose constraints on military operations that have the potential for inflaming a crisis.

8

Post-Hiroshima Crises

This chapter is intended to be a historical data base for the remainder of this volume. It is neither encyclopaedic, nor an original piece of scholarship.[1] Of the crises in which the superpowers confronted each other frontally, we discuss only three of the most serious examples: the Berlin Blockade of 1948–49, the Cuban Missile Crisis of 1962, and the Yom Kippur Crisis of 1973. In addition, there is a brief examination of the Korean War, even though it only involved one of the superpowers directly, because it illustrates several features that recur at the outbreak of conflict. Our treatment will be purposely uneven. Because of its singular severity and importance, the bulk of the chapter is devoted to the Cuban Crisis, for which we provide a detailed narrative in an effort to convey some feeling for the psychological texture of crisis.

THE BERLIN BLOCKADE

The most serious East–West confrontation in Europe thus far took place in Berlin from 1948 to 1949. Even though it erupted at the epicenter of tension, this crisis never began to approach the gravity of the Cuban Missile Crisis. Nevertheless, it was a watershed in East–West relations. The birth of NATO and the Warsaw Treaty Organization, the political and economic status of the Federal (West) and Democratic (East) Republics of Germany, and the relations between these states and the two alliances were all shaped by the crisis.

A number of developments presaged the blockade.[2] East–West relations deteriorated steadily following the defeat of Germany. Stalin perceived America's nuclear monopoly, and the demonstrated will to use atomic weapons, as ominous challenges to Soviet security. The unsuccessful Soviet attempts to absorb the Iranian province of Azarbaijan and to exploit the

Greek civil war, and the coup of February 1948 that replaced the democratic government in Prague by a puppet regime, had created profound apprehension in the West. In Germany, the four occupying powers—France, Great Britain, the United States and the Soviet Union—were in increasingly rancorous disagreement concerning the political and economic future of their former enemy. The Western allies, partially out of concern for Germany's faltering economy, were moving toward consolidation of their occupied zones into one nation whose economy would be linked to that of Western Europe. During the winter and spring of 1948 economic aid under the Marshall Plan was extended to the Western occupation zones. The Soviet Union, concerned that Germany could again pose a threat, sought to keep Germany economically weak,[3] and made it clear that it considered these Western initiatives as violations of the Potsdam Agreement[4] between the victors of 1945.

A decision to introduce currency reforms in the Western occupation zones was the immediate cause of the crisis. The Soviets claimed that this act rendered Western rights to Berlin null and void. On March 31, 1948, the Soviets imposed the "baby blockade" by demanding inspection of military trains bound for Berlin through Soviet-occupied territory, but they did not interfere with other traffic. The Allies responded by dispatching a train with armed guards with orders not to submit to search, but the Soviets shunted it onto a siding from which it eventually had to be withdrawn. The Allies then mounted a small airlift to carry supplies to the military garrison. Soviet harassment resulted in a midair collision with some fatalities. Allied cargo planes were then given fighter escorts, whereupon the Soviets formally apologized for the incident and stated that no interference with air access had been intended.[5] Ten days after its inception, the baby blockade was suddenly lifted without explanation.

The two sides then engaged in a complex sequence of competing initiatives regarding currencies. During this same period two steps that foreshadowed the creation of NATO were taken: In April France, Great Britain, and the Benelux countries committed themselves to military cooperation for 50 years, and on June 11 the U.S. Senate passed a resolution that indicated America's readiness to participate in Europe's defense. On June 24, 1948, the Soviets imposed the "real" Berlin Blockade by halting all military and civilian surface traffic to West Berlin. The Soviets did not hide their objective: The Soviet military governor told his American counterpart, General Lucius Clay, that the blockade "would continue until the West abandoned plans for a West German government."[6]

Despite the baby blockade, the Allies were caught unprepared on June 24. The airlift was reinstated, and grew to massive proportions:[7] 2,500 tons daily by late July and twice the city's minimum daily requirements of 4,000 tons by the time the blockade ended on May 12, 1949. By then the Soviet Union had abandoned its original demands, and was reduced to accepting the lifting of a token counterblockade imposed by the Allies as the *quid pro quo* for permitting unhindered traffic to Berlin.

It is clear why the Soviets sought to prevent the formation of a separate

West German government by means of the blockade. As George and Smoke[8] summarized it:

> The Soviets hoped that the blockade would help to achieve their primary objective by shattering Western unity. The blockade provided almost perfect leverage for exerting political–diplomatic pressure. It squeezed the Western powers in a painful fashion without using Soviet military force. It placed the Western Allies in the invidious position of having to pay a heavy diplomatic price to get the blockade lifted; and it confronted them with the alternative of having to use force or to make aggressive moves to challenge the blockade that might result in bloodshed or war.

Furthermore, in the event that the blockade failed to achieve its primary objective it could be expected to at least remove the West from Berlin. Neither objective was achieved, however. Instead, the airlift kindled public attitudes in the West that facilitated the birth of NATO and the Federal Republic. The Berlin Blockade, therefore, culminated in a serious setback for the Soviet Union.

Was this outcome due to Soviet bungling? Or was it the result of prescient American insights into Soviet intentions and tactics, the fruit of skillful crisis management, or some combination thereof?

The Soviets did not bungle—they played their cards well. What they had failed to foresee was Washington's determination to hang on to Berlin, which is understandable since that determination was not in evidence during the baby blockade, and only crystallized in Washington's mind *after* the real blockade was imposed. For its part, the U.S. government had failed to anticipate Soviet moves, and apparently overestimated Stalin's willingness to risk war. The final outcome resulted from political decisions taken by the Truman administration after the gauntlet had been thrown down, from Soviet reluctance to up the ante, and from resourceful, if ad hoc, crisis management. In short, the Berlin Blockade was really a *failure* by the United States to exert deterrence recouped by ex post facto innovation.[9]

We must now substantiate these assertions. General Clay and the senior U.S. civilian official in Germany, Robert Murphy, had been warning since the fall of 1947 that Western policy toward Germany could result in "Soviet action to force our withdrawal from Berlin."[10] Three weeks before the inception of the baby blockade Clay cabled Washington[11] that he had "a feeling that [war] may come with dramatic suddenness." The consensus in Washington was that this was an alarmist viewpoint, as subsequent Soviet actions showed it to be. But the baby blockade had transformed Clay's "strategic" warning into "tactical" warning. Nevertheless, despite further warnings and requests for explicit instructions from Clay and Murphy,[12] the 3 months between the baby and real blockades saw no systematic assessment of Western objectives or Soviet intentions, nor planning for the contingency[13] of a renewed and more stringent blockade. No protest regarding the baby blockade was ever lodged.[14] As we shall see, this is par for the course.

Indeed, the Truman administration did not reach a definitive position regarding its commitment to Berlin until *after* the imposition of the blockade on June 24. This hiatus stemmed primarily from disagreements concerning the basic issues: Was Berlin really vital to Western interests? If so, to what extent? Given Soviet military dominance on the scene, and the fragile link between the isolated city and the Western military zones, what level of commitment to Berlin was prudent? Disagreements regarding Soviet intentions were another impediment to decision. Was the baby blockade merely an exploratory jab[15] that had no larger purpose? Were Soviet moves against Berlin bluffs that could be faced down by showing the flag? Or was Stalin prepared to risk bloodshed to thwart Western policy in Europe?

The administration was unable to resolve these interwoven dilemmas in a coherent manner before the Soviet move made further procrastination impossible. Following the imposition of the full blockade, Truman made an unambiguous decision to maintain the Western position in Berlin, and his strong leadership ended the debate within his government. In the light of hindsight we can now see that Stalin was not ready to risk conflict at any level, as the scrupulous observance of Allied rights to air access demonstrated. That meant that the air corridor, slender reed though it was, was sturdy enough to support the policy that Truman adopted, a fact that was anything but obvious when his decision was taken.

The paucity of experience in dealing with the Soviet Union, the absence of a West German political entity, and the ill-defined nature of the embryonic Atlantic alliance, all combined to make firm decision making prior to the blockade very difficult. Nevertheless, the total absence of anticipatory policy formation deserves comment; indeed, it was openly criticized at the time. The administration could have formulated some set of alternative plans that would have addressed the most likely contingencies even if it was impossible to agree beforehand on a particular course of action. Such an exercise might have elucidated the significance of Berlin to Washington's strategic objectives in Europe, and what risks it was willing to take in pursuit of those larger aims. That, in turn, might have led to a diplomacy that would have prevented the blockade. At worst, a failed attempt to sort through the alternatives would have left the government in the position that it held on June 24.

Finally, some facts that were not of much importance in the Berlin crisis, but which invoke themes that recur throughout this book, should be noted. In 1948 the United States had some 50 unassembled fission weapons of the Nagasaki (implosion) type, and about 30 B-29 bombers, based in New Mexico, configured to deliver such munitions.[16] The Soviets still had to test their first fission device, but they enjoyed overwhelming conventional superiority in Central Europe due to Western demobilization following Germany's defeat in 1945. Sixty B-29s were sent to Britain in July with considerable fanfare as a token of U.S. determination. At the time, this was widely regarded as momentous because it was left purposely ambiguous as to whether or not the B-29s were nuclear capable.[17] These particular aircraft were not suitable for nuclear bombing, however, nor were any weapons released from civilian custody at that time.[18] Aside from this B-29 deployment, and the activities

related to the airlift, there were no military moves or alerts of any significance, and Clay's desire to send an armored supply column into the city dis-
appeared with the success of the airlift.

THE KOREAN WAR

Although the Korean War did not produce any face-to-face confrontation
between the superpowers,[19] this major turning point in East–West relations
merits our attention because it provides striking illustrations of phenomena
that often accompany the transitions from peace to war.

General MacArthur's landing at Inchon on September 15, 1950 was a
highly significant watershed of the Korean War. The pre- and post-Inchon
phases had very different military and political complexions, and therefore
shed light on rather different aspects of crisis behavior. Before Inchon, the
United States was reacting defensively to a violent breech of the status quo.
After Inchon, the United States was on the attack, and it sought an outcome
that would have given it a much stronger position than it held before the
outbreak of hostilities. The domestic political climate was very important
throughout, but it changed its coloration after Inchon. In the opening phase,
rather broad political considerations served to define the Truman administration's objective—a return to the status quo antebellum. After Inchon, however, the increasingly torrid domestic political climate unsettled the government, and it failed to base policy on its military resources and the potential
threat being created by its own actions.

The Invasion of South Korea

A capsule history of the Korean War is provided in the caption to Figure 8.1.
After the fall of China to Mao Tse Tung's communist forces, and before the
invasion of South Korea by the communist North, the Truman administration conducted a comprehensive review of the geopolitical situation in the
Far East.[20] This had led it to conclude that Korea was of little strategic importance to the United States in the event of a major war in that region, an
assessment that was publicly stated by Secretary of State Acheson on January
12, 1950, when he defined the U.S. "defense perimeter" in the Orient and
excluded Korea from it.[21] Northern incursions into the South, a Northern
military buildup, and CIA reports that an attack might occur, did not lead
the administration to review its policy, nor did domestic political pressure
cause it to significantly enlarge its commitment. Nevertheless, when the
North struck, the administration quickly reversed itself because it then
decided that the international and domestic *political* repercussions of an
armed conquest of South Korea were unacceptable, even though it continued
to adhere to its earlier *strategic* assessment. In coming to its aid, Truman
declared that the U.S. war aim was a return to the status quo antebellum, with
Korea divided along the 38th Parallel. United Nations endorsement for this

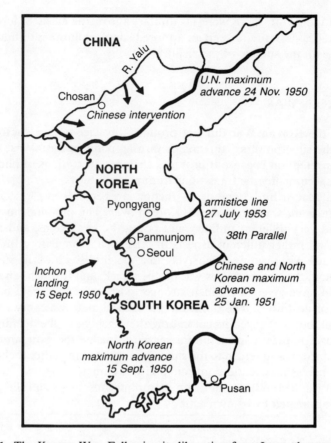

Figure 8.1. The Korean War. Following its liberation from Japan the peninsula was divided along the 38th Parallel, with the South being associated with the United States and the North under communist control. The American and Soviet occupation armies were withdrawn during 1948 and 1949. On June 25, 1950, North Korea invaded, quickly captured the South's capital at Seoul, and had reached the line shown by September 15. On that day, General MacArthur's forces landed at Inchon, and inflicted a major defeat on the North Korean army. He had nearly captured all of North Korea when the Chinese attacked en masse. That offensive threw the UN army back as far as the line shown. Subsequently the North–South border was reestablished by the Panmunjon armistice agreement of July 27, 1953.

objective was gained, after which American military involvement in Korea was formally under UN auspices.

The similarities to the Berlin crisis of the preceding year are striking. Intelligence indicated the possibility of forceful action against another exposed Western outpost to which there was no clear-cut commitment; the military logic that had argued against such a commitment again proved to be untenable in the face of political factors, and yet there was no policy review to force a resolution between these conflicting perspectives. Such a review might well have anticipated the decision that was taken as soon as the fat was in the fire since the dominant political factors, especially the threat from the administration's powerful domestic critics, were readily visible beforehand. That exercise could have led to diplomatic and military measures that might have deterred an invasion of the South, or, alternatively, a decision that it would not intervene in Korea, no matter what.[22] In another analogue to Berlin, the North Koreans and their mentors[23] failed to recognize that their invasion would shatter Washington's passivity—that the assumptions on which the risks of that act were reckoned were rendered invalid by the act.

The Chinese Intervention

The tide of events that impelled China to intervene[24] had their origin in the resounding success of MacArthur's daring landing at Inchon. That victory created formidable domestic political pressure on the Truman administration to permit the general to cross the 38th Parallel, which soon transformed the modest aim of compelling a return to the status quo antebellum into the grander objective of unifying Korea by force of arms.

From the outset some senior American officials[25] warned that this radically enlarged objective could provoke China to intervene, but in the euphoria created by Inchon these cautions went unheeded. Indeed, China had begun to build up its strength in bordering Manchuria before Inchon, and had taken pains to make these movements visible to Western observers.[26] Chou En-lai repeatedly issued public statements and diplomatic messages that Peking would not tolerate an American occupation of the North. Military intelligence on the scene, however, which was under MacArthur's control, grossly underestimated the Chinese buildup and painted a picture for decision makers that was, for a considerable period, much less realistic than that provided by the Western press. Until too late, the CIA's assessment of China's intentions and military capabilities did not contradict MacArthur's proclaimed conviction that he "understood the Oriental psyche," and that his show of power would suffice to convince Peking that it could not afford to engage his forces.

As MacArthur marched northward,[27] apprehension that China might intervene grew, particularly among the Chiefs, and in the newly appointed secretary of defense, George Marshall. These concerns peaked in early November when large Chinese formations attacked the advancing army. On November 9 the NSC decided that diplomatic contact with China should be made because a purely military policy was no longer tenable. But no such initiative appears to have been taken, nor was there any modification of MacArthur's standing orders, which allowed him[28] "to continue the action as long as, in your judgment, action by forces now under your control offer a reasonable chance of success." On that very day the Chinese troops broke off all contact and appeared to vanish into thin air. On November 21 the NSC met again, but took no definitive action;[29] apparently the Chinese disengagement had allayed fears. MacArthur announced his final push to the Yalu on November

24. Two days later the Chinese struck, and forced the longest retreat in U.S. military history, with American fatalities alone numbering in the tens of thousands.

Given that only America had nuclear weapons in 1950, it is hardly surprising that the question of their use to stave off the Chinese surfaced quickly. At his weekly press conference[30] on November 30, Truman, in response to a question, said that the use of nuclear weapons was always under "active consideration," but that he did not want this "terrible weapon" to be "used on innocent men, women, and children." When asked whether consideration was being given to civilian or military targets, however, he answered that "was for the military authorities to decide." He "was not the military authority that passed on those things." This caused an uproar, and the White House quickly issued a "clarifying statement," which "emphasized that by law, only the president can authorize the use of the atomic bomb, and that no such authorization had been given." From that statement,[31] and Acheson's memoirs,[32] it appears that use of nuclear weapons was considered by the Truman administration. They could not have been used to directly repel the Chinese onslaught, however, because the nuclear weapons of the era were not suitable for use against moving tactical targets.[33] Hence, the only available nuclear option was attack on fixed targets in China.

Postmortem

A major military disaster usually has a multitude of intertwined causes. This was no exception. Obviously there was a major failure of intelligence at both the tactical and strategic level. In sharp contrast to the pervasive micromanagement that was later to mark Vietnam, there was little central management. Instead, there was an astounding willingness to have[34] "the general [MacArthur], not the president, become the judge and arbiter of White House risks." Of greater significance, there was a widespread American inability to perceive that the newly installed regime in Peking would see the creation of an American client state on its border as a grave threat to its security, and that Washington might therefore have grossly underestimated the sacrifices China might countenance to remove that threat.[35] This misconception was abetted by Chinese tactics in the 2 weeks following their first forays: due to U.S. hegemony in the air, Chinese troop movements were brilliantly disguised,[36] which bestowed the deadly element of surprise on their devastating assault of November 26, but by that token precluded those movements from deterring MacArthur's advance.

The domestic political scene, and MacArthur's unique personal power, were at least as important as the miscalculation vis-à-vis Peking, however. After the fall of China to the communists in 1949, foreign policy in the Far East became a highly partisan and divisive issue that plagued American politics for two decades until the rapprochement with China. Already before the invasion of Korea, Truman, Marshall, and especially Acheson, were exposed to vitriolic attack in the press and in Congress. Although Truman's decision to intervene in Korea had quieted this drumbeat momentarily, the president and his cabinet believed, with good reason, that it would quickly return should they fail to exploit any military opportunity, such as that offered by Inchon, to its fullest. Under these circumstances, it is understandable why the administration found it so difficult to properly assess the implications of the turbulent scene in Korea, and to shape a sound policy. This disarray was compounded by MacArthur's ascendancy over JCS Chairman Omar Bradley and the other Chiefs after his triumph at Inchon, for they had opposed the landing and only acceded to the General's plan with great reluctance. As a result, MacArthur effectively held a carte blanche, which the charismatic, formidable, popular, and politically ambitious general[37] did not shrink from exploiting.

In short, as its armies marched toward China, the government was reduced to calming its fears by issuing protestations of American good will toward the Chinese people,[38] and to hoping that MacArthur's prophesies would be confirmed once again. The general had come to embody the government's worst fears and best hopes. He might bring about a bloody Chinese attack; to reign him in short of the Chinese border would unleash a hurricane of criticism, but were he to succeed the administration's stock would be restored.

In retrospect, the decision to land at Inchon was decisive for that operation's success inexorably led to the enlargement of the war aims, which then unleashed forces that Washington and Peking were unable to control, even though neither sought the war that ensued. After Inchon, the course of events came to resemble a Greek tragedy.

THE CUBAN MISSILE CRISIS

Khrushchev's abortive attempt to base nuclear-armed missiles in Cuba led to the most dramatic and hazardous confrontation of the nuclear age. The Cuban Missile Crisis—henceforth referred to simply as *the* Crisis—appears to have been the only time when a nuclear exchange between the superpowers was more than a distant contingency. While the Crisis may have been a tame and leisurely affair in comparison to what even a prosaic imagination could concoct, no other experience since July 1914 offers as vivid an illustration of phenomena that lie at the heart of this study. Furthermore, the extensive documentation that is available allows one to gain some feeling for the texture and tempo of a major crisis in human terms.[39] For these reasons we shall describe the Crisis in considerable chronological detail. Since we know vastly more about American decision making, events will first be viewed from the vantage point of President Kennedy and his entourage, followed by a summary of what is known about the view from the Kremlin.

Since the tale is gripping, the reader should not lose sight of themes that recur in crisis: the often-unrecognized influence of deeply held attitudes and long-term policies on the manner in which the crisis breaks, and on the adversaries' first actions; the tensions imposed on policy formation by dissension within a political culture and government; the formidable ambiguities that cannot be removed by the wizardry of modern intelligence; the problem of defining the nature of the threat and one's own objectives while contending with the often incompatible requirements of valuable allies; the insuperable difficulty of maintaining detailed control over the prodigiously complex organizations at the disposal of modern governments; and the weighing of diplomatic versus military options amidst uncertainty of how the other side will react, not to mention the enigma of what to do should that reaction intensify the conflict.

The Strategic and Political Setting

As in any major political collision, the historical backdrop was one of the dominant factors in the Crisis itself. Two developments, initially quite distinct, merged to form the volatile mixture that spawned the Crisis. One was the competition in strategic weapons; the other a popular revolution in Cuba that eventually led to a considerable Soviet military presence merely 90 miles from U.S. soil.

As we saw earlier, the U.S. built a large bomber fleet that could deliver thousands of hydrogen bombs against Soviet targets during the 1950s. The Soviet Union, however, staked its future on the new technology of long-range missiles.[40] The Soviets conducted the first ICBM test in August 1957, and launched the first earth satellite, *Sputnik,* several months later, which aroused a form of hysteria in significant segments of American opinion. The Kremlin mounted a campaign of propaganda and misinformation that resonated with these fears, and created the perception of an ever-widening "missile gap," while Khrushchev also developed a propensity for "missile rattling" during crises. Eisenhower took all this quite calmly, but in 1960 the missile gap was an important campaign theme in John F. Kennedy's victory over Eisenhower's vice president, Richard Nixon.

In reality, the strategic competition had a very different complexion. The first Soviet ICBM, the SS-6, was so cumbersome and inaccurate that only four were ever deployed.[41] While their ICBM development work proceeded, the Soviets deployed medium- (MRBM) and intermediate- (IRBM) range ballistic missiles that could reach all NATO targets, and assiduously cultivated the myth of a missile gap. A fair picture of Soviet strategic power was actually available to the United States during much of this period thanks to U-2 overflights, but Eisenhower could not rebut Soviet claims without revealing these operations. Furthermore, the overflights stopped in 1960 after a U-2 was shot down and its pilot captured.[42]

Kennedy entered office in January 1961 and quickly expanded the U.S. strategic procurement program.[43] Shortly thereafter, the first generation of U.S. photographic intelligence satellites established that the missile gap had the opposite sign: the United States was comfortably ahead in deployed ICBMs. Since Khrushchev was still engaging in missile diplomacy, the administration made the true picture known in October 1961.[44] Given its 10-

to-1 advantage in intercontinental bombers, and the impending Minuteman and Polaris deployments, the United States therefore held a large and growing margin of strategic superiority that, at least as seen from Moscow, could soon pose a credible first-strike threat. While the Kremlin did not acknowledge the collapse of the missile gap, statements by Soviet spokesmen quickly became much less flamboyant.[45]

Let us now turn to Cuba. Following a protracted guerilla war, Castro took power on January 1, 1959. Relations with the United States deteriorated steadily, and diplomatic relations were severed just before Kennedy's inauguration.[46] During this same period ties between Cuba and the communist bloc grew. Soviet arms shipments began in the summer of 1960, and were accompanied by statements from Moscow supporting Havana. In April 1961 Cuban exiles, with covert and overt help from the Kennedy administration, staged a disastrous landing in the Bay of Pigs. Not only did this poorly executed and ill-conceived operation expose the government to derision at home and abroad, but it also shook its self-confidence and created distrust between the newly installed president and his military and intelligence advisors. Kennedy himself saw Cuba as his[47] "heaviest political cross."

Just 2 months after the Bay of Pigs a contentious summit was held in Vienna from which many people—including the president himself—gained the impression that Khrushchev doubted Kennedy's strength of character. In August 1961 the long-festering Berlin situation took a dramatic turn when the Berlin Wall was installed overnight to stem the exodus from East Germany,[48] a fait accompli that Kennedy was obliged to accept.

During the summer of 1962 the Soviet involvement with Cuba changed its character. A cornucopia of Soviet equipment began to arrive, although the security guarantees that Havana requested were never granted. Aside from the missiles that caused the Crisis, by October these shipments were to include enough surface-to-air missiles (SAM) for a ring of 24 bases surrounding the island, guided-missile patrol boats, 42 state-of-the-art supersonic MIGs, 42 IL-28 jet bombers that could carry nuclear or conventional bombs, about 150 tanks, antitank missiles, short-range tactical missiles,[49] and heavy construction equipment. Some 22,000 Soviet technicians and soldiers, the latter ill-disguised as civilians in quarters sporting their units' insignia, had also arrived by the time the Crisis broke.[50]

No operation of this size can remain hidden, and the administration's domestic opponents were soon demanding a response to this breach of the Monroe Doctrine, which Khrushchev had the temerity to label as "dead." The administration was exquisitely vulnerable: Not only had it bungled the Bay of Pigs operation, but Kennedy had repeatedly attacked his Republican predecessors for permitting the establishment of a Soviet military presence in Cuba during his campaign against Nixon. In September 1962 the Republicans declared that Cuba would be "the dominant issue" in the November elections.

The administration sought to deflect domestic criticism by scratching a line in the sand that it was convinced that Khrushchev would not cross, and to that end it drew a distinction between "defensive" and "offensive" capabilities in Cuba.[51] It thereby acknowledged that the Bay of Pigs had given Castro reason to fear an invasion, and that the U.S. would acquiesce to Soviet arms for repelling such an attack. On the other hand, "offensive" weapons, particularly surface-to-surface missiles, would not be countenanced. This policy was personally announced by the president on September 4:

> There is no evidence of any organized combat force in Cuba from any Soviet bloc country; of military bases supplied to Russia . . . ; of offensive ground-to-ground missiles; or of other significant offensive capability either in Cuban hands or under Soviet direction and guidance. *Were it to be otherwise, the gravest issues would arise.*[52] (Emphasis added.)

Congress quickly granted the president's request for stand-by authority to call up 150,000 reserves. The Soviet government attacked this measure as provocative, but reaffirmed its policy of not transferring nuclear weapons to another country, and explicitly mentioned Cuba in this context. Furthermore, both before and after the September 4 statement, the president privately received assurance from Khrushchev, conveyed by Soviet Ambassador Anatoly Dobrynin and other diplomats via his closest associates, Robert F. Kennedy and Theodore Sorensen, that the Soviet government would not make any trouble anywhere before the forthcoming elections.[53] Nevertheless, during a press conference on September 6, the president again warned that should Cuba "become an offensive military base for the Soviet Union, then this country will do whatever must be done to protect its own security." The new policy hardly silenced Congressional criticism, however.[54]

The Discovery of the Missiles

In the 6 weeks that followed the president's policy statement of September 4, the intelligence assessment on which it was based collapsed: The Soviets were stationing "offensive" missiles in Cuba!

On August 22 Director of Central Intelligence John McCone met with the president, Secretary of State Dean Rusk, and Secretary of Defense Robert McNamara, and told them "that the only construction I can put on the material going into Cuba is that the Russians are preparing to introduce offensive missiles."[55] His premonition was not based on any direct evidence, and the two secretaries countered with the conventional wisdom that the Soviets would not embark on so reckless a venture. Nevertheless, the next day McGeorge Bundy, Kennedy's assistant for national security affairs, issued a presidential directive[56] ordering "an analysis of the probable military, political, and psychological impact of . . . surface-to-surface missiles that could reach the U.S.," and "of the various military alternatives . . . to eliminate [such] installations in Cuba . . . ;" furthermore, since Khrushchev had castigated the United States for deploying Jupiter missiles in Turkey that the administration wanted to remove for its own reasons, Bundy also asked "what action can be taken to get Jupiter missiles out of Turkey?" This request elicited[57] "the unanimous consensus of Soviet affairs experts in the intelligence community and elsewhere in the government that the Soviets would *not* deploy missiles in Cuba."

On August 29 a U-2 brought back the first hard evidence of a SAM installation. The biweekly tempo of overflights was then stepped up, but on September 10 the Committee on Overhead Reconnaissance (COMOR) restricted these missions to the eastern half of the island to *avoid* the SAMs being installed in the west because on the other side of the globe a U-2 had been shot down over China the day before. We now know[58] that the first MRBM shipments arrived in Cuba aboard the *Omsk* and *Poltava* on September 8 and 15, respectively, and that they were destined for installation *alongside* the SAMs, as McCone had suspected.

The United States Intelligence Board, which coordinated activities of the intelligence community,[59] was convened on September 19 to consider the Cuban situation, and issued the famous[60] "September Estimate," which concluded, without dissent, that the Soviet Union would not install offensive missiles in Cuba because of the great risk of exposure and the high probability of a strong U.S. reaction. It supported this assessment by noting that the Russians had never stationed strategic nuclear weapons outside the Soviet Union, not even in Eastern Europe where they would be less provocative and much easier to defend.[61] McCone, who normally chaired the Board, was abroad; he had sent a flurry of telegrams to his deputy expressing his concerns while the Estimate was being drafted, but they were not pressed at the Board's meeting.

A report from a reliable agent[62] claiming the sighting on September 12 of the rear of a large missile in transport reached senior officials in the CIA and the Defense Intelligence Agency (DIA) on September 21. By then a DIA specialist had noted the resemblance between the unfinished SAM installation photographed by the last U-2 overflight of western Cuba on September 5, and the trapezoidal configuration of SAM launchers protecting missile bases in the Soviet Union. On October 3 the CIA certified central and western Cuba as a high-priority target for aerial reconnaissance. The following day COMOR ordered overflights of the western areas despite concerns that the loss of a U-2 would have serious repercussions.

A 10-day delay then ensued due to poor weather and a dispute between the CIA and the Defense Department as to who would conduct the operation.[63] Finally, on October 14, two planes flew the famous mission. By the following afternoon the photographs had been analyzed.[64] They showed the telltale trapezoid of SAM launchers, as well as missile transporters and erectors—the construction of a standard Soviet missile base was under way at San Cristobal! (See Figure 8.2.)

These facts were conveyed to senior officials during the evening of October 15. The president was not told since he had just returned from a campaign trip—"a quiet evening and a night of sleep was the best preparation you could have in light of what you would face in the days ahead."[66]

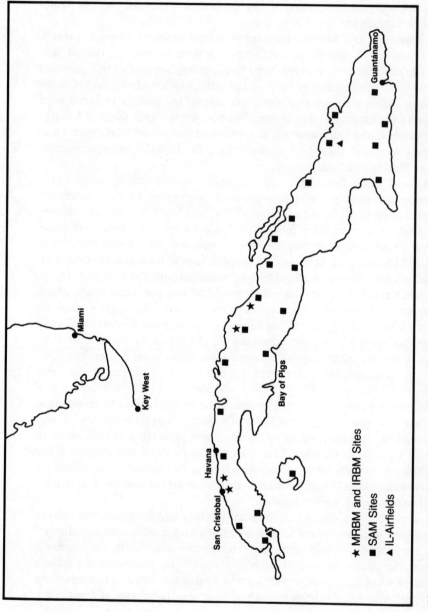

Figure 8.2. Major Soviet military installations in Cuba, including the missile site near San Cristobal discovered on October 15, 1962. The MRBMs were SS-4s with a range of approximately 1,000 nautical miles; 24 launchers with two missiles per launcher were under construction, and 42 missiles had arrived in Cuba when the quarantine was imposed. The IRBMs were to be SS-5s, with a range of 2,200 nautical miles; 16 launchers were under construction but none of the missiles ever arrived in Cuba. The airfields were bases for the IL-28 dual-capable jet bombers.[65]

The Blockade Decision

Early Tuesday morning, October 16, Bundy informed the president. A relatively small group was convened in the White House at noon: Rusk, McNamara, Bundy, McCone, JCS Chairman General Maxwell Taylor, Robert F. Kennedy, the president's "alter ego" and speech writer Theodore Sorensen, Vice President Lyndon Johnson, Charles Bohlen, and Llewellyn Thompson, who had both served as ambassadors to Moscow,[67] Deputy and Assistant Secretaries of Defense Roswell Gilpatric and Paul Nitze, Under Secretary of State George Ball, Secretary of the Treasury Douglas Dillon, and several others. This group came to be called the Executive Committee (ExComm); it did not meet formally as the National Security Council (NSC) for nearly a week. Strict secrecy measures were imposed, which turned out to be astonishingly effective. The press, virtually the whole government, and the Russians were kept in the dark, which gave the administration time to fashion a coherent response and allowed it to consider options that relied on an element of surprise.

ExComm met twice that day. White House meetings were secretly recorded during that period, and declassified transcripts of these two sessions have been published.[68] Since the themes that dominated deliberations throughout the Crisis surfaced on this first day, we shall often let the participants speak for themselves, although the unspoken thoughts so vividly recalled in their memoirs will also be drawn upon.

The first ExComm meeting began with a review of diplomatic and military options. Rusk sketched a concerted political offensive involving the Organization of American States (OAS) and NATO coupled with the most explicit warnings to Khrushchev, and a separate attempt to deal directly with Castro by convincing him that "Cuba is being victimized." McNamara described a spectrum of military alternatives from an air strike to a full-blown invasion. He emphasized that an air strike required complete certainty that the missiles were not yet operational, and that the air strike would have to be massive, and could incur as many as several thousand Cuban and Soviet casualties, to attain confidence that no hidden missiles or aircraft survived to deliver a nuclear reprisal.

General Taylor underscored the importance "of a strike with all the benefit of surprise," recommended that the air strike be accompanied by a naval blockade, and that a decision whether to invade be left for later. The question of whether such a large air strike was needed immediately arose, and recurred throughout the Crisis, but McNamara was adamant: "We don't know what kinds of communications the Soviets have with those sites. We don't know what kinds of control they have over the warheads," so "if I saw a warhead on the site and we knew that the launcher was capable of launching that warhead, . . . I would strongly urge against an air attack." He also mentioned that there might be no nuclear warheads in Cuba—that the Soviet deployment might be a bluff. At the outset, therefore, the question whether or not the missiles were equipped with nuclear warheads and were operational was viewed as a critical factor in selecting a course of action.

The drawbacks of a purely diplomatic approach were also examined: It would take a long time and sow division in the alliance. Also, "the chance of getting through this thing without a Russian reaction is greater under a quick strike than building the whole thing up to a climax." But, as Rusk remarked, the Soviets might up the ante after a strike; the latter would thus expose the allies without prior consultation.

Naturally, there was speculation concerning Soviet motives: Were their "rather defective ICBMs" being supplemented by missiles in Cuba? Would there be a proposal for some sort of trade between Cuba and Berlin? Or, McCone asked Rusk, did Khrushchev want the United States to be under the psychological pressure that NATO's Jupiter missiles in Turkey might be exerting on him? Rusk nevertheless found the action irrational unless the Soviets had "grossly misunderstood the importance of Cuba to this country."

The president's thoughts converged toward the air strike, but he wondered whether destruction of every conceivable means for delivery of nuclear weapons was necessary, and Bundy emphasized the "enormous premium" of "as small and clear-cut an action as possible." The president finished by saying that preparations for taking out the missiles should begin immediately, "because that's what we're going to do *anyway*," but he reserved judgment on a general air strike, let alone an invasion.

The evening meeting on October 16 began with a review of the alternatives by McNamara, in which the option that would finally be adopted was first raised: one that "lies in between the military . . . and the political course of action . . . a blockade against *offensive* weapons." He then warned that any direct military action could "lead to a Soviet military response of some type some place in the world," that one should try to deter such a response by alerting SAC and other units, although "these bring risks of their own."

Rusk held that there is no "such thing as a nonpolitical course of action," and that one must consider "what political preparations, if any, are to occur before . . . any military action. . . . " The president's reaction to the purely political option was that it would then impede any military move, and that Khrushchev would not respond to political pressure.

There were widely differing assessments of the strategic impact of Soviet MRBMs in Cuba. McNamara reported that the Chiefs felt the impact was substantial, whereas "my own personal view is, not at all." General Taylor disagreed: While these might be "just a few more missiles targeted on the U.S." they could "become a very important adjunct" to the Soviet's strategic capability. The president found this telling—that in the absence of a U.S. action an ongoing build-up in Cuba was a plausible and unpleasant prospect. Furthermore, Paul Nitze pointed out (see Figure 8.3) that SAC bomber bases in the South would only have several minutes warning for missiles launched from Cuba as compared to 15 minutes from the Soviet Union.[69]

Nevertheless, there was a consensus that the Soviet initiative was primarily a political and psychological, as compared to a military threat. Or, as Ken-

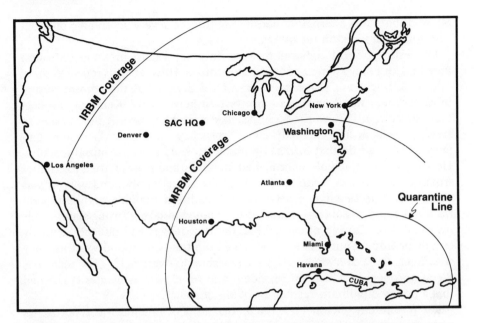

Figure 8.3. Regions of the United States reachable by various missiles based in Cuba. The smaller circle (MRBM Coverage) refers to the SS-4s that were actually deployed, whereas the larger circle refers to the SS-5s that never arrived because of the blockade imposed at the "Quarantine Line" on the morning of October 24.

nedy put it, amidst some laughter, "I should have said . . . that we don't care. But when we said we're *not* going to and then they go ahead and do it, and then we do nothing, then . . . I would think that our risks increase." The discussion thus reverted to the air strike, whose large size was justified by the observation that the missiles were mobile and could be pulled "under trees . . . and disappear almost at once," while their 20- to 40-minute countdown meant that undestroyed missiles could be fired promptly. Nevertheless, the president and Bundy continued to probe whether a small air strike would not do.

McNamara then returned to the blockade, by saying that he too didn't "think there *is* a military problem here, . . . this is a domestic, political problem" created by the president's commitment to act should Cuba acquire the capacity to attack the United States, but that did not mean "we'd go in . . . and kill them, we said we'd *act*." The act must prevent the use of the missiles, and the arrival of further offensive weapons. That would require surveillance "twenty-four hours a day from now and forever," combined with a naval blockade that would search ships and remove any offensive weapons, and that the initiative should be announced with an ultimatum stating that the missiles were under constant surveillance, and that "if there is ever any indication that they're to be launched . . . we will respond not only against Cuba, but we will respond against the Soviet Union with a full nuclear strike." He allowed that "this alternative doesn't seem to be a very acceptable one, but wait until you work on the others."

Domestic political constraints were only alluded to in these ExComm meetings, but they loomed large in many minds. Hilsman thus reflected that[70] "the U.S. might not [have been] in mortal danger but the administration most certainly was," and in a conversation between the Kennedy brothers they agreed that JFK would be impeached were he to permit the missiles to stay.[71] Indeed, at first Kennedy saw Khrushchev's move as a personal challenge: "He can't do that to *me!*" was said to have been his initial reaction. He was highly vulnerable since he had, in public and private, tried to counter what he thought was a paranoid view of the Soviet Union, and now he was being shown up as naive. Furthermore, his administration's credibility with the allies could be severely damaged if he failed to take a strong stand in his own bailiwick. On top of everything, the Bay of Pigs had put the Kennedy entourage into a double bind:[72] "Having been tried and found wanting, they were liable to be overwhelmed by the pressures to overreact." This, then, was the atmosphere in which the president and his closest associates concluded that a purely diplomatic response would not suffice.

On Wednesday, October 17, the first sighting of missiles was reported, as was other work indicating that the MRBM site construction was proceeding rapidly. The next day two more missile installations were discovered by the U-2s, whose overflights had been sharply increased.

To maintain secrecy the president stuck closely to his schedule. ExComm met through most of Wednesday while the president was on a campaign trip, and three times on Thursday. Dean Acheson and Robert Lovett, who had been secretary of defense under Truman and a senior War Department official during World War II, were asked to join the group. The blockade and air strike were calibrated against a number of political and military requirements. One faction that came to be called "the doves" placed highest priority on minimizing the likelihood that Khrushchev would respond in a theater where he held the advantage, such as Berlin or Turkey, which could lead to further escalation. Others, dubbed "the hawks" and led at the outset by Acheson, were, in General Taylor's words, convinced that[73] "we had 'em over a barrel" and "never worried much about the final outcome," but were deeply concerned that Khrushchev would engage in other adventures if the missiles were not eliminated swiftly by a coup de main. To many the blockade was enticing because it offered a half-way house between diplomacy and deadly force, and, furthermore, would put the decision of whether or not to commence shooting into Soviet hands. In addition, the blockade would exploit U.S. hegemony at sea, allow graduated increases in military pressure, and be much more likely to isolate Castro in Latin America than a military action. The blockade, however, was seen to have its own drawbacks—it took little advantage of surprise and could not stop construction of bases, nor did it get rid of the missiles already in Cuba. In short, once the blockade was announced it could acquire the shortcomings of the discarded purely diplomatic approach. The pros and cons of the air strike were just the converse—

though a fait accompli, it would kill a large number of Russians without warning, which, according to Thompson, the ExComm's highly regarded Kremlin guru, could provoke Khrushchev into a rash response. The advocates of the air strike lost ground,[74] not in the least because the Chiefs continued to insist that a surgical strike would not do. There seemed to be wider agreement on one thing: both options were dangerous and difficult.[75]

On Thursday Foreign Minister Andrei Gromyko paid a previously scheduled visit. Whether Gromyko should be told about the discovery of the missiles was considered and rejected. The government had not yet decided on its course of action, and did not want to lose the initiative.[76] Furthermore, Bundy and Sorensen had tried but failed to formulate a satisfactory private message to Khrushchev.[77] The president, therefore, simply warned Gromyko forcefully about the Soviet shipments to Cuba, and even read the operative passages from his statement of September 4. Gromyko responded with the assurances Dobrynin had already delivered.

Late Thursday the president met ExComm and came out openly in favor of the blockade. He was increasingly concerned by the danger of escalation, and had come to feel that Khrushchev needed more room for maneuver. The blockade minimized these concerns but was still a tangible act that forced Khrushchev to make the next move. That seemed to settle the matter. Nevertheless, the next morning the air strike was argued again by the Chiefs while an annoyed president delayed his departure for another campaign trip, and then in the all-day ExComm session. Robert Kennedy eventually made it clear that his brother simply would not order a large air strike as the first move. The blockade's advocates, however, had come to see that it would have to be accompanied by clear signs that further military actions would follow if U.S. demands were not met.

A considerable effort, led by Robert Kennedy, was devoted to building support for the president's decision within ExComm so that the administration could hope to maintain cohesion in the turmoil it anticipated once the decision was announced and the Soviet counter moves began to unfold. There was also an elaborate effort to document that alternative courses had been fully explored. A Saturday session was therefore devoted to detailed presentations of the two options, after which the president formally stated his decision. Because the Chiefs[78] favored the air strike and opposed the blockade, the president was briefed yet again on the air strike on Sunday, and heard the Tactical Air Command confirm that the attack would have to include many targets beyond the missile sites, and that even then the elimination of more than 90 percent of the missiles could not be guaranteed.[79] During the same meeting McCone informed the President that some 8 to 12 missiles had become operational,[80] but by this time the thought that nuclear warheads would actually be fired against the United States from Cuba had apparently been dismissed, and the precise status of the missiles no longer seemed to be a significant factor in decision making.[81]

After the president's military briefing ExComm held its first formal NSC meeting, and chose the blockade having heard the chief of naval operations explain the procedure: Each approaching ship would be signaled to stop and a boarding party would inspect it. If the ship failed to respond to orders a shot would be fired across its bow. If that failed, the ship would be disabled by a shot to the rudder or propeller. Finally, the group commented on Sorensen's latest draft of the speech that the president would deliver the next day, Monday, October 22, at 7:00 PM.

The administration went to great lengths to enhance its prospects for international support. Dean Acheson was sent to brief President deGaulle and Chancellor Adenauer about the impending action. Both gave their unqualified support, as did Prime Minister MacMillan, who had been kept abreast by his ambassador. On the evening of the speech, the State Department gave separate intelligence briefings, complete with U-2 photos, to the ambassadors of allied, Latin American, and nonaligned nations. These photos were released to the press shortly thereafter, and played an important part in the administration's effort for garnering public and diplomatic support. Finally, since a blockade is an act of war in international law, it was decided to call the measure a "quarantine,"[82] and to seek the support of the OAS, which astonished the United States on the day after Kennedy's speech by voting 19 to 0 "for the immediate dismantling and withdrawal from Cuba of all missles." This diplomatic success tended to place the U.S.–Soviet conflict in the context of collective self-defense, and provided some legal basis for the blockade, a point that the administration sought to emphasize by delaying the proclamation of the quarantine until after the OAS action.

The text of the president's speech was given to Dobrynin, and to the Kremlin, 1 hour before delivery. The Russians' behavior—in particular, that of Dobrynin—indicated that the discovery of the missiles, and the U.S. response, had caught them completely by surprise.[83] Secrecy had been maintained despite a growing awareness of what was afoot in the press and in Washington diplomatic circles.[84]

Congressional leaders were finally briefed by the president, McCone, McNamara, Rusk, and Taylor, but the administration's decision received a cold reception from them. The election was 2 weeks off. That the Republicans would find the blockade too weak had been anticipated, but the president was surprised by the reaction of the two most influential Democratic senators, Fulbright, chairman of the Foreign Relations Committee, a consistent softliner on Cuba, and Russell, the powerful chairman of the Armed Services Committee. Fulbright supported Russell's rebuff of the blockade as an ineffectual move that would merely irritate the allies. Despite explanations that the decision was the result of week-long deliberations that had painstakingly examined more forceful actions, the consensus of the Congressional leadership was that the blockade would not work and might well be more dangerous than an invasion. When the meeting ended, just 1 hour[85] before the most important speech of his life, Kennedy was in a foul mood.

The president's address spelled out the "steps to be taken immediately," and should these fail to attain the removal of the missiles he implied that further action would be taken. In addition to announcing the "quarantine on all offensive military equipment," Kennedy stated that:

> It shall be the policy of this nation to regard any nuclear missile launched from Cuba against any nation in the Western Hemisphere as an attack by the Soviet Union on the United States, requiring a full retaliatory response upon the Soviet Union.

The president ended with a

> call upon Chairman Khrushchev to halt and eliminate this clandestine, reckless, and provocative threat to world peace . . . by returning to his government's own words that it had no need to station missiles outside its own territory, . . . by refraining from any action which will widen or deepen the present crisis—and then by participating in a search for peaceful and permanent solutions.

From Face-Off to Denouement

Military preparations had begun well *before* the discovery of the missiles on October 15.[86] On October 1 Atlantic Command was ordered to be prepared for a blockade of Cuba, and on October 6 its forces assumed a higher state of readiness. Two days later a fighter squadron was deployed to Key West. These were not intended as "signals"; they were disguised as part of the large annual amphibious assault exercise PHIBRIGLEX '62 originally scheduled to begin on October 21, whose objective that year was the overthrow of a mythical republic ruled by a tyrant with the puzzling name of Ortsac. At the start of the exercise—the day before the speech—1,000 Marines were airlifted to Guantánamo. On that day SAC quietly began to increase its readiness. A portion of the quarantine fleet was put to sea before the speech, but every effort was made to maintain secrecy, to the extent that some vessels left port seriously undermanned not to raise suspicions by a hasty recall of crews. On the day of the speech the JCS issued its orders: lists of prohibited actions, rules of engagement, detailed instructions for conducting searches, and plans for the defense of Guantánamo.

The moment the government's action became public, military operations went into high gear, with many carried out in a manner that would make them apparent to the Russians. The president mobilized 150,000 reserves. Except in Europe, a worldwide rise to DEFCON 3 was ordered. On October 24 SAC assumed DEFCON 2 for the only time in its history.[87] Polaris submarines left port, the B-52 fleet began a large airborne alert, and SAC then proceeded to generate its entire spectrum of forces. Without doubt these vast operations quickly became known to Moscow, and underscored the threat to retaliate should any missile be fired from Cuba. Whether this flaunting of the strategic forces also deterred a blockade of Berlin, or a conventional military riposte there or elsewhere, has fueled unending speculation.[88] One point is undisputed: there was never a hint that Soviet strategic forces had been put on alert.

The day after the speech the president signed the proclamation imposing the quarantine, which was to take effect the following morning, October 24, at 10 AM EDT. At that time some two dozen Soviet ships were known to be en route to Cuba. The Kremlin had already replied to Kennedy's speech, calling the quarantine "piracy" that would not be respected, but announced no concrete response.

The quarantine was imposed with a massive display of force: destroyers, patrol boats, antisubmarine warfare units, naval aviation, and units involved in PHILBRIGLEX '62, including an amphibious force of 40,000 Marines. A military encounter with the Soviet Union appeared to be imminent when the quarantine took effect, as we learn from Robert Kennedy's recollections:[89]

It was now a few minutes after 10:00 o'clock [the commencement of the quarantine]. Secretary McNamara reported that two Russian ships . . . were within a few miles of our quarantine barrier. . . . the expectation was that at least one of the vessels would be stopped and boarded between 10:30 and 11:00 o'clock.

Then came the disturbing Navy report that a Russian submarine had moved into position between the two ships. . . . The carrier *Essex* was to signal the submarine by sonar to surface and identify itself. If it refused, said Secretary McNamara, depth charges with a small explosive would be used until the submarine surfaced.

I think these few minutes were the time of gravest concern for the President. Was the world on the brink of a nuclear holocaust? Was it our error? A mistake? Was there something further that should have been done? Or not done? His hand went up to his face and covered his mouth. His face seemed drawn, his eyes pained, almost grey. We stared at each other across the table.

. . . The voices droned on, but I didn't seem to hear anything until I heard the President say: "Isn't there some way we can avoid having our first exchange with a Russian submarine—almost anything but that?" "No, there's too much danger to our ships. There is no alternative," said McNamara. "Our commanders have been instructed to avoid hostilities, if at all possible, but this is what we must be prepared for, and this is what we must expect."

We had come to the final decision . . . I felt we were on the edge of the precipice with no way off. . . . One thousand miles away in the vast expanse of the Atlantic Ocean the final decisions were going to be made in the next few minutes. President Kennedy had initiated the course of events, but he no longer had control over them. He would have to wait, we would have to wait. The minutes in the Cabinet Room ticked slowly by. What could we say now—what could we do?

The first hint that the Russians would not breach the quarantine came shortly after this traumatic moment, at 10:25. Naval aviation reported that five Soviet ships with large hatches had changed course, while all other suspect ships heading for the proscribed zone (see Figure 8.3) had stopped dead in the water.[90] The navy warned, however, that they might merely be waiting to be escorted by Soviet submarines. ExComm decided then and there that the navy be instructed not to intercept any vessel without explicit orders from the president, and that direct contact be made with the *Essex* "not to do anything."

The controversial craft of micromanagement, which this same administration had introduced in the previous year's Berlin Crisis,[91] and that would become endemic in Vietnam, thus swung into operation. The president had acquired every incentive not to find himself again "on the edge of the precipice" without control over events he had initiated. Not only did he and his civilian advisers thereafter ponder which ship would get precisely what treatment, but they exploited modern technology to circumvent the military chain of command by speaking directly with skippers in the quarantine operation. Naturally, this unprecedented[92] intrusion into the domain of the professional military was not warmly received.[93] Matters boiled to a head that evening when McNamara visited Flag Plot, the navy's command center in the Pentagon, and had his famous altercation with the chief of naval operations, which established that no action was to be taken—in particular, no firing on any ship—without an explicit presidential order.[94]

As the week progressed it became clearer that the Soviets would accommodate themselves to the quarantine. Following lengthy deliberation, JFK decided that the Russians should be given a bit more time, so the *Bucharest,* a Soviet tanker, and therefore not a likely carrier of "offensive weapons," was allowed to pass through the quarantine line after simply identifying itself.[95] At 7:50 AM on Friday the *Marcula,* a Lebanese freighter under charter to the Soviet Union, was boarded and searched, following which it was allowed to proceed.

In retrospect Friday, October 26, was the turning point, although that was not to be known until Sunday. For some time apprehension had been growing that the blockade critics were being vindicated. Already at the ExComm meeting[96] that morning the president had said "we will get the Soviet strategic missiles out of Cuba only by invading Cuba or by trading. [I doubt] that the quarantine alone would produce a withdrawal of the weapons." Pressure for action mounted, and it was agreed that a military initiative could not be delayed by more than several days. The State Department was ordered to participate in planning for an invasion, and for the replacement of the Castro government.[97] But at midday a possible breakthrough began to unfold.[98] Aleksander Fomin, known to be the senior Soviet intelligence official in the United States, asked ABC correspondent John Scali to quickly explore how his excellent contacts would respond to a Soviet offer to dismantle and remove all offensive weapons from Cuba under UN supervision in return for an American pledge not to invade. Scali went directly to Hilsman and Rusk, who cleared a response with the White House to the effect that the proposal had "real possibilities" but "that time is very urgent." Scali immediately conveyed this to Fomin with the assurance that it had come "from the highest sources."

At 6 PM Khrushchev's famous "secret" letter, which has never been officially released in toto, began to come in over the teletype.[99] It was long, rambling and emotionally charged—clearly not the output of any bureaucracy, let alone the Kremlin's. Some have called the letter the "nightmare outcry of a frightened man."[100] To us it reads more like the unedited thoughts of an unusually imaginative politician, keenly aware of the gravity of his predicament, and searching for a face-saving escape. Insofar as policy is concerned, the letter contained Fomin's proposal buried twice among long passages describing Khrushchev's experiences in two wars, the dangers of nuclear war, Khrushchev's intent to only defend Cuba, etc., etc. The final passage is surely one of the most memorable utterances of our precarious age:

If you have not lost your self-control, and sensibly conceive what this might lead to, then, Mr. President, we and you ought not to pull on the ends of the rope in which you have tied the knot of war, because the more the two of us pull, the tighter the knot will be tied. And a moment may come when the knot will be tied so tight that not even he who tied it will have the strength to untie it, and then it will be necessary to cut that knot, and what that would mean is not for me to explain to you, for you yourself understand perfectly of what terrible forces our countries dispose. Consequently, if there is no intention to tighten that knot, and thereby to doom the world to the catastrophe of thermonuclear war, then let us not only relax the forces pulling on the ends of the rope, let us take measures to untie that knot. We are ready for this.

The State Department spent the night analyzing this letter, and no booby traps having been found, a resolution appeared to be in sight when ExComm convened next morning at 10 AM. But those hopes evaporated within 15 minutes because Moscow radio then began to broadcast a letter from Khrushchev to Kennedy of quite different substance and tone. It attached a crucial string that the administration had feared from the beginning:[101] The United States would have to remove its Jupiter missiles in Turkey, in addition to the pledge not to invade Cuba, as the price for the removal of the missiles in Cuba. Furthermore, it did not have Khrushchev's unmistakable personal stamp. Had Khrushchev raised the ante? Or had his earlier proposal been rescinded by the Politburo? Had he been overruled? For the first time Thompson was unsure of his reading of Soviet actions. This was to be the one of several events that, in the memory of most participants, made Saturday, October 27, the most harrowing day of the Crisis.[102]

Recent revelations have clarified the deliberations and decisions of Black Saturday. The ExComm minutes for that day,[103] released in 1985, already demonstrated that Kennedy tenaciously considered acceptance of the terms of Khrushchev's *second* letter, whereas the participants' memoirs and the "oral tradition" would have it that he would not countenance such a missile swap.[104] Furthermore, the verbatim (declassified) transcript has now appeared,[105] and it contains important nuances of substance and tone not captured by the minutes. Finally, Dean Rusk has disclosed that there is little reason to doubt that Kennedy was prepared to openly trade the Jupiter missiles despite the severe damage to himself and to the political position of the United States that such a resolution would have entailed. Taken together, this new data has altered our picture of the crisis as it reached its climax. Indeed, it should give us pause that an episode of such historical significance should still be susceptible to significant "revisionism" despite a quarter century of scrutiny, analysis, and reminiscences by an army of journalists, scholars, and key participants.

During the morning of Black Saturday several developments raised the suspicion that Khrushchev's second letter was part of a coordinated plan to increase pressure for a settlement more favorable to the Soviet Union, or, worse still, to create a breathing space while the Soviets prepared a military move. At the outset of the morning's ExComm meeting McCone reported that the construction of the missile sites was now proceeding around the clock, including work on storage bunkers for nuclear warheads,[106] and, more significantly, that low-level reconnaissance was coming under antiaircraft fire while SAM bases had become operational. Robert Kennedy was then informed of FBI reports that the Soviet UN mission was preparing to burn documents, a standard precaution in anticipation of war.[107]

The president, noting that Khrushchev's second letter was public whereas the first was private, was quick to see that [108] "if this [second letter] becomes his proposal . . . we're going to be in an insupportable position . . . In the first place, we last year tried to get these missiles out of there because they're not militarily useful,[109] Number 1. Number 2, it's going to—to any man in the UN or any other rational man—look like a very fair trade." Furthermore, he was concerned that if he rebuffed the trade he might quickly find himself with no option other than an attack on Cuba, which would then give Khrushchev almost a[110] "blank check to take action against Berlin on the grounds that we were wholly unreasonable." He argued that NATO as a whole, and Turkey in particular, should be made aware of the peril it would be in were the United States to attack Cuba, and that consultations should be used to induce the NATO allies to take an accommodating stance. Although he agreed that "we're not in a position today to make a trade—maybe in three or four days, I don't know, we have to wait what the Turks say,"[111] he proposed that in the interim the *sole* precondition for further negotiations should be that missile construction in Cuba must stop forthwith.

His advisors were of a different mind. The simultaneous removal of missiles in Turkey and Cuba would not only be a humiliating retreat from the president's speech of 5 days before and from his earlier pronouncements, but it would also cast a shadow over NATO since the allies, who were living within range of Soviet missiles, could hardly be expected to maintain confidence in U.S. commitments were the president to withdraw missiles that supposedly protected them as a quid pro quo for the removal of missiles that threatened America. Bundy therefore spoke for the government's foreign policy establishment when he said[112] "Mr. President . . . to our NATO people and to all the people who are tied to us by alliance, we are in *real* trouble . . . I think we should tell you that that's the universal assessment of everyone in the government that's connected with these alliance problems." Kennedy, the professional politician, had a more cynical view:[113]

> I'm just thinking . . . what we're going to have to do in a day or so, which is [an air attack] and possibly an invasion, all because we wouldn't take the missiles out of Turkey, and we all know how quickly everyone's courage goes when the blood starts to flow . . . and they grab Berlin, and everybody's going to say, "Well, that was a pretty good proposition." Let's not kid ourselves . . . Today it sounds great to reject it, but it's not going to, after we do something . . . if we take no action or if we take action—they're all going to be saying we should have done the reverse—

Various maneuvers that might induce the Turks to "offer" to remove the missiles were discussed, but came to naught when the Turks issued a press statement rejecting Khrushchev's proposal while ExComm was meeting.[114]

Amid the discussion as to how the second Khrushchev letter should be dealt with, a number of ExComm members evolved the idea that it should not be rejected, but ignored: Khrushchev's preferable offer—to remove the missiles in return for a pledge not to invade—buried ambiguously[115] in the *secret* letter should be accepted as if the *public* letter did not exist! This came to be called the Trollope Ploy for the Victorian novelist whose heroines were prone to interpret compliments as marriage proposals. It's lead exponent, Thompson, thought that the second letter might be[116] "just pressure on us . . . [and that] the important thing for Khrushchev, it seems to me, is to be able to say "I saved Cuba, I stopped the invasion," and that he can get *away* with this, if he wants to." Although Kennedy continued to worry that even a tacit rejection of Khrushchev's second offer might mark the end of negotiations, he eventually agreed that a message responding only to the first letter should be formulated.

During the afternoon session Taylor, in the knowledge that forces could not be kept at peak readiness indefinitely and that antiaircraft fire would soon restrict U.S. reconnaissance, argued that further delay should be avoided, and presented the position of the Chiefs:[117]

> That the big strike—OP Plan 3-12—be executed no later than Monday morning the 29th unless there is irrefutable evidence in the meantime that offensive weapons are being dismantled . . . [and that its] execution be part of the execution of 3-16, the Invasion Plan [deleted] days later.

The only reaction to this formal recommendation that appears in the transcript is: "(Pause.) RFK: "That was a surprise. (Laughter.)." Indeed, reconnaissance over Cuba was the only military issue considered in depth by

ExComm. It had previously been decided that should a U-2 plane be downed the SAM site responsible would be attacked, and that the second such incident would make it necessary to attack all sites.[118] McNamara recommended that[119] "if our reconnaissance planes are fired on [tomorrow], we will attack the attackers," and Taylor backed that by noting that "to be ready to invade Monday, we must continue intensive air surveillance." But Kennedy would not go along: "The President directed that our air reconnaissance missions be flown tomorrow without fighter escort . . . We will decide tomorrow how we return fire after we know if they continue their attacks."

The question of reconnaissance took an ominous turn when it was learned that a U-2 had been shot down that morning and the pilot killed.[120] Lyndon Johnson pointed out that it was essential to know who was responsible[121]— "you could have an undisciplined Cuban antiaircraft outfit, but to have a SAM-site and a Russian crew fire is not any accident." Although no definitive answer was forthcoming, it seemed to be accepted that this was a purposeful Soviet action.[122]

While the president was absent, McNamara urged examination of what might be in store should a settlement not be reached quickly:[129]

> We're going to send surveillance aircraft in tomorrow. Those are going to be fired on without question . . . we're going to lose airplanes . . . so we must be prepared to attack Cuba—quickly . . . with an all-out [air] attack . . . and I personally believe that this is almost certain to lead to an invasion . . . the Soviets *may,* and I think probably will, attack the Turkish missiles . . . the minimum military response by NATO . . . would be with conventional weapons . . . against Soviet warships and/or naval bases in the Black Sea area. Now that to me is the absolute minimum, and I would say that it is *damned dangerous* to do . . . I'm not sure we can avoid anything like that if we attack Cuba.

That war might be so close provoked outspoken reactions. To Lyndon Johnson, it was absurd to risk calamity by rejecting what he saw as a bargain:[124] "what we were afraid of was that he'd never offer this [missile trade], but what he'd want to do was trade *Berlin.*" McCone, supposedly the staunchest of hawks, said he would[125] "trade those Turkish things out right now. I wouldn't even talk to anybody [i.e., NATO] about it." After Kennedy returned, the meeting ended with the agreement that the Trollope Ploy would be played immediately in a letter to Khrushchev.

ExComm reconvened again at 9 PM. Taylor reported that the Chiefs had reexamined the surveillance problem and that they could do without low-level overflights for one day. The president did not accept McNamara's recommendation[126] "that if our planes are fired on tomorrow, we ought to fire back," and reaffirmed that "if tomorrow they fire at us, and we don't have an answer from the Russians" to the U.S. acceptance of the terms of Khrushchev's first letter, we can "then go in [on Monday] and take all the SAM-sites out."

This sketch is no substitute for the actual transcript. At first sight, chaos seems to reign: many topics are discussed simultaneously amid telephone calls to and from Kennedy; people leave to write statements and messages, and return to read drafts and to report the latest intelligence; presidential decisions do not spring forth with pristine clarity, as in the ExComm minutes. Thus, whether and precisely how to bring an ill-formed U.S. position to NATO was considered all day and continually postponed. According to legend, the afternoon of Black Saturday saw a struggle between hawks and doves, and growing support for military action. Neither theme, however, is in evidence in the transcript,[127] while the transcriber of the tapes, McGeorge Bundy, reports that[128] "I heard no voice raised in anger and no rancorous exchange." On reflection, however, the image we gain is that of a group struggling through a swirling fog of hazardous ambiguities, led by a man who cannot see through them either, but who is determined to postpone any step that might lead to combat while he is searching for a termination of the confrontation before military imperatives gain the upper hand.

The crucial maneuver of the day took place between the afternoon and evening ExComm meetings when Robert Kennedy met privately with Dobrynin. In addition to transmitting the president's letter guaranteeing that Cuba would not be invaded if Soviet offensive weapons were removed forthwith, RFK made two other crucial points to the Ambassador.[129] First, when Dobrynin raised the issue of the missiles in Turkey, RFK said that there could be no quid pro quo "under this kind of threat," but that "it was our judgement that, within a short time after the Crisis was over, those missiles would be gone."[130] And second, although claiming not to be issuing "an ultimatum but a statement of fact. He should understand that if they did not remove those bases, we would remove them," his parting assertion was that "time was running out. We had only a few more hours—we needed an answer immediately from the Soviet Union. I said we must have it the next day". To the ambassador, this must have been indistinguishable from an ultimatum.

The next morning at 10 AM Washington time, Sunday, October 28, Khrushchev's reply was delivered to the embassy in Moscow, and broadcast shortly thereafter: "the Soviet Government . . . has given a new order to dismantle the arms which you describe as offensive, and to crate and return them to the Soviet Union . . . I regard with respect and trust the statement that you made . . . that there would be no attack, no invasion of Cuba." By noon Kennedy's acceptance of Khrushchev's offer[131] was broadcast, and released to the press with Rusk's off-the-record admonition "we don't want the word 'capitulation' used or any gloating." As for the Soviets, they[132] "moved promptly to begin dismantling the missile facilities, without even waiting for a response from Kennedy confirming agreement."

The Trollope Ploy had worked. What was not known until very recently is that it was probably a bluff—that President Kennedy was predisposed to find some way to accept the terms of Khrushchev's second letter had the "ultimatum" transmitted by Robert Kennedy been rejected. For in February 1987

Dean Rusk revealed that after ExComm disbanded on Saturday evening, President Kennedy

> instructed me to telephone the late Andrew Cordier, [a former senior UN official] then at Columbia University, and dictate to him a statement which would be made by U Thant, the Secretary General of the United Nations, proposing the removal of both the Jupiters and the missiles in Cuba. Mr. Cordier was to put that statement in the hands of U Thant only after a further signal from us. That step was never taken and the statement I furnished to Mr. Cordier has never seen the light of day. So far as I know, President Kennedy, Andrew Cordier, and I were the only ones who knew of this particular step.[133]

The View from Moscow

In comparison to the information available regarding the U.S. government's activities, we still know very little about those of the Soviet Union. Nevertheless, a tentative sketch can now be drawn.

Garthoff's new study[134] presents what an acute observer can discern from the public record and from private sources. His analysis has been complemented, and largely confirmed, by the October 1987 Cambridge Conference[135] in which, for the first time, ExComm members and U.S. scholars were able to discuss the Cuban Crisis with Soviet "eyewitnesses": Fedor Burlatsky, one of Khrushchev's principal speech writers at the time; and Sergei Mikoyan, a diplomat, an intimate of the Khrushchev family, and the son of Anastas Mikoyan, one of the most powerful members of Khrushchev's politburo, who accompanied his father to Cuba in connection with the Crisis.[136] It should be noted, however, that these two men were not at a level comparable to that of ExComm, that there are large gaps in their knowledge that cannot be ascribed to discretion, and that they disagree on a number of essential points of judgment, although not of fact. But above all, we have no documentary Soviet evidence, and we have just seen that such evidence has substantially altered our picture of what happened on the U.S. side despite many accounts by the president's closest intimates.

The first question, of course, is what motivated the Soviets and how was their decision reached? Two desires were dominant: to counter U.S. strategic superiority and to deter the U.S. from acting against Castro. Burlatsky and Mikoyan disagree strongly, however, as to which was uppermost in Khrushchev's mind, and that is what was important because the notion of sending missiles to Cuba was apparently Khrushchev's and he dominated decision making at the time.

The desire to escape from strategic inferiority had both a psychological and a military dimension. That U.S. Jupiters were deployed just across the Black Sea from Khrushchev's summer retreat while the United States was virtually a sanctuary angered him. The preceding spring he had voiced such sentiments in public, and then in private to the new U.S. ambassador on the very day that Kennedy learned of the Cuban deployment.[137] Furthermore, the administration's public revelation that the "missile gap" was large but in its favor was seen in Moscow as an attempt at coercion that it had to counter. Khrushchev, however, did not think that the numerical imbalance mattered—he felt that the capability to deliver some weapons is what counted. Hence even a small deployment that could strike into the United States was seen as politically significant.

As for Cuba, it seems that Soviet leaders did not see the Bay of Pigs as a sign that Kennedy would be afraid to act; on the contrary, they assumed that to erase the humiliation he would invade Cuba to liquidate Castro's regime. We now know that the United States never made any decision to invade Cuba, even contingently, during the Crisis.[138] Such Soviet perceptions were hardly paranoid, however. The United States had mounted extensive covert activities[139] and sizeable readiness operations by the Tactical Air Command against Cuba,[140] both of which predated the Crisis, and were surely known to Soviet intelligence.

Khrushchev apparently thought that missiles in Cuba would solve both problems: as a first cheap step toward psychostrategic parity, with merchant ships turning off-the-shelf MRBMs into ICBMs; and as a deterrent against a humiliating U.S. defeat of his ally Fidel Castro. It is true that this "explanation" does not withstand logical analysis. First, if the United States wanted to remove Castro, why offer it such a wonderful pretext? Second, if the

Figure 8.4. Targets in the Soviet Union and Eastern Europe covered by Jupiter missiles deployed in Turkey.

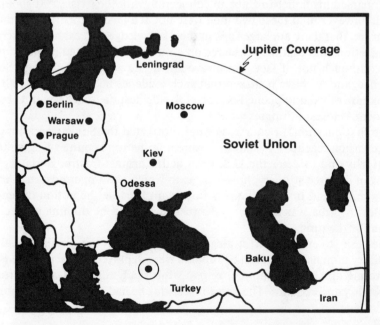

roughly 17-to-1 U.S. advantage in deliverable warheads had created an understandable Soviet fear of a U.S. first strike,[141] why make the move most likely to provoke such a strike? But, we are told by those who knew him, and as is already clear from many events and his own memoirs,[142] Khrushchev did not explore the likely consequences of his actions systematically, and he often allowed his emotions to reign.

How did he gain support for his scheme? Contrary to some Western speculations, Khrushchev was at the peak of his power in the period preceding his Cuban misadventure; he could not be challenged directly in the Politburo. Those in the Politburo who believed the operation would fail—Mikoyan in particular—assumed that Castro and the military would refuse to go along. Unfortunately, they had not only misjudged Castro's willingness to take risks, but also the competence of the military mission dispatched to Cuba to explore the feasibility of the plan. Once Castro and the military mission had approved Khrushchev's plan, the opposition had to swallow its misgivings.

Kennedy's speech clearly caught Moscow by surprise—there was no response whatsoever for more than half a day. There was no contingency plan for coping with the blockade even though Khrushchev was aware that the United States might take precisely that action.[143] Tension mounted to the point where Khrushchev slept in his office fully clothed so that he would not be "caught literally with his pants down"; he and his colleagues also attended the opera to reassure their compatriots and to "disguise our own anxiety, which was intense."[144]

The Soviet government apparently decided that it would avert escalation no matter what happened in Cuba, and according to Garthoff's sources, the Politburo formally recorded a vote to that effect.[145] Although Khrushchev's second letter—the proposal of a missile trade—was probably written in the Foreign Ministry, there is no evidence that it represented a "palace revolt," but rather an attempt to get better terms, triggered, perhaps, by a Walter Lippmann column on October 25 that had made the same proposal and was misread by Moscow as a Kennedy trial balloon.[146] Robert Kennedy's statements to Dobrynin on Saturday evening were perceived by the Kremlin as an unambiguous ultimatum.[147] The response accepting a pledge not to invade Cuba as the quid pro quo for the removal of the "weapons you describe as offensive" was formulated in great haste under Khrushchev's personal supervision and immediately broadcast to assure that it would be known to Washington when ExComm convened on Sunday morning since fear of a U.S. military action was running very high.

Assuming that the Soviet government had really decided not to respond to an attack on Cuba, it can never be settled whether it would have adhered to that policy—witness the U.S. reversal of its firm decision not to defend Korea. Soviet opinions regarding this question are divided,[148] with some convinced that Khrushchev could not have avoided a military reaction if American forces had killed Russians in Cuba. What we do know is that Khrushchev faced internal problems immediately after the crisis, and suffered an irreversible loss of power even though there were no Russian casualties.[149]

Postmortem

The Missile Crisis has been scrutinized repeatedly by the Kennedy administration,[150] the Congress, some of the leading participants, and by a host of journalists and scholars.[151] While there has been criticism of certain operations and decisions, and especially of some of the U.S. government's underlying assumptions, the handling of the Crisis by the Kennedy administration has generally received warm reviews. These have produced a rather widespread acceptance of the notion that crisis "management" is a politicomilitary art that governments can learn to master. Our postmortem argues that this is an unwarranted and dangerous inference.

U.S. Intelligence: "Tactical" Warning. What could have been the earliest date for obtaining *hard* evidence that missiles had *arrived* in Cuba? This question has a fairly straightforward answer: Perhaps a week after the arrival of the *Omsk,* or in mid-September, some *4* weeks before the actual discovery.[152] Such prompt apprehension would have required hard evidence that the Soviets were installing missiles in Cuba, however, and also no turf contests between the Defense Department and the CIA. Evidence, not mere suspicion, was needed because in all eyes but McCone's the notion that missiles were about to be installed flew in the face of common sense: The Soviets had never based such missiles on foreign soil, let alone in the jaws of overwhelming U.S. conventional forces. Furthermore, as we saw, in September Khrushchev had sent assurances through Dobrynin to Robert Kennedy and Sorensen: in these conversations Dobrynin was explicitly warned not to introduce surface-to-surface missiles. But even if the administration had harbored rather stronger suspicions by mid-September, it would have taken some degree of recklessness to conduct U-2 missions over Cuban airspace protected by SAMs, since the loss of a plane might well have raised a storm that would have shut off this irreplaceable source of intelligence.[153]

Nevertheless, one "superficial" criticism regarding intelligence has merit. Apparently McCone's suspicion was not based on any direct evidence,[154] but on a shrewd hunch. As his deputy explained,[155] McCone could not understand why the Soviets would go to the trouble of installing SAMs where there was nothing valuable for them to protect, "which led him *then* to the belief that they *must* be coming in with MRBMs." It seems that McCone's ingenious speculation was not translated into directives that sought to extract supporting data from the intelligence colossus.[156] Indeed, the postmortems revealed that the *Omsk* and *Poltava,* which had uncommonly large hatches, had been observed to be riding unusually high in the water, and intelligence specialists had noted that they must have carried "space-consuming" cargoes.[157] Had this *hint* been available at the appropriate level, been *judged* as ominous, *and* been corroborated by more direct evidence, as much as a month might have been saved, and eased the time-pressure in the ensuing crisis. On the other hand, the actual discovery could easily have come later than it did.[158] The identification of the SAM configuration with bases in the Soviet Union was not straightforward—the officer who did this was subsequently decorated.

U.S. Intelligence: Soviet Intentions. With the benefit of hindsight a deeper criticism can be lodged: whether the September Estimate had given enough thought to how things looked to a man standing in the Kremlin, particularly to the fact that *that* man was Nikita Khrushchev. Intelligence, it has been argued, should have been more sensitive to the possibility that Khrushchev would recognize that the ambiguous distinction between "defensive" and "offensive" weapons was, to a large degree, a ploy for coping with domestic critics, and that he would therefore read Kennedy's warnings as meant for domestic consumption—that the United States would somehow accommodate itself to a fait accompli. Several observations have been made in support of this charge: The president's handling of the Bay of Pigs could be taken by the Kremlin as a sign that JFK would not use armed force; the administration's emphasis on missiles appeared to be artificial since it indicated that nuclear-capable aircraft would be countenanced;[159] it had also made the disingenuous claim that it had no evidence of Soviet military units in Cuba; and in Khrushchev's private reassurances there had been an unseemly emphasis on causing the president no trouble *while* the election campaign was in progress. From such considerations one might have concluded that the missile deployment was not implausible because Khrushchev would assess the worst possible outcome to be what actually transpired, which he might have deemed as an acceptable risk in view of the payoff should he have won his gamble.

We are not persuaded that in the real world this is a compelling criticism of U.S. intelligence. It is a tall order to discern the intentions of a leader who is unable to estimate risks in his own backyard, for Khrushchev had apparently not recognized that a failed Cuba adventure could contribute to his political demise, nor did he seem to realize that his position was in jeopardy at the time of his downfall.[160] While everything should be done to learn from the experience of Cuba, it would be imprudent to base policy on an expectation of better—or indeed, equally good—overall performance by the nation's intelligence services.

Soviet Intelligence. However one views the U.S. intelligence effort, Soviet intelligence suffered from much more serious failures. The behavior of the Kremlin, the UN mission, and of Dobrynin demonstrate that they received no warning that something big was afoot before the October 22 speech. Soviet intelligence therefore, did not do as well as leading journalists, nor as well as the British Embassy, despite a spate of telltale signs: windows lit at all hours in the Pentagon, an epidemic of broken appointments, rows of official limousines constantly parked outside the State Department, etc. It is unlikely that all this went unnoticed. It has long been suspected,[161] and now confirmed,[162] that the Cuban adventure was a closely kept secret known only to a very small high-level group that did not include Dobrynin.[163]

Turning to political assessment, Soviet intelligence apparently had not recognized the impact that acquiescence to the unveiling of Soviet nuclear-armed missiles in Cuba would have had on the American body politic, and thus on the administration—assuming, that is, that intelligence was consulted before Khrushchev made his decision. Furthermore, those most likely to correctly interpret these implications of the Soviet plan were in the Washington embassy, and were not privy to it.

Military Operations. Two weeks before the discovery of the missiles McNamara and the JCS met to consider plans for a blockade, for the removal of offensive weapons from Cuba, and even for the removal of the Castro regime itself.[164] The air strike described in the first ExComm sessions was the one envisaged in these plans, and as we saw, the air force adhered to the necessity for the large strike throughout the first week when the decision for a blockade was being formed. In the second week further analysis led to a reappraisal: the Soviet missiles were mobile, but it would take days and not hours to move them, so a smaller "surgical" strike would have sufficed. Indeed, air strike advocates subsequently complained that they had been obliged to go along with the quarantine because of the air force's refusal to abandon the large strike. But when an air strike finally became an imminent prospect on September 27 the newly operational SAMs were hindering reconnaissance; in McNamara's view[165] that had "made a limited air strike . . . impossible."

Turning from contingency plans to operations,[166] the navy's planes flew 30,000 flight hours in imposing the quarantine, while the 90 ships directly involved steamed a total of 780,000 miles. SAC moved to DEFCON 2 by placing one-eighth of its B-52 force on continuous airborne alert within 36 hours, with some 50 planes carrying more than 180 nuclear bombs in position for execution of an attack, battle staffs on round-the-clock alert duty, 183 B-47s dispersed to 33 civilian and military airfields, and 136 liquid-fueled ICBMs at a heightened state of readiness. During the course of the alert SAC flew some 50,000 flight hours in 2,000 B-52 and tanker sorties. There was no major accident during this vast naval and air operation.

As we have seen, submarines were a serious concern. Even before the quarantine went into effect an unexpected movement of Soviet submarines toward the Caribbean had been detected. Antisubmarine warfare activities were then pursued with great vigor and efficacy: At least five of the six Soviet submarines in the area were located, forced to surface, and kept under surveillance.

Soviet operations before and during the Crisis were very complex and ambitious. Not only was a massive array of equipment shipped to Cuba, but the installation of the SAM and MRBM bases proceeded at a pace that astonished and impressed U.S. experts. On the other hand, many features of these operations were puzzling.[167] For example, while great pains were taken to hide the missile shipments, no attempt to hide the construction work was made before Kennedy's speech, yet camouflaging began after the whole world knew. At the height of the Crisis IL-28 trainers were being assembled, but combat IL-28 bombers were left in crates. Construction work on MRBMs *and* IRBMs proceeded simultaneously until the bitter end, even though not one IRBM ever arrived in Cuba!

What is one to make of this? Allison[168] offered the explanation that this behavior is characteristic of an assembly of organizations adhering to their standard operating procedures: military intelligence (GRU) was in charge of shipments, from whence came the meticulous attention to secrecy;[169] the Strategic Rocket Forces were responsible for constructing the bases, which they did with the plans and procedures perfected back home, where there was no need for camouflage; the air force followed its normal practice of first assembling trainers when foreign pilots would have to be trained; and so on. Allison observed that the SAMs should logically have been installed first to impede aerial reconnaissance, and that the subsequent construction of the missile bases should have been done at night and covered by camouflage during the day. He concluded that the Soviet behavior pattern is characteristic of a closely guarded decision made at the highest levels, and then implemented by the separate portions of the Soviet military machine executing their orders as they would any operation, whereas what was required would have crossed entrenched boundaries between bureaucracies. The recent revelations confirm this interpretation:[170] The Soviet units had no inkling where they were going—they brought all their standard equipment, including skis!

It should be recognized, however, that speed was indispensible; this required the large organizations necessary for the mission to follow well-practiced routines. Had the operation been "logically" planned ab initio, it would have taken considerably longer and been more prone to foul-up. The probability of evading detection in a nation infested by American agents would then have been nil.

Thus, we are left with the disturbing conclusion that what the Soviet Union attempted in Cuba was not only risky because of its likely repercussions, but also relied on an operation that stood little chance of achieving its mission— the clandestine installation of six dozen missiles as tall as a six-story building figuratively within view of U.S. soil.

Control by Central Authorities. To what degree were operations understood and controlled by the White House and the Kremlin?

We recall that considerable friction between the civilians and the military arose in the implementation of the quarantine. Nevertheless, there is little if any evidence that the president's quarantine orders were not followed, and it is clear that these operations were well understood in ExComm. The antisubmarine (ASW) operations that accompanied the quarantine have been the subject of controversy, however, with some claiming that the navy had exceeded its authority.[171] There is no clear evidence for this. It appears, however, that ExComm did not fully comprehend the implications of the orders it had approved since they authorized the undersea equivalent of "the shot across the bow" without the case-by-case approval from Washington required for interception of surface vessels. Perhaps no one outside the navy appreciated the speed and thoroughness with which ASW operations would proceed. In any event, it was a likely consequence of the rules of engagement that the first military contact with the Soviet Union[172] could well have been with a submarine, and that the president would not have known it was happening.

The only known and major unauthorized action by the United States has been revealed recently: the order to assume DEFCON 2 was issued unencoded ("in the clear") to SAC by its commander, General Thomas Powers. This purposely provocative breach of a standard procedure was not known to Defense Secretary McNamara and other ExComm veterans.[173]

The only unambiguous example of an inadvertent U.S. military action that could have had serious consequences occurred on Black Saturday when a U-2 on a reconnaissance mission from Alaska lost its bearings and overflew the Soviet Union.[174] Soviet fighters scrambled to intercept the U-2, whose pilot radioed for help in the clear, and U.S. fighters in Alaska flew to its assistance, but nothing untoward happened. It appears that while very close attention was paid to U-2 flights over Cuba, reconnaissance elsewhere followed standard operating procedures, as did the fighters that rushed to the straying U-2's aid, even though that could have triggered a skirmish at the very tensest moment.[175] There were also potentially provocative intelligence missions in and near Cuba that were not fully monitored by central authorities, although in one instance the president ordered an intelligence vessel (like the famous *Liberty*) to put more distance between itself and Cuba.[176]

Surprisingly there was also what could be called an inadvertent loss of diplomatic control: unknown to the White House, the key to the Jupiters were handed over to the Turkish authorities in a ceremony on October 22, the day of Kennedy's quarantine speech.[177] As a further coincidence, the quarantine just prevented the *Poltava* from reaching Cuba, and it is possible that this was the ship that carried the first nuclear warheads to Cuba. As Garthoff observes,[178] the timing of Kennedy's speech may therefore have appeared as far more threatening to Moscow than Washington could have perceived.

The Kremlin, however, suffered the most serious instance of loss of control over forces—the shoot down of the U-2. As we saw, this was interpreted in Washington as ominous. It is now established[179] that the Cubans had control over conventional antiaircraft batteries and were responsible for the fire against low-altitude reconnaissance on October 27. The SAMs, on the other hand, were in Soviet hands, and the destruction of the U-2 that day was an unauthorized act, perhaps due to ambiguous rules of engagement or faulty communications.

We have no other evidence regarding any loss of central control by Soviet authorities. As we have seen, operations in Cuba followed standard operating procedures for the disparate organizations involved, with no sign of micromanagement from Moscow. But it is quite possible, some would say virtually certain, that Khrushchev maintained total control over the crucial component of his forces, the nuclear warheads, by not sending any to Cuba! Two considerations lead to that conjecture. First, in 1962 the Soviets did not have the technical means (PALs) that would have allowed the Kremlin to control the arming of warheads in the field, so that unauthorized use could not have been ruled out with complete assurance. Second, firing a few missiles against the United States would have been sheer madness. Equipping the missiles with nuclear warheads, therefore, would have made little sense given that the

United States could hardly afford to assume that Khrushchev was only bluffing.[180]

Fear of Escalation. Finally, to what extent did U.S. nuclear superiority and mutual fear of escalation play a role in the Crisis? A vast literature has been devoted to this issue,[181] but we shall be brief.

Despite the enormous strategic disparity that then existed, it is clear that by Black Saturday escalation to combat, albeit conventional, had ceased to be a remote and abstract apprehension. The scenario painted by McNamara that afternoon depicted a plausible chain of events of unknown likelihood but of high risk because it linked the relatively modest air strike against Cuba to war between the dual-capable forces of NATO and the Warsaw Pact. Without entering into such specifics, JFK that day said to his brother: "It isn't the first step that concerns me, but both sides escalating to the fourth and fifth step— and we don't go to the sixth because there is no one around to do so."[182] Khrushchev's secret letter had made the same point: "If indeed war should break out, then it would not be in our power to stop it, for such is the logic of war. . . . If people do not show wisdom, then in the final analysis they will come to a clash, like blind moles, and then reciprocal extermination will begin."

In retrospect, most ExComm veterans believe that the threat of nuclear escalation was actually remote, and that the fear thereof was exaggerated at the time:

> The decisive military element in the resolution of the crisis was our clearly available and applicable military superiority in conventional weapons within the area of the crisis . . . American nuclear superiority was not in our view a critical factor . . . nuclear war, in 1962, would have been an unexampled catastrophe for both sides . . . No one of us ever reviewed the nuclear balance for comfort in those hard weeks.[183]

On the other hand, there is no consensus within this group—nor, it would seem, among Soviets—whether an attack on Cuba would have led to Soviet conventional escalation.[184]

To what extent Khrushchev was inhibited by his strategic inferiority, as compared to his untenable military position in Cuba itself, is difficult to say. There was never the slightest hint of a Soviet move in any region where she would have enjoyed the advantage in a conventional conflict. From all the evidence[185] Khrushchev had no intention to up the ante, and it is therefore unlikely that the flexing of America's nuclear muscles—the strategic alert of SAC and the departure of the Polaris submarine fleet—contributed significantly to his caution.

When all is said and done, both leaders feared a loss of control over events by some route or other, with losses that could vastly outstrip any benefits that they sought. Both were willing to pay a heavy price to extricate themselves from a predicament they had come to see as intolerably hazardous. Khrushchev paid that price. Kennedy's decisions on Saturday, October 27, indicate quite unambiguously that he too had decided that despite the strong cards in his hand, he could not afford to risk war. His preparation of an escape hatch that would have permitted him to acquiesce to a *public* request for a missile trade made to himself and to Khrushchev simultaneously by the UN secretary general was designed to limit the severe political damage that would surely have accompanied that decision.

THE YOM KIPPUR CRISIS OF 1973

In comparison to the Cuban Missile Crisis, the U.S.–Soviet confrontation that accompanied the Yom Kippur War in October 1973 could be called a tempest in a teapot. Nevertheless, it had two remarkable features. First, these events coincided with the most traumatic American domestic political crisis since the Civil War. As a result, foreign policy was dominated by one unelected official, Henry Kissinger, who was *simultaneously* secretary of state and assistant to the president for national security affairs, and who, with his colleagues, apparently acted without presidential authority at the critical juncture. Second, at that point the tempo of events was perceived to preclude a proper review of the potential consequences of the U.S. military actions taken to deter the threatened introduction of Soviet troops into Egypt. Had the Soviet Union proceeded to do so, the crisis could have taken a much more hazardous turn. In consequence, the Yom Kippur crisis raises questions of broad significance.

The publicly available evidence regarding U.S. decision making in this episode is fragmentary compared to that for the Missile Crisis. We have only the detailed memoirs of Kissinger,[186] the leading actor, in contrast to three for the Missile Crisis, not to mention the paucity of declassified documents and the absence of a tape recording or minutes of the critical White House meeting.[187] An authoritative history therefore remains to be written.

The Yom Kippur Attack on Israel

The crisis was a delayed aftershock of Israel's capture of the Sinai in the Six Day War of 1967. In the early 1970s Anwar Sadat decided that the status quo was intolerable, and set out to regain the Sinai by a combination of diplomacy and armed force.[188] The strategy he devised embodied several assumptions: that negotiations in some form with Israel would be necessary; that Egypt had to regain a degree of self-respect by force of arms before it could enter into such negotiations; that the Soviet Union, despite its long-standing support for Egypt, did not have the leverage necessary for his purpose; that only the United States had the required degree of influence on Israel; and that the superpowers would not intervene effectively unless Egypt were to demonstrate that Israel's continued presence in the Sinai was a threat to world peace.

Acting on this assessment, Sadat expelled some 20,000 Soviet military advisers in July 1972, and sharply reduced the Soviet military presence in

Egypt. Although formal diplomatic relations between Egypt and the United States did not exist, he established quiet contacts with Washington. At the same time, he made secret arrangements for a coordinated attack on Israel with Syria. During the spring and summer of 1973 Sadat launched a barrage of threats against Israel. Both American and Israeli intelligence eventually decided that he was only posturing, but Brezhnev and Kosygin, apparently fearing that he would attack and be trounced, repeatedly cautioned Sadat. At the Brezhnev–Nixon summit in June 1973, Brezhnev was at pains to express concern about the Middle East and advocated a joint U.S.–Soviet initiative to prevent a conflict. Nixon and Kissinger deflected his suggestion; they were not about to resuscitate the Soviets' diminishing diplomatic role in the area, and they also suspected that Brezhnev's worries were not authentic.

On October 3 Sadat informed the Soviet Union that Egypt and Syria would attack Israel shortly. On October 4 and 5 civilian dependents of Soviet personnel in Cairo and Damascus were evacuated by air, and Soviet ships steamed out of Alexandria and Port Said. Israeli (and U.S.) intelligence interpreted this as either a sign of a sudden deterioration in Arab–Soviet relations, or of Soviet fear of an attack by Israel, but it surely reflected a Soviet assessment that the impending attack on Israel would be a disaster. During the early morning of October 6, Israeli intelligence finally decided that an attack would occur that afternoon,[189] but that warning did not suffice to prepare Israel for the highly effective Egyptian–Syrian assault.

Superpower Diplomacy

During the next 2 weeks the largest tank battle since World War II was fought in the deserts of Sinai. Moscow and Washington eventually cosponsored a cease-fire under the aegis of the UN Security Council, although each superpower's fluctuating enthusiasm for an end to hostilities was closely correlated to its ally's fortunes on the battlefield, and both mounted massive airlifts of military supplies. Toward the end of this first phase of the war, with Israel irrevocably gaining the upper hand, Moscow became very alarmed that it would suffer a grievous setback. Pressure from Moscow, and Israel's crossing of the Suez Canal, induced Sadat to accept a cease-fire to take effect on October 18, but Kissinger purposely procrastinated in bringing U.S. influence to bear on Israel. Kissinger then accepted Brezhnev's invitation to come to Moscow, where he arrived after further delays on October 20, negotiated a cease-fire proposal, flew directly to Tel Aviv to extract Israel's reluctant acquiescence to the arrangement, and returned to Washington at 3:00 AM on October 23.

These negotiations proved to be significant in the subsequent confrontation between Moscow and Washington, and a few words concerning them are therefore in order. The Yom Kippur War coincided with two of the spectacular events that compelled Richard Nixon to abandon the presidency 9 months later: Vice President Agnew resigned 4 days after the outbreak of the war, and the Saturday Night Massacre—the firing of the Watergate special

prosecutor, and the resignations of the attorney general and his deputy—
occurred during Kissinger's stay in Moscow.

As one might imagine, Nixon was not engrossed in foreign affairs during
this period. But on October 20 he did send Kissinger a message in Moscow
instructing him to accept Brezhnev's old position that the two leaders, acting
personally in the name of the superpowers, should impose a settlement.[190]
Kissinger was appalled: he saw no reason why the United States should abandon its goal of becoming the sole arbiter of peace in the Middle East. He
therefore ignored Nixon's instructions, and presented a cease-fire proposal
within the framework that he and Nixon had agreed to before his departure!
To his surprise, the Russians quickly accepted, thereby revealing that their
first priority was to stop the Israeli advance. In Tel Aviv Kissinger then told
the Israelis that[191] "I would understand a few hours 'slippage' in the cease-fire
deadline while I was flying home."

The cease-fire, jointly sponsored by the superpowers in the Security Council, collapsed within hours after it took effect on October 23 for reasons that
remain murky. Israel reopened its offensive, which quickly threatened the
survival of the Egyptian 3rd Army Corps, and put the credibility of both
superpowers in jeopardy. There were more diplomatic maneuvers, and a second Security Council cease-fire resolution, which was also ineffective. On
October 24, Sadat called on the United States and the Soviet Union to send
forces to impose the cease-fire.

As the plight of the 3rd Army deteriorated, concern mounted in Washington that the Soviets would feel compelled to intervene militarily, and this
became acute with Sadat's appeal. As early as October 12, U.S. intelligence
had a confirmed report that all seven Soviet airborne divisions, some 50,000
men, had been alerted. The Soviet Mediterranean fleet had been steadily reinforced and had reached a complement of 85 ships by this time, including several vessels that could land marines. On October 22 a Soviet merchantman
carrying a radioactive cargo was reported to have passed through the Bos-
porous.[192] On the critical day, October 24, the Soviets set up an airborne command post in southern Russia, and halted transport flights to Egypt.

Brezhnev's "Ultimatum" and the U.S. Alert

These then were the circumstances at 9:35 PM on October 24 when the brief
superpower crisis was precipitated by a telephone call from Dobrynin to Kissinger conveying a message from Brezhnev. The essential points[193] were, first,
a demand for "an immediate and clear reply"; second, a proposal to "urgently
dispatch" Soviet and American troops "to insure the implementation" of the
Security Council's cease-fire resolutions; and third, a warning:

> I will say it straight that if you find it impossible to act jointly with us in
> this matter, we should be faced with the necessity urgently to consider the
> question of taking appropriate steps unilaterally.

Kissinger interpreted this as "in effect an ultimatum . . . one of the most serious challenges to an American president by a Soviet leader," and in view of the intelligence just cited, he decided that the proposal must be rejected "in a manner that shocked the Soviets into abandoning the unilateral move they were threatening."

The decisive meeting that formulated the American response was chaired by Kissinger, and was attended by Secretary of Defense James Schlesinger, Director of Central Intelligence William Colby, JCS Chairman Admiral Thomas Moorer, White House Chief of Staff Alexander Haig, Deputy National Security Adviser Brent Scowcroft, and Kissinger's military assistant, Commander Jonathan Howe. This group constituted the so-called Washington Special Action Group (WSAG).[194] From a careful examination of the memoirs and public statements of Haig, Kissinger, and Nixon, Garthoff[195] concludes that it is quite certain that the president first learned about Brezhnev's note, the WSAG meeting, its decisions, and the messages it sent to Brezhnev and Sadat in Nixon's name the following morning at 8 AM.

Shortly before WSAG convened[196] at 10:40 PM on October 24, Kissinger called Dobrynin to warn him that[197] "if any unilateral action is taken before we have a chance to reply that will be very serious." The time constraint was judged to be exceedingly tight: given the time difference, should the Soviets have planned to land troops in Egypt at daybreak, any action to deter them would have to occur no later than midnight in Washington, that is, within an hour and a quarter after the start of the meeting.

The meeting's dominant themes were the pressure of time, fear that the Kremlin might believe that the administration would be paralyzed by the political chaos in Washington, and the perception that a response would have to be more than verbal if it were to attain its objective. According to Kissinger,[198] WSAG rapidly reached a consensus that the reply to Brezhnev should be "conciliatory in tone but strong in substance," and that this would have to be backed up by "some noticeable action that conveyed our determination to resist unilateral moves." Hardly any time was available for assessing the dangers that might accompany such "noticeable action." Two alternatives were considered: an alert of conventional forces in the Mediterranean, in Europe, and in the Indian Ocean; or a worldwide alert effecting the entire spectrum of U.S. conventional and strategic forces. The conventional alert was seen to have the advantage of being more credible considering what the Soviets were expected to do. The advocates of a global alert argued that readily available U.S. conventional strength was not that credible either, and that the message traffic accompanying the more dramatic action would immediately send out an unambiguous signal to Soviet intelligence that would shock Brezhnev into at least delaying any action, and thereby provide time for diplomacy.

A decision in favor of the stronger alternative was reached within the hour, and at 11:41 PM Secretary Schlesinger and Admiral Moorer ordered all military commands to move to DEFCON 3. The resulting pulse in signal traffic was the Soviet Union's first indication that the United States was alerting its forces around the globe. At SAC all training missions were canceled, some refueling tankers were dispersed, certain airborne command posts were readied for takeoff, additional B-52s were placed on heightened ground alert, and the command and control system was tested. There are unconfirmed reports that some ballistic missile submarines suddenly left port for the Atlantic. Somewhat later that night WSAG received intelligence indicating that Soviet aircraft capable of transporting 1,600 men were about to leave for Egypt, so the 82nd Airborne Division was alerted, the carrier *Franklin Delano Roosevelt* and its escort were sent from the western to the eastern Mediterranean to join the carrier *Independence,* and the carrier group *John F. Kennedy* was ordered from the Atlantic into the Mediterranean.[199]

During the night WSAG also took two diplomatic initiatives in the president's name. Immediately after calling the alert, it sent a message to Sadat expressing strong opposition to the introduction of superpower contingents, and threatening to withdraw the United States as a mediator in the peace talks with Israel that would have to follow.[200] In contrast, it purposely delayed its verbal response to the Soviet Union to allow time for the military alert to sink in at the Kremlin. Then, at 5:40 AM on October 25, the reply to Brezhnev's message was delivered to Dobrynin; its essence is captured by the following fragments:[201]

> I have carefully studied your important message of this evening. I agree with you that our understanding to act jointly for peace is one of the highest value. . . . I must tell you, however, that your proposal . . . of sending Soviet and American military contingents to Egypt is not appropriate in the present circumstances. . . . We have no information which would indicate that the cease-fire is now being violated on any significant scale . . . Mr. General Secretary, in the spirit of our agreement this is the time for acting not unilaterally but with cool heads . . . we could in no event accept unilateral action . . . such action would produce incalculable consequence which would be in the interest of neither of our countries and which would end all we have striven so hard to achieve.

At 8:00 AM (Washington time) on October 25 Sadat replied to the "president's" message by appealing for an international peacekeeping force in place of an American–Soviet joint force, thereby effectively withdrawing the invitation to which Brezhnev was proposing to respond, which then made a unilateral Soviet intervention highly unlikely.[202] But to Kissinger's surprise and chagrin,[203] the morning news reported the worldwide alert of U.S. forces, which, in his words,[204] "would inevitably turn the event into an issue of prestige with Moscow . . . seriously complicating the prospect of a Soviet retreat." These fears were soon shown to be unfounded, for at 2:40 PM Brezhnev responded, saying that the Soviets would send "representatives" to observe compliance with the cease-fire, and making no mention whatever of the U.S. alert!

The crisis subsided in several days, although intense interactions between U.S. and Soviet naval units persisted for some time. The U.S. alert was lifted on October 26, by which time the cease-fire was in effect. After further pressure by Kissinger on the Israelis a UN convoy was permitted to supply food and water to the 3rd Army Corps, and Egypt and Israel agreed to direct negotiations in the guise of meetings between military delegations to work out cease-fire arrangements. On October 28 the Egyptian foreign minister came to Washington to discuss further diplomatic moves, followed 3 days later by Golda Meir.

Kissinger had gained all his objectives: he had prevented the Soviets from recreating their military presence in Egypt, excluded Moscow from the diplomatic game, and demonstrated that the road to peace ran through Washington—a road that eventually led to Camp David. Nevertheless, the performance of the U.S. government before the Yom Kippur War, and its handling of the superpowers' interaction, justify further scrutiny.

Intelligence Assessments

As we have seen, U.S., Soviet, and especially Israeli intelligence had serious lapses. Israel, in particular, came to a dangerously flawed assessment because of a remarkable confluence: its own intelligence estimate regarding Sadat's intentions appeared to be confirmed by a reliable source in the Egyptian government. The resulting misperception was further reinforced by adroit Egyptian deception. The fundamental misconception was that Sadat would only attack from a military position that *Israel* would deem propitious, which implicitly assumed that Sadat's objective was a military victory, whereas he actually sought a limited political objective by military means. Israel, within this frame of reference, concluded that Sadat would not attack unless he could attain air superiority over the battlefield, but as it was clear that he could not achieve such superiority, this logic led to the conclusion that he could not afford to attack. This assessment was shared by the commanders of the Egyptian air force, and disclosed to Israel by a high-level source, but one not sufficiently well-placed to be privy to Sadat's calculations. To compound the problem, the postmortem of the Six Day War had led Israel to conclude that its preemptive attack of 1967 on Nasser had not been necessary,[205] and that, as a consequence, Egypt would tend to read Israeli defensive preparations as an indicator of imminent preemption. Acting in concert, these facts and misconceptions created a situation wherein Israel would be most unlikely to abandon its assessment that, first, it would not be attacked,[206] and second, that visible preparations in anticipation of an attack would be likely to provoke it.[207]

The failure to read Sadat's mind, to comprehend that his bombastic threats created a noisy background against which he could make his preparations, and to recognize that Egypt and Syria were in collusion, emanated from a conviction that Israel was impregnable. As a result, U.S. and Israeli intelligence misread clear signs that pointed to an Egyptian–Syrian attack. As Kissinger puts it, "we had become too complacent about our own assumptions. We knew everything but understood too little,"[208] which he illustrates with a retrospective probe of the Soviet evacuation on the eve of the war: Why would a *political* crisis require the pell-mell *evacuation of dependents* simultaneously from Damascus *and* Cairo, *leaving military* advisers and technicians behind? The grip of such "complacent assumptions" is illustrated by the fact that WSAG, which happened to be meeting as the attack began, was given the latest intelligence estimate that could "find no hard evidence of a major, coordinated Egyptian–Syrian offensive."[209] Furthermore, during the first days of the war, *both* superpowers operated on the assumption that a quick Arab defeat was a foregone conclusion.

What the Soviet intentions were when Brezhnev's message triggered the American alert is still being debated. In particular, Garthoff[210] argues that Brezhnev's note was not an ultimatum, but rather an appeal for cooperative enforcement of the cease-fire jointly sponsored by the United States and the Soviet Union, the breakdown of which was a serious problem for both. The threat of unilateral Soviet intervention was meant to shock the United States into pressuring Israel to abide by the cease-fire. In his view, Kissinger's representation of the Soviet note as an ultimatum served a number of other ends: it publicly allowed him to blunt domestic criticism of detente by demonstrating resolve "to face down any Soviet threat," while it privately provided leverage against the Israelis. We do not know whether this critique is on the mark.[211] All that is certain is that when the U.S. note was delivered to Dobrynin some 6 hours after the alert was called it was midday in the Middle East, and the Soviet troops whose daybreak arrival had been feared were not in sight,[212] but we do not know whether this was due to the alert, which must have been known to Soviet signals intelligence long before then, or because there was no Soviet intention to insert its forces that day.

American Contingency Planning

Kissinger had ordered the NSC to begin contingency planning during the preceding summer, when he asked[213] "what to do to keep the Soviets out" should they intervene, but by his own admission, his "prescience for raising questions that defined fairly accurately the very issues that were to confront us . . . was not matched by a sense of urgency," and the contingency study was not finished when war broke out. These incomplete plans[214] apparently envisioned the introduction of American troops for the purpose of demonstrating a willingness to match a Soviet deployment, and as "quid pro quo for parallel withdrawals of Soviet and American troops" once the situation had been stabilized. As such, these plans imply that the landing of Soviet troops in Egypt was not seen as an irrevocable reversal for U.S. policy.

To our knowledge, there was no high-level anticipatory planning in the period immediately preceding the "ultimatum," even though there was mounting apprehension in Washington that the flimsy cease-fire and the plight of the Egyptian 3rd Army could provoke a Soviet military intercession that would compel an American response. As early as October 12, almost 2 weeks before the risk of such a Soviet action became acute, Kissinger warned

Dobrynin that[215] "any Soviet intervention—regardless of pretext—would be met by American force."

Why, then, did WSAG not use its regular daily meetings, and especially those of October 23 and 24 after Kissinger's return from Moscow and Tel Aviv, to explore alternative options in the event of a Soviet intervention? Had it done so, it would not have been reduced to a 1-hour consideration of the alert and its ramifications on the night of October 24.

These are not idle remarks, for the actions taken by WSAG were not credible in military terms, but were only intended as a political signal, a point that Admiral Moorer made to the unified and specified commanders in a telephone conversation right after calling the alert.[216] Such signals, however, can cause unexpected reverberations. Had the Soviets ignored these actions, and moved troops into Egypt, the United States would have found itself in an embarrassing position because the naval balance in the region was not favorable,[217] nor could the United States have countered the Soviet's ability for putting 5,000 troops per day into Egypt, in part because the NATO allies were solidly opposed to the movement of materiel or troops from Europe to the Middle East. Given Kissinger's long-standing apprehensions, it should have been possible to devise a policy that would have achieved U.S. objectives with less exposure to potentially dangerous Soviet countermoves. For example, even greater pressure on Israel to cease and desist might have emerged as an urgent priority before the arrival of Brezhnev's note.

In the light of these observations, the manner in which the alert decision was taken is therefore consistent with the conjecture that Kissinger did view Brezhnev's "ultimatum" in much the same way as Garthoff:[218] a warning that Israel must be reigned in, with little danger of a military confrontation between the superpowers provided the United States could impose its will on Israel. Kissinger's response to Brezhnev, therefore, could safely be mounted with a flourish to satisfy a variety of secondary political objectives. Nevertheless, even if all this is granted, one must still ask whether those who had just learned that they had misread the mind of the Sphynx should have been confident that they understood the psyche of the Kremlin.

The Washington Scene

During this crisis the government was not operating in accordance with the rules laid down by Founding Fathers, but that was not the fault of Kissinger and his colleagues. The president was fighting for his political life—articles of impeachment were approved by the House Judiciary Committee on the critical day of October 24. Furthermore, Nixon was trying, although not with great vigor or persistence, to take advantage of the crisis; that presumably was his purpose in altering Kissinger's instructions at the time of the Saturday Night Massacre, for had that led to success it would have put Nixon into the limelight.

Without minimizing the difficulty of this unprecedented situation, it is nonetheless disturbing that a group of appointees should have made potentially momentous decisions in the name of a 200-year-old democracy without establishing any legal line of authority for their actions. For example, Gerald Ford, who was sworn in as vice president on October 12, could have been asked to join WSAG meetings, empowered by Nixon to act in his name. In addition to the question of legitimacy, the concentration of power was remarkable; WSAG could be compared to an ExComm in which Bundy and McNamara were one and the same person, while President Kennedy, his brother, and Sorensen were all in the hospital, for there was no one in WSAG who was primarily a Nixon loyalist.

There are other noteworthy contrasts to the handling of the Missile Crisis, which can only be sensed by reading the Kissinger memoirs. Where Kennedy's ExComm might spend a hundred "high-priced man-hours" in grappling with some decision, Kissinger would often go through an exercise of comparable complexity by himself, or with the help of a few aides and telephone calls, and make a decision within the hour, or often right on the spot. And where communications from Kennedy to Khrushchev were usually separated by a day or so, and painstakingly drafted, Kissinger and the Soviet leaders were in incessant contact. On the day before the "ultimatum" there were six separate U.S.–Soviet contacts at the highest level, all in effect via Kissinger. And on October 24, *before* the delivery of that message, there were again six messages, with three more afterward before the formal U.S. response, totaling eleven in all! To this one must add a stream of messages, telephone calls, and personal meetings between Kissinger and the representatives of the other governments involved. So, in some sense, the Yom Kippur ExComm was the opposite of small—it was global, with Kissinger as its maestro. Within the U.S. government this meant that Kissinger held a virtual monopoly on the information and connections vital to the rendering and implementation of decisions.

EPILOGUE

The confrontations between the superpowers have led to only one purposeful killing[219]—that of Major Rudolf Anderson, who was shot down over Cuba on October 27, 1962. Considering both sides' capacity for slaughter, this is a remarkable record. Nevertheless, below this tranquil surface one can see symptoms of the volatile interplay between threat and fear that led states to destruction in 1914, but only rare glimpses of the reckless adventurism of 1941. Can we recognize common patterns in these symptoms to help ward off a grotesque reincarnation of 1914?

This question can be addressed by first identifying a variety of common threads linking the pre- and post-Hiroshima crises that we have considered— for example, the role of domestic tensions and the performance of intelligence. The threads of greatest significance involve human perceptions, as experienced both by individuals but especially by groups, and are therefore not sensitive to the ever-changing technologies that can turn intangible perceptions into tangible armed force.

The intensity of perceived threat is the natural independent variable for characterizing not only different crises, but also the evolution of a particular crisis. Two distinct empirical observations then become apparent: as the perceived threat intensifies the threads weave a pattern that becomes increasingly complex; furthermore, increasing intensity is accompanied by a growing likelihood that governments will lose control over events. This correlation between growing complexity and loss of control is not fortuitous, but stems from the increasing ambiguity created by the growing complexity of events. As the perception of threat intensifies so does the call for swifter decisions, despite mushrooming ambiguity. In addition, a quickening pace amid deepening uncertainty intensifies the perception of threat, and can thereby create a catastrophic feedback loop.

What are the common threads to which we have alluded? The interplay between domestic politics and the conduct of relations with adversaries was seen to be a recurring theme. The external threat, both real and imagined, was widely exploited to repress domestic fragmentation before the outbreak of war in 1914. Furthermore, since World War II internal dissension during crises has often been a major preoccupation of American governments. Fear of domestic opposition was a serious factor in the conduct of the Korean War and the Missile Crisis. To demonstrate that domestic political tension can be influential it suffices to observe that a government led by men of the stature of Harry Truman, George Marshall, Dean Acheson, and Omar Bradley could not "manage" the Korean War after Inchon in large part because they were hounded by adversaries whose threat to their power hinged on its outcome. While domestic schisms were not as deep in 1962, fear of what its opposition would do should the administration take a soft stance on Cuba was unquestionably significant in defining Kennedy's position before the crisis and in his initial actions when it broke, although other factors came to play a dominant role as the crisis intensified.

Alliance politics is another common thread. To a very considerable degree alliances were the raison d'être of World War I. The perception that America's allies would lose confidence in its leadership were, in the last analysis, the reason why the United States did not abandon Berlin and South Korea even though it saw neither as strategically important. Once the Missile Crisis reached its climax, Kennedy's deepest quandary was to find a course that neither ran the risk of damaging confidence of NATO in U.S. commitments nor of provoking war with the Soviet Union—two almost incompatible requirements.

The tension between internal and external policy is much more noticeable in democracies than in authoritarian regimes, but the latter are not immune to the problem. There is no need to document this in the cases of Austria, Germany, and Russia in 1914, but it is not so widely known that Japanese foreign policy in 1941 was strongly affected by internal power struggles.[220]

And the demand of Castro on Khrushchev for support was certainly a factor, although of uncertain weight, in creating the Cuban Missle Crisis, while friction between Havana and Moscow was a serious problem for the Kremlin in reaching its settlement with the United States.

Intelligence, in the broad sense of the term, constitutes a set of critical common threads. Knowledge of tangible actions by an adversary that have occurred or are imminent are often quite sound, as was demonstrated in 1914. But this is no rule, as illustrated by the failure of strategic and tactical warning before the attack on Pearl Harbor or across the Yalu, and the Soviet failure to recognize that the United States had discovered the missiles in Cuba. Once we leave the recognition of actions that have been or are about to be taken and ask for predictions of future moves or assessments of intangible factors, intelligence, quite understandably, becomes a much more fallible instrument. For then intelligence must peer through the mists laid down by history and mythology regarding not only the adversary, but also the state it is serving.

The problems faced by these more profound tasks of intelligence are already evident in the relatively simple problem of assessing the adversary's capabilities. Thus, U.S. strength was discounted through sheer denial by Japanese intelligence in 1941, while the United States failed to recognize Japan's superb military competence; the U.S. underestimated China's military prowess in 1950; and Israel, the Soviet Union, and the United States all underestimated Egypt's and Syria's military capabilities in 1973.

Israel's intelligence failure on Yom Kippur 1973, while partly at the level of predicting Egypt's and Syria's tactics and capabilities, actually ran much deeper. Ultimately it was due to her inability to comprehend the motives that shaped her opponents' plans and actions—a psychological barrier that blocked the vision of the contestants of 1914, of Stalin on the eve of Hitler's attack, and remains a prominent feature of international conflict in the post-Hiroshima period. Thus, the United States did not recognize that Stalin's goals were quite limited when he first blockaded Berlin; those who decided to invade South Korea presumably did not realize that their action would impel the United States to intervene because of considerations that were unrelated to Korea's intrinsic value to the United States; and the disaster on the Yalu stemmed from the American failure to perceive the threat that MacArthur's northward march was creating in China's mind.

In the case of Cuba, misperceptions were rife on both sides, especially in Moscow. The Kremlin showed a remarkably poor understanding of American political psychology when it failed to comprehend that by deceiving the president personally and deploying its missiles clandestinely it would, quite apart from all other considerations, create an unacceptable situation for Kennedy,[221] and that a more promising and safer course of action would have been to declare openly that it would send missiles to Cuba *unless* the United States undertook not to invade and to remove its Jupiters targeted on the Soviet Union from nearby bases.[222] For its part, the United States was insensitive to the possibility that by publicly proclaiming its overwhelming strategic superiority it might not deter Khrushchev, but rather provoke him to a reckless attempt to improve his position. Furthermore, U.S. intelligence could never bring itself to recognize that fear of an invasion of Cuba might have been one of Khrushchev's motivations, because the United States had no invasion plans—just provocative covert operations and threatening military exercises and preparations!

As an aside, however, it should be noted that astoundingly good intelligence can be an impediment. This can be seen in Israeli decision making in 1973, when a source at very high levels in the Egyptian military yielded an image of Egyptian thinking that confirmed Israel's own military analysis, but failed to reveal the critical variable—Sadat's political motivations; indeed, Israel's actions on the eve of war give the impression that more weight was given to this single source than to her formidable intelligence community.[223] As another example, MAGIC gave such a penetrating insight into Japanese decision making in 1941 that it was held so closely as to undercut the effectiveness of key diplomats and commanders not privy to this information. The millstone of inordinate secrecy is also illustrated by the Kremlin's understandable decision to restrict knowledge of the Cuban adventure to a minute group, for it thereby hobbled one of its most valuable intelligence resources— its embassy in Washington.

The most impenetrable obstacle faced by intelligence is the possibility that the adversary may have goals and intentions that he himself does not understand or know, for then his objectives may change dramatically and unpredictably as a result of what is about to happen! This problem is especially acute for opponents of democracies because it is the very nature of democracy to foster improvisation. As we have seen, in July 1914 England could not formulate its policy vis-à-vis Germany until its decision had essentially become irrelevant to the outbreak of war, although not to its subsequent course, while in 1950 the United States underwent an overnight change of heart once Korea's survival was in imminent jeopardy. But sudden changes in policy forced by a chilling confrontation with reality are not confined to democracies. While we still have no documented understanding of Soviet decision making during the Missile Crisis, there is good reason to believe that Khrushchev's objectives changed radically after the United States imposed the blockade—that avoidance of war then became his reigning priority even though he had inveighed against a blockade before the Crisis.

This brings up the question of whether or not these common threads form recognizable patterns. For this purpose crises can be classified in terms of the intensity of perceived threat to vital interests. The crises we have considered fall into three groups of increasing intensity: Yom Kippur and the Berlin Blockade, post-Inchon Korea and Cuba, and July 1914. This sequence immediately indicates one such pattern: the ability of governments to control the course of events declines with mounting intensity of threat. Obviously this is not a deterministic law of nature, like Newton's equations of motion, but an empirical correlation that history points to.

Before we go any further, we must explain our use of the term *control*. It does *not* refer merely to the prevention of unauthorized military actions before central authorities order contact to be made with the enemy, for such "bottom-up" loss of control is a remarkably rare occurrence in modern armies. Even in 1914, when real-time communications to forces in the field—especially reconnaissance by cavalry—was essentially nonexistent, the cheek-by-jowl proximity of armies numbering in the hundreds of thousands deployed along three long fronts did not lead to any loss of control in this narrow sense. By *loss of control* we mean the phenomenon whereby at least one government finds itself careening toward a war that it had not intended to wage, or which it no longer wants to fight. Precisely how it fell into that predicament—whether through unauthorized actions by its own diplomats or forces, or with far greater likelihood, in a "top-down" fashion because of some intricate combination of poor assessments of its own resources and political support, inadequate awareness of the implications of its own policies, incompatible military plans and political objectives, flawed intelligence about its adversaries, incompetent leadership, or unpredictable actions by its adversaries provoked by its own initiatives—is not of importance to the point we seek to make.

That July 1914 was the gravest of crises and was also marked by the most catastrophic collapse of control in this broad sense needs no discussion.[224] It is also clear that the Berlin Blockade and the Soviet–U.S. confrontation during the Yom Kippur War were low-intensity crises. While there was fear at the outset that the Blockade intimated a threat to the Western position in Germany as a whole, this concern soon receded when the Soviet Union did not impede the airlift, while in the Yom Kippur crisis the risk of an armed superpower confrontation on the Suez Canal was a remote risk. Turning to control, except for a single incident in the air-corridor to Berlin stemming from a Soviet action, the Blockade saw no loss of military or political control by either side. As for Yom Kippur, even though Washington had considerable difficulty in exerting control over Israel, the superpowers fully controlled their own actions except for a *potential* erosion of control that might have emerged from the decision by Kissinger and his colleagues to call a global alert of U.S. forces within a deadline that did not allow examination of the escalatory countersteps that the Soviets might plausibly have taken.

While all would agree that Cuba and post-Inchon Korea were much graver crises than Berlin or Yom Kippur, and modest by the standards of 1914, their relative gravity is a matter of judgment and perspective. Most denizens of Washington would say that Cuba was graver because they would not assess a Chinese intervention in Korea as a threat to vital American interests, whereas for Peking the arrival of a hostile American army on her border was such a threat. Furthermore, from the viewpoint of both superpowers, Cuba was far more serious than Korea because it threatened to embroil them in direct combat and even entailed a risk of nuclear escalation.

Quite apart from their relative gravity, Cuba and especially Korea were marked by appreciable loss of control. Neither China nor the United States sought war against the other. Nevertheless, they could not avert it: the U.S. government, beset by turmoil at home, unable to grasp the impact on Peking of MacArthur's northward thrust, and confused by poor and probably purposely distorted military intelligence, in effect surrendered control to its field commander; China tried vigorously but failed to convey her determination not to accept an American army standing on the Yalu.

In the Missile Crisis both Khrushchev and Kennedy ultimately found themselves faced by a choice between actions that, on one hand, could start a war that neither intended, and on the other an ignominious retreat that would imperil their own political fate and damage the strategic position of the states they led. The two governments had reached that point because they could not comprehend the motives that ruled the other's intentions, and above all, because Khrushchev had taken the one step most likely to lead to loss of control—he had gambled against heavy odds. Furthermore, at the climax, even "bottom-up" loss of control for once became a serious hazard when a U-2 strayed inadvertently over Soviet territory at the same time as Major Anderson's U-2 was destroyed by Soviet forces in contravention of standing orders, which in turn nearly unleashed a counterattack on Soviet SAM sites in Cuba.[225]

Two other observations regarding the relationship between gravity and control, and the significance of perspective, are also appropriate. First, as seen from Cairo and Jerusalem the Yom Kippur War was an extremely grave crisis; both governments had the greatest of difficulty in maintaining control over events that posed a threat to their survival. Second, while U.S. nuclear forces were readied, for the one and only time, for imminent combat during the Cuban crisis, the Soviet Union did not respond by alerting any of its forces, whether conventional or nuclear. To gain some appreciation for the interactions between the superpowers' forces that two-sided alerts might have triggered in 1962, the reader should peruse the lists of anticipated alert operations that will be discussed in the next chapter.

The pattern formed by the common threads do not only show a correlation between crisis intensity and a propensity for loss of control, but also between intensity and the texture of events. The national security organizations of a modern state constitute an enormously complex organism, but that complexity is largely dormant in peacetime. When the organism perceives a rising threat of attack it responds by arousing a progression of ever more threatening capabilities from their peacetime repose—increased reconnaissance, alerts, dispersal of commands and forces from vulnerable peacetime positions, mobilization of reserves, and so forth. The adversary's intelligence services quickly sense these activities, and must assess them as potentially threatening. Once these interactions are permitted to amplify each other and to accelerate the pace of events,[226] governments find themselves astride an organism of ever-swelling complexity facing adversaries and allies undergoing a similar metamorphosis.

The difficulty of maintaining command over one's own security apparatus is rarely a primary propellant toward loss of control, as we have seen. What drives this process is the increasingly ambiguous decision-making environment created by the rise in complexity on all sides, resulting in behavior that departs ever further from the familiar and benign patterns of peacetime. The arousal of ever more variables can also produce the impression of ominous coordinated activity where there is none. The Cuban Crisis had two such coincidences. For the Kremlin that may have occurred on October 22, when the president's speech announcing the blockade happened to coincide with the commissioning of the Jupiters in Turkey, while the blockade itself prevented the vessel that may have been transporting the first nuclear warheads to Cuba from reaching its destination. For Washington October 27 was an analogous experience: Khrushchev's second letter demanding the trade with the Jupiters coincided with the unauthorized shoot-down of the U-2 because the first Soviet SAM radar happened to become operational that day and the order from Moscow not to attack U.S. reconnaissance had been irrelevant until then.

The multinational decision process that forms the crisis trajectory can thus be visualized as a tree whose firm trunk is peacetime. As the threat intensifies, adversaries feel compelled to climb out along forked branches of increasing fragility. The further they move from the trunk the more insistent the demand for prompt decisions of greater moment and the less adequate their understanding of these decisions, as if the branches of the tree reached out into a thickening fog of ambiguity. Confrontations between states are thus not to be viewed as engagements between ships of state commanded by rational captains, but more akin to the intermingling of streams of chemically active, turbulent fluids that are likely to interact in ways that cannot be foreseen with a degree of confidence commensurate with the risks.

NOTES

1. For comparative studies of crises, see George and Smoke; Lebow, *Between Peace and War;* Betts, *Nuclear Blackmail,* and Blechman and Kaplan. George and Smoke, provide the most comprehensive narrative survey of the period from 1945 to 1962, whereas Lebow also treats crises that did not involve the superpowers and/or occurred before World War I. Betts is a comparative study of the role of nuclear weapons in crises.

2. For a recent study, see Avi Shlaim, *The United States and the Berlin Blockade, 1948–1949* (Berkeley, CA: University of California Press, 1983).

3. During 1946 and 1947 France pursued a policy that was dominated by fear of German resurgence, but by the time of the crisis it had largely come to agree with the position of Great Britain and the United States concerning the future of Germany. During the Blockade there were no significant disagreements between the Western allies.

4. This agreement stipulated that Germany would be completely disarmed and demilitarized, and limited the establishment of a central German government.

5. Allied access by air was formally guaranteed, whereas road and rail access were not embodied in any document.

6. Lucius D. Clay, *Decision in Germany* (New York: Doubleday, 1950), p. 367.

7. Daniel Yergin, *Shattered Peace: The Origins of the Cold War and the National Security State* (Boston: Houghton Mifflin, 1977), p. 387.

8. George & Smoke, p. 118.

9. Ibid., pp. 134–136.

10. Clay, p. 239.

11. W. Phillips Davison, *The Berlin Blockade* (Princeton, NJ: Princeton University Press, 1958), p. 73.

12. George and Smoke (loc. cit., p. 127) speculate that inconsistencies between Clay's and Murphy's assessments, compounded by the fact that the former reported through the military chain of command, whereas Murphy's reports went to the State Department, may have contributed to top-level indecision.

13. Col. Howley, the commander of the American garrison, did, however, prepare for another blockade by stockpiling supplies and taking other measures; see Frank Howley, *Berlin Command* (New York: Putnam's, 1950).

14. In the wake of the baby blockade, a warning against further Soviet initiatives was considered, but dropped because Truman was reluctant, apparently concerned that it might provoke Stalin.

15. George and Smoke (loc. cit., p. 122) make the intriguing speculation that the baby blockade only became a blockade because the West refused to allow Soviet inspection of military trains, and that it is therefore not clear what the Soviets had in mind with their action of March 31. No such ambiguity surrounds June 24.

16. David A. Rosenberg, "U.S. Nuclear War Planning, 1945–1960," in Ball and Richelson, pp. 38–39.

17. Shlaim, op. cit., pp. 238, 359. This forward deployment of SAC B-29s was however the precursor for a subsequent network of SAC bases within ready striking distance of the Soviet Union.

18. David A. Rosenberg, "U.S. Nuclear Stockpile, 1945 to 1950," *Bulletin of Atomic Scientists* (1982), *38:*5, 25.

19. The final phase of the Korean War is noteworthy in its own right because it provides the only known instances of serious consideration of the use of nuclear weapons by an American president since Nagasaki (see p. 48).

20. For this phase of the Korean War, see George and Smoke, pp. 140–183.

21. Acheson (p. 358) contends that this widespread interpretation of his speech is "specious" because "Australia and New Zealand were not included either, and the first of all our mutual defense agreements was made with Korea." On the other hand, the geographical detail of the speech is hardly ambiguous (p. 357): " . . . our line of defense runs through the chain of islands fringing the coast of Asia. It starts from the Philippines and continues . . . [to] Okinawa. Then it bends back through Japan and the Aleutian(s) . . . ," which explicitly skirts the Korean Peninsula. On the other hand, in his March 7 testimony before the Senate Foreign Relations Committee, Acheson stressed the strategic importance of South Korea and the U.S. commitment to the country. (Dept. of State Bulletin, March 20, 1950; pp. 454–5). Nevertheless, the administration's internal communications reflect the conventional view of its position. Thus, in a memorandum of May 2, Assistant Secretary of State Dean Rusk cautioned against any future reference to the "Japan–Ryukyus–Philippines defense perimeter." He indicated that past reference to the defense perimeter had resulted in requests from the Korean government to extend the line to include South Korea. He went on to state that "inasmuch as this Government is not in a position to provide the Korean government with such a commitment, any public reference to the Japan–Ryukyus–Phil-

ippine line can serve only to undermine the confidence of the Korean government and people, and consequently their will to resist the ever-present threat of Communist aggression." (*Foreign Relations,* 1950, Vol. VII, pp. 64–65.)

22. For a full analysis of this point, see George and Smoke, pp. 165–166.

23. It is widely believed that Moscow at the very least approved the invasion of the South.

24. See George and Smoke, pp. 184–234; Lebow, pp. 148–164, 172–184, 246–247; and references cited therein.

25. In particular, George Kennan and Paul Nitze, who were successive directors of the State Department's Strategic Planning Staff during this period, as well as the heads of the Department's Offices of Chinese and Northeast Asian Affairs. A concern more widespread in the administration was that a deeper military embroilment on the Asian mainland in pursuit of a secondary objective would play into Stalin's hands, for it would severely limit the ability of the United States to discharge its more important responsibilities in Europe.

26. In July there were reports that 180,000 troops had been moved to Manchuria, and in October *The New York Times* reported that 250,000 were deployed along the Yalu, with 200,000 reserves elsewhere in Manchuria.

27. The official military histories of the campaign are Ray E. Appleman, *United States Army in the Korean War: South to the Naktong, North to the Yalu* (Washington: Department of the Army, USGPO, 1961); John F. Schnabel, *United States Army in the Korean War, Policy and Direction: The First Years* (Washington: Department of the Army, USGPO, 1972); Lynn Montross and Nicholas A. Canzona, *U.S. Marine Operations in Korea* (Washington: U.S. Marine Corps, USGPO, 1957).

28. From the October 9 JCS directive to MacArthur, quoted in Harry S. Truman, *Memoirs, Vol. II: Years of Trial and Hope, 1946–1952* (New York: Doubleday, 1956), p. 362. On November 6 the JCS authorized MacArthur to bomb in Korea near the frontier, including targets at the Korean end of the Yalu bridges, but urged him to use extreme care to avoid violation of Manchurian territory and airspace. (*Foreign Relations,* Ibid., pp. 1075–1076.)

29. On November 24 Army Chief of Staff Collins, alluding to the NSC meeting, informed MacArthur that "the consensus of political and military opinion was that there should be no change in your mission." He went on to give vague instructions to seek "a course of action which would permit the establishment of a unified Korea and at the same time reduce the risk of general involvements." (*Foreign Relations,* Ibid., pp. 1222–1223.)

30. *The New York Times,* December 1, 1950.

31. The statement also said that "Naturally, there has been consideration of this subject [atomic weapons employment] since the outbreak of hostilities in Korea. . . . Consideration of the use of any weapon is always implicit in the very possession of that weapon."

32. Acheson, p. 472.

33. Furthermore, Far East Command was not to obtain any nuclear-capable aircraft until the following spring; David A. Rosenberg (private communication and forthcoming book).

34. Richard E. Neustadt, *Presidential Power: The Politics of Leadership* (New York: Wiley, 1960), pp. 138–139.

35. Concerning these misperceptions, see especially Lebow, pp. 205–216; and George and Smoke, pp. 212–216.

36. See Appleman, loc. cit.

37. MacArthur's remarkable role on the world scene of the time was aptly put by James Reston, "a sovereign Pacific power in his own right" (*New York Times,* July 9, 1950), a judgment that was confirmed when the general addressed a joint session of Congress following his dismissal by Truman, an honor normally reserved for presidents and heads of friendly states. In addition to commanding the UN forces in Korea, he was the commander of all U.S. forces in the Far East, and the de facto ruler of Japan. MacArthur was widely considered to be a serious candidate for the presidency in the forthcoming 1952 election; he was intellectually brilliant and a superb orator. During the war against Japan he had conceived and successfully executed several daring—some would say reckless—operations. He dominated his subordinates to the extent that they often suspended their own military judgment.

38. The administration took no concrete measures that might have given substance to these statements. Indeed, the only tangible move regarding China during this whole period was a reversal of policy concerning Formosa, which undoubtedly enhanced Peking's suspicions of U.S. intentions. On January 5, 1950, Truman had announced that Formosa (Taiwan) was considered to be part of China, and that the United States would not intervene in the civil war between Chiang Kai-shek's Nationalists, who controlled the island, and the communist regime. Subsequently, when the administration came to the help of South Korea, it changed its attitude toward Formosa by stating that its future would have to be decided by the UN, and dispatched the Seventh Fleet to "neutralize" Formosa. This circumstance offered opportunities for providing Peking with tangible reassurance, but none was forthcoming. There is also no doubt that such a move would have led to an outcry from the powerful "China lobby" in the United States.

39. There is a vast and ever-growing literature on the Missile Crisis. In addition to George and Smoke, Blechman and Kaplan, and Lebow, we refer the reader to monographs by Abel, Allison, Robert F. Kennedy, Dinerstein, Horelick and Rush, and Larson. The twenty-fifth anniversary of the crisis also elicited a considerable body of new and important material, and an excellent up-to-date study by Raymond L. Garthoff (*Reflections on the Cuban Missile Crisis,* see bibliography), who was an official in the State Department at the time with responsibilities for Soviet affairs and intelligence analysis. Material that refers to specific aspects will be cited in due course.

40. In addition to Chapter 7, see Holloway, Chapter 5; Horelick and Rush, especially Part 2.

41. Lawrence Freedman, *U. S. Intelligence and the Soviet Strategic Threat* (London: Macmillan, 1977), p. 73.

42. See Abel (pp. 21–22) for a description of the U-2. These planes were optimized for range at a height where they could not be reached by the SAMs of the era. They carried high-resolution stereoscopic cameras.

43. For evidence that Kennedy was aware before his election that there was no missile gap, see Desmond Ball, *Politics and Force Levels: The Strategic Missile Program of the Kennedy Administration* (Berkeley: University of California Press, 1980).

44. Garthoff, p. 25.

45. See Horelick and Rush, pp. 83–96.

46. For a Cuba chronology see Larson, pp. 271–331.

47. Sorensen, p. 669.

48. For the Berlin crises of the Eisenhower and Kennedy administrations see George and Smoke, pp. 392–444.

49. Contrary to many reports, there are no indications that these dual-capable missiles were equipped for nuclear operations; see Garthoff, p. 22.

50. This data was given to the Senate Armed Services Committee by Secretary of Defense McNamara in a special briefing on Feb. 6, 1963. For further details based on this and other Defense Department testimony see Allison, pp. 106–109, and Garthoff, pp. 20–22.

51. Theodore Sorensen has recently said that "the line was drawn between offensive and defensive weapons" not "to leave the Soviets any ambiguity," but because U.S. intelligence "thought the Soviets weren't going to deploy any [missiles] there anyway," and he suggested, furthermore, that the line would have been drawn elsewhere had intelligence indicated otherwise. See James G. Blight, Joseph Nye, Jr. and David A. Welch, "The Cuban Missile Crisis Revisited," *Foreign Affairs* (1987), 66:1, 170; p. 181.

52. When we give no reference for important public pronouncements, the full text can be found in *The New York Times*.

53. Garthoff, pp. 15 and 27.

54. There was considerable skepticism in Congress regarding the president's assertion that there was no Soviet combat personnel in Cuba. A State Department press briefing had also provided a good deal of information about the arms shipments and intimated that they might include SAMs. According to Garthoff (p. 15), JFK's statement on September 4 was partially motivated by skepticism regarding Khrushchev's private assurances.

55. Abel, p. 18.

56. National Security Action Memorandum No. 181, August 23, 1962, declassified.

57. Garthoff, p. 26.

58. Ibid., p. 19.

59. The USIB is now replaced by the National Foreign Intelligence Board; see Richelson, p. 280.

60. SNIE 85-3-62, "The Military Buildup in Cuba," September 19, 1962, declassified.

61. See Hilsman, p. 172. Hilsman was then the Director of Intelligence and Research in the State Department, and State's representative on the USIB.

62. During this whole period there was a flood of human intelligence, the bulk of which was known to be unreliable. It was also reported that Castro's personal pilot had boasted about long-range nuclear-armed missiles in a Havana bar.

63. Both organizations had a point: the mission was dangerous and appropriate to a military pilot, but the CIA's planes were better suited to the purpose. In the end air force pilots received some training on CIA U-2s. See Allison, pp. 121–123, 192.

64. For these and other photos, see Abel, p. 128.

65. Garthoff, pp. 20, 138–146.

66. From a memorandum by Bundy to the president, cited by Abel, p. 31.

67. Robert McNamara recalls that a third former envoy to Moscow, George Kennan, then ambassador to Yugoslavia, was also consulted during the crisis (interview, August 21, 1985).

68. M. Trachtenberg, "Documentation: White House Tapes and Minutes of the Cuban Missile Crisis," *International Security* (1985), 10:1, 164. In all 18 tapes covering the Crisis exist, of which eight are of ExComm meetings. There appear to be no tapings of the many ExComm meetings held in the State Department. All words emphasized in our quotations are emphasized in the transcripts, and signify that the speaker has raised his voice.

69. Hilsman, p. 195. An examination of the military value of the Cuban missile deployment prepared for ExComm on October 27 can be found in Garthoff, pp. 138–146.

70. Hilsman, p. 197. He also opined that it would be "the greatest illusion of all" to think that the Congressional advocates of belligerency would support such a policy for long, for "no one could forget that Senator Taft, leader of the opposition during the Korean War, had praised President Truman's decision to fight in the twenty-four hours after it was made, but within weeks had begun to call it Truman's War."

71. Kennedy, p. 67.

72. Allison, p. 188.

73. Blight, Nye and Welch, op. cit., p. 174.

74. The blockade vs. air strike division did not have a pattern set by the participants' organizational roles, as is evident from the positions taken by McNamara, Nitze and Taylor. Some ExComm members changed their minds more than once.

75. A memorandum by Sorensen of October 17, in summarizing the various options, lists fourteen "questions or points of disagreements."

76. Garthoff, pp. 26–29.

77. *Proceedings of the Cambridge Conference on the Cuban Missile Crisis,* October 11–12, 1987, edited by James G. Blight and David A. Welch, to be published; cited as *Cambridge Conference* henceforth.

78. The term "the Chiefs" does not mean that they held their positions unanimously. In his memoirs RFK claims that the Chairman, Maxwell Taylor, supported the blockade, and afterwards (see *New York Times,* October 26, 1968) the Marine Commandant, General David M. Shoup, objected to the notion that the Chiefs were one voice, and stated that he had "fought against invasion of Cuba from the start." Nevertheless, there is no question but that Taylor was an advocate of the air strike and opposed the blockade, although naturally he always supported presidential decisions. Apparently the Chiefs were unanimously in favor of the air strike (although, it seems, not an invasion) at the critical juncture on October 27; see *Cambridge Conference.*

79. Declassified memorandum by Robert S. McNamara, October 21, 1962, *The National Security Archive.*

80. McNamara memorandum, Ibid.

81. Indeed, Dean Rusk has already argued on October 16 that the status of the missiles was not critical; see Trachtenberg, op. cit., p. 176.

82. During September 1962, Richard Nixon, followed by five senators, had actually advocated a quarantine to halt the flow of arms to Cuba (Garthoff, p. 16).

83. See Garthoff, pp. 15 and 34.

84. The British Ambassador had not only recognized that a serious crisis was afoot, but on Friday morning he had informed his Government that he presumed that Soviet missiles had been discovered in Cuba. By Saturday evening James Reston and Alfred Friendly had put two and two together, but agreed to requests not to disclose what they knew. Many journalists had recognized that there was a crisis by Sunday. That evening the President and McNamara called the publishers of *The New York Times* and *Herald Tribune,* and the *Washington Post,* and asked them not to print what they had learned in their Monday papers.

85. This timing was chosen for two reasons: To minimize the danger of leaks, and to give opponents no time to mount a campaign in favor of some other policy.

86. Concerning U.S. military measures, see Adam Yarmolinsky, "Department of Defense Operations During the Cuban Crisis," *The Naval War College Review* (1979), *32*:4, 83; and Scott D. Sagan, "Nuclear Alerts and Crisis Management," *International Security* (1985), *9*:4, 100.

87. Recall that SAC is normally at DEFCON 4.

88. See Horelick and Rush; and Marc Trachtenberg, "The Influence of Nuclear

Weapons in the Cuban Missile Crisis," *International Security* (1985), *10:*1, 137, which cites the newer literature on Soviet policy.

89. Kennedy, pp. 61–70.

90. Hilsman, p. 215; Garthoff, p. 49.

91. Direct telephone links were established from Washington to a convoy on the Autobahn to Berlin.

92. "Unprecedented" really means within living memory: Lincoln intervened deeply into military matters in the Civil War.

93. Insight into how civilian management of the quarantine was viewed in some military quarters is offered by the Office of Air Force History's taped interview of General David Burchinal: " . . . so there was a phone from the Secretary of Defense's office right to the deck of the damn destroyer . . . the first ship comes up to the blockade line. He's a Swede. They give him the signal 'heave-to'. . . . And he said, 'Go to hell!' Full steam ahead and right through the damn blockade . . . 'nobody tells me what to do on the high seas with my ship.' So they just looked at each other, these people who were now learning how to 'manage crises' and run wars. 'That didn't work very well. What do we do now?' . . . So the next ship comes along [the *Marcula*] . . . 'Oh, I'm very happy to comply . . . I'm just a poor Lebanese. . . . ' So they went aboard and opened up his hatches, and he's got a bunch of military electronic gear, and they shut the hatches down, pretend it wasn't there, and said, 'Pass friend.' And he steamed merrily into Havana. That was our naval blockade. And that's the way it was being run under the kind of civilian control we had." Cited by Trachtenberg, loc. cit., pp. 152 & 156.

94. The secretary first sought to impress on Admiral Anderson that the quarantine was in essence a political operation, and then posed a sequence of questions concerning procedures—for example, whether there would be Russian speaking men on board to communicate orders—that finally drove Anderson to say that all blockade procedures were spelled out in the navy's manual. McNamara responded by saying he "did not give a damn for what John Paul Jones would have done," only in what would be done now, and that under no circumstance was a ship to be fired on without a presidential order. This account has been confirmed by Mr. McNamara (private communication). According to Abel (p. 155), someone actually had had the foresight to assign foreign language instructors from Annapolis to blockade duty, but this was not known to the CNO!

95. Apparently two other ships were allowed to pass through at about this time. One was an East German passenger ship, the other a Swedish ship mentioned in Burchinal's reminiscences (loc. cite.).

96. Quotation from minutes of NSC Executive Committee Meeting No. 6, October 26, 1962, 10:00 AM, by Bromley Smith, reprinted in Trachtenberg (loc. cit.), pp. 194–196.

97. Garthoff, p. 45.

98. Ibid., p. 51.

99. An extensive reconstruction from quotes and paraphrases in various memoirs can be found in Allison, pp. 221–223.

100. Abel, p. 178.

101. Recall Bundy's memo of August 23, p. 172.

102. In a television program commemorating the fortieth anniversary of Hiroshima, Robert McNamara said that on that Saturday evening, as he was going home, he wondered whether he would live to see another Saturday. According to Abel (p. 201), unflappable Ambassador Thompson told his wife that if he did not return the next day he would let her know "at the first opportunity" where to join him "when

capital was evacuated." It is reported that at the end of Saturday's meeting Kennedy distributed sealed evacuation instructions, as did Khrushchev at about the same point. Since it now appears that both were determined to avoid hostilities, one may wonder whether they were simply being cautious, or manipulating fear to marshal support for the politically unpalatable steps that faced them.

103. The minutes of the 10 AM and 4 PM ExComm meetings on October 27 in the White House are available in Trachtenberg (loc. cit.), pp. 196–203, but not for the 2:30 PM State Department session.

104. The new documentation also tends to validate Allison's speculation (p. 209) that JFK had "sacrificed the Ambassador to the hawks in order to allow himself to choose the moderate, golden mean" when, on the preceding Saturday, the president had summarily rejected UN Ambassador Adlai Stevenson's suggestion of such a missile tradeoff.

105. McGeorge Bundy and James G. Blight, "October 27, 1962: Transcripts of the Meetings of the ExComm," *International Security* (1987/88), *12*:3, 30, referred to as Bundy henceforth. See also David A. Welch and James G. Blight, "An Introduction to the ExComm Transcripts," Ibid., 5.

106. The documentation is inconsistent regarding the operational status of the MRBMs. McNamara's October 21 memo states that the CIA estimated 8 to 12 operational missiles, whereas the minutes for the October 25 ExComm meeting have McCone reporting that some of the missiles are "now operational." See also Garthoff, p. 21.

107. Kennedy, p. 93.

108. Bundy, p. 36.

109. Here "Number 1" referred to the fact that the Jupiters were both obsolete and vulnerable, and that the Turkish government had refused to consider their removal. (See Welch and Blight, op. cit., p. 17, for a recent statement by Dean Rusk on this point.)

110. Bundy, p. 46.

111. Ibid., p. 49

112. Ibid., p. 49. In the ExComm meeting Nitze asserted that if the negotiations were to involve NATO "the whole questions as to whether we are going to denuclearize NATO" would soon arise (Ibid., p. 36). A memorandum prepared by Raymond Garthoff on October 25 for the head of the State Department Policy Planning Staff stated that "a week ago we were concerned about strangulation of West Berlin, missile firings and exchanges of cities within the U.S. and USSR. . . . Now the danger that looms is not exchange of cities, but exchange of bases—at the extreme, the unhinging of our whole overseas base and alliance structure," and that this possibility has arisen because "we have to our peril neglected one particular contingency: that the Soviets would react mildly and with great caution." (Garthoff, p. 133.) Note that this was written *before* Khrushchev's offer of a trade.

113. Bundy, p. 58.

114. Trachtenberg, op. cit., p. 199.

115. On carefully rereading this rambling document, McNamara proclaimed that it "was twelve pages of fluff. That's no contract. You couldn't sign that and say we know what we signed. And *before* we got the damned thing read the whole deal changed— *completely changed.*" (Bundy, p. 79)

116. Ibid., p. 59. Indeed, a memorandum by Garthoff dated October 27 points out that Khrushchev's second letter "clearly evades any commitment to military action if the U.S. should decline its offer and eliminate the missile site by unilateral action . . .

[this] can scarcely be an oversight . . . ," so that even if the Soviets cannot be compelled to withdraw the missiles their destruction "would almost certainly not provoke even limited military escalation." (Garthoff, pp. 136–137)

117. Bundy, p. 63.

118. ExComm Minutes, October 23, 1962, 10:00 AM, by McGeorge Bundy; the National Security Archive.

119. Trachtenberg, pp. 202–203.

120. Major Rudolf Anderson, who had taken the famous photo that first revealed the missiles.

121. Bundy, p. 71.

122. That U-2s were beyond the reach of anything but SAMs did not seem to be known at that point in ExComm.

123. Bundy, pp. 74–75.

124. Ibid., p. 76.

125 Ibid., p. 78. McCone was however adamant that Khrushchev had to stop fire on reconnaissance "or we're going to take those SAM-sites out *immediately.*"

126. Ibid., p. 87.

127. Welch and Blight, op. cit., p. 21.

128. Bundy, p. 31.

129. Kennedy, pp. 85–87. The pledge to remove the Jupiters was unknown even to ExComm members until the publication of RFK's memoirs in 1969.

130. He reportedly also "made it plain . . . that any attempt to treat the President's unilateral assurance as part of a deal would simply make the assurance inoperative"; Dean Rusk, Robert McNamara, George W. Ball, Roswell L. Gilpatric, Theodore Sorensen, and McGeorge Bundy, "The Lessons of the Cuban Missile Crisis," *Time,* September 27, 1982, pp. 85–86.

131. This was followed by an official letter of acceptance later that day, and negotiations involving the UN that hammered out the details of the arms withdrawal, which eventually *included* the IL-28 bombers. Because Castro refused inspections in Cuba, Soviet ships at sea withdrew tarpaulins so that the missiles could be photographed by U.S. aircraft (see Abel). The quarantine was maintained while the sites were dismantled, and lifted on November 21. At Christmas Castro released the 1,100 prisoners taken at the Bay of Pigs, and received a sum of $52 million. But in the end the Kennedy administration never provided the formal noninvasion pledge that the Soviet government sought because of disagreements regarding Cuban–Soviet compliance with the minutae of U.S. demands. For a detailed account of the settlement negotiations, see Garthoff, pp. 61–83.

132. Garthoff, p. 58.

133. Blight, Nye and Welch, op. cit., p. 179.

134. See note 39.

135. See note 77.

136. Georgi Shaknazarov, a current member of the Central Committee, who did not participate in the Crises, but who has apparently been involved in a Cuba postmortem ordered by Gorbachev, also participated in the conference.

137. Garthoff, pp. 6, 7, and 13. As we saw, McCone had either been made aware of, or had surmised, Khrushchev's views on this score (see p. 176).

138. Garthoff, p. 54.

139. Ibid., p. 16. As a by-product of these covert operations a score of Russians were killed by Cuban emigres.

140. "The increased seriousness of the Cuban situation during the summer of 1962

alerted the Tactical Air Command (TAC) to the necessity of preparing a well-planned, thoroughly coordinated tactical air offensive launched against Cuba . . . By 10 October TAC forces had already commenced training exercizes . . . and the build-up of war readiness materiel . . . "; *The Air Force Response to the Cuban Crisis,* USAF Historical Division, declassified, p. 22.

141. In this context, see the interview of Robert McNamara in Robert Scheer, *With Enough Shovels* (New York: Random House, 1982), p. 217.

142. Strobe Talbott, ed. and transl., *Khrushchev Remembers* (Boston: Little, Brown, 1970). Garthoff (p. 6) states that the authenticity of the memoirs is now "established beyond doubt."

143. Garthoff, p. 48.

144. *Khrushchev Remembers,* op. cit., p. 497; Garthoff, p. 41.

145. Garthoff, p. 51.

146. Llewellyn Thompson had recognized that this might be the origin of the second Khrushchev letter in the October 27 ExComm meeting; see Bundy, p. 83.

147. According to Soviet accounts, such as those published by Burlatsky (see Garthoff, p. 126), RFK had warned of a military takeover of the U.S. government. It is not credible that RFK would have made such a preposterous statement to Dobrynin, or that the latter would have believed it. As Sorensen speculated at the Cambridge Conference (op. cit.), various links in the chain between JFK and Khrushchev may have embroidered what they heard with melodramatic touches since they had a common interest in a quick resolution. Furthermore, it was to Khrushchev's advantage to claim that he had prevented a catastrophic *putsch* in Washington.

148. *Cambridge Conference.*

149. Castro was furious about the Soviet offer of a missile swap as it turned Cuba into a bargaining chip, and doubly so after the settlement because he had been refused entry into the Warsaw Pact and told that the missiles, which were now to go, would give him protection equivalent to membership. Indeed, Cuban troops surrounded the missile bases for several days, and the Soviets had great difficulty in getting Castro's acquiescence to the settlement (Garthoff, pp. 63–65).

150. In addition to classified reviews within separate departments, Paul Nitze and Walt Rostow conducted an unpublished inter-agency postmortem for the administration in 1963; cf. Edward Weintal and Charles Bartlett, *Facing the Brink: An Intimate Study of Crisis Diplomacy* (New York: 1967), p. 62. The article by Yarmolinsky (loc. cit.) is actually a report, declassified in 1979, that he had prepared for McNamara's testimony to the Subcommittee on Department of Defense Appropriations of the House Appropriations Committee, "Defense Department Appropriations for 1964," February 6, 1963.

151. In addition to Allison, George and Smoke, Lebow, and especially Garthoff, see Roberta Wohlstetter, "Cuba and Pearl Harbor," *Foreign Affairs,* July 1965, p. 700; Blight, Nye and Welch, op. cit.; a forthcoming book by Richard Ned Lebow and Janice Stein; and the *Cambridge Conference.* Intelligence operations are discussed in Laqueur, Chapter 5.

152. This is also Hilsman's conclusion (p. 190), based on his inside knowledge and not just guesswork. This leaves aside whether more data on the progress of SAM installations in western Cuba would have sufficed to bring other members of the administration to agree with McCone.

153. Indeed, the COMOR meetings of September 10 and October 4 struggled with just that tradeoff.

154. McCone never alluded to intelligence from agents in this connection, and tried

hard to get Senator Keating, who was making charges that missiles were going into Cuba, to quietly reveal his sources to him (see Allison, pp. 190–191).

155. Trachtenberg, p. 185.

156. In this connection, see the statement by Admiral Bobby Inman on p. 272.

157. Hilsman, p. 186.

158. The president, and other senior officials without intelligence experience, were somewhat incredulous that the October 14 photographs were solid evidence that missiles were to be deployed (Kennedy, p. 2; Abel, p. 43).

159. In a television appearance on October 14 McGeorge Bundy mentioned that the Soviets had supplied IL-28 bombers to Egypt and Indonesia, from which one could infer that the United States would acquiesce to such shipments to Cuba.

160. Myron Rush, private communication.

161. Allison, p. 135.

162. *Cambridge Conference.*

163. Note that Adlai Stevenson had no inkling of the Bay of Pigs operation until it was in the newspapers even though (or perhaps because) it was his job to defend his government against charges that it was intervening in Cuba!

164. This conformed with the Presidential directive of August 23; see p. 172. See also note 140 concerning the Tactical Air Command.

165. Trachtenberg, p. 201.

166. See Yarmolinsky, op. cit.

167. These and other peculiarities of the Soviet buildup are abstracted from Allison's discussion (pp. 102–106).

168. Ibid., pp. 109–117.

169. Allison points out that secrecy and deception was also used in arms shipments to Egypt and Indonesia, even though there was no need for it: these were the GRU standard operating procedures.

170. *Cambridge Conference.*

171. The most complete analysis of ASW operations is in Sagan, pp. 112–115. That JFK and McNamara were aware of ASW procedures is clear from RFK's memoirs quoted on pp. 182. The ASW orders were further clarified on October 24; they explicitly permitted surfacing, including the dropping of "harmless explosive sound signals." (A submarine can be ordered to surface with sonar signals using international codes; alternatively, a diesel submarine can be tracked until it surfaces since it cannot stay submerged for more than about 48 hours; and finally, depth charges can be used.)

172. The published record does not say when the first submarine contact took place, but it presumably preceded the boarding of the *Marcula* 46 hours after the quarantine began.

173. Garthoff, p. 38.

174. For a detailed account, see Sagan, pp. 118–121.

175. The president wondered afterward whether Khrushchev may have thought that this U-2 flight was a prestrike reconnaissance mission of Soviet air bases, and that this frightened him and contributed to his decision to come to terms that evening (see Sagan, p. 119).

176. Ibid., p. 121.

177. Garthoff, p. 37.

178. Ibid., p. 36. In this connection, see also Richard Ned Lebow, "Was Khrushchev bluffing in Cuba?", *Bulletin of the Atomic Scientists* (1988), *44*:3, 38.

179. Ibid., p. 52; *Cambridge Conference.*

180. Recall that in the first ExComm meeting McNamara raised the possibility that

there were no warheads in Cuba. U.S. intelligence was rather confident that no nuclear warheads ever reached Cuba (Garthoff, p. 21), but whether warheads were on their way at the time of the blockade is uncertain. The Soviet participants in the Cambridge Conference (op. cit.) disagree as to whether Khrushchev intended to ever send warheads to Cuba. The question is examined in detail in Lebow, op. cit.

181. For a bibliography, see Trachtenberg, loc. cit.

182. Kennedy, p. 98.

183. Rusk et al., op. cit. This should be contrasted with McNamara's postmortem to Congress, in which he said that during the night of October 27–28 Khrushchev "knew without any question whatsoever that he faced the full military power of the United States, including its nuclear weapons . . . and that is the reason, and the only reason, why he withdrew those weapons." (Subcommittee on Department of Defense Appropriations, House Appropriation Committee, "Defense Department Appropriations for 1964," February 6, 1964.) McNamara did not, however, know that Kennedy had promised to remove the Jupiters from Turkey.

184. Blight, Nye and Welch, op. cit., pp. 173–178; *Cambridge Conference.*

185. In addition to what has already been cited, in November 1962 Mikoyan reportedly told Warsaw Pact ambassadors in Washington that "after evaluating the strong American reaction during the crisis, however, the Presidium had decided against risking the security of the Soviet Union and its allies for the sake of Cuba"; Garthoff, p. 11.

186. Kissinger, Chapters 11 and 12.

187. On the other hand, an official Israeli inquiry (the Agranat Commission), and memoirs by several Israeli leaders, provide considerable information regarding Israeli decision making, intelligence, and military operations. See Betts, *Surprise Attack,* pp. 68–80; Van Creveld, pp. 203–231; and Stein (in Jervis, Lebow and Stein), pp. 60–88. A good deal is also known about decision making in Cairo (see Stein, Ibid., pp. 34–59). Virtually nothing is available regarding Soviet policy formation.

188. For an account of the events leading up to the Yom Kippur War in the broader context of U.S.–Soviet relations, see Garthoff, *Détente and Confrontation,* Chapter 11.

189. For a detailed account of the outbreak of war, see Van Creveld, loc. cit. Israeli intelligence had predicted H-hour as 18:00 on the basis of an agent's report, whereas the attack began 4 hours earlier, which had very serious consequences for the early course of the campaign. According to Van Creveld (p. 205), even so there was actually enough warning to initiate the fully rehearsed plan of defense, but permission to carry this plan out was postponed at noon because of lingering uncertainty as to Egypt's intentions and fear that such an action might provoke an attack. In a message to Kissinger on October 7 (Kissinger, p. 477), Golda Meir stated that the postponement was ordered on purely political grounds to place full onus for the war on Egypt. Her own memoirs, and the Agranat Commission's report, are not consistent with this claim, however (Stein, loc. cit., p. 77).

190. While Kissinger was flying to Moscow, Nixon also informed Brezhnev that Kissinger had the authority to cut a deal. This "horrified" Kissinger, for it made it impossible for him to request pauses for consultation with Washington in order to give Israel the time that he had promised for the advance of its armies. Despite this "handicap," Kissinger was able to delay the pace of the negotiations considerably (Kissinger, pp. 552–557).

191. Ibid., p. 569.

192. Garthoff (p. 378) states that this intelligence was not an important factor in U.S. decision making.

193. Kissinger, p. 583.

194. WSAG had been formed by Kissinger in Nixon's first term. It "was an inter-departmental group responsible for coordinating policy during crises and reviewing contingency plans" (Kissinger, p. 316). During the Yom Kippur War it met daily.

195. Op. cit., pp. 378–379. The question of Nixon's participation is a byzantine one. According to Kissinger, Haig recommended that Nixon not be awakened as he was too distraught; furthermore, Haig did not tell Kissinger whether he had discussed the matter with Nixon. When the fact that Nixon had not participated in the decision became known, there was a howl of criticism, which makes some of the accounts of the episode suspect. In his memoirs, Nixon states that Haig had informed him, and that he then told Haig that "we need action, even the shock of a military alert"; (Richard M. Nixon, *RN: The Memoirs of Richard Nixon* [New York: Grosset and Dunlap, 1979], p. 938). But Garthoff, who was a senior member of the Foreign Service at the time, apparently has sources that led him to write that in the WSAG meeting "neither Kissinger nor Haig ever said" that "Nixon approved in advance the idea of a military alert."

196. On this phase of the crisis, see Scott D. Sagan, "Nuclear Alerts and Crisis Management," *International Security* (1985) 9:4, pp. 122–128; Barry M. Blechman and Douglas M. Hart, "The Political Utility of Nuclear Weapons: The 1973 Middle East Crisis," Ibid. (1982) 7:1, pp. 132–156; and John Steinbruner, "An Assessment of Nuclear Crises," in Franklyn Griffith and John C. Polanyi (ed.), *The Dangers of Nuclear War* (Toronto: University of Toronto Press, 1979), pp. 34–49.

197. Kissinger, p. 585.

198. Ibid., p. 587.

199. The 6th Fleet had already been ordered to concentrate in the eastern Mediterranean on October 6.

200. Ibid., pp. 588, 592.

201. Nixon, op. cit., pp. 939–940.

202. This is also Kissinger's view (pp. 592–593).

203. That such an alert could not be kept quiet was well understood in many circles. According to interviews conducted by Sagan (op. cit., p. 128) it seems that some WSAG members probably expected the alert to become known to the public, but refrained from saying so since they did not want that to stand in the way of the action.

204. Kissinger, p. 591.

205. Stein, loc. cit., pp. 37, 69.

206. This is actually an oversimplified rendition of Israel's intelligence assessments. For example, in the spring of 1973 important elements of the military and intelligence leaderships came to a completely correct interpretation of Sadat's actions, but the attack that was then anticipated did not materialize, and everyone reverted to the conceptions sketched in the text (see Stein, loc. cit., p. 67).

207. Expense, and the desire not to disrupt Israeli society, were other factors in Israel's lack of readiness, because it had previously called a sizeable mobilization in response to strategic warning of an attack that did not occur.

208. Kissinger, p. 467. In this connection, we note that Kissinger (p. 462) reports that in May 1973 the State Department's Bureau of Intelligence and Research estimated that a continuing diplomatic stalemate could lead to resumption of hostilities for political purposes by the following autumn, but that it "abandoned its prediction as war actually approached."

209. Kissinger, p. 458.

210. Garthoff, pp. 382–384. Furthermore, Garthoff (p. 374) points to a number of Brezhnev messages preceding the "ultimatum," including one addressed *personally* to

Kissinger, urging the United States to force Israeli compliance with the cease-fire, and remarks that the Soviets must have been suspicious that "the U.S., and specifically Kissinger . . . [was] quietly giving Israel a free hand."

211. After receiving Brezhnev's "ultimatum," Kissinger and Scowcroft called Dobrynin three times before conveying the U.S. response to him in the early hours of October 25, but the ambassador never took these opportunities to soften the impact of the Brezhnev message. Kissinger, pp. 585, 588–590.

212. In addition to the reports about Soviet airborne troops available to WSAG when the alert was called, there was subsequently an unconfirmed report that a Soviet transport landed at Cairo and immediately took off again.

213. Ibid., p. 462.

214. Garthoff, p. 376.

215. Kissinger, p. 510.

216. Sagan, p. 128. Furthermore, items on the alert checklist were immediately rescinded (our interviews).

217. Elmo R. Zumwalt, Jr., *On Watch* (New York: Quadrangle, 1976), p. 446, who was then CNO, states that Admiral Moorer told WSAG "that we would lose our ass in the eastern Med under these circumstances."

218. Garthoff, op. cit., especially p. 374.

219. Here we do not include inadvertent casualties when there is no crisis—for example, along the inter-German border, nor the fatalities resulting from a mid-air collision during the Berlin Blockade.

220. Michael Barnhart, "Japanese Intelligence before the Second World War: 'Best Case' Analysis," in May, Chapter 14; and Scott D. Sagan, "The Origins of the Pacific War", *Journal of Interdisciplinary History* (1988), *18*:4, 893.

221. Note that the first adjective used by Kennedy in the quarantine speech of October 22 when he called on Khrushchev to "halt and eliminate" the "threat to world peace" was *"clandestine";* see p. 181.

222. This view was expressed by both the Soviet and former ExComm participants in the *Cambridge Conference* (op. cit.).

223. See Stein, in Jervis, Lebow, and Stein, Chapter 4.

224. An important explanatory observation is in order here. In contrast to the other cases in our sample, in the July crisis one of the principals—Germany—had a policy that willingly ran the risk of war (cf. Chapter 3). Nevertheless, in our sense of the term, Germany had lost control over events within a month when the Schlieffen plan failed because she had no intention of fighting the war that then ensued. In 1941, on the other hand, Germany and Japan were determined to go to war in the knowledge that they ran enormous risks, and for that reason we have not considered these outbreaks of war to be crises.

225. On October 25 ExComm had adopted a standing order that in the event of the downing of a U-2 the SAM site responsible would be attacked—an order that JFK rescinded on October 27. This last decision barely reached the air force in time to prevent the attack (Garthoff, p. 62).

226. Many ExComm veterans believe that the quality of crisis decisionmaking is directly related to the length of time available, and that they were exceedingly fortunate in 1962 to have so much time. Robert McNamara has suggested that "within certain limits, the longer the time taken to form the decision, the more sound the decision will be"; see "A Retrospective on the Cuban Missile Crisis," Alfred P. Sloan Foundation, New York, January 22 and 28, 1983.

9

Potential Arenas for Crisis and Conflict

The preceding chapter on crises of the nuclear age, together with Chapter 3 on the outbreak of the two World Wars, constitutes our historical data base. There is another data base that is probably more germane to the problem of assessing the risks entailed in future crises: the constant, *objective* factors defined by the superpowers' military deployments, alert operations, command organizations, and political commitments in the various geopolitical arenas were friction exists or can be anticipated. These tangible factors are likely to play a significant role in a future crisis whatever its peculiarities may be, and this chapter is devoted to describing them. The next chapter will then examine context-dependent *subjective* features that may dominate some actual chain of events.

Crisis arenas may be divided into categories having quite distinct characteristics: Europe, where both superpowers have large forces in constant and close contact; the Middle East and other circumscribed regions where they do not; and the global arenas—the oceans and space. In view of these distinctions, we shall impose this geographic division on our discussion of the objective factors.

EUROPE

East and West stand face to face on Europe's central front as nowhere else. There they permanently deploy two armies much stronger in even their non-nuclear firepower, and far more mobile, than those of 1914 or 1939. This show of force reflects each superpower's assessment that any significant deterioration in its position in Europe would threaten its vital interests. The magnitude of the stakes, the proximity and lethality of those forces, their immersion in a large civilian population, and the short distance from the front to valuable territory, combine to allow little time for diplomacy should shooting ever begin. In addition, the intermingling of conventional and nuclear forces on both sides implies that once fighting starts there would be a serious risk of escalation to nuclear conflict.

The several Berlin crises, and NATO's caution whenever Soviet control of Eastern Europe has been challenged, show that Washington and Moscow are keenly aware of these hazards. Both exercise very tight control over their forces. Neither has allies that show any disposition to reckless action. Hence stability in Europe is dominated by two opposing factors: on one hand, forces that have the capacity for vast and quick destruction; on the other, a very tight leash. Under normal circumstances the leash dominates. In that sense the European and strategic confrontations resemble each other.

Nevertheless, hostile armies almost within earshot are not silos half a globe apart, and should there ever be a flagrant departure from "under normal circumstances" that difference could spell trouble. These armies are not machines, but hundreds of thousands of human beings. They are not immune to political events of great emotional impact. They must be fed and supplied even if their lines of communication are threatened by popular upheaval. One can therefore conjure up chains of events that might compromise that control. And then the inflammation might reach into the silos.

The scenarios that seek to flesh out these speculations largely hang from a common thread:[1] Loss of full political control by the Soviet Union in Poland or East Germany; infusion of Soviet reinforcements that aggravates the upheaval, and simultaneously threatens NATO, thereby triggering a chain reaction of escalating military preparations, viewed as defensive by each side but threatening to the other; culminating in the outbreak of fighting, either by a preemptive attack on NATO, or through a process resembling spontaneous combustion.

But would it not be reckless for the Soviets to launch an attack from so slippery a footing? Or for West German troops to cross the frontier because their East German compatriots were being cut down? Perhaps it would be, but wars have begun in equally implausible ways. Of greater importance, such scenarios can elicit questions whose relevance transcend the plausibility of some fictitious sequence of events. In particular, they highlight features of the political and military setting in which any European crisis would start and then evolve. Such features can be discerned from what is known about NATO and Warsaw Pact strategy, forces, and command, the behavior of the two sides in past crises and in military exercises, and from NATO's anticipated alerting operations.

NATO Strategy, Forces, and Command

To a great extent geography determines strategy. The strongest member of the NATO alliance is separated from the potential battlefield by an ocean whose shores are largely in Western hands, and to which the Soviet Navy has poor access. On the other hand, the depth of NATO territory on the continent is nowhere more than 500 miles from front to sea, whereas the Soviet Union stands on terrain that, in any nonnuclear campaign, is effectively infinite in extent.

In order to impose control over the vital Atlantic sea lanes, the United States and Great Britain have always maintained navies far stronger than those of the Soviet Union. They would keep the Atlantic supply route functioning; all that is open to debate is the degree of disruption that Soviet air and naval forces (especially its growing fleet of attack submarines) could achieve.

On land the tables are reversed. NATO is inferior in that it lacks the wherewithal to mount a successful conventional offensive against the Warsaw Pact. Furthermore, the Pact can afford to absorb deep penetration to trade space for time, whereas NATO cannot. But the fact that NATO cannot mount a successful offensive against the Pact does not establish that NATO could not defend itself were the Soviets to attack: a capable defense can repel attack by stronger forces.

Whether NATO's conventional forces have that capability has long been debated. It would clearly depend on many factors, some of which (especially timely political decision making) can only be known a posteriori. But the widespread belief that NATO would quickly succumb to a massive conventional attack stems from analyses that ignore a number of subjective factors in NATO's favor that are difficult to quantify in simple terms, but are significant nonetheless. Among these are:

- The questionable loyalty of the Soviet Union's allies, which could require the Soviets to retain large forces in rear areas.
- Soviet–Chinese hostility, which has led the Soviet Union to maintain about a quarter of a million troops in proximity to China even when its European flank is tranquil, and would compel a close watch over her shoulder during a European campaign.
- The problem of maintaining the momentum of an armored offensive across increasingly industrialized and urbanized West Germany.
- The air surperiority that NATO could attain over the battlefield if planned reinforcements in combat aircraft are flown in from the United States, an advantage, especially in all-weather operations, that would severely jeopardize the Pact's ability to sustain an armored offensive.
- The high quality of U.S., British, and especially West German ground forces.
- The certainty that France would honor its commitments to NATO should Germany be invaded, which would not only add another excellent fighting force to the Western side, but also provide NATO with a deeper theater of operations.

Finally, while Pact ground forces would remain numerically superior to NATO at all comparable levels of readiness, the Soviets could not expect to attain the highly favorable ratios at the front on the eve of battle that their planners appear to consider necessary for a successful offensive unless NATO had a catastrophic failure in apprehending Pact preparations or in raising its own combat readiness. Obviously, this caveat also applies to our statement concerning air superiority.

In the light of these considerations, and despite their unquestionably strong military and strategic position in Europe, cautious Soviet planners should be inclined to conclude that a conventional attack on NATO would be a high-risk undertaking. In that case the greatest risk of war would be posed by a political crisis that runs out of control and impels a Soviet decision to attack because they perceive their other options as even more forbidding.

NATO's very considerable potential for repelling a Pact attack by conventional means, and the desire to avoid nuclear escalation until other options are closed, has led NATO to adopt a strategy that envisions a conflict as having distinct nonnuclear and nuclear phases.[2] At the outset of war, NATO's air forces, and a nonnuclear "covering force" consisting largely of light armored units deployed well forward, would have the task of trading some space for time while awaiting the arrival of reinforcements. The main defensive battle would then be fought, with the objective of halting the Pact advance. Success would result in a major counterattack aimed at clearing NATO territory. Should the conventional defense fail, however, consideration would be given to the use of tactical nuclear weapons.

The guidelines for such use have been drafted by NATO's Nuclear Planning Group. They are reportedly very general and emphasize terms such as "appropriate use," "low yields," and "low collateral damage." Furthermore, they also call for clear commmunication to the adversary of NATO's intention to keep military violence at the lowest possible level and in the service of limited goals—namely, a return to the prewar status quo.[3]

While NATO strategy embodies a clear demarcation between conventional and nuclear conflict, the composition of its forces and command infrastructure does not reflect that differentiation. Following the withdrawals mandated by the INF Treaty, NATO will have approximately 4,000 U.S. tactical nuclear warheads, while Great Britain and France will have about 700 and 500 nuclear warheads, respectively. These run the gamut from battlefield weapons to missiles that can reach deep into the Soviet Union. The majority of these munitions are intended for delivery by ships, planes, and guns that are "dual-capable," that is, which must also drop or fire conventional munitions in the prenuclear phases of conflict. In large measure, this is a legacy of the period when the United States enjoyed a substantial advantage in nuclear weapons. Furthermore, to this day, this intermingling of nuclear and conventional forces is widely (although by no means universally) perceived as essential to NATO's ability to deter aggression.[4] On the other hand, the presence of thousands of weapons on or near the battlefield places great demands on command, an issue to which we will return in the next chapter.

Because of its political composition and traditions, NATO's military chain-of-command is actually more akin to a web than a chain, especially in its nuclear aspects (see Figures 9.1 and 9.2). On top stands the Supreme Allied

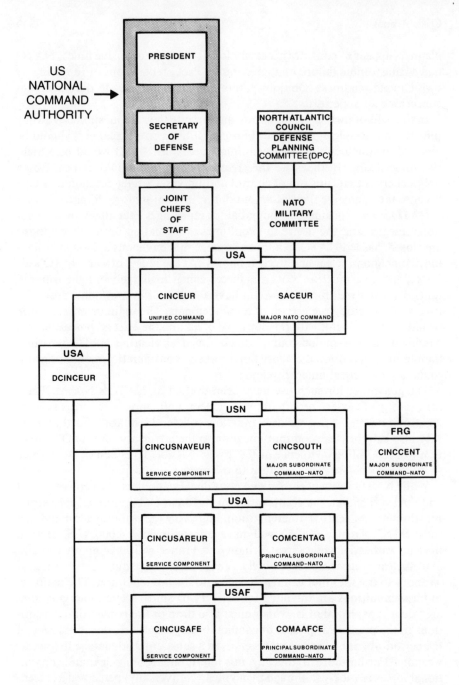

Figure 9.1. NATO's political and military chain-of-command, as viewed from a U.S. perspective.[5] In peacetime the allies' forces are under their own national commands, but in crisis or war they are to be committed to SACEUR, the NATO commander-in-chief, in the so-called command "chop." Each state retains the sovereign right to decide at what point it is willing to chop. NATO can only *acquire* nuclear weapons by a decision of the U.S. or British governments.[6] The decision to *employ* nuclear forces can only be made by SACEUR (or one of the two other major NATO commanders)[7]

Commander, Europe (SACEUR), with headquarters at Mons, Belgium. That post is always held by a U.S. general who is *simultaneously* the commander-in-chief of all American forces in Europe (CINCEUR), with headquarters at Stuttgart, more than 200 miles from Mons. As CINCEUR he reports to the U.S. president, while in his role as SACEUR he reports to the NATO Defense Planning Committee (DPC) headquartered in Brussels, which provides political control over NATO forces. The DPC is composed of ambassadors from the member states, and is permanently in session there. It has a staff and facilities that would immediately come into action should a crisis erupt in Europe or a related theater. In particular, a group of senior officials is responsible for assessing intelligence, declaring crisis conditions, and notifying the DPC.

Two groups at the apex of the U.S. government would assemble to handle any crisis involving the Soviet Union, whether in Europe or in some other arena.[9] The president and his senior advisors constitute the first group. In the past, presidents have either convened the NSC, or formed ad hoc groups, such as Kennedy's ExComm during the Cuban crisis. The second senior group is the JCS, and in particular, its personnel responsible for implementing the so-called emergency operating procedures (EOP).[10] In the event of a serious confrontation with the Soviet Union, this emergency group consisting of about 150 people would be called together. The formation of the EOP organization would take place at the Pentagon within 4 hours.[11] If the situation appeared to be rapidly deteriorating with imminent prospects of war, the EOP would be implemented at the ANMCC at Ft. Ritchie.[12]

Warsaw Pact Strategy, Forces, and Command

The growth of Soviet strategic forces[13] has had an important impact on Soviet doctrine regarding the relationship between nuclear weapons and conventional warfare. During the period when the West placed primary reliance on early use of its superior nuclear arsenal, the Soviets sought to assure the West and themselves that they would not be intimidated—that they anticipated rapid escalation to an all-out nuclear war in which NATO rear areas and the U.S. homeland would not escape nuclear attack, Western nuclear superiority notwithstanding. War with the United States would start with nuclear-missile strikes deep into the enemy interior, Khrushchev warned. But after his fall from power and the emergence of strategic parity, this insistence on a single pattern was abandoned.

---

subsequent to release authorization by the warheads' "owner": the president or the prime minister. In addition, the views of the owners of the delivery vehicle (say a Belgian artillery unit) and the launch point (say Germany) would carry great weight in the employment decision. Nuclear weapons consigned to other than American and British forces are under a "dual-key" arrangement, which gives the nonnuclear power a veto right over the use of the weapon.[8]

By 1967, the Soviets were taking the possibility that war might begin with a conventional phase seriously. This change in doctrine came in response to NATO's adoption of the doctrine of flexible response in 1967, which had been forced on NATO by the Soviet acquisition of an assured retaliatory capability that denied the West the option of using its strategic forces with impunity to defend Western Europe.

By the mid-1970s, the Soviet interest in conventional operations at the beginning of war had broadened to the point where the possibility that nuclear weapons would not come into use at all was being considered.[14] The General Staff Academy lecture materials of the period, however, noted that "it is not likely that strategic operations in European theaters of military operations without the employment of nuclear weapons will be conducted for the duration of the war. Every consideration suggests that a war initiated in [Europe] will transform into a nuclear war at a certain stage."[15] Moreover, a war in Europe would, in Soviet eyes, probably escalate into a general nuclear war involving the homelands of the superpowers.[16]

More recently, Soviet military thinking and planning has deemphasized the role of nuclear weapons even further, to the point where serious consideration now appears to be being given to a strategy that would seek to avoid any use of nuclear forces. For example, Marshal Ogarkov has stated[17] that the growth in the number, diversity, and quality of nuclear weapons since the early 1970s has "led to a radical revision of the role of these weapons, to a break with former views of their place and significance in war, of the methods of conducting combat and operations, and even of the possibility of conducting war at all with nuclear weapons." In 1982, Lt. Gen. M. M. Kir'ian, one of the leading Soviet military theorists, summarized the Soviet view by writing that "a future war may be unleashed both by conventional and by nuclear weapons; started by conventional weapons it may at a certain stage develop into nuclear war," and that "Soviet military thought has worked out methods for the conduct of military operations both with the use, and also without the use of nuclear weapons."[18] Although these theoretical options had been inherent in Soviet doctrine since the mid-1960s, the Soviet capability to carry out large-scale conventional operations on a theater-wide scale grew in the late 1970s as a result of significant changes in Soviet forces, especially in their command.

Every Soviet discussion of conventional war nevertheless notes the possibility that NATO will resort to nuclear weapons. Even Colonel-General Gareev, who is an outspoken proponent of the conventional option, concludes that "it cannot be excluded that the imperialists will unleash nuclear war."[19] Moreover, there seems to be disagreement in the High Command about the risk of escalation once war has begun. Marshal Ogarkov appears to have concluded that war could be confined to the conventional level, whereas Marshal V. Kulikov, the commander-in-chief of the Warsaw Pact, argues that "no matter with what means a new world war begins, it will inevitably end in a nuclear catastrophe."[20]

The growing, but far from unanimous, view in military circles that violence could be kept below the nuclear threshold coexists with progressively stronger statements by Soviet political leaders that nuclear war cannot be fought to any rational purpose.[21] It is unclear to what extent such public utterances only seek a mutual cancellation of the nuclear threat so as to enhance the benefits of the Soviet Union's conventional military advantage in the European theater.

Finally, while most details, and even many important facets, of the Soviet chain-of-command in the European theater are obscure to us, a number of significant features are unambiguous. There can be little doubt, therefore, that whatever multinational superstructure the Warsaw Pact might sport in peacetime, it would be totally dominated by the Soviet Union in a serious crisis, let alone war. Most specialists therefore believe that in wartime non-Soviet divisions would be incorporated into Soviet armies (consisting of four or five divisions plus support units), or even that non-Soviet armies might be incorporated into Soviet "fronts," consisting of four or five armies. Furthermore, all of the Pact's nuclear weapons belong to the Soviet Union, and there is presumably no counterpart to the elaborate NATO consultations involving nuclear weapons. The "Pact" should therefore be expected to make crucial decisions in a more timely fashion than NATO. Whether that would make them sounder is, of course, another matter.

The Soviet Union's chain-of-command has already been discussed in Chapter 7. Precisely how the peacetime Warsaw Pact structure would transform into the wartime command is unclear. Three separate TVDs correspond to the theater commanded by SACEUR: the Southwestern, Western, and Northwestern TVDs. It is believed that at this time Marshal Ogarkov is the commander-in-chief of the Western TVD covering the region from the Alps to the Baltic, but given his rank, he may be senior to the other two TVD commanders, in which case he would be the counterpart of SACEUR.

Turning to nuclear command, ground-based missiles with a range of more than 1,000 km, including the mobile SS-20s to be eliminated by the INF Treaty, belong to the Strategic Rocket Forces. Their employment is probably under the direct control of *Stavka* and the General Staff. The line of authority over short-range nuclear weapons is obscure; release authority is presumably held by *Stavka,* but employment decisions may rest with the TVD commander, in close analogy with NATO's arrangement.

Warning

As a crisis intensifies, both sides can be expected to mount complex alerting operations. Two considerations would largely determine the level of military readiness sought in a particular crisis: political objectives; and the intelligence assessment of threat and opportunity. These are not independent variables. Furthermore, anomalies that cannot be put on organizational charts or be foreseen in contingency plans might turn out to be crucial, such as an inability of the allies to agree on the desirable degree of readiness.

The Pact's day-to-day military posture is continually monitored by Western imaging reconnaissance from aircraft and satellites; ground, air, and space-based electronic listening posts; underwater sound detectors for surveillance of naval movements; airborne radars that can detect moving metallic objects, such as aircraft and vehicles; as well as human sources of intelligence. Given the manifold operations involved in preparing a major conventional attack, it is anticipated, therefore, that warning indicators would signal significant departures from the Pact's peacetime posture within hours. Alarms would then go off at the European Command (EuCom) headquarters in Stuttgart, which has automated facilities for integrating signals intelligence from the entire theater, and for fusing and displaying warning indicators from all sources. EuCom is linked to the intelligence centers of its subordinate army, navy, and air force commands, and to the National Military Intelligence Center at the Pentagon serving the JCS Operations Directorate.[22] This vital hub of military intelligence is tied into a larger network called the National Operations and Intelligence Watch Officers Net, which provides secure voice conferencing between the operations centers of the CIA, DIA, the State Department, the National Security Agency (NSA), the White House Situation Room, and the recently created NSC Crisis Coordination Center.[23]

This timely and extensive warning, supposedly available in a matter of hours, is to be contrasted with a standard planning *assumption* that the Pact would require about 4 days to mount an attack by its standing forces with very limited goals, 9 days following mobilization to prepare an offensive with ambitious territorial objectives, and 2 weeks for a campaign that threatened all of Western Europe.[24] These intervals between decision and attack are to be compared with the 3 days that are considered as the minimum required by NATO for deployment of its covering force to the inter-German border. If NATO defenses are to attain their theoretical optimum, deployment of forces in being and mobilization of reinforcements must begin on the very heels of Pact mobilization. Failure to detect Pact preparations, or to react with dispatch, would have dire consequences were an attack in the offing.

Turning to the Pact's awareness of NATO activities, in a crisis the vast human and technical resources of the Soviet intelligence services[25] would be brought to bear on NATO, with a particular focus on its nuclear forces. As already mentioned, Soviet strategy places a premium on discovering the level and progress of U.S. and NATO preparations for the possible use of nuclear weapons; discerning the shift of the U.S. and NATO command systems to a wartime footing; monitoring the movement of bombers and tankers to secondary dispersal bases and submarines to sea; and on determining whether and when military commanders would acquire authority to use U.S. and NATO nuclear weapons. It would be prudent to assume that the Soviet intelligence services would be at least as successful in providing warning as their Western competitors.

Alerting Operations

The alert operations that NATO and the Pact are likely to mount provide a great deal of insight into the interactions that could inflame a European crisis.

NATO's operations are officially organized into alert conditions (LERT-CONs), and are the NATO counterpart to the U.S. DEFCON alert ladder described in Chapter 4. There are also five LERTCON rungs. The first step above the peacetime posture is called *military vigilance*.[26] SACEUR can move to the three higher rungs (LERTCON 3, 2, and 1) on his own authority, but is expected to consult first with NATO's Defense Policy Committee. The higher three alert postures are roughly equivalent in readiness to that of the corresponding DEFCONs. Because of the close coupling between U.S. and NATO strategy and forces, and the likelihood that a NATO alert would be accompanied by the alerting of U.S. forces outside the European theater, the DEFCON and LERTCON rungs will be discussed together. Most aspects and implications of the naval components of these operations will be considered in a later section devoted to the oceans.

In brief, these rungs have following significance. The peacetime posture is 5/4, with SAC at DEFCON 4, while all other forces are at 5. NATO's military vigilance is a counterpart of DEFCON 4. At level 3 units are to heighten readiness and standby for further orders. Level 2 signifies readiness for combat, while level 1 is deployment for imminent combat. For perspective, we recall that at the peak of the Yom Kippur Crisis a mild version of DEFCON 3 was declared, while during the Cuban Missile Crisis U.S. forces outside of Europe were at DEFCON 3, but SAC was at DEFCON 2. NATO has never moved beyond military vigilance.

Were the two military organizations to climb the alert ladder, they would undergo a sequence of profound changes that would transform them from a reservoir of immense but largely latent power into a vast array of forces ready for immediate use. This process would be inordinately complex, so only its broad features will be examined here.[27] To provide a digestible overview, the spectrum of alert operations have been summarized in Tables 9.1 through 9.3, which divide these measures into three categories of increasing combat readiness. This is a hypothetical and context-free depiction of what is inherently a context-dependent process. Nevertheless, the tables reflect the broad military and political objectives that the various readiness conditions are intended to attain. These goals impose a rough ordering on the alert measures—an ordering that, at the lowest rungs, can also be discerned in the operations conducted by U.S. forces in the Cuban and Yom Kippur crises.[28] The step to the highest state of NATO readiness is interpreted in this illustration as the response to strategic warning of a conventional Pact attack, so that most alert measures should be in place before then. This supposition results in the remarkable brevity of the list of NATO operations in Table 9.3 and would imply that LERTCON 2 represents a step of profound gravity.

Several facts should be kept in mind while examining these tables. First, alerting systems have considerable flexibility and provide considerable opportunity for adapting the military posture to the needs of the moment. For example, both sides have the ability to emphasize or deemphasize measures involving strategic forces; steps that would "normally" be part of a certain rung may be postponed to a higher rung (or vice versa); the alert status

Table 9.1   Heightened Readiness

U.S./NATO

Strategic C³I and Forces

Preparations for emergency evacuation of leadership.
Increased readiness of NEACP and other principal command aircraft.
Enhanced readiness of communication networks.
Overseas relocation of reconnaissance aircraft.
Conversion of sensors (e.g. radars) to wartime warning status.

SAC: relocation of airborne command posts and formation of back-up crews
    and battle staffs; enchanced readiness of Minuteman crews; more bombers
    and refueling aircraft on strip alert and dispersed.

Navy: In-port missile submarines (SSBNs) readied for departure, may leave.

Theater C³I

Activation and testing of command networks.
Intensified reconnaissance, including AWACS.
Activation of 24-hour battle staffs.
Intense processing of intelligence data.
CINCEUR's airborne command posts alerted and dispersed.

Tactical Nuclear Forces

Marginal changes of battlefield weapons (custodial units alerted).
Increased readiness of theater-range missiles at peacetime locations, and of
    nuclear-capable aircraft.
Missile submarines (SSBNs) assigned to NATO leave port.

Conventional Forces

Recall of personnel, accelerated maintenance.
Gain control of Greenland–Iceland–Norway straits to impede passage of Soviet
    naval units.
Reinforcement of carrier groups.
In-port attack submarines (SSNs) surged to sea.
ASW forces alerted and strengthened.
Intense reconnaissance and trailing of Soviet ships and SSBNs.
Enhanced runway alert of aircraft.

could vary geographically,[29] even within Europe; and so forth. Second, little
is known about Soviet and Pact alert operations—the tables merely reflect
what Western analysts regard as plausible.[30] Finally, many terse phrases in
the tables represent truly major undertakings, such as the "arrival in Europe
of 1,000 combat aircraft from the United States" or "General Mobilization,"
operations that are of a magnitude not seen since 1945. The tables, therefore,
merit scrutiny and contemplation; their entries—individually and collec-
tively—have a multitude of military, political, and psychological
implications.

SOVIET/WTO

Likely

Nuclear forces largely exempted from alert.

Continental air defenses alerted.

C^3 largely peacetime, but tactical command posts at heightened readiness for deployment.
Intensified reconnaissance by satellites (additional launches) and aircraft of NATO ground and naval forces.
Enhancement of early warning capabilities.

Increased protection of SSBNs in homewaters against ASW. Anticarrier air and naval deployments.

Stepped-up field training of forward deployed ground units.
Covert reinforcement of rear-area forces.
Alert exercises of rear-area ground forces; increased garrison readiness.

Possible/Partial

Some SSBNs leave port.
Airborne troops alerted.
Forward deployment of attack aircraft.
Naval units at sea move to and beyond choke points.
Preparation for attacks on naval C^3.

The alert ladder has a number of general features that the tables illustrate. The most obvious and significant feature is that while each side's vulnerability drops as its alert level rises, its capability to attack also rises, and the other side is therefore bound to perceive a mounting threat. This can already be seen in the entries that refer to command, even though they involve no fire-power as such.

Civilian and military command organizations at their peacetime status are not designed to cope immediately with crisis circumstances. Both the capability and the endurance of the command system can be significantly

Table 9.2   Readiness for Combat

U.S./NATO

Strategic C³I and Forces

Formation and dispersal of alternate national leadership teams and evacuation of other officials; national level command distributed between Washington and alternate command posts.

Rendezvous between vice president and NEACP; another NEACP moves to Andrews AFB near Washington.

Reinforcement of SAC airborne command and reconnaissance network, and that of other commands (e.g., Pacific Command forward-deploys airborne command post to Japan).

Remainder of SAC bombers and tankers brought to alert status and dispersed; possibly partial airborne alert, some forward deployment to Great Britain.

Remainder of SSBNs leave port; communication relay aircraft for SSBNs dispersed and on heightened airborne alert.
Whole fleet on heightened alert, much leaves port.

NATO Command

"Chop": alliance forces, conventional and perhaps nuclear, put under command of NATO SACEUR. U.S. CINCEUR headquarters staff in Stuttgart splits, goes to wartime command bunkers for SACEUR and CINCEUR.

Transition to wartime covert communication.

Tactical Nuclear Forces

Pershing IIs and Ground Launched Cruise Missiles (GLCMs), if still deployed, dispersed to covert field locations.

Covert dispersal from storage 75 to 100 km behind inter-German border of battlefield weapons (mainly shells for dual-capable artillery and Lance short-range missiles).

Conventional Forces

Alerted "covering" ground forces dispatched to wartime positions as rapidly as logistics permit.
United States and allies mobilize reserves and reinforce standing forces.
Arrival in Europe of perhaps 1,000 combat aircraft from United States, many dual-capable.
Intensification of ASW (surveillance only).

enhanced in a manner that does not project threat, at least at first blush; furthermore, the adversary may not be able to detect a good portion of these steps. Many measures fall into this lowest readiness category, such as the alerting of key civilian and military leaders and advisors, and preliminary

SOVIET/WTO

Strategic C³I and Forces

Most SSBNs with long-range SLBMs to sea in homewaters.
Long range bombers dispersed to Arctic bases.
Increased sorties by Yankee SSBNs with shorter-range SLBMs to U.S. coasts.
Intensive reconnaissance by aircraft and satellites.

Theater C³I

Intrusive reconnaissance of NATO airspace; excitation of air defense.
Soviet marshalls assume command of WTO forces.
Activation of TVD commands.
C³ and logistics exercised from field locations.

Should nuclear war appear imminent, electronic warfare against satellites,
    radars, and AWACS begins.

Tactical Nuclear forces

Dispersal of warheads to field locations.
Launchers leave garrison for changing field locations.

Conventional Forces

Intensified field training of first echelon forces.
Ground forces reinforce, leave garrison in strength, drawing war stocks.
Dual-capable surface vessels and subarines may sortie beyond choke points.
Intensive harrassment and target acquisition against carrier groups by ships and
    aircraft.
Continental air defenses fully alerted; forward deployed SAMs dispersed,
    launchers leave garrison.

preparations for their possible evacuation; enhanced readiness of wartime
command posts for national leaders and major military combat commands;
the readying of backup communication networks;[31] the conversion of peacetime intelligence sensors to attack detection sensors;[32] the formation of 24-

Table 9.3   Deployment for Combat

U.S./NATO

Conventional Forces

Defensive preparations (digging in, setting barriers, mining bridges, etc.) rushed to completion by "covering" forces.

Theater C³

Maximum reconnaissance activities and target acquisition.

Tactical Nuclear Forces

Warheads and launchers collocated and/or mated.

---

hour battle staffs, and the dispersal of alternate staffs; and the like. The synergism between these relatively modest steps results in command systems that are much better prepared to cope with a surprise nuclear attack, and to disseminate intelligence and orders, than when they are at their peacetime posture.

Further increases of command readiness greatly reduce vulnerability and enhance combat effectiveness, but it is also difficult to conceal many of these measures from electronic intelligence. Whether by intent or not, such changes in the status of the command system can project at least as intense a perception of threat as operations involving the forces themselves. These general remarks are illustrated by the dispersal of at least a portion of leaderships from their peacetime locations; deployment of airborne and ground-mobile military command posts and communications relays by NATO and the Pact, as well as by other major U.S. and Soviet commands around the world; acti-

---

SOVIET/WTO

Command

Evacuation and relocation of leadership groups; national command exercised
  from alternate command posts.
Activation of wartime communications networks; adoption of wartime standard
  operating procedures (encryption, silence).

Strategic Forces

Wartime command for Strategic Rocket Forces activated.
All SSBNs leave port with ASW escort.
Long-range bombers fully alerted and loaded.

Other Nuclear Forces

Tactical launchers leave garrison for covert positions.
Tactical warheads collocated with launchers.
Nuclear weapons stockpiles emptied.

Conventional Naval and Air Forces

Air Force at full force and stood down; fire control raders stand down.
Naval units move into close proximity with US and NATO fleets.
Further intensification of airborne and satellite fleet surveillance, and of
  electronic warfare against NATO satellites, radars, AWACS, etc.

Ground Forces

First echelon forces assume battle positions in attack formation.
Second echelon forces advance to forward assembly areas.
Allocation and dispersal of war material and stocks.
Covert insertion of sabotage (Spetznas) commando units behind NATO lines.

---

vation of wartime military chains-of-command, such as that of the Soviet
Western TVD and the "chop" of allied forces to the command of SACEUR;
the shift of communication traffic from peacetime to wartime command posts
and networks, accompanied by increased encryption; and perhaps most omi-
nously, the sudden suspension of certain activities, such as communications
silence.

   Reconnaissance would also display a change in character as the alert level
rises. At first, only marginal departures from peacetime would occur, such as
forward deployment of reconnaissance aircraft and a heightened tempo of
AWACS surveillance by NATO. In view of the vulnerability of U.S. command to SLBM attack, intensified surveillance of Soviet SSBNs patrolling off
U.S. shores should also be expected at moderate alert levels. If we are to judge
from past crises, such as the Falkland Islands War, Soviet space activity is
likely to change markedly because many Soviet surveillance satellites have

short mission lifetimes and must be launched in response to demand, whereas U.S. space-born intelligence would undergo far less change unless the Soviet Union were to engage in antisatellite operations. Should the risk of war appear to be rising, reconnaissance would become increasingly intense and intrusive, and eventually seek to provoke reactions to reveal information about the adversary's readiness and defenses—for example, the location and frequency of radars.

Electronic warfare, especially jamming of communications and of radars, could become intense should actual war appear to be imminent. Harassment and intimidation of reconnaissance operations in international airspace and waters would also be likely.

The readying of nuclear forces would not follow a uniform pattern. The alerting of U.S. strategic forces has already been discussed in Chapter 4, so we shall confine ourselves to a few additional remarks. As we saw, ICBMs are essentially always ready; unless they are mobile their vulnerability cannot be altered significantly short of launch. Missile submarines (SSBNs) in port are highly vulnerable, as are bombers not on strip alert. Consequently, the disposition of these two elements of the strategic forces is likely to change dramatically and visibly. This is especially true of the Soviet Union since, in contrast to the United States, it keeps the great majority of its SSBNs in port and does not have bombers on strip alert in peacetime.

The U.S. in-port SSBN force can sail on very short notice because every submarine has two complete crews. If previous crises are taken as indicative, essentially the whole U.S. SSBN force is likely to be at sea even if the risk of war was deemed to be moderate. As a crisis intensifies, SAC bombers and tankers would be dispersed, an increasing number of bombers would go on strip alert, and eventually some portion of the fleet might be consigned to an airborne alert, as they were during the Cuban crisis. Furthermore, SAC's nuclear-armed FB-111 bombers could be forward-deployed to bases in Great Britain.

United States SSBNs patrol over vast ocean areas, but, as we shall see, the bulk of the Soviet SSBN fleet is expected to leave its ports for nearby home water "sanctuaries" in a crisis where Soviet ships and naval aviation are to provide defense against U.S. attack submarines and other ASW activities. It is anticipated that Soviet long-range bombers would be dispersed to airfields in the Arctic in a severe crisis.

The readying of tactical nuclear forces can be expected to follow a quite different pattern from that of the strategic forces. The immediate threat posed by the strategic forces is already enormous in peacetime. Alert operations by strategic forces, therefore, have a considerably greater impact on their survivability than on their offensive capability. Furthermore, the strategic forces are well-isolated from other forces. As it is unlikely that war would begin with a strategic strike, a rise in the alert status of strategic forces that is not accompanied by other potentially aggressive measures stands a reasonable chance of being interpreted as a protective step by the adversary.

In comparison to the strategic forces, the tactical nuclear forces are at a much lower state of readiness and far more vulnerable in peacetime. They are also thoroughly intermingled with the forces that would be engaged in the conventional phase of a war. As a result, many of the alert measures for tactical nuclear forces would be an ambiguous indicator to the adversary, and therefore pose dilemmas for either side.

Neither alliance appears to contemplate the use of tactical nuclear forces at the outset of a European campaign. Furthermore, visible preparations for such use would be read as an especially grave warning indicator, and could also stimulate public unrest. Both sides store nuclear warheads for artillery and short-range missiles in depots that are vulnerable to conventional attack, and from which they must be dispersed and mated to their means of delivery. As we have seen, the Soviet Union would presumably seek to prevent nuclear escalation in a European campaign, and would be likely to resort to a preemptive conventional attack on NATO's nuclear forces should there be indications that they are about to be dispersed.[33] For all these reasons, it is likely that NATO would not disperse such warheads in the early stages of a crisis, even though that would leave them vulnerable.[34] It also appears that the Soviet alerting system is designed to allow conventional readiness to rise to high levels without entailing the strategic nuclear forces.[35]

The conundrum between vulnerability and provocation is far less onerous for dual-capable aircraft based on airfields and carriers far from the battlefield, and their readiness for nuclear missions, therefore, can be heightened at a lower level of alert. Indeed, even in peacetime a considerable number of U.S. and NATO aircraft loaded with some 150 nuclear weapons are routinely kept on quick reaction alert (QRA), ready for takeoff on short notice.

Finally, a few words regarding conventional forces. Their state of readiness is of paramount importance whether or not nuclear forces would actually see action because war cannot be waged with nuclear forces alone. While crucial elements of the command infrastructure and of the nuclear forces (both strategic and tactical) can be prepared for war clandestinely, it has become virtually impossible to ready the large units involved in conventional operations without offering a loud warning to the adversary. A watershed of truly historic proportions would therefore be crossed should any combination of the following steps ever be taken: first-echelon Pact forces currently deployed within striking distance of the inter-German border reinforce and leave garrison; NATO's covering forces take up forward defensive positions; combat aircraft from the United States arrive in Europe in large numbers; the bulk of the U.S. and British navies leave port; and either or both sides mobilize reserves. Should a crisis of such a high intensity escalate still further, Table 9.3 summarizes the operations that could be expected to follow before war actually breaks out.

THE MIDDLE EAST

As a crisis arena, the Middle East has very different characteristics from Europe. Neither superpower has standing armies in the region. Their past actions indicate that even dramatic changes of fortune, such as Egypt's several switches in alliance between the East and the West, do not pose a threat to vital interests sufficiently dire to demand massive, direct armed intervention. These factors favor stability; chronic and violent turmoil strain stability.

Israel has long been a superpower in miniature, but its superiority over Syria has undergone some erosion.[36] Should a deep shift in that balance ever be perceived as imminent, the risk of warfare at an unprecedented scale, including chemical and perhaps even nuclear weapons, could become appreciable. The superpowers could be drawn into this cauldron. Each has solemn commitments to states that are often at each other's throats, whose demise would bring into question the value of those commitments, and which could thereby produce a global shift in the balance of power.

Following Israel's devastation of the Soviet-equipped Syrian Air Force and air defenses during the 1982 invasion of Lebanon, the Soviet Union mounted a vast reequipment program.[37] Damascus has acquired weapons of a caliber not previously deployed by Arab states, especially missiles that can strike deep into Israel, and sophisticated SAMs that cover all of Lebanese and much of Israeli airspace. The missile and SAM batteries are manned by thousands of Soviet combat personnel who are training Syrian crews. Syria has also set out to develop and produce toxic gases.[38] In conjunction with its panoply of missiles, this could yield a potent chemical warfare capability.

While Israel still remains distinctly superior militarily to Syria, its qualitative advantage is slipping, and its poor economic performance has forced unprecedented cutbacks. For the first time Syria poses a threat to Israel even if it were to attack alone.

While the conventional balance may have shifted somewhat toward Syria, Israel appears to be the only nuclear power in the region. Her 1981 air raid that destroyed the Iraqi nuclear reactor indicates that she is determined to prevent the Arab states from aquiring such weapons. Until recently authoritative estimates[39] put Israel's arsenal at 20 aircraft-deliverable weapons with yields in the 20-kiloton range that are ready for prompt assembly. Now detailed reports[40] indicate that the Israeli arsenal holds 100 to 200 sophisticated warheads, some of which are likely to have appreciable yields.[41] On one-way unrefueled flights Israeli aircraft could attack targets as distant as Kiev, a fact that may be germane to reports that the Soviets have promised to provide nuclear weapons to Syria should Israel resort to their use.[42] A new longer-range model of the Jericho missile has also been a cause for concern to the Soviet Union because recent tests have demonstrated a range sufficient to deliver nuclear weapons not only to distant Arab capitals, but with further improvements also to targets inside Soviet territory.[43]

In such a setting one can imagine chains of events that are not outrageously implausible and would entrain a dangerous confrontation between the superpowers. The members of this study explored one such scenario in some detail.[44] It began with the death of King Hussein, which spurred both Israel and Syria to step into the vacuum. This soon escalated to a major Israeli–Syrian conflict in which Israel conducted a highly successful offensive that threatened Damascus. Syria responded with chemical weapons delivered via

Soviet-supplied rocket launchers, which caught the Israel army unprepared. At the same time Israel failed to maintain air superiority. As a result, a Syrian counteroffensive, reportedly accompanied by heavy casualties among Israeli civilians, carried deep into the Galilee and threatened Haifa. Soviet intelligence was informed by a highly placed agent that Israel was about to use nuclear weapons, possibly even against Soviet targets. Amid considerable confusion and ambiguous intelligence, the Soviet government ordered a "surgical" strike with several subkiloton nuclear weapons against Israeli facilities that were supposedly staging the impending attack; the Soviet strike produced virtually no collateral damage. The United States thereupon intervened to stabilize Israel's deteriorating situation by unilaterally establishing an enclave covering all of Israel except the terrain already held by Syria, to be protected by U.S. naval and air power. Furthermore, the U.S. government announced that it was committed to a return to the status quo antebellum. A spectrum of Soviet–Syrian responses to this U.S. initiative were considered, and various options for fulfilling the U.S. commitment were explored in some detail.

This exercise indicated that even in a crisis considerably more intense than the Cuban Crisis—involving not only chemical warfare but even a nuclear strike by a superpower, and with both superpowers taking military measures on behalf of warring parties—there is nevertheless a reasonable chance that direct U.S.–Soviet fighting could be avoided. The superpowers hold no territory in the region, and their forces are at sea and in the air, so they could carry out extensive military operations with relatively little friction. Conflict between them, therefore, may be avoidable even through a few steps in crisis escalation. Furthermore, the United States enjoys air and naval superiority in the region, which gives it considerable freedom to maneuver and imposes a high threshold on Soviet intervention. This optimistic assessment, however, rests on the assumption that both superpowers would be following a fundamental rule of the Middle Eastern road—that they are prepared to protect an ally from destruction but not to support an ally's quest for total victory, nor to dramatically alter the political landscape by use of their own forces. Were either to violate that rule, the risks would be far higher.

Compared to the Mediterranean, in the Persian Gulf the lines in the sand are blurred, the rules of the road are ill-defined by precedent or commitment, and the balance of power is less favorable to the United States. Recent events, such as the attack on the USS *Stark,* and the remarkable effectiveness of short-range missiles, small armed craft, and vintage underwater mines, have driven home the hazards of projecting military force into this region. In a confrontation with the Soviet Union, U.S. naval operations in the Gulf would be hampered by lack of room and poor access, and would be endangered by aircraft based in the Soviet Union. Indeed, this region may well be more dangerous than the eastern shores of the Mediterranean.[45] On the other hand, the Soviet Union also faces imposing obstacles to effective military intervention. The Gulf's shores are separated from Soviet ground forces by several imposing mountain ranges traversed by a small number of poor roads.[46]

Although the superpowers also confront each other outside Europe and the Middle East, we shall not explore other areas where a severe superpower crisis could originate. Most of the known phenomena that could have an impact on crisis behavior already appear in the two arenas we described, and relatively little of generic value would probably be added were we to explore scenarios set, say, in the Far East. Thus, fear that conflict between China and the Soviet Union could entrain the United States in a nuclear confrontation has been forcefully expressed by no less an observer than Richard Nixon;[47] others have concerns about the Indian subcontinent. In all cases, however, it is nuclear proliferation that causes anxiety, just as proliferation greatly aggravates the dangers that exist in the Middle East even in its absence. Furthermore, should events in any theater run out of hand, the crisis might spread to the European vital center.

GLOBAL ARENAS

The oceans and space share characteristics that distinguish them from geographically circumscribed theaters. The superpowers' widely dispersed fleets and naval aviation are continuously within range and often in contact. The high seas, therefore, are a medium in which a crisis could rapidly propagate, even if it did not have its origin there. Should powerful means for destroying satellites become available, space would take on a character akin to the high seas: an arena where a crisis might originate, or a medium that could rapidly spread a crisis from a mundane terrestrial beginning.

The Oceans

On the oceans the United States enjoys clear superiority—a much more capable surface fleet, more comprehensive coverage and shore facilities, and a virtual monopoly in sea-based air power. Figure 9.2 provides a succinct summary of the military balance at sea.

Of perhaps greater significance than the naval balance itself, Petropavlovsk on the Pacific is the only Soviet port from which ships can reach open ocean without passing through choke points. In addition, most Soviet harbors are icebound many months of the year.[48] The Soviets' impressive effort to develop a strong blue water navy must always contend with these geographic handicaps, which are shown in Fig. 9.3. This Western geographic advantage is offset to some extent by the West's incomparably greater dependence on sea traffic, brought about by centuries of profitable exploitation of that advantage.

To see what these immutable facts of geography can imply, consider the deployment of Soviet submarines into the Mediterranean. Because of the Montreux Convention, only diesel-powered Soviet submarines can pass through the Dardanelles, and must do so on the surface. Soviet nuclear-powered submarines based in the Baltic or at Murmansk must therefore pass not only by Gibraltar, but also through the Danish Straits or the Greenland–Iceland–Norway (G–I–N) gaps, all of which are under intense Western surveillance. Similarly, ships based at Vladivostock can only reach the open ocean by passing through the narrow straits that connect the Seas of Japan and Okhotsk with the Pacific.

Quite aside from the strategic weapons on SSBNs, the nuclear arsenals at sea are formidable. The United States and Soviet Union have about 250 and 200 nuclear capable ships and submarines, respectively, not counting SSBNs.[49] American naval forces could carry about 3,500 tactical nuclear warheads compared to at least 1,500 for the Soviet Navy. The two nations deploy these weapons on a large variety of dual-capable surface ships, attack submarines, carrier-based aircraft, and land-based naval aviation. The United States has nearly 1,000 nuclear-capable high-performance aircraft on carriers, whereas relatively low-performance vertical takeoff and landing planes (VTOLs) now constitute the Soviet Union's sea-based air power. The Soviet's first large carrier is slated to enter service in 1989, and it is presumably intended for high-performance fixed-wing aircraft.[50]

A significant recent development is the U.S. decision to deploy a large number of nuclear armed sea-launched Tomahawk cruise missiles (SLCMs) on surface ships and attack submarines. Current plans call for the deployment of 750 SLCMs on 140 surface ships and submarines by the early 1990s. The Tomahawk's high accuracy and range of 1,350 miles will give a large number of vessels that are not part of the strategic forces the capability to attack hard military targets on the shores and well into the interior of the Soviet Union. The Soviets are expected to deploy similar weapons in the near future.[51]

Broadly speaking, in wartime each superpower should be expected to place highest priority on the maritime objectives that are consistent with its strategic position and naval power. Given the West's dependence on oceanic lines of supply, the paramount Western goal would be to bottle up the major Soviet fleets in their home waters north of the G–I–N gaps, and behind the straits connecting the Seas of Japan and Okhotsk to the Pacific. In particular, NATO would seek to prevent passage of Soviet ships, especially attack submarines, through the G–I–N gaps.

The highest priority for the Soviet Union would be the protection of its home waters, which are to serve as sanctuaries for Soviet SSBNs. In contrast to U.S. SSBNs, most Soviet strategic submarines stay within range of Soviet air and surface fleet support because of superior U.S. ASW capabilities. The primary Soviet objective, therefore, would be to prevent the passage of U.S. surface ships and submarines through those same choke points into Soviet home waters.

Were both sides to confine themselves to these complementary priorities, the oceans might not be a particularly fertile ground for crisis interactions or escalation. But each side appears to have further objectives that are potentially dangerous: the disruption by Soviet submarines of the sea traffic carrying supplies and reinforcements to Europe;[52] and the large-scale deploy-

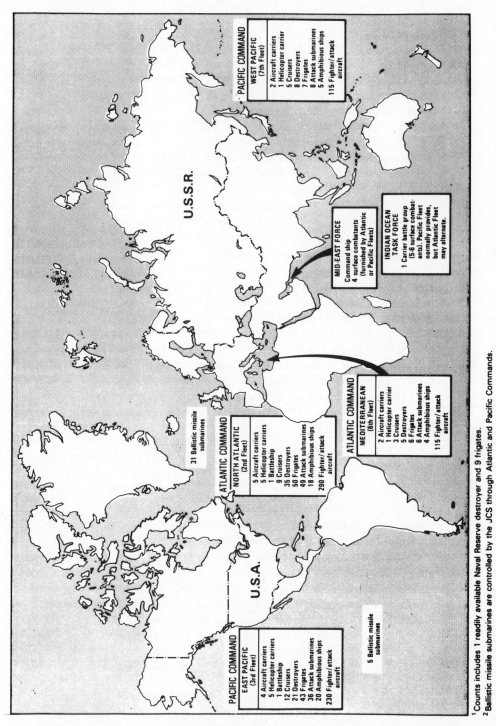

Figure 9.2. U.S. and Soviet naval deployments as of 1985. These maps are from John M. Collins, *U.S.-Soviet Military Balance, 1980–1985,* published by Pergamon-Brassey's International Defense Publishers, Inc., 1985, and reprinted by permission of the publisher.

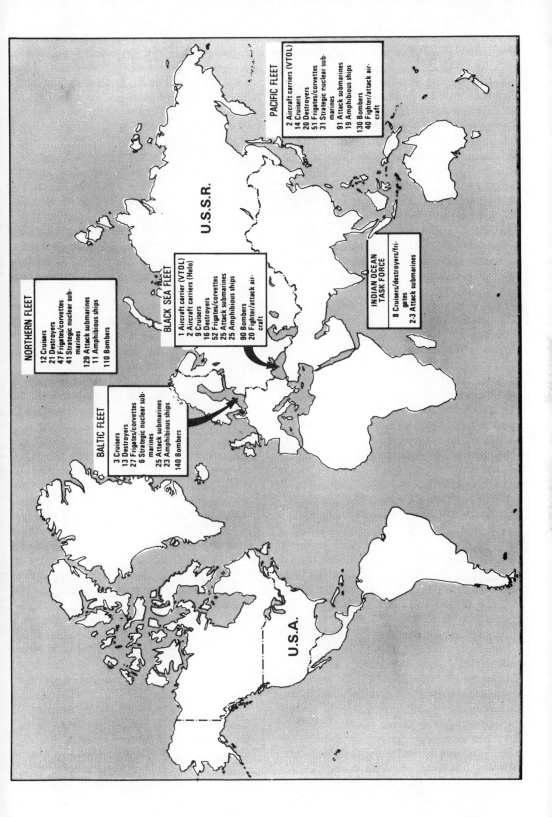

NORTHERN FLEET

12 Cruisers
21 Destroyers
47 Frigates/corvettes
41 Strategic nuclear submarines
129 Attack submarines
11 Amphibious ships
110 Bombers

BALTIC FLEET

3 Cruisers
13 Destroyers
27 Frigates/corvettes
6 Strategic nuclear submarines
25 Attack submarines
23 Amphibious ships
140 Bombers

BLACK SEA FLEET

1 Aircraft carrier (VTOL)
2 Aircraft carriers (Helo)
9 Cruisers
16 Destroyers
52 Frigates/corvettes
25 Attack submarines
25 Amphibious ships
90 Bombers
20 Fighter/attack aircraft

PACIFIC FLEET

2 Aircraft carriers (VTOL)
14 Cruisers
20 Destroyers
51 Frigates/corvettes
31 Strategic nuclear submarines
91 Attack submarines
19 Amphibious ships
130 Bombers
40 Fighter/attack aircraft

INDIAN OCEAN TASK FORCE

8 Cruisers/destroyers/frigates
2-3 Attack submarines

U.S.S.R.

U.S.A.

Figure 9.3. a. Access to the Atlantic Ocean for the Soviet Union's Baltic and Northern Fleets. The Greenland–Iceland–Norway (G–I–N) gaps, frequently mentioned in the

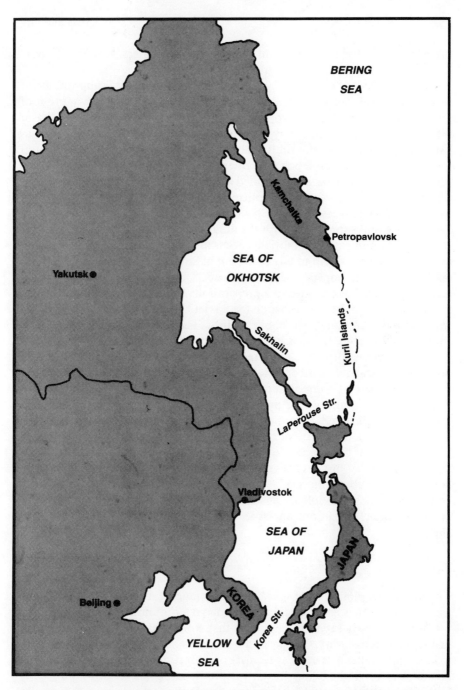

text, refers to the relatively shallow waters between these major land areas, which are further punctuated by small but strategically important islands (especially the Faeroes and Bear Island). It should be noted, however, that Soviet nuclear-powered submarines can circumnavigate Greenland under the polar ice cap. b. Access to the Pacific Ocean for the Soviet Pacific Fleet, whose home bases are at Vladivostok and Petropavlovsk.

ment of NATO naval units into Soviet home waters.[53] Each of these
endeavors would threaten vital interests.

Aside from these "constants" in the maritime situation, it is appropriate to
reconsider naval facets of the alert operations to be expected in the event of
an escalating crisis in the European theater. In view of the vulnerability of
the U.S. national command system to nuclear attack from nearby submarines, Soviet missile submarines that normally patrol in the Atlantic would
quickly find themselves exposed to intensified surveillance; should the crisis
intensify this would be accompanied by aggressive harassment. American
SSNs can set sail on very short notice, as was demonstrated during a recent
exercise.[54] Surface vessels and SSNs already at sea would pick up and trail
Soviet ships and submarines with the aid of intelligence transmitted via fleet
satellite communications.[55] Initially, SSNs and other naval forces might concentrate on the relatively small contingent of Soviet forces beyond the natural
choke points that impede the Soviet fleets.[56] The United States and allied
navies could also begin extensive preparations for interdicting Soviet vessels
transiting through these gaps, while the Soviet Union might decide to quickly
surge vessels through these choke points. Therefore, abrasive encounters
short of shooting are likely in such regions before war breaks out.

The positioning of U.S. carrier task forces within striking range of Soviet
ports and anticarrier bomber bases, and the deployment of U.S. attack submarines into Soviet home waters, can be expected to stimulate a variety of
responses. The Soviets would probably launch satellites specifically designed
for naval surveillance.[57] Soviet dual-capable naval forces and naval aviation
would move to a high state of combat readiness, Soviet SSBNs would leave
port, and the units assigned to their protection would be reinforced. Both
sides would carry out intensive and probably provocative reconnaissance
below, on, and above the sea.[58] In short, as a crisis mounts the risk of inadvertent or purposeful violence at sea would multiply, and could contribute to
or even trigger escalation, an issue to which we shall return in the next
chapter.

Space

The military exploitation of space is approaching a turning point, and its role
as a potential crisis arena could soon undergo a profound transformation.

Current military satellites play roles that would change markedly as political circumstances vary. In peacetime satellites are invaluable to arms control, in many other activities of security organizations, and in confirming that
an attack is not in the offing. In wartime, those same spacecraft would greatly
amplify the effectiveness of the military forces they serve; hence, they would
become tempting targets as soon as even conventional hostilities appear
imminent. Yet destruction of those satellites would make escalation more
likely and a negotiated end of hostilities more difficult.

At this time the Soviet Union has a primitive capability for ASAT warfare
against low-orbit satellites passing over two sites in the Soviet Union.[59] The

United States has successfully tested, but not deployed, a ground-based ballistic missile interceptor that could also attack low orbit satellites.[60] Of greater significance for the ASAT competition, the United States is developing a low-orbit air-launched weapon that is intended solely as a satellite interceptor. Airborne basing is superior to launch from the ground since it provides the possibility of simultaneous attack on widely separated satellites with little warning.[61]

In addition to these low-orbit interceptors, both nations presumably have some capabilities for nondestructive interference with satellite operations, such as jamming. To our knowledge, neither nation has tested ASATs that could reach the high-orbit satellites vital to strategic command, nor have they tested or deployed space mines—satellites carrying conventional or nuclear explosives maintained in orbit within range of their prospective victim, which they would destroy on radio command.[62]

It is unclear whether these ASAT interception techniques will lead to deployed systems capable of comprehensive attacks on low-orbit satellites, or whether space mines, which could threaten satellites in any orbit, will be tested or deployed, but the long-term trend toward greater reliance on satellites by military units of all sorts appears to be irreversible. Consequently, ASAT deployments would create growing opportunities for crisis inflammation;[63] for example, one side might view the destruction of the other's unmanned satellites as relatively harmless, while the other might read it as an indicator of imminent escalation. The erosion of the current regime, in which space has been treated as a sort of sanctuary, would also encourage the development of nondestructive techniques for interfering with satellites, which could then be employed during a crisis.

The repercussions of space-based ballistic missile defenses (BMDs) would be much more significant than ASAT deployment alone. The architecture and infrastructure of the entire strategic command system may then have to be refashioned. In particular, it would have to become very highly automated because the defense must be engaged very promptly; on the other hand, since the defense might fail, command of the offensive forces would presumably require integration with that of the defense.[64] Conventional low orbit satellites would be at the mercy of the opponent's BMD weapons, and it is doubtful that any low orbit satellite that did not carry active defenses could be made secure in such an environment. If the BMD systems had directed-energy weapons (lasers, etc.) of very high performance, they could threaten the high orbit satellites of the strategic command systems with virtually instantaneous destruction.[65]

A BMD system that relies on space weapons, therefore, poses very serious and unresolved problems for command and control, and for stability at the threshold of strategic warfare. It is unclear whether command vulnerability, even if narrowly defined as the endurance of some set of critical facilities, would be decreased or increased by such BMD systems—whether the inherently small number of vital C³I nodes would gain protection from "active" defenses beyond that available through mobility, communications security, covertness, and redundancy, or whether such space weapon technologies will ultimately increase the net threat to command. Indeed, a proper assessment of vulnerability would have to include the increased demands on the command mission, especially the further compression of the time available for critical decisions.

NOTES

1. See especially Alexander L. George, et. al., *Inadvertent War in Europe: Crisis Simulation,* Center for International Security and Arms Control, Stanford University, June 1985; and references cited therein. This report describes a week-long simulation conducted by Stanford faculty and students. It begins with an uprising in East Germany that leads to the closing of the autobahn to Berlin and to large-scale Soviet military exercises that could be construed as preparations for the seizure of West Berlin. The simulation explored an escalating spiral of alerts by NATO and the Pact, punctuated by violent incidents amid ineffective diplomacy and misperceptions by political leaders regarding the implications of various military steps, as well as other phenomena to be discussed in this and the next chapter.

2. The following assumes that the Pact does not use nuclear weapons first. Were it to do so, NATO policy calls for nuclear retaliation. For a review of NATO nuclear policy, see Legge. For the most recent comprehensive official statements, see James R. Schlesinger, *The Theater Nuclear Force Posture in Europe: A Report to the U.S. Congress,* USGPO, April/May 1975; and Frank C. Carlucci, *Support of NATO Strategy in the 1980s,* A Report to the U.S. Congress, January 25, 1988.

3. These guidelines, first drawn up in the Healy-Schroeder Report of 1969 and subsequently refined for the Nuclear Planning Group, have changed little since 1975. See Catherine McArdle Kelleher, "NATO Nuclear Operations," in *MNO;* and Legge.

4. For example, highly concentrated formations for overwhelming NATO defenses would present a very lucrative target to nuclear attack. It is therefore argued that mere awareness that such tactics could invite a nuclear attack strengthens NATO's conventional defense.

5. *Defense Organization: The Need for Change,* Staff Report to the Committee on the Armed Services, U.S. Senate, October 16, 1985, 290. This depicts the situation when CINCEUR is an army officer; he can also be a USAF officer.

6. In addition, 400 U.S. SLBM RVs are consigned to SACEUR.

7. An American admiral who simultaneously holds the U.S. Atlantic Command, and a British admiral who heads the Channel Command.

8. There is a de facto veto whether or not the delivery vehicles of the nonnuclear allies have been chopped to SACEUR control because the allied command authorities could simply order their own forces not to release the means for delivering nuclear weapons. This operational veto is strengthened by the involvement of allied security, transportation, and other units in dispersing nuclear weapons prior to use. Cooperation in this preparation as well as release for launch could be withheld. See Kelleher, p. 463.

9. Normal mechanisms for notifying the president's senior advisors of situations that warrant immediate attention are illustrated by the Mayaguez and Korean incidents. In the former case, the message from the overseas embassy carried several

addresses—the NMCC, the White House Situation Room, and the State Department. The message arrived simultaneously at all three destinations approximately 2 hours after the Mayaguez radioed for help. A similar pattern of notification followed the Korean incident in which an American soldier was killed in the Demilitarized Zone. This time the NMCC was informed directly by military rather than diplomatic sources. Shortly after the assault, the NMCC received the message from Seoul and activated an interagency network now called the National Operations and Intelligence Watch Officers Net, which allows for remote secure voice conferencing between the operations centers of the CIA, DIA, J-3 (Director for Operations, JCS Joint Staff), State Department, White House Situation Room, and the recently created NSC Crisis Coordination Center in the Old Executive Office Building adjacent to the White House (Richard G. Head, Frisco W. Short and Robert C. McFarlane, *Crisis Resolution: Presidential Decision Making in the Mayaguez and Korean Confrontations* (Boulder CO: Westview, 1978), p. 63; Thomas G. Belden, "Indications, Warning, and Crisis Operations," *International Studies Quarterly* (1977), 21, pp. 192–193; R. Jeffrey Smith, "Crisis Management Under Strain," *Science* (August 31, 1984), pp. 907–909; Stephen E. Becker and J. Michael Landrum, "Survey and Appraisal of Current Crisis Management," Naval War College, unpublished manuscript, pp. 24–26; and interviews).

For a crisis involving NATO, the Situation Center at NATO Headquarters in Brussels would receive warning from the various national governments. The center is permanently manned by military and civilian staffs from the member countries and depends on the exchange of intelligence among the permanent delegations. NATO itself possesses no independent intelligence gathering machinery. See Julian Critchley, *Warning and Response* (Crane, Russak, 1978), p. 93.

10. Discussion of EOP in this chapter draws entirely on Joint Chiefs of Staff, *Crisis Staffing Procedures of the JCS,* sanitized manual in accordance with FOI, 1983; cited hereafter as CSP.

11. CSP, 4-1.

12. CSP, 3-9, 4-1, 4-9, 5-1. When the EOP are in effect, the JCS meet in the NMCC or ANMCC conference rooms. If necessary, the NCA would join the JCS in emergency conference at one of these locations, or at a wartime command center such as the National Emergency Airborne Command Post, or via telephone.

13. This discussion of Soviet doctrine and strategy is largely based on David Holloway and Condoleeza Rice, "Soviet Military Doctrine and its Implications for Crisis Management" (unpublished). On the shift towards a conventional strategy see also David M. Glantz, "Soviet Offensive Ground Doctrine since 1945," *Air University Review,* March–April 1983, pp. 25–35; and Stephen M. Meyer, *Soviet Theater Nuclear Forces, Part I: Development of Doctrines and Objectives,* Adelphi Papers No. 187 (London: International Institute for Strategic Studies, 1984).

14. James M. McConnell, "Shifts in Soviet Views on the Proper Focus of Military Development," *World Politics* (April 1985), pp. 317–343.

15. Notra Trulock III, "Weapons of Mass Destruction in Soviet Military Strategy," (unpublished) 1984, p. 69.

16. Ibid., p. 55.

17. *Istoriia uchit bditel 'nost'* (Moscow: Voenizdat, 1985), p. 51. Remarks along the same line have been made in an official pronouncement by the former Minister of Defense, Marshal Ustinov, and by leading military commentators.

18. M. M. Kir'ian, *Voenno-tekhnicheskii progress i vooruzhennye sily SSSR* (Moscow: Voenizdat, 1982). pp. 312–313.

19. M. A. Gareev, *Frunze-voennyi teoretik* (Moscow: Voenizdat, 1985), p. 240.

20. *Krasnaia zvesda,* February 21, 1984.

21. Furthermore, Gorbachev and other Soviet spokesmen have stressed that the Chernobyl catastrophe is minuscule compared to any nuclear conflict, and they have pointed to the danger of attacks on nuclear power plants by terrorists or in the midst of a conventional war (*The New York Times,* 22 August 1986, pp. 1,3,4).

22. U.S. Congress, House, Committee on Appropriations, "Department of Defense Appropriations for 1980," pt. 3, 817.

23. Head, et. al., op. cit., p. 63; Belden, op. cit.; R. Jeffrey Smith, op. cit.; and Seymour M. Hersh, *"The Target Is Destroyed": What Really Happened to Flight 007 and What America Knew about It* (New York: Random House, 1986), pp. 66–67.

24. See William W. Kaufmann, "Nonnuclear Deterrence," in *Alliance Security: NATO and the No-First-Use Question,* John D. Steinbruner and Leon V. Sigal, editors (Brookings, 1983), pp. 58–61.

25. See Chapter 7, Notes 68 and 69, for references.

26. *Military Vigilance* could include activation and testing of communication networks, placing aircraft on heightened ground alert, activation of crisis operating procedures at command centers, and intensified nonintrusive surveillance (e.g., by AWACS). Such steps were taken during the invasion of Czechoslovakia in 1968 (Betts, *Surprise Attack,* p. 86).

27. For a much more detailed description see Bruce G. Blair, "Alerting in Crisis and Conventional War", pp. 75–120, in *MNO.*

28. For a more detailed discussion than that presented in Chapter 8, see Scott D. Sagan, "Nuclear Alerts and Crisis Management," *International Security* (1985), 9:4, 113.

29. During the Cuban Crisis SACEUR decided not to increase the alert status of forces in Europe for political reasons.

30. See Douglas M. Hart, "Soviet Approaches to Crisis Management: The Military Dimensions," *Survival,* 26:5, Sept/Oct 1984, pp. 214–223; and Richard I. Wiles et al., *A Net Assessment of Tactical Nuclear Doctrine for the Integrated Battlefield,* Defense Nuclear Agency #5452Z, September 1980.

31. For example, this might include the deployment of TACAMO aircraft beyond the two that are always on station over the Atlantic and Pacific, and enhanced readiness of PACCS relay aircraft and of airborne command posts for CINCEUR and other unified and specified combat commands.

32. For instance, the Cobra Dane radar in the Aleutians reverts to a BMEW radar at DEFCON 3; U.S. Congress, Senate, "Department of Defense Appropriations, FY1974," pt. 4, 483.

33. NATO's land-based theater range missiles (Pershing II and GLCM), which would be removed by the INF agreement, are vulnerable unless dispersed, and that dispersal could be difficult to conceal. They can, however, be fired on very short notice from their peacetime location, and can also be launched during transport.

34. Safekeeping and dispersal of nuclear warheads for NATO ground forces is the responsibility of special custodial units. Should the order for dispersal be issued in the midst of a conventional campaign, nuclear artillery shells would be brought to covert locations at some distance from the artillery units for subsequent delivery upon receipt of authorization and unlock codes. The other major battlefield weapons are Lance missile launchers assigned to both U.S. and allied units.

35. Joseph J. Kruzel, "Military Alerts and Diplomatic Signals," in Ellen P. Stern, ed., *The Limits of Military Intervention* (Sage, 1977), p. 98.

36. Ze'ev Schiff, "Israel's Defense in a Changing World," *Defense and Foreign*

Affairs (1987) *15*:1, p. 8; and "Israel's Eroding Edge in the Middle East Military Balance," *Policy Paper,* No. 2, Washington Institute for Near East Policy, 1985.

37. Robert G. Neumann, "Assad and the Future of the Middle East," *Foreign Affairs* (1983/84), *62*:2, 237.

38. Schiff, "Israel's Eroding Edge . . . ", op. cit., p. 13. See also Michael R. Gordon, "U.S. and Soviet to Meet Again on Curbing Chemical Weapons," *The New York Times,* August 26, 1986, p. A4.

39. Leonard S. Spector, *The New Nuclear Nations* (Random House, 1985).

40. See *The Sunday Times* (London), October 5 and 12, 1986, for detailed data supplied by a technician formerly employed at the Dimona reactor, and an interview with F. Perrin, the "father" of the French nuclear weapons program, revealing that France and Israel collaborated in the 1950s, and constructed a clandestine plutonium separation plant at Dimona. The technician was tried in camera in Israel.

41. Leonard S. Spector, *Going Nuclear* (Cambridge, MA: Ballinger, 1987), pp. 130–141.

42. Ze'ev Schiff, "Dealing with Syria," *Foreign Policy* (Summer 1984), p. 94.

43. Private communication with Israeli defense expert.

44. For a fuller description, see Bruce G. Blair, David S. Cohen, and Kurt Gottfried, "Command in Crisis: A Middle East Scenario," *Bulletin of Peace Proposals* (1986), *17*:2, p. 113.

45. It could also provoke "horizontal escalation," since the United States would have to bring forces from other theaters, such as units of the Rapid Deployment Force based in Turkey, a member of NATO.

46. A Soviet invasion of Iran, to cite the most dangerous contingency involving Soviet power projection into this region, "would be an exceedingly low-confidence affair," according to Joshua M. Epstein, *Strategy and Force Planning: The Case of the Persian Gulf* (Washington, DC: Brookings, 1987), p. 104.

47. *Foreign Affairs* (1985), *64*:1, 3.

48. Petropavlovsk is too remote to be accessible by road or rail and is supplied by sea and air.

49. Great Britain has more than 60 nuclear-capable surface and undersea vessels, and nearly 200 sea- and land-based nuclear-capable naval aircraft. France and China have considerably smaller nuclear naval forces.

50. *Soviet Military Power 1986* (Washington, DC: USGPO, 1986), pp. 81–83.

51. Ibid., p. 33.

52. Air strikes against NATO ports may actually be a graver threat to the transatlantic supply lines than interdiction at sea.

53. The role of forward operations in U.S. naval strategy is examined in the following references: Bruce G. Blair, "Arms Control Implications of Anti-Submarine Warfare (ASW) Programs," in Library of Congress, Congressional Research Service, Foreign Affairs and National Defense Division, *Evaluation of Fiscal Year 1979 Arms Control Impact Statements,* prepared for the Subcommittee on International Security and Scientific Affairs of the House Committee on International Relations, 95th Congress, 2nd session (GPO, 1978); Barry R. Posen, "Inadvertent Nuclear War?: Escalation and NATO's Northern Flank," *International Security* (1982) *7*:2, p. 28; Desmond Ball, "Nuclear War at Sea?: Ibid. (1985/86) *10*:3, p. 3; John J. Mearsheimer, "A Strategic Misstep: The Maritime Strategy and Deterrence in Europe," Ibid. (1986) *11*:2, p. 3; and Linton F. Brooks, "Naval Power and National Security: The Case for the Maritime Strategy," Ibid., p. 58.

54. Admiral James Walker, then Chief of Naval Operations, told Congress that

"this year, for the first time, we surged our own SSNs, and in 24 hours put 44 SSNs in the Atlantic, at sea, fully loaded" (William Arkin, "Provocations at Sea," *Bulletin of the Atomic Scientists* (1985), *41*:11, 7.

55. Bruce G. Blair, "Arms Control Implications of Anti-Submarine Warfare Programs," *Evaluation of FY 1979 Arms Control Impact Statements,* in Report of the Committee on International Relations, U.S. House of Representatives (January 3, 1979), p. 111. Available through GPO, 1978.

56. In peacetime, typical Soviet naval deployments outside of home waters and adjacent seas are approximately 25 to 30 combatants (Pacific), 8 (Indian), 15 (Atlantic), 20 to 30 (Mediterranean), and nominal numbers scattered in other regions of the world. The vast majority of combatants in the four Soviet fleets would be in port or operating in home waters.

57. The Soviets have two types of satellites for such missions: RORSAT, which carries a radar powered by a small nuclear reactor, and EORSAT for electronic intelligence.

58. Concentrations of American naval power in areas close to Soviet territory during the peacetime exercises has drawn responses from anticarrier Soviet forces, such as Backfire bombers. During the 1982 exercise, the Soviets dispatched Backfires on mock attacks against the carriers for the first time—100 sorties to within about 100 miles of the task force ships. The subsequent two exercises also drew responses from Backfires in the Soviet's Pacific and Northern Fleets. (U.S. Congress, House, Committee on Armed Services, "Authorization for Fiscal Year 1984 Department of Defense Appropriations," pt. 1, p. 1253.)

59. Successful Soviet ASAT tests have all used radar homing, which is susceptible to jamming; and interception after two complete orbits, which gives more than 2 hours of warning for evasive maneuvers by the quarry.

60. This is the U.S. Army's Homing Overlay Experiment, conducted on June 10, 1984. The nuclear-armed Galosh interceptors deployed in the Moscow ABM system could also be used to attack low-orbit satellites, perhaps even with conventional warheads.

61. The U.S. ASAT uses a passive infrared homer that cannot be detected and hence is difficult to counter; furthermore, the approach to the target is so rapid that evasion would be difficult, See *Anti-Satellite Weapons, Countermeasures, and Arms Control,* U.S. Congress, Office of Technology Assessment, OTA-ISC-281 (Washington, DC: USGPO, September 1985), pp. 58–62.

62. Both nations could attack satellites and their ground-stations with nuclear-armed missiles, but such acts hardly come under the rubric of crisis behavior.

63. Kurt Gottfried and Richard Ned Lebow, "Anti-Satellite Weapons: Weighing the Risks," in Long, Hafner and Boutwell; Ashton B. Carter, "Satellites and Anti-Satellites," *International Security* (1986), *10*:4, 46.

64. See Charles A. Zraket, "Strategic Defense: A Systems Perspective," in Long, Hafner and Boutwell.

65. Attacks on geosynchronous satellites with projectiles would take hours to execute, and are therefore of dubious value. On the other hand, a BMD scheme like the ground-based Free Electron Laser with relay mirrors in geosynchronous orbit could threaten satellites in high altitude orbits even if it were not powerful enough to destroy ICBM boosters.

10

Crisis Phenomena and Sources of Instability

What are the most likely paths that might carry a crisis to nuclear war between the superpowers? Are those paths marked by critical junctures or patterns that recur and are amenable to analysis? These questions form the crux of this study, but history provides a meager data base for answering them. Only once, during the Cuban Missile Crisis, did nuclear war appear to be a conceivable consequence of steps already taken or under serious consideration. Furthermore, the interactions between the superpowers' forces during the Missile Crisis were marginal in comparison to what would be likely to occur should both sides take a sizeable portion of the imposing array of alert operations summarized in the tables on pp. 236–241. We must therefore extrapolate far into the unknown in addressing these questions.

To prepare a springboard for that extrapolation, we must first examine the settings in which leaders have coped with crises, and identify features that are likely to recur in future confrontations. These features include the environment that in the past has differentiated crisis from peace and war; the dominant factors that have been (or should have been) assessed either at the outbreak of crisis or as events unfolded; the human dimension of crisis; domestic and alliance politics; intelligence; and the trade-offs between diplomacy and military measures that have chronically perplexed leaders during a crisis.

Finally, we must consider confrontations of an intensity with which the world has no experience: direct conflict, either conventional or nuclear, between the superpowers. Admittedly, this is an exercise in speculation, but we shall base our discussion on existing realities—the crisis arenas, forces, command structures, and alert operations that have been described in the preceding chapters.

The persistent currents of the adversaries' foreign and security policies will loom over the course of any crisis. The examination of most of these policies

259

falls outside the scope of this book. We shall simply assume a rule that has often been honored in the breach: That those policies have a plausible relationship to the objectives that both sides seek, and that the means each will use are in contact with geopolitical realities. By that token, crises that appear to start far below the nuclear threshold will be emphasized. Even in resolving such altercations, however, the two sides are bound to strive for terms that are as favorable as possible, and they may therefore be willing to run risks that neutral observers might judge as unjustified or even reckless.

A NO-MAN'S LAND BETWEEN PEACE AND WAR

History has taught us a good deal about the psychological and political atmosphere that defines "crisis," and how it differs both from peace and war.

Crisis is sensed as a sudden and marked departure from the norm. It may come as a great surprise, as with the installation of missiles in Cuba, or it may confirm the worst of fears, as with the mobilizations of July 1914. Today's vast electronic networks notwithstanding, crisis is an inherently human phenomenon; some of this century's most formidable leaders have collapsed under the trauma of crisis. Perceptions and misperceptions, impelled by fear and haste, and amplified by interactions within and among leadership groups, bureaucracies, governments, the media, and public opinion, will always be the stuff of crisis.

An isolated event can attain astonishing prominence in an incipient crisis. The assassination of an archduke may ignite a conflagration that alters the fate of an entire civilization, but had some other incident triggered a different chain of events that led to the Great War, and had the archduke been shot in Sarajevo during the Battle of the Marne, the story might never have made the front pages. Chaos and destruction are accepted as normal once war breaks out. What government could survive the loss of its industrial heartland or the death of millions of its citizens were it not at war? Crisis is not nearly so fault-tolerant, nor does it yield time for the learning process that governments and armies have always gone through in wartime.

An unholy brew of ignorance pervades warfare, and is aptly called "the fog of war." In some ways, however, that fog is more ominous still in crisis, when nations teeter on the edge of the precipice that drops into the abyss of war.[1] Uncertainty looms over at least one adversary in virtually every crisis—perplexing questions concerning the intentions of the other side and the understanding of the implications of his actions; the validity of one's own previously defined vital interest; the cohesion of alliances at home and abroad; the confidence with which one could carry out the contending proposals for action; the responses they might elicit, and what the options would be then. This swamp is all the more forbidding when strong voices argue that it must be crossed immediately, yet history offers examples where hesitation was fatal, as well as others where haste led to disaster.

Tactics tend to overwhelm strategy in crisis. During war a decision to counterattack would be left to the military. But in crisis, tactical minutiae may determine which of several quite distinct outcomes is actually achieved because the various trappings in which a given action may be clothed can convey different political goals to the adversary. Hence, the apex of government becomes involved in decisions for which it is usually ill-equipped. Yet, to surrender such decisions to "the experts" is unattractive when so much is at stake and there are no certified experts.

THE OUTBREAK

Initial Conditions

The dynamics of crises have tended to be governed by the adversaries' prior objectives, and by the extent to which these were (or were not) reevaluated at the outbreak. These objectives and reassessments largely determined the first steps, which in turn set the psychological atmosphere and the political tone of subsequent events.

All past crises illustrate the importance of initial conditions. The most extreme example of how the outcome of a crisis can almost be preordained is July 1914. Incompatible political goals and commitments and military plans that left no room for hesitation once an adversary began to move conspired to make the crisis essentially uncontainable.[2] In today's Europe an analogous "preordained" chain of events might result from the security concerns of NATO and the Warsaw Pact. As we saw, both alliances have elaborate plans for attaining various levels of readiness in response to warning. A crisis could initiate an interlocking sequence of escalating alerts, for as one side sought to enhance its security it would also be magnifying the threat to the other.

The post-Hiroshima crises have also displayed the significance of initial conditions, although in aspects that differ greatly from 1914. Kennedy's pre-crisis statement that "the gravest issues would arise" if Soviet missiles were installed in Cuba came to mean that his administration could not confine itself to a purely diplomatic response. The Berlin Blockade of 1948, and the invasion of South Korea in 1950, shocked the United States into making immediate commitments to defend both—commitments that it had previously considered but not been willing to accept despite warnings that Berlin and South Korea could be in jeopardy. Those new commitments largely determined how the Truman administration then dealt with the blockade and the invasion. In the latter case, however, MacArthur's landing at Inchon, and his crossing of the 38th parallel, suddenly created entirely new initial conditions that transformed the dynamics of the Korean War and led, almost inexorably, to the Chinese intervention.

The sudden U.S. policy shifts at the inception of the Berlin Blockade and the Korean War illustrate that the risk entailed in an action cannot be calculated with confidence on the basis of an adversary's standing policy if the action contemplated upsets the tacit assumptions on which the policy was based. This observation also applies to Britain's decision to enter the war against Germany in 1914, although not in quite as clear-cut a fashion.

Gravity and Pace

In view of the crucial role of the initial conditions, every effort must be made to choose the first responses as well as circumstances permit. For that purpose, a quick and rough assessment of the gravity and pace of the crisis is essential, where at the outbreak "pace" can be calibrated by the time until the first move *must* be made because of the "objective" situation created by the adversary. This quick appraisal should be viewed as a first step in a sequence of approximations; whether more refined assessments will be possible may not be known at the outset. If this first assessment is wide of the mark, the risk that the crisis will turn into a circumscribed defeat, or even run amok, increases markedly. For example, the crisis that resulted in the massive Chinese attack on North Korea really began several weeks before that when Chinese units engaged MacArthur's forces and then broke off contact. Failure to grasp the gravity and tempo of events was paid for in tens of thousands of human lives and the longest retreat in U.S. military history.

Experience demonstrates that a prompt assessment of gravity is difficult since it requires insight into the opponent's motives, and a reexamination of the validity of one's own commitments and policies. Is the enemy hell-bent on attack, as when Hitler prepared to invade Russia? Soviet deterrence had already collapsed, but Stalin did not yet know that. Or will the enemy only attack if circumstances are propitious, as in Sadat's crossing of the Suez? Presumably, the Egyptian attack would have been postponed—perhaps even abandoned—had Israel mobilized in time. Does the adversary believe that vital interests are threatened and is therefore preparing to preempt because of inadequate reassurance? That was China's motivation in crossing the Yalu. Did Khrushchev understand the threat to the United States posed by his missiles in Cuba? In what dimension—military or political—were they a threat? What were Stalin's intentions in the Berlin Blockade? Was he behind the invasion of South Korea? Did the Truman administration's prior lack of commitment to Berlin and South Korea remain appropriate once their survival was at stake?

It may be clear in retrospect how grave these crises were, but they often were not at the time. In most cases where the gravity was seriously underestimated, as in Hitler's invasion of Russia, the Chinese intervention in Korea, and Sadat's crossing of the Suez, the error ultimately stemmed from a deepseated inability to comprehend other nations' political attitudes, and not from poor intelligence about military preparations.

Gravity is not only determined by the degree of conflict between the opponents' objectives, but also by their actions in support of those goals prior to the crisis. If the crisis begins because one side makes it clear that it is *considering* an initiative, the other side need only to deter it from an action that has *not yet* upset the status quo. This type of outbreak is illustrated by the Yom

Kippur Crisis, when Brezhnev's note warned that the Soviet Union was contemplating the insertion of troops into the Suez Canal area. The Berlin Crises of 1959 and 1961 were of a similar character.[3] In such cases the initiator must only be "encouraged" to adhere to his prior policy. A crisis is much more dangerous if one side has *already* committed itself to a course of action, so that the adversary must try to coerce it into *abandoning* that commitment. That was the situation in Cuba—Khrushchev had to remove missiles, not to refrain from installing them. The historical evidence[4] indicates that it is much more difficult to reverse actions already taken than to forestall them.

Once the time available for critical decisions has been estimated, the opponent's intentions have been evaluated, and one's own vital strategic objectives have been framed, existing contingency plans can be reviewed. That should be the order of business, not the reverse. If time is of the essence, much will depend on whether the crisis resembles any of the contingencies for which preparations exist. That does not mean, however, that a crisis that conforms with contingency plans will be coped with successfully! If those plans were misconceived, they could be worse than no plan at all, as 1914 demonstrates, for the July crisis ran wild precisely because of meticulous contingency plans that were designed for the events that actually occurred. Since 1945, however, U.S. contingency plans have rarely been used in a crisis.

Strategy Versus Tactics

The assessment of gravity and pace, the definition of objectives, and the selection of diplomatic and military steps toward those ends, is a formidable set of tasks, especially under the stress of a serious crisis. If they are not to be overwhelmed, leaders must recognize that they have one constant responsibility: to maximize the dominance of strategy over tactics. The chance that this platitude will actually be heeded can be greatly improved if an orderly process for decision making is already in place so that the apex of government can devote itself to matters that only it can settle.

Ideally, the core leadership group that is to cope with the crisis should have been in operation beforehand. They should have carefully scrutinized all salient information and been involved in the preparation and review of contingency plans, among which there is at least one that is crudely appropriate to the situation at hand. The group should also understand how to command the government to a common action, while remaining aware that no government behaves like a rational individual.

The existence of such a body, however, would violate all tradition. It would be more realistic to assume that leaders will be presented with military contingency plans that they have never seen, or which are clearly inappropriate, or both, and that they would only have a rough knowledge of the vast and potentially destructive machine that they are to employ with surgical precision to deal with the pressing and ominous problem of which they only have a fuzzy image. This is neither a caricature nor a snide criticism of the U.S. government, or that of other nations. Governments are chronically unprepared for crisis, unless they have planned to initiate it. Leaders usually face too many urgent problems to prepare systematically for improbable circumstances, no matter how serious, even though they may be quite aware of the hazards they thereby run.

Despite all these handicaps, governments have sometimes been able to assess the pace and gravity of a breaking crisis in a competent fashion, although many a government has failed to do so. For example, McGeorge Bundy was hearing a fairly reliable metronome when he decided not to disturb President Kennedy with the news of the Cuban missile installations until he had a good night's sleep. At this point the administration had ascertained that the missiles could not be operational for at least 2 weeks, and that it could impose a blockade or launch an air strike within a matter of days. This estimate concerning the operational status of the missiles turned out to be off base. Nevertheless, the perception that the tempo of events was to be measured in many days proved to be correct. This perception, however arrived at, combined with overwhelming U.S. military superiority in the region, yielded a timely and reasonably sound assessment of the gravity of the crisis. Furthermore, Kennedy's ExComm had identified the urgent priorities and a plausible spectrum of options by the end of the first day of the crisis. Had circumstances forced a decision in, say, 36 hours instead of 96, the ExComm records indicate that the blockade may well have been chosen at that point anyway, although the air strike was then the favored option among the president's advisors. Whatever the option chosen, such a collapse of the time-scale would have made the crisis much more dangerous. It would not have permitted U.S. measures to be put into effect with much diplomatic or military refinement, and the assessment of likely Soviet reactions would have been much more superficial. An accelerated tempo, especially if accompanied by deadly force, would also have put the Kremlin under greater duress, and increased the likelihood of a Soviet response against Berlin or Turkey, with consequences that remain unclear even in hindsight.

To take another example, recall that on October 26, 1973, the U.S. government felt it had an accurate measure of the pace of the Yom Kippur Crisis from the start, and that Kissinger seemed confident that he had assessed its gravity before it broke. The pace was set by the apprehension that the Soviets could land troops in Egypt within several hours, while the gravity was judged as sufficiently low to call for a largely symbolic initiative. The foregoing views the crisis from Washington. From the perspectives of Jerusalem and Cairo, however, it was exceedingly grave.

History also records abominable first assessments. Even if the July 1914 crisis had smoldered on for months it is doubtful that Berlin, St. Petersburg, and Vienna would have altered their *Weltanschauung* sufficiently to evade the disaster that eventually swept away their empires. July 1914 also illustrates how calculations, not done in haste but enshrined in years of meticulous planning by most of the participants, can submerge all other considerations in a tide of tactics.

THE HUMAN FACTOR

Command systems have three distinct but totally interdependent components: hardware, operational procedures, and humans. There is a tendency to devote great attention to the technical and organizational aspects of command organizations, and to mention the human element only in passing.[5] The reason is clear. Organization and machines can be modified or even replaced by entirely new structures and technologies, whereas human behavior is ill-understood, unpredictable, and apparently immutable. The strength and frailties of leaders have often been a highly significant factor in a crisis—the roles played by the kaiser and Moltke in 1914, MacArthur in 1950, Kennedy and Khrushchev in 1962, and Kissinger, Nixon, and Sadat in 1973 illustrate this observation. In consequence, bureaucracies and legal systems find it difficult to cope with all the astonishing contingencies that human idiosyncracy often unleashes whenever opportunity knocks.

For these reasons, the human component of command represents something of a paradox. Humans have a critical role in the command network, but human failure at critical junctures is commonplace. Yet flaws in the technical and procedural elements of the command system are tempered by the "man-in-the-loop"; for example, false warning incidents at NORAD are contained routinely by human intervention.[6] From the two-man rule in Minuteman Launch Control Centers to the concentration of launch authority in the NCA, humans provide the essential element in command and control.

On the other hand, many powerful and experienced leaders have undergone complete psychological withdrawal from reality at the height of a crisis. Even the formidable Joseph Stalin apparently suffered a breakdown when Hitler struck. Since Stalin terrorized his subordinates, the Soviet government was crippled for several crucial days until he regained his composure. Other recent examples of normally stable leaders who suffered mental paralysis induced by severe crises are Moltke, Nehru, and Nasser. Moltke, the German chief-of-staff, was a vigorous and persistent proponent of war in the years leading up to 1914 and during the July crisis itself. But he never recovered from the trauma of the outbreak of the War, had to be replaced, and died without ever regaining his full composure. The fragility of the human component of the command system is also illustrated very graphically by the problems that plagued the Israeli Defense Forces at the outset of the Yom Kippur War. Many of the leaders of the brilliant campaigns of the Six Day War of 1967 were still in senior positions, including Defense Minister Moshe Dayan. Nevertheless, what might seem like a minor change of cast sufficed to produce a clash of personalities and disputed lines of authority that rendered the highly skilled and seasoned IDF remarkably ineffective.[7]

Decision making is subject to a wide range of pathologies. While many of the common maladies have been studied and described, human behavior, especially under severe stress, is poorly understood. Nevertheless, history and psychology offer some insights that are relevant to the issues at hand.

Crisis, by its very definition, contains the nutrients for stress: momentous threats, obscure circumstances, and the demands for total concentration and rapid reactions. In addition, there may be an ambiguity of responsibility and authority, leading to personality clashes. If the crisis is prolonged, there is bound to be both mental and physical fatigue. Each of these separate features are classic inducers of stress. Grave threats challenge an individual's mental construction of reality. The "cognitive maps" that guide (among other things) the formulation of national policy come under attack if it becomes apparent that the policy is failing. Such a dramatic alteration in the structure of one's perception of reality can induce stress. Furthermore, ambiguous threats induce stress by posing problems that either defy definitive answers or only allow makeshift resolutions. Finally, crisis demands immediate attention— or so it seems. A combination of fatigue and the perceived necessity to reach *some* decision quickly is likely to induce stress.

The effect of stress on individuals is difficult predict. It is not true that stress always impedes performance. There are rare individuals who seem to be immune to stress. Napoleon, in particular, displayed none of the classic symptoms. As was his habit, he slept during the hours preceding the battle of Waterloo. Stress is internally derived, and not an intrinsic property of a given situation, and for that reason the response to stress will vary among a set of individuals exposed to the same circumstances. Robert Kennedy noted this regarding the members of ExComm during the Missile Crisis: "For some there were only small changes, perhaps varieties of a single idea. For others, there were continuous changes of opinion each day; some, because of the pressures of events, even appeared to lose their judgment and stability."[8] Despite this unpredictable variability, there are some general features of stress-related behavior.

As a rule, stress enhances performance, but only up to a point. There is a certain level of stress, which varies with the individual, the task, and the circumstance, beyond which coping processes are initiated and performance is materially impaired. *Coping* refers to behavior patterns used to ease the psychological burden of stress. These strategies can be categorized into four rough sets of behaviors: contending, denial, hypervigilance, and bolstering.[9]

Contending consists of increased attention and activity in the attempt to assess the problem and select the solution from those that are available that, after as careful a consideration as possible, appears to offer optimal satisfaction. Obviously, this coping strategy is essential to sound decision making, but the others represent impediments.

Denial is perhaps the most appealing psychologically and the most common. Stress is avoided by evading the situation, or by minimizing its importance. Denial cannot often be sustained, however, because reality becomes too obvious. If the collapse of denial does not lead to contending, it may give way to hypervigilance or bolstering. *Hypervigilance* is a frenetic but ultimately futile search for alternatives. In contrast, *bolstering* is the seizing on a particular alternative without adequately assessing the range of available options, and the downgrading of the discarded options so that the decision taken seems, in retrospect, to be manifestly correct.

In addition to these coping patterns, there are decision-making pathologies that are prevalent even in absence of stress, but they are still more likely to arise under crisis conditions because of the pressure for critical decisions on the basis of inadequate evidence. First, there is a tendency to interpret ambiguous evidence as a confirmation of expectations—to "see what one *expects* to see"; this is called *cognitive distortion*. In addition, there may be the urge to "see what one *wants* to see, which is called *motivational distortion*.[10] Both appear with great clarity in Roberta Wohlstetter's account of Pearl Harbor; for the American commanders in Hawaii "the only signal that could and did spell 'hostile action' . . . was the bombing itself . . . the noise of the explosions was necessary before anyone identified the aircraft as Japanese";[11] as for the Japanese, they played elaborate war games that incorporated their motivational distortions regarding the expected American response to Japanese expansion.[12] It should be noted that stress and fatigue were not contributors to these examples of flawed decision making before Pearl Harbor, nor to the motivational bias that marked much of the planning prior to World War I.[13]

That various combinations of stress, perceptual distortions, and fatigue have been important factors in crises of the past is well established;[14] indeed, if they are all absent, there is no crisis. Thus, Sir Edward Grey, the British foreign secretary in 1914, "like so many of the leading participants in the crisis, including Bethmann Hollweg [the German chancellor], gave the impression to those who saw him in these days of a man near the end of his nervous resources."[15] That profound perceptual distortions flourished in all the capitals of Europe in 1914, and in Tokyo, Washington, and Moscow in 1941, has already been recounted in Chapter 3, and, with regard to the post-Hiroshima crises, in Chapter 8. Some participants have reported that as the Missile Crisis reached its climax, ExComm meetings were marred by short tempers and discord. Fatigue—the crisis had been on for almost 2 weeks at this point—presumably contributed to this atmosphere, but it should be added that there is no evidence that stress and fatigue actually undermined decision making.

Fatigue is likely to play an important role in any crisis involving the United States and the Soviet Union. The time difference of 6 to 7 hours between Washington and Moscow means that when one side is trying to sleep, the other is working. In the Yom Kippur crisis, for instance, Kissinger was repeatedly awakened to respond to Soviet queries. Sleep deprivation, coupled with the exceptionally draining demands of crisis, can severely impair decision making.

A structured decision-making process by a sufficiently diverse group would also optimize the probability that the group will come to recognize the motivational and cognitive distortions that are likely to be present in its thinking. In looking back to the Missile Crisis, many ExComm veterans concur with Robert McNamara's view that "within certain limits, the longer the time taken to form the decision, the more secure the decision will be."[16] Given enough time, people are more likely to put themselves into their adversary's shoes, which is indispensible to recognizing one's own biases: "as the crisis wore on, President Kennedy expressed increasing curiosity about Khrushchev, and about the ways this man's personality might interact with the Soviet system and with the deep crisis they both were in."[17] This emphasizes the importance of assessing "the initial conditions" of a crisis, and in particular its initial pace as the time available for the first serious decision. A structured group process would seem to have the best chance of avoiding the pitfall of decisions that are flawed because they were made more hastily than circumstances actually warranted.

This cursory discussion of the human factor has been based on what little understanding we have of past decision making in difficult circumstances. Whether this gives us any insight into the performance of leaders and chains of command should they be faced with imminent nuclear war is, of course, quite another matter. Suffice it to say that history informs us that even under far-less-stressing circumstances there is usually a good deal of play in the tiller of the ship of state.

DOMESTIC AND ALLIANCE POLITICS

Solidarity on the home front was already a high-priority objective before nuclear weapons or short wave radios existed:

Any government, even the most dictatorial, needs to be sure of popular support before starting a war. For this reason, . . . each of the governments which declared war in 1914 was concerned to present its decision in such a way as to win the maximum public approval: the French were fighting to defend the soil of France against a German invasion; the Germans were fighting to defend the soil of Germany against the Cossack hordes, and so on.[18]

The belligerents of 1914, therefore, sought to maneuver their opponents into making a move that would be militarily indecisive, but which could offer the pretext for a decisive step of their own. Germany was able to accomplish this vis-à-vis Russia, and France vis-à-vis Germany. In the latter instance, the French government was particularly anxious to convince its hesitant ally across the Channel that France was the victim of aggression, and French political authorities had enough clout to delay some militarily significant preparations and operations so as to place the onus on Germany.

These features of 1914 are likely to recur. American and Soviet allies are likely to be on the front lines of a crisis, and alliance and domestic solidarity would then be essential to both superpowers. While internal cohesion would appear to be a more serious problem for the West, since Stalin's death the Kremlin can no longer take obedience for granted, even under conditions that are more benign than a severe crisis.

As we saw, domestic politics, foreign alliances, or both, have played a significant role in every important post-1945 crisis involving the United States. The domestic opposition was a dominant factor in the Korean War, and fear of such opposition hung over the Kennedy administration throughout the Missile Crisis. Domestic support for Israel was of significance in the Yom Kippur Crisis, and the travails of Agnew and Nixon had a great bearing on the actual prosecution of that crisis. Bolstering alliance cohesion was a dominant U.S. goal in all the Berlin crises and in its decision to intervene in Korea, while lack of alliance support reduced the room for maneuvering available to the United States in the Yom Kippur Crisis.

These historical patterns can give only a premonition of what could be in store in a severe crisis. For example, should chemical weapons in the hands of a Soviet client state ever kill large numbers of Israelis, that would create an emotional cauldron that could spill into the streets of America's largest cities, and put great pressure on the government to come to Israel's aid. Such intervention would presumably have solid support as long as it did not appear to be on a collision course with the Soviet Union. That consensus could quickly dissolve should fighting between Americans and Russians appear likely, for the fear of nuclear conflict that would then arise could produce a second faction that would fervently oppose intervention. It would not be farfetched to imagine violent clashes between the two U.S. camps, or massive demonstrations in Europe opposing U.S. policy.

Americans behaved very calmly throughout the Missile Crisis, but the media in 1962 had a smaller impact on daily life and were more restrained than they are today. Indeed, it would be prudent to anticipate dramatic departures from normal life in any severe superpower crisis. As the primarily symbolic alerting of SAC during the Yom Kippur Crisis demonstrated, large military operations cannot be kept secret in a free society, unless they are preceded by imposition of censorship, which in itself could affect public behavior. Should dependents of American personnel abroad be evacuated to the United States, or troops be sent to Europe, even censorship would be unlikely to prevent the news from spreading. A prolonged crisis could disrupt financial and commodity markets, and cause chronic absenteeism from work. In areas where fighting could be anticipated, panic might break out, especially if there were reports or rumors—possibly spread by the adversary—that nuclear weapons were being prepared for use. Panic could well be widespread should fear of nuclear war become palpable.

In short, the political environment in which Western leaders would be operating is likely to be very demanding. While they can impose martial law and censorship, their parliaments are not tightly constrained by emergency powers, and a "loyal opposition" could be active. There could also be deep disagreements between NATO governments. These could stem from long-standing differences, or be created by the crisis itself since its impact is likely to vary significantly from state to state. While one cannot predict how Western governments would cope with their publics or each other in an intense crisis, it is likely that problems internal to the alliance would be among the most vexing issues faced by all NATO capitals.

The governments of Warsaw Pact states might also face domestic turmoil in a severe crisis. Millions in East Germany and Czechoslovakia regularly watch Western television, tens of millions throughout the Soviet bloc listen to Western radio, and the grapevine is known to spread rumors with astonishing speed in the Soviet Union itself.

Political control over its Warsaw Pact satellites, especially Poland and East Germany, would also be of grave concern to Moscow in a severe crisis, whatever its origin. Breakdown of such control is the most popular scenario for crisis outbreak in Europe since that might trigger intervention by Soviet forces already in place or dispatched for that purpose. There has often been speculation that in Poland such intervention might lead to fighting between Soviet and Polish troops, especially if civilians were being killed in the attempt to regain control. Given Soviet aversion to any scent of political chaos, similar speculations probably thrive in the minds of Soviet leaders.

Whether Soviet determination to maintain its position in Eastern Europe would be a moderating or exacerbating factor in a crisis is not clear. Some highly experienced Western leaders[19] believe that Moscow would never attempt to project power westward unless it was confident of its Eastern European springboard, and that turmoil in Eastern Europe, therefore, could not produce a serious superpower crisis. But that is only a well-informed belief.

INTELLIGENCE: PEERING THROUGH THE FOG

The marshaling and exploitation of intelligence resources is crucial to crisis management. The problem is primarily human, not technical. Enormous advances in intelligence technology have been a hallmark of our age, but there has been no corresponding advancement in the analysis of political intelligence.[20] This art may even have regressed because the ideological and cultural distance between today's contenders for world power is far larger than those that separated the enemies of World War I.

In the U.S. government the Central Intelligence Agency, the NSA, and the National Reconnaissance Office (NRO) are the major intelligence organizations.[21] The CIA is responsible for creating a comprehensive worldwide picture and assessment ("national" intelligence), NSA produces signals intelligence (SIGINT), and NRO manages satellite reconnaissance. The State Department's Bureau of Intelligence and Research, both a producer and consumer of intelligence, is also very relevant to our concerns.[22] In addition, the Defense Department has its own intelligence agency, the DIA. The separate services each have intelligence arms, as do the unified commands; the latter deal primarily with theater intelligence and tactical intelligence.

Overall intelligence goals are set by general directives issued by the president. Implementation requires further specification by the NSC, coordinating committees of the intelligence community, and the directors of the various agencies. As the directives flow down these chains-of-command, they come into sharper focus, with the result that many of the detailed orders for intelligence gathering tend to be generated at a fairly low level.

Beyond data acquisition, intelligence involves integration, evaluation, and analysis. The process follows a fairly regular pattern. The first step in the cycle is task definition, followed by the collection of raw data from open sources, clandestine agents, and by technical means. The mass of data must then be sifted and cataloged, after which analysis can begin. Finally, analyses and estimates are produced in a variety of forms for various leadership echelons.

Daily intelligence analyses are presented in the *President's Daily Brief* to the very highest officials, and in the *National Intelligence Digest,* a more complete discussion distributed to the top 200 policymakers. The *Weekly Watch Report* provides in-depth analyses of "front-burner" issues. *National Intelligence Estimates,* issued periodically, predict future trends and estimate their impact on U.S. national security. In a crisis *National Intelligence Situation Reports* provide net assessment of the immediate status; in addition, *Special National Intelligence Estimates,* which predict the longer-range impact of the crisis, may be ordered, as has been mentioned already in the context of the Missile Crisis.

A number of factors tend to distort political intelligence. While intelligence officers and diplomats have a far more realistic view of an adversary than does the man in the street, or even their own superiors, they too may wear ideological blinders. In addition, political intelligence competes for attention with the seemingly unambiguous "hard facts" produced by technical intelligence, even though estimates of fundamental trends are essentially political. Ultimately intelligence lands on the desks of frenetically busy leaders—people who often hold their posts because they are thought to have the ability to decide complex matters that they barely understand.

There is also a tendency among senior decision makers to disregard intelligence that runs counter to their policy commitments, which can induce analysts to exercise self-censorship to enhance their chance to be heard, thereby compromising their product. Intelligence services may even come under direct pressure to provide a politically palatable product. For example, in the pre-1914 era German diplomats learned that their careers would not flourish if they filed reports that contradicted basic assumptions held by the Foreign Ministry in Berlin.[23] Japanese intelligence that accurately predicted America's overwhelming capacity for arms production was purposely shut out by the government as it prepared to go to war in 1941. During its advance to the Yalu in 1950, U.S. tactical intelligence was distorted to conform with General MacArthur's conviction that China would not intervene.[24] And during the Iran–Contra hearings the secretaries of state and defense testified that elements of the U.S. intelligence community misrepresented the course of the Iran–Iraq war in a manner that rationalized the shipment of arms to Iran. These examples demonstrate that the purposeful distortion of intelligence has afflicted governments of every type in a wide variety of circumstances, and that this insidious habit should not be expected to disappear.

In a crisis, the value of intelligence is determined by the skill with which it is focused, the speed with which it can be produced, the quality of the final product, and the extent to which that product influences decision makers. For a variety of reasons, senior officials may have failed to properly frame and focus the work of their subordinates. While intelligence resources can quickly be marshaled, the final product may be of poor quality because crisis can create difficulties beyond those that already exist in peacetime, especially for analysis. Greater collection resources are brought to bear, while the time available shrinks, so the problem of separating the wheat from the chaff increases. Acute crises would also induce fatigue and stress in those that must discern significant patterns against a noisy and shifting background when making the difficult judgments embodied in intelligence estimates.

Some of these problems have been pointed to by Admiral Bobby Inman, who served in intelligence for 30 years, and rose to be director of NSA and then deputy DCI:[25]

> It is in my experience the relatively rare policymaker who takes the time to tell you, particularly in a crisis, precisely the elements of information that would make the most difference if you could pin down some knowledge in the next few hours in that area. But most often you operate in a vacuum without any feedback, either on whether what you are providing is relevant or on new guidance on where you ought to go.

The allusion to the lack of political context that often hamstrings intelligence analysis is noteworthy. A vast capacity for data collection can be an impediment if it is not complemented by guidelines as to what is likely to be salient in a particular situation. Such guidelines may be missing or inadequate for a variety of reasons. Senior officials have often failed to realize that the manner in which they pose questions to the intelligence services can have an important impact on the estimates they subsequently receive. On the other hand, some officials are so sensitive to that danger that they may purposely refrain from issuing guidance; it may be that this motivated John McCone not to ask the CIA to investigate his suspicion that missiles were being installed in Cuba.[26] A prevalent cause of the problem is the desire, or even the need, to confine an understanding of the political context to a small body of decision makers. Thus it is likely that the Soviet government was surprised by the American discovery of the missiles in Cuba because the whole Soviet scheme was so secret that Soviet intelligence in the United States was unaware that it should be on the lookout for signs of such a discovery. Quite generally, the compartmentalization that is indigenous to intelligence, and which has its own powerful rationale, must find a modus vivendi with the need to provide political context for the process of intelligence analysis.

Another facet of intelligence that should be mentioned is that the role of high-ranking intelligence officials tends to change in crisis. In peacetime they are executives—they may not have had any hands-on intelligence experience. In a crisis, however, they are the ones who brief the decision makers. The officers who are expert in a given area may not be consulted by the leadership, or even by the heads of their own agencies; therefore, even if high-quality intelligence is produced, it may reach decision makers in a degraded form. Furthermore, during a crisis the community's sophisticated skills may be largely ignored because the latest raw data, and not refined analysis, is often preferred by decision makers who may think that their intuition and powers of analysis are superior to those of professional subordinates. When that occurs, the meat of intelligence is neglected. Decision makers should recognize an obligation to be aware of the capabilities and insights of those diplomats and intelligence officers who have spent years observing an adversary's leaders and the political milieu in which they operate. While political leaders have the power and right to make decisions that run counter to expert judgments, they have a responsibility to first weigh those judgments.

In the last analysis, however, the interpretation of political intelligence is exceedingly difficult, even when there are no self-imposed obstacles. Deepseated and rational preconceptions may prevent entire intelligence communities from uncovering an adversary's intent, especially if that adversary is engaging in skillful deception. As we saw in Chapter 8, such a combination of misconception and deception led U.S. and Israeli intelligence not to anticipate Egypt's and Syria's attack on Israel, even though both intelligence services had a good picture of Egyptian and Syrian military preparations. The failure stemmed from the rational assumption that Egypt would not attack unless its prospects were *militarily* propitious, whereas Sadat actually sought a *limited political* objective. A similar rational misconception confounded the American government before the attack on Pearl Harbor.

Finally, a word concerning the widespread belief that open societies have an inherent disadvantage when it comes to intelligence vis-à-vis totalitarian and authoritarian adversaries. The historical evidence does not bear this out. Germany in 1914, Japan in 1941, and the Soviet Union in 1961, had deeply flawed images of their democratic adversaries' objectives and intentions. This pattern has a number of explanations. Whereas closed societies emit a paltry signal that makes it very difficult to ascertain their inner workings, democracies produce a babel of voices that create a formidable background against which it is hard to hear what is actually salient. The latter problem is compounded when, as is often the case, a democracy is divided on its foreign policy. Then its government often does not know its own mind until an adversary's sudden initiative makes further procrastination impossible. This was the behavior of the British government in July 1914, and of the American government in the Berlin Blockade, in the invasion of Korea, and, to a considerable extent, in the Cuban Missile Crisis. Furthermore, the suppression of intelligence that does not bear out political preconceptions occurs in all types of governments, as we have seen. It is likely to be an especially pernicious syndrome if fear of punishment for dissenting views is the glue that bonds a political system.

In the light of the historical record, therefore, accurate intelligence estimates of an adversary's intentions should not be expected as the norm by the government of any state, no matter what its political complexion may be.

THE SOLDIER–STATESMAN DILEMMA

We now turn from the process, however imperfect, that seeks to identify a nation's objectives, to the means that are to attain those ends.[27] The choice of means is bedeviled by a perplexing question[28] that chronically arises in confrontations between states: To what extent is diplomacy to be supported by military measures?

This question raises a swarm of dilemmas. In the absence of all military measures an adversary may dangerously underestimate one's intentions. On the other hand, political signaling by means of military activities may be misinterpreted as preparation for attack, unless the operation is designed to avoid such an interpretation, in which case it may have little effect, or even be treated as a bluff waiting to be called. Furthermore, diplomacy may become impossible in the aftermath of a military initiative, but the converse can also be true.

The actions of states are often based on the belief that in a tight corner diplomacy becomes more efficacious if supported by at least symbolic military measures. This is evident in the best-documented case—American foreign policy,[29] but the pattern is not confined to the United States. Indeed, pure diplomacy may fail to convey a state's intentions—to give two examples, political warning that appeared to be crystal-clear to the sender was not heeded by Khrushchev before the Missile Crisis, or by Nasser before the Six Day War. Even deadly force has been ignored—as exemplified by China's forays into North Korea before its devastating intervention on November 27, 1950. In contrast to 1914, however, military signaling between the superpowers has rarely provoked escalation. A possible exception to this rule occurred in the Yom Kippur Crisis, when the alerting of Soviet airborne troops was one of the factors that led the United States to call a strategic (DEFCON 3) alert; on the other hand, it is unclear whether the Soviets were "signaling."

That a priority on diplomacy may preclude military options was evident in the Missile Crisis. A purely diplomatic U.S. initiative would have disclosed knowledge of the Soviet action in Cuba, and relinquished the benefit of surprise considered crucial to any military step.

It is therefore necessary to strike a balance between the attitudes of the statesman and the soldier. Such decisions are usually not the outcome of contests between civilians and the military.[30] This is illustrated by Eisenhower, who, as president, tried to impose restrictions on military operations that he would have resented or rejected as a general.[31] The two attitudes have their own logic; their marriage, although often necessary, is always difficult.

The statesman focuses on negotiation. To strengthen his position, the statesman is willing to threaten military action, but the accent is on the threat as opposed to the action. The statesman views war and peace as a continuum, rather than a dichotomy, with military operations being an extension of policy formation, not merely the implementation of policy. Affecting the opponent's intentions by modulating applied force, whether veiled or barefaced, takes precedence over destroying the opponent's military capabilities. The statesman, therefore, wants to postpone the decision to apply force to the last moment. And even after the troops have been ordered to march, the statesman will try to preserve flexibility by asserting detailed control over commanders in the field. In relatively simple situations, that option has become feasible with modern communications.[32] Once military operations begin, however, communications silence may become essential, whereas the control sought by political leaders requires continuous reports from forces in the field.

The soldier's attitudes are shaped by awareness of the fog and fortunes of war, by the requirement to achieve goals imposed from above, and by the tradition that those under his command are not to be exposed to unnecessary risks. The soldier, therefore, seeks to minimize uncertainty, so enemy capabilities are of greater concern than are intentions. The soldier disdains bluff and opposes threats that must be carried out if the bluff is called, as well as shows of force that give higher priority to political signaling than to operational success. The soldier agrees that the use of force is a last resort, but wants an early decision. Elaborate preparations are needed to attain combat readiness, gaining the initiative can be critical to success, and a sustained high alert can erode readiness due to fatigue and the suspension of maintenance. If force is to be used, the soldier demands well-defined objectives, resources determined by a pessimistic assessment of enemy capabilities, and firm political commitment. And once operations begin, the soldier expects them to be conducted by military professionals in accordance with plans that are not to be altered in midstream for extraneous reasons. The soldier holds to the tradition that the decision to employ force is the prerogative of the national leadership, but implementation of that decision is a professional military responsibility.

The tension between the priorities of the statesman and the soldier can crop up at every juncture and in a variety of dimensions. At the outbreak of a crisis the military will usually be able to offer detailed contingency plans, whereas the diplomatic community will not.[33] Foreign services do not engage in detailed operational planning for alternative contingencies, whereas such planning is a raison d'être for military staffs.[34] That difference is intrinsic: military operations are tangible and quantifiable, whereas political goals are relatively inchoate and ambiguous.

Even before any decisions are taken, military and political tactics can pose conundrums. A contemplated military operation can hinge on timely information obtained by intrusive reconnaissance, but the adversary will read such intrusions as an indicator that an attack may be imminent.[35] Awareness that martial overtones may elicit more political cohesion on the home front than a purely diplomatic environment can lead a government to adopt such a tone, but if that consideration is given undue weight it can lead to disaster. Both of these quandaries arose in the Missile Crisis. President Kennedy refused to allow the use of flares in nighttime reconnaissance since that might have been mistaken as gunfire; on the other hand, his government's posture had a military coloration that forced his domestic opponents to hold their tongues, whereas a purely diplomatic stance would have exposed him to a barrage of "advice."

The dilemmas do not dissolve once military operations begin unless all diplomatic avenues have been abandoned and there is no need to convince citizens or allies that war is unavoidable. Recall that France, Germany, and Russia in 1914 had to balance the requirement to attain combat readiness by prompt mobilization against their desire to portray themselves as victims of aggression. Pressures in both directions were intense. For example, the French General Staff estimated that France would lose about 10 kilometers of territory for every day of delay in mobilization. Nevertheless, the French government postponed full mobilization and restricted reconnaissance near the frontier in order to convince England that France had not started the war.

Such trade-offs between political and military imperatives are resolved in a rather abstract guise in high-level policy decisions, and must then be translated into concrete orders governing military measures. That translation process is crucial and complex. It is crucial because the visible military operations that are mounted, the manner in which they are carried out, and the diplomacy that accompanies them paint the picture from which the adversary must read one's intentions. It is complex because the spectrum of military options and the variety of forces is so large.

One important aspect of this conversion of political decisions into military orders—changes of alert status—was already discussed in Chapter 9. The DEFCON system offers a large menu of military steps, and the particular combination that is chosen will be one highly significant feature in the picture presented to the adversary. Another important element in that picture is formed by the wartime operations that the adversary will anticipate as the potential sequel to the chosen alert measures. In addition, there are the *rules of engagement* at the nuts-and-bolts level. Whether in peacetime, crisis, or war, all military forces operate under such rules.[36] They are a set of detailed instructions that specify under what circumstances each combat unit is permitted to engage in a particular type of action against the enemy—for example, whether an aircraft is permitted to approach a certain type of enemy ship to within some specified distance and then open fire should that ship have "painted" the aircraft with its fire-control radar. The rules can embody a spectrum of broad goals, from minimizing contact with the adversary to maximizing tactical effectiveness. The former increases the danger of tactical surprise, the latter that of escalation.

The enormous variety of weapons and weapon platforms, the various threats they face, and the different political environments in which contact with an adversary may occur, imply that the rules of engagement are highly complex. If they are to be useful to combat units, they must be formulated in detail by expert staffs that continuously modify them in the light of evolving military technology. In a particular crisis situation, the rules of engagement for the units involved should seek to capture the desired mix of combat readiness and political tone. Finally, the rules must be modified in a timely fashion should the situation change.

Because so much may ride on the rules of engagement in a crisis, at least the overall character of the rules is chosen at the highest levels of government by civilians and their military advisors. If the crisis is localized and slow-paced, the finer details of the rules may be negotiated at such levels. As with other aspects of micromanagement, this runs the risk that not only civilian decision makers, but even senior military leaders, will not be sufficiently conversant with the current status of these rules to grasp their full implications. This problem is again illustrated by the Cuban Missile Crisis, when the secretary of defense and other senior officials were deeply involved in formulating the minute details of the rules of engagement for surface ships enforcing the blockade, but were relatively unaware of the rules under which U.S. anti-submarine forces were operating, even though these latter activities probably sent a far more threatening message to Moscow than the precise deportment of boarding parties.

To summarize, the selection of the many variations in alert operations that the DEFCON system can accommodate and the associated rules of engagement are of central importance to crisis "management." The host of mundane details that they embody form the concrete, operational manifestation of the abstractions discussed in high government offices—the political objectives that are to be sought and the psychological context in which they are to be pursued. Once again, the apex of government is faced with a task for which it is ill-equipped but which it can hardly delegate. If it is to discharge that responsibility, the leadership must see to it that it has the advice of officers fully conversant with the current status and military implications of alert operations and rules of engagement, and also with the details of military activities that may not appear to be at center stage so that they do not inadvertently compromise the objectives being sought.

ESCALATION

Despite the tensions between the priorities of the soldier and the statesman, crises between the superpowers[37] have been benign enough so that policy-makers could create a political environment that produced a pattern of military operations largely consistent with that environment.[38] The interleaved dilemmas we have considered, however, imply that the probability of successful "management" decreases sharply as a crisis intensifies because the political atmosphere would then grow more ominous, and the attitudes of the soldier could gain the upper hand over those of the statesman.

Were that to occur, we would enter terra incognita: crises that could escalate to war between the superpowers. That terrain seems to have two continental divides—one between peace and conventional war, another between conventional and nuclear war, although once the first threshold to war is crossed the nuclear divide might not loom large. Whether the various subdivides inside the nuclear watershed would be sturdy firebreaks is unclear. Of these, the most significant is the one between tactical and long-range nuclear conflict. It is likely that the distinction between theater-range and intercontinental nuclear war would disappear as soon as U.S. warheads struck targets inside the Soviet Union; many Western observers tend to believe that the Soviets would view such attacks as de facto strategic whether or not they are launched by U.S. strategic forces.

The Standing Taboos

Before we speculate about escalation we should ask why it has not yet emerged from the post-Hiroshima crises.[39] Fear of nuclear war is surely one fundamental reason, if not the only one:

> The development of nuclear weapons has had, on balance, a stabilizing effect on the postwar international system. They have served to discourage the process of escalation that has, in other eras, too casually led to war. They have had a sobering effect upon a whole range of statesmen of varying degrees of responsibility and capability. They have forced national leaders, every day, to confront the reality of what war is really like, indeed to confront the prospect of their own mortality . . . [40]

On the other hand, both superpowers have sought to exploit that fear—Khrushchev against various nations other than the United States, the Soviet Union against China in 1969,[41] and the United States against China in the final phase of the Korean War, as well as against the Soviet Union in several crises. A large literature[42] and heated debates have examined the efficacy of such "nuclear diplomacy." In every instance, however, a spectrum of plausible assessments can be defended because virtually nothing is known about the impact U.S. nuclear signals have had on Soviet decisions, and also because factors unrelated to nuclear weapons were of evident importance in all superpower crises. Thus, many leading American participants in the Missile Crisis hold a different view today of what impelled Khrushchev to withdraw his missiles than they themselves did at that time. For example, in testimony before Congress on February 6, 1963, Secretary of Defense McNamara said that at the critical juncture in the Missile Crisis, when it appeared that the blockade had failed to induce the Soviet Union to comply with U.S. demands, and an invasion of Cuba was becoming a serious option, the risk of subsequent escalation implied that "we faced that night the possibility of launching nuclear weapons and Khrushchev knew it, and that is the reason, and the only reason, why he withdrew those weapons." Today, he and many of the Cuba veterans believe that U.S. conventional superiority in the theater, which was overwhelming, was the fundamental coercive factor.[43] Until we hear tapes of Politburo meetings we cannot really know whether either interpretation is correct.

What can be said without fear of contradiction about nuclear diplomacy is therefore very brief:

- Superpower crises were quite common before the Missile Crisis in 1962, but in the quarter-century since that gravest of post-Hiroshima confrontations there has only been one such event, the far milder 1973 Yom Kippur Crisis.

- The United States alerted nuclear forces during the 1973 and 1962 crises, and in several crises before that. The Soviet Union has never held a nuclear alert during a superpower crisis.
- In 1962 the United States had overwhelming strategic superiority, but the Soviet Union had essentially attained strategic parity by 1973.

For whatever reason, the superpowers seem to have evolved a tacit code of conduct that has prevented war:[44] While doing your utmost to advance your own interests:[45]

1. Don't use deadly force against the adversary.
2. Don't paint the adversary into a corner so that he must choose between humiliation and escalation.
3. Don't use military means to undermine the opponent's dominance in geographical areas he deems vital.
4. Don't use your own forces against an adversary's ally or protectorate.
5. Don't use your own forces to dramatically alter the status quo in a region (such as the Middle East), where both superpowers have significant stakes, but their spheres of influence are not carved in stone.
6. Don't engage in "horizontal escalation"—a response in a region other than the one in which the crisis began.

Since the superpowers lay claim to global power and influence, an encounter that does not remain localized is likely to be perceived as a challenge to that stature, and, therefore, as a strategic threat. As we recall, the Truman administration interpreted the invasion of South Korea in that light, and that was a prime factor in its decision to engage itself militarily, despite prior decisions not to do so.

The Missile Crisis was serious from the start because the Soviet Union was ignoring Taboo No. 3, and were on the way to violating No. 2. It would have become far more serious had Kennedy used an air strike against the missile installations manned by Soviet personnel, for that would have breached Taboo No. 1, as well as No. 2, and carried a high risk that the Soviets would have responded by violating No. 6 with a move against a distant Western soft-spot, such as Berlin or Turkey.

Whether by design or not, these taboos have produced an important rule of engagement: *keep things simple!* Tight control by national leaderships requires simplicity. No superpower crisis has seen more than one major escalatory step by each side or any gross attempts to stampede the adversay into decisions.

Such a courtly etiquette for dealing with crisis is not free of risk, however. Henry Kissinger has argued that[46]

What seems "balanced" and "safe" in a crisis is often the most risky. Gradual escalation tempts the opponent to match every move; what is intended as a show of moderation may be interpreted as irresolution; reassurance may provide too predictable a checklist and hence an incentive for waiting, prolonging the conditions of inherent risk. A leader must choose carefully and thoroughly the issues over which to face confrontation. He should do so only for major objectives. Once he is committed, however, his obligation is to end the confrontation rapidly. For this he must convey implacability. He must be prepared to escalate rapidly and brutally to a point where the opponent can no longer afford to experiment.

This critique of crisis management may be justified, but the prescription with which it culminates assumes that subsequent moves by both sides can be adequately calculated in advance. Unfortunately, international relations are less tractable (and more dangerous) than chess, and even masterful statesmen can rarely plan their next move with care, let alone the one after that.[47] For that matter,[48] in the brief meeting on October 24, 1973, in which Kissinger and his colleagues decided on diplomatic and military measures to forestall a possible insertion of Soviet troops into the Suez, there simply was no time to consider what was to be the next U.S. move had the Soviets not yielded.[49] That is par for the course. From a comprehensive review of nuclear signaling by the United States, Betts finds a striking pattern of initiatives *"taken after collegial discussions that did not carefully evaluate or even address what all the possible military consequences could be, especially if the object of the threats refused to accede to basic demands."*[50]

That syndrome is not confined to ambiguous threats, or to the United States. Governments find it difficult to assess unwelcome but plausible responses to their actions, as Khrushchev's adventure in Cuba and MacArthur's march to the Yalu illustrate.[51] The syndrome stems, in large part, from the assumption that the adversary's intentions are understood. MacArthur was confident that he knew the oriental mind; Khrushchev presumably believed that he had read the minds of the Kennedy entourage. The decisions by Kissinger's WSAG in the Yom Kippur Crisis are consistent with an assessment that Moscow had no intention of challenging a show of force—a highly plausible hypothesis given that the United States was trying to satisfy Moscow's basic demand that Israel's destruction of the Egyptian army be stopped.[52] But as we already remarked in Chapter 8, WSAG was at the apex of a government that had operated on an equally plausible but utterly wrong reading of Sadat's intentions in that very same crisis! Had its interpretation of Soviet intentions also been wide of the mark, it might have discovered that the Kremlin still had options with which it could "afford to experiment," and that would have made the crisis far more dangerous. In short, Kissinger's actions assumed that the Soviets would adhere to the unwritten code.

Were the cooperative regime defined by that code to fissure, the risks would be far greater than in the crises of the past. How large these fissures would have to become to produce various levels of escalation is difficult to assess. Many imponderables would come into play.

The Conventional Threshold

The question then arises as to how the political, organizational, and military context is likely to evolve as the intensity of threat and violence increases.

That evolution would be strongly influenced by what is thought to be in store should escalation continue. Whether that anticipation would be a moderating or exacerbating influence would depend on circumstance—on the degree to which diplomatic reassurance fortified by fear of nuclear war could compete with visible preparations for combat.

Were the risk of conflict to mount, activities that border on warfare would be likely to occur: jamming and other forms of electronic warfare, passive interference with satellite surveillance, antisubmarine operations, harassment of surface fleets, and so forth.

Maritime operations have unique features that could bear on escalation. While a skirmish at sea would take place in relative isolation from other forces, and is unlikely to lead to civilian casualties, other aspects of naval operations imperil stability. Communications with ships, especially submarines, are more tenuous than those with air and ground forces. Furthermore, opposing naval forces shadow each other and mingle as no others do; there are, on average, about 40 serious U.S.-Soviet naval incidents per year, including some collisions.[53] Such proximity demands virtually instantaneous reactions to aggressive tactics even in peacetime, and has led to tense encounters during crisis. During the Yom Kippur Crisis, Soviet naval squadrons, consisting of surface and submarine units, maintained close contact with four U.S. carrier and amphibious groups for a week *after* the DEFCON 3 alert was over; the two fleets continually targeted each other for immediate attack. In the Jordanian crisis of 1970 Soviet Navy crews assumed battle stations, loaded SAM launchers, and locked their fire control radars on U.S. aircraft. In recent years U.S. Navy exercises in the Atlantic and Pacific have elicited mock attacks from Backfire bombers.

Tenuous communications, isolation, and the need for prompt decisions have established a deeply entrenched resistance in skippers to "rudder orders from shore." Political authorities tend to try to hold the tiller from afar because of apprehension that the rules of engagement, even though approved by themselves, do not fit the circumstances. Should conflict appear likely, control by higher levels of command would become looser because ships may have to maintain radio emission silence for their own protection. As the pace and complexity of events, or the level of violence, intensifies, rudder orders from shore would become increasingly divorced from tactical realities.

Should a crisis erupt in Europe, naval interactions could occur if the Soviets sought to thwart an effort by NATO to block the G–I–N gap with mines or by antisubmarine tactics such as those used in the 1962 blockade of Cuba. Attack submarines engaged in intrusive reconnaissance before the outbreak of war could also cause inflammatory incidents. Should war break out, with nuclear weapons not yet used, conventional firepower based below, on, and above the sea would try to bar and penetrate maritime choke points. Lethal antisubmarine warfare by both sides would also begin at once, especially along the Atlantic sea lanes, the U.S. coasts, and probably in Soviet home waters.

On the Continent a severe crisis would pose a variety of intertwined political and military problems for NATO. Warning of Pact military preparations can be expected, but its political interpretation, and of when and how to respond, would involve NATO's leadership in very difficult decisions.

Were the Pact to attack, one must assume that it would seek to achieve surprise by disguising the location, time, and nature of the onslaught. As Betts has emphasized,[54] "in the past forty years there have been few if any examples of failures by major powers to inflict effective shock in the initiation of war." In essentially every instance of successful surprise, the victim's problem did not stem from stupidity or treachery, but from a puzzle created by deception compounded with political misperceptions. It would be hazardous to presume that modern technology can eliminate surprise in conventional (as compared to strategic) warfare, as demonstrated by the failure of NATO intelligence to recognize that Soviet armies engaged in large-scale "exercises" were about to move massively into Czechoslovakia in 1968: it was the Kremlin that notified President Johnson that was happening![55] Surprise at the outset hardly guarantees ultimate success, however, as aggressors often discover. Furthermore, NATO's air superiority and the nature of the terrain gives it a considerable degree of insurance against surprise on the ground. The agreement concluded at Stockholm in September 1986 also hinders the masquerading of attacks by military exercises, a classic means for attaining surprise.[56]

Response to warning could become a political problem for NATO since the allies may differ in their interpretation of events and in their willingness to act. While SACEUR has the authority to call alerts, in practice he would have to gain the support of the governments affected,[57] especially if he requested a "chop" of forces to his command. Another potential source of tension is that a NATO nuclear alert virtually mandates increased readiness of U.S. strategic forces, which might then be answered with a Soviet strategic alert.

If war appeared imminent, there might be panic and spontaneous evacuations, particularly near the inter-German border. The familiar photos of refugees sharing roads with armies in World War II do not begin to give an adequate picture of what would ensue today should spontaneous flight occur since very few Europeans owned automobiles in 1940. Because NATO's operations could be seriously disrupted if the population were allowed to take to the autobahns, such behavior might be provoked and stoked by the purposeful spreading of rumors.

These observations imply that as a crisis increases in intensity and complexity, the number of decisions required to steer vast security organizations would grow swiftly, and micromanagement would have to be abandoned by national leaderships. The two-way signal traffic required for detailed command from the very top during a severe crisis could probably not be accommodated even if the necessary decisions could be made at an adequate pace by so small and remote a group. That may sound implausible given modern automated data processing and transmission, but the electronic revolution has not only increased the supply but also the demand for information.[58] Even minor crises tend to flood communication networks—a famous example is that of the 1967 Israeli attack on the U.S. intelligence vessel *Liberty*.[59]

That such problems persist in the U.S. commands system is documented in an interview with Lt. Gen. Clarence E. McKnight Jr. while he served as director of C^3 System, JCS.[60]

Although many would view the hobbling of micromanagement as a blessing, ever greater reliance would then have to be placed on previously established rules of engagement whose details could not be reviewed by political authorities, and on military plans whose implications could not be carefully weighed in the light of a rapidly changing situation. Furthermore, leaders may have anticipated that they would directly manage the crisis, and be unprepared for the role they would actually play.

At the psychological level, a point could come where pressure to accept ambiguous warning could overwhelm the desire for certainty, and the imperative for combat readiness could take priority over that for reassurance of the adversary. Anticipation of war could thus become a self-fulfilling prophecy. In all likelihood, war would begin as a deliberate and conscious act, but in a deeper sense it could arise through inadvertence from such an environment.

Nuclear Thresholds

Nuclear escalation would, presumably, only emerge from the midst of a major conventional conflict, but the readying of nuclear forces would certainly have begun before that. Strategic forces are likely to be near a wartime status even before hostilities break out, but that does not present the most dangerous path to escalation. As we shall argue, alerting ground-based tactical nuclear forces is a more hazardous and perplexing issue whether or not war had begun.

In a major conventional war, both sides would have to maintain control over thousands of nuclear weapons, possibly up to the brink of defeat, while the front might be shifting through regions where such weapons are based. Commanders would have to prevent unintended use of any nuclear weapon, and simultaneously prepare their large and diverse arsenals for possible use. These two opposing requirements would have to be met in the face of conventional attacks on the nuclear forces and on their command system.

Soviet plans for a purely conventional European campaign apparently envisage a fast-paced armored offensive with air support using conventional and possibly chemical munitions, augmented by sabotage carried out by commandos (Spetsnaz) inserted behind NATO lines. Their two major objectives appear to be the suppression of NATO ground-based tactical nuclear forces before they could be dispersed from vulnerable peacetime locations and the swift disruption of NATO's command infrastructure. By that token, the Soviets also anticipate concentrated attacks by NATO on their own command facilities.

NATO command suffers from a number of long-standing vulnerabilities to conventional attack. The dearth of protected modern command posts, insufficient communications between NATO headquarters and tactical commands that are secure in the face of electronic warfare, and incompatibility between tactical command networks of the member states are seen as the most serious problems.[61] On the other hand, NATO air superiority would pose a threat to Soviet command, even if it is more robust than NATO's.

The Soviet conventional strategy is apparently based on the observation that the more deeply Pact forces penetrate into NATO territory, the more difficult it would be for NATO to employ nuclear weapons against those forces for fear of putting NATO forces and populations at risk. This does not mean that the Soviets now rule out the possibility of nuclear escalation. Rather, it appears that should escalation be "forced upon them," they foresee it as a sudden, major step that would move the conflict into an entirely different phase in which they would endeavor to exploit their nuclear forces in a decisive fashion, in contrast to the smoothly graduated "controlled" transition that has been prominent in NATO planning.[62]

Paradoxically, Soviet plans for a purely conventional campaign carry a large risk of nuclear escalation. They rely on deeply ingrained principles of Soviet offensive strategy that could place great pressure on Soviet political leaders to order the use of force before NATO attained combat readiness, while those same pressures might call for nuclear preemption were there any suspicion that NATO was about to resort to its nuclear forces if war should break out.[63] Such a strategy, however, could not preclude NATO from going nuclear even if had not yet dispersed its ground-based nuclear weapons. A large number of land- and carrier-based nuclear-capable aircraft would always be available, as would SLBMs on British, French, and U.S. missile submarines assigned to NATO, and nuclear-armed SLCMs on U.S. surface vessels and attack submarines. Until the Pershing II, ground-launched cruise missiles (GLCMs), and shorter-ranged nuclear-armed ground-based missiles are removed in accordance with the INF arms control agreement, these could also be launched from their peacetime locations prior to dispersal. Even after their removal, French nuclear-armed surface-to-surface missiles would remain. In the light of all these NATO options, it is hardly surprising that at least some senior Soviet officers have made it clear that they do not accept the notion that a war between the superpowers could remain purely conventional.[64]

Turning to the sea, we have already noted that in the Atlantic the United States and the Soviet Union have primary objectives that are compatible— protection of the Atlantic sea lanes and of Soviet home waters. But they also have secondary objectives that could stoke escalation. The Soviet Union has invested heavily in attack submarines, and to a lesser degree in other blue water naval units. Were Soviet forces to surge through the G–I–N gaps in an attempt to imperil the Atlantic sea lanes, any crisis would be greatly aggravated. The same statement would apply should the United States execute those operations called for by the "Maritime Strategy" in which U.S. surface ships and/or attack submarines would be deployed into the Soviet Navy's Arctic sanctuary,[65] where they would pose an imminent threat to Soviet strategic submarines. Should those U.S. vessels carry the highly accurate long-range Tomahawk cruise missiles, they would also threaten targets deep inside the Soviet Union. Tomahawks launched from the Norwegian Sea can reach targets from the shores of the Arctic (Murmansk, the Kola Peninsula, etc.) to the Moscow region; launched from the Eastern Mediterranean, they could cover Southern Russia from the Ukraine to Baku on the Caspian Sea.

The combatants in both superpower navies are largely dual-capable. Given the problems with communications with naval forces, their operations in a conventional war are a potential spawning ground for escalation. Long-range nuclear-armed cruise missiles (the Tomahawk and its forthcoming Soviet counterpart) are especially worrisome, for any vessel that carries them could, without notice, shift from being a conventional combatant to a platform for strategic nuclear warfare.

Nuclear use would be on the agenda of Western decision makers as soon as war had begun, and probably even before then. Given the possibility of a disrupted command system, and the pace of multinational political deliberations, it would be prudent from a military viewpoint to request and obtain authority for nuclear use well before the situation on the battlefield would warrant exploitation of such authority by SACEUR. Thus, General Bernard Rogers, when he served as SACEUR, stated[66] that he would expect to request nuclear release authority[67] within days following the outbreak of war, and that this request would be *preceded* by a series of messages warning political authorities of the decision they might soon face.

NATO political leaders are quite aware of the many quandaries that have been mentioned. They would be concerned that the dispersal of nuclear weapons would become known to the public, and might initiate panic; this is especially true of the large theater-range missiles that would be removed by an INF agreement.[68] They also know that it would be prudent to assume that Soviet signals intelligence would be aware of major operational shifts by NATO, as was demonstrated during the 1976 Reforger exercise when the Soviets announced[69] "that NATO was going nuclear during the exercise" 2 hours before NATO troops received word of the approval! The dilemma that it is dangerous to keep nuclear weapons at their peacetime locations and also dangerous to disperse them typifies issues that could cause serious dissension if various governments were to insist on different cuts through these Gordian knots. General Rogers has reportedly sought permission to develop standard operating procedures for dispersal of nuclear weapons early in a crisis, but the idea was not pursued because of political resistance.[70] This can be taken as an indication of what could be in store.

This array of political hurdles that the United States and its allies would face does not mean that NATO would inevitably be paralyzed by internal disarray in a nuclear crisis. The chain of command allows decisions to be taken even if dissension is rife. Thus, some Englishmen with extensive government and military experience related to NATO hold the view that the United States would resort unilaterally to the use of its own nuclear weapons should NATO be unable to reach a timely decision.[71] SACEUR serves many masters, but when all is said and done, if nuclear weapons are to be used the owners of the warhead and the means of delivery will issue his orders.[72] The political realities of an association of free nations have led to the intricate command structure depicted in Figure 10.1. It seeks to satisfy two incompatible requirements: effective decision making and full consultation. The former has ultimate precedence, but the need to maintain alliance cohesion could easily come into serious conflict with the demands of the military situation and impose exceedingly difficult and urgent choices on decision makers. The other side of that coin is that a Soviet expectation that NATO may hesitate fatally could lead to Soviet actions that would precipitate NATO decisions, and lead to nuclear escalation.

While it is unlikely that the outbreak of war would be inadvertent, nuclear escalation might occur in that manner. Once large-scale conventional combat had caused serious damage to command facilities and personnel on both sides, and if commanders had already received contingent authority to use nuclear weapons, the environment in which decisions would be taken could lead to escalation. Both sides would be attuned to rapid response to tactical warning, and very sensitive to any indication of nuclear attack. Both would be giving the highest priority to successful execution of combat missions. In such circumstances, fully legitimate actions by local commanders, as seen from a broader perspective, could be imprudent because they might reverberate through the opponent's entire command system and trigger a swift and powerful response.

Had nuclear war already begun, all those escalatory factors would be stronger still. If Soviet declaratory doctrine is taken at face value, the use of NATO nuclear weapons on the battlefield would impel the Soviets to large-scale response with their longer range nuclear forces. If those were missiles or aircraft based on Soviet soil, a NATO counterattack on them could be the precursor to strategic nuclear war.

The considerations that are likely to dominate at the brink of strategic conflict were already discussed in a context-free setting in Chapter 5. Now we have some inkling of the political, military, and human environment in which the decision to initiate strategic war would be faced. As we saw, today's strategic forces have imposed a great incentive on both sides not to ride out a strategic attack before initiating a response, even though such a prompt-

---→

Figure 10.1. The U.S.–NATO command system. This figure is a schematic depiction, not an organizational chart. It portrays those components that would be most relevant to a European conflict; thus, it does not show the U.S. "out-of-area" unified commands shown on p. 50, and it also suppresses the lower command echelons shown on p. 230. For the sake of clarity, not all NATO member states appear separately, and the chain-of-command for NATO nuclear forces is only shown for Great Britain. The switch "Peace→War" depicts the "chop" of forces to the operational command of SACEUR, in this case of British units equipped with U.S. nuclear warheads. The link with question marks represent the somewhat ambiguous status of France within NATO. It should be noted that this scheme leaves out the important links provided by diplomacy.

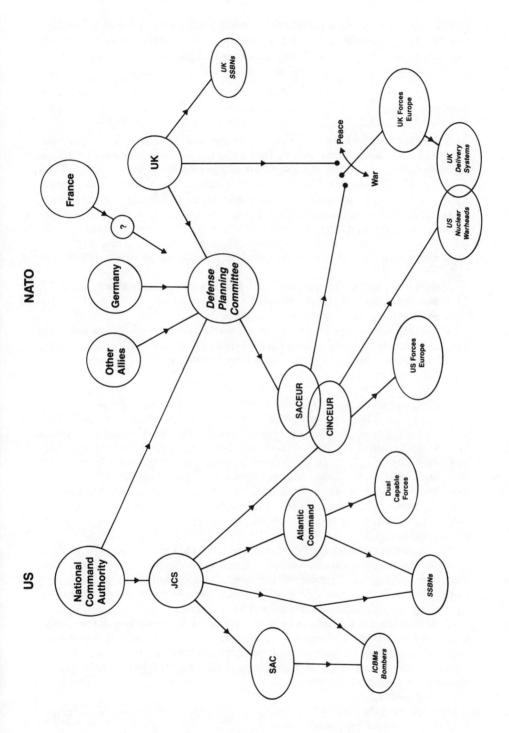

NATO

US

France

UK
UK
SSBNs

Peace
War

UK Forces
Europe

UK
Delivery
Systems

Germany

Defense
Planning
Committee

?

Other
Allies

US
Nuclear
Warheads

SACEUR

CINCEUR

US Forces
Europe

National
Command
Authority

JCS

Atlantic
Command

Dual
Capable
Forces

SSBNs

SAC

ICBMs
Bombers

launch posture has a formidable list of chilling drawbacks. To that list we may now add leaders awash in the chaos brought on by a torrent of violent events that they had failed to stem, facing decisions of a gravity unknown to history.

NOTES

1. Perhaps because crisis is so unstable a condition, a juxtaposition of unrelated events may have a significant impact. Thus Sadat did not synchronize his 1973 Yom Kippur attack on Israel with the resignation of Agnew and the Saturday Night Massacre, but that coincidence meant that Kissinger and not Nixon would make virtually all of Washington's decisions. By a second simultaneous coincidence, a terrorist attack on a train in Austria carrying Jewish emigrants from Russia distracted the Israeli cabinet just before Sadat attacked. As another example, the Chinese shot down a U-2 just before a crucial White House meeting on overflights of Cuba, a happenstance that curtailed reconnaissance, and delayed the discovery of the Soviet missile installations in Cuba.

2. This is not meant to imply that World War I broke out inadvertently. See p. 29.

3. See George and Smoke, pp. 390–446.

4. See Blechman and Kaplan, pp. 524–525.

5. For imporant exceptions to this rule see Jervis; Lebow; Jervis, Lebow and Stein; and Alexander George, *Presidential Decisionmaking in Foreign Policy: The Effective Use of Information and Advice* (Boulder: Westview Press, 1980).

6. See Chapter 4, Note 30.

7. Van Creveld cites these factors as the main cause of the IDF's poor performance on the first day of the war. The chief-of-staff was forced to contend with a flood of unsolicited advice; he "was surrounded by a galaxy of generals, the heroes of 1967; although for the most part they were out of uniform, they had dropped in to lend a hand. Unable or unwilling to drive these men away, among whom were several of his own former superiors, [he] had to put up with—at the least count—three former chiefs of staff as well as . . . the former head of Military Intelligence" (p. 209). On the battlefield, the commander of the Southern forces had to cope with "two subordinates who had both been his superiors and one of whom (Sharon) was constantly bypassing him and talking directly to the chief of staff" (pp. 217–218).

8. Kennedy, p. 32.

9. This discussion of coping strategies draws on Irving Janis and Leon Mann, *Decision Making: A Psychological Analysis of Conflict, Choice, and Commitment* (New York: The Free Press, 1977); Margaret Hermann, "Indicators of Stress in Policymakers During Foreign Policy Crises," *Political Psychology* (Spring 1979) *1*:27–46; Lebow, op. cit.; George, op. cit.; and Jervis, Lebow and Stein, op. cit.

10. Motivational bias tends to be institutionalized in intelligence bureaucracies: intelligence officers are not demoted for overestimating the threat. The bureaucratic incentives encourages the perception of threat: if you are wrong, the threatening action does not materialize, and no obvious harm is done, whereas if you are right, you are decorated and promoted.

11. Wohlstetter, p. 68.

12. Ibid., pp. 355–356.

13. See, in particular, Snyder, Chapter 1.

14. See, in particular, Lebow; and Jervis, Lebow and Stein.

15. Joll, p. 25.

16. *A Retrospective on the Cuban Missile Crisis* (New York: Alfred P. Sloan Foundation, 1983).

17. James G. Blight, Joseph S. Nye, Jr., and David A. Welch, "The Cuban Missile Crisis Revisited," *Foreign Affairs* (1987), *66*:1, 70; p. 82.

18. Joll, p. 171.

19. Interviews.

20. For a review of some recent literature on intelligence matters, see Robert Jervis, "Intelligence and Foreign Policy: A Review Essay," *International Security* (1987), *11*:3, 141.

21. For a comprehensive description of the U.S. intelligence services from an organizational viewpoint see Richelson; their history and operations are described by Laqueur. The history and current structure of the Soviet intelligence apparatus is described in Jeffrey T. Richelson, *Sword and Shield* (Cambridge, MA: Ballinger, 1986).

22. According to Laquer (p. 225), the 1973 composition of the major intelligence services was approximately as follows: CIA, 15,000; NSA, 20,000; DIA, 5,000; air force, 60,000; navy, 10,000; army, 38,500; State Department, 335. Richelson (p. 20) esitmates that NSA had from 50,000 to 60,000 employees in 1985.

23. Lebow, pp. 125–132.

24. Ibid., pp. 158–163.

25. *Avoiding Inadvertent War: Crisis Management,* Hilliard Roderick, editor (Austin: University of Texas, 1983), p. 74.

26. Interview (not with Mr. McCone).

27. This section draws heavily on Betts, *Soldiers, Statesmen.*

28. See especially Jervis; also Thomas C. Schelling, "Confidence in Crisis," *International Security* (1984), *8*:4, 55.

29. For a compendium see Blechman and Kaplan.

30. There is a folklore that in a confrontation the military always presses for action while the politicians and diplomats urge caution. The U.S. record does not support that picture (see Betts, *Soldiers, Statesmen*). When the issue of committing troops to combat has arisen, military advice to presidents has, on the whole, resembled that of civilians, although the Cuban Crisis was a significant exception to this rule. In any event, military leaders have only dominated decisions concerning the use of force when they *vetoed* intervention outright, or did so by setting force requirements that had no chance of being accepted. Once battle is joined, however, as in Korea and Vietnam, the military usually adopts a much more aggressive stance, and calls for a level of support and freedom of action that the political leadership rarely grants.

31. During the 1958 Quemoy-Matsu crisis, Eisenhower rejected repeated requests to give commanders on the scene authority to commit forces to combat in the event of a Chinese assault. After authorizing the 1958 landing of Marines in Lebanon he asked whether the operation could be halted, to which his chief of naval operations retorted that "this thing doesn't start and stop. It's like a missile. You let her go, it's gone" (Betts, *Soldiers, Statesmen,* pp. 90 and 248).

32. Telephone links from Washington to units in the field were first used by the Kennedy administration to speak to a military convoy on the Berlin autobahn in 1961, and as we saw, to vessels enforcing the blockade of Cuba, in 1962.

33. This is a compression of Betts, *Soldiers, Statesmen,* p. 157.

34. The much smaller resources of the diplomatic community amplify this difference.

35. Because such trade-offs should reflect national policy, all U.S. reconnaissance

operations are under close supervision of senior military and civilian officials; see Richelson, pp. 276, 305–306.

36. For a good discussion of rules of engagement in the context of the Cuban Missile Crisis, see Scott D. Sagan, "Nuclear Alerts and Crisis Management," *International Security* (1985), 9:4, 113.

37. Note the qualification "between the superpowers." The U.S.–China crisis that preceded China's intervention in Korea ran out of control. From China's perspective U.S. military operations posed a threat to her vital interests and were incompatible with U.S. declaratory policy, which claimed no hostile intent.

38. See John D. Steinbruner, "An Assessment of Nuclear Crises," in *The Dangers of Nuclear War* (University or Toronto, 1979), Franklyn Griffiths and John C. Polanyi, editors, pp. 34–39.

39. See especially John Lewis Gaddis, "The Long Peace: Elements of Stability in the Postwar International System," *International Security* (1986), 10:4, 99.

40. Ibid., p. 123.

41. Following the clashes on the Sino-Soviet border in March 1969, the Soviet Union hinted through its news media that nuclear weapons could become involved if the skirmishes turned into warfare. Soviet diplomats also tried to ascertain what the U.S. position might be should the Soviet Union use nuclear weapons against China. For details and references, see Betts, *Nuclear Coercion,* pp. 79–81. In this connection we note that Glenn Seaborg, chairman of the Atomic Energy Commission during the Kennedy and Johnson administrations, reports that in 1963–64 the U.S. government explored the possibility of U.S.–Soviet joint action to prevent China from acquiring a nuclear capability. [Glenn T. Seaborg, *Stemming the Tide: Arms Control in the Johnson Years* (Lexington, MA: Lexington Books, 1987), pp. 111–112.]

42. Comprehensive accounts of U.S. nuclear diplomacy are provided by Blechman and Kaplan, and by Betts, *Nuclear Coercion.* See also Marc Trachtenberg, "The Influence of Nuclear Weapons on the Cuban Missile Crisis," *International Security* (1985), 10:1, 137.

43. Dean Rusk, Robert McNamara, George Ball, Roswell Gilpatric, Theodore Sorenson, and McGeorge Bundy, *Time,* September 27, 1982.

44. In this connection see Alexander L. George, "Crisis Management: The Interaction of Military and Political Considerations," *Survival* (Sept./Oct. 1984), 223; and Gaddis, op. cit., pp. 113–140, who argues that the code has arisen from "a mixture of custom, precedent, and mutual interest that takes shape quite apart from the realm of public rhetoric, diplomacy, or international law. They require the passage of time to become effective; they depend, for that effectiveness, upon the extent to which successive generations of national leadership on each side find them useful. They certainly do not reflect any agreed upon standard of international morality: indeed they often violate principles of "justice" adhered to by one side or the other."

45. As Gaddis remarks (Ibid., p. 133), "No two observers of superpower behavior would express these 'rules' in precisely the same way; indeed it may be that their very vagueness had made them more acceptable ... "

46. Kissinger, p. 622.

47. As JFK put it during the Missile Crisis, "it isn't the first step that concerns me, but both sides escalating to the fourth and fifth step—and we don't go to the sixth because there is no one around to do so." (Robert F. Kennedy, p. 98.)

48. In his memoirs Kissinger's statement is *not* made in connection with the Yom Kippur Crisis, though it is clearly intended as a general, if not universal, observation.

49. Interviews with most of the principal participants reported in Barry M. Blech-

man and Douglas M. Hart, "The Political Utility of Nuclear Weapons: The 1973 Middle East Crisis," *International Security,* (1982), 7:1, 132.

50. Betts, *Nuclear Coercion,* p. 9, our emphasis.

51. Janis (see bibliography) reports that leadership groups of various types (i.e., not only in government) seldom dwell on how their chosen policy might fail.

52. Garthoff, Chapter 11.

53. In 1984 a U.S. carrier collided with a Soviet attack submarine; Fred Hiatt, "Soviet Sub Bumps into US Carrier," *The Washington Post,* March 22, 1984, p. 1.

54. Betts, *Surprise Attack,* pp. 8 and 13. Successful surprise at the outset of a major campaign was attained despite the victim's awareness that an attack was likely: by the Germans against France on May 10, 1940, and against Russia on June 22, 1941; by Japan at Pearl Harbor, and in the Philippines 9 hours later despite warning; by China's attack on the U.S. and Korean armies in November 1950; by Israel in destroying the Egyptian Air Force in May 1967; and by Egypt on the Suez Canal and Syria in the Golan on Yom Kippur 1973. With the exception of May 1940 and 1967, these attacks are described in Chapters 3 and 8.

55. Betts, *Surprise Attack,* pp. 81–86.

56. See Chapter 11.

57. Well before such decisions are on the table the Defense Planning Committee should have received formal notification that a crisis situation existed, and the NATO states should have set up their own crisis management teams.

58. Van Creveld, Chapter 8.

59. Hirsh Goodman and Ze'ev Schiff, "The Attack on the *Liberty,*" *The Jerusalem Post Magazine,* August 31, 1984, 1.

60. Richard Halloran, "Military's Message System Is Overloaded, Officers Say," *The New York Times,* November 25, 1985.

61. See John H. Cushman (Lt. Gen., U.S. Army, ret.), "The Specified and Unified Commands C^3—Problems of Centralization," in *National Security Policy: The Decisionmaking Process,* Robert L. Pfaltzgraff, Jr. and Uri Ran'anan, editors (Archon, 1984), 270–274. See also interview with Gen. McKnight, preceding note.

62. See Legge, pp. 19 and 27.

63. For a critique of these aspects of Soviet doctrine, and a detailed bibliography, see Richard Ned Lebow, "The Soviet Offensive in Europe: The Schlieffen Plan Revisited?," *International Security* (1985), 9:4, 44.

64. Thus Marshall V. G. Kulikov, commander-in-chief of Warsaw Pact forces, has stated that "no matter with what means a new world war begins, it will inevitably end in a nuclear catastrophe." But Legge (p. 46) cautions against inferring Pact strategy from military statements, field manuals, and the like, by pointing out that one could not infer NATO policy from such sources.

65. Under what circumstances the United States would actually deploy large naval forces in Soviet home waters, as called for by the strategy described by Admiral James D. Watkins, the former CNO (see *The Maritime Strategy,* Supplement to U.S. Naval Institute Proceedings, January 1986, pp. 4–17), has been a subject of debate. The two sides are represented by John J. Mearsheimer, "A Strategic Misstep: The Maritime Strategy and Deterrence in Europe," *International Security* (1986), 11:2, 3; and by Linton F. Brooks, "Naval Power and National Security: The Case for the Maritime Strategy," Ibid., 58.

66. *Department of Defense Authorization for Appropriations for FY83,* U.S. Senate, Committee on Armed Services, pt. 7, 4334; "A Peril Seen by NATO Forces Chief," *Los Angeles Times,* July 13, 983, p. 4.

67. Such a request, or one by the other two NATO commanders with nuclear authority, must specify the weapons to be used and the targets. Use of other weapons, or targeting changes, mandate a separate request.

68. Thus dispersal of one GLCM flight (of 16 missiles) would require a convoy of 22 vehicles. GLCMs and Pershing IIs, however, can be fired from their peacetime location (and also during transport).

69. House Committee on Armed Services, *Authorization for Appropriations for FY1981,* 96th Congress, 2nd. session, pt. 4, p. 1946.

70. Daniel Charles, *Nuclear Planning in NATO: Pitfalls of First Use* (Cambridge, MA: Ballinger, 1987), p. 50.

71. Interviews.

72. Legge (p.23) emphasizes that full alliance consultation is not mandatory, but has been subject to the qualification "time and circumstances permitting" since the Athens meeting of NATO defense ministers in 1962.

11

Technical Developments and Arms Control

This chapter explores the contributions that arms control could make to crisis stability. In principle, arms control could ameliorate at least three aspects of the confrontation between the superpowers and their allies by placing constraints on new technologies that threaten stability, by restructuring and reducing existing forces, with particular emphasis on those well-suited to surprise attack, and by creating verifiable limitations on military operations that would reduce the threat of surprise attack and of sudden mobilizations or other activities that could endow a would-be attacker with the equivalent of surprise.

The strategic command system illustrates the interconnections between technical innovation, stability, and arms control. In describing the U.S. government's strategic command modernization program in Chapter 6, we observed that this effort would, by itself, not suffice to eliminate prompt launch from the list of likely strategic options. Some combination of reductions of Soviet offensive forces, and of a less vulnerable basing mode for the U.S. ICBM force, would also be required, as well as confidence that vital space-based portions of the modernized command system would retain their current security against ASAT attack. Only carefully constructed and verifiable agreements between the superpowers are likely to produce this reduction in the threat.

In short, investments in the command system will yield a net gain in performance only if the improved system can pull ahead of the competition. That competition stems from new threats posed by the adversary, and from increasingly taxing missions that the command may be required to accomplish. New threats may actually be reactions by the adversary to one's own force modernization. Thus, during the 1960s, U.S. strategic command improved greatly in sophistication and survivability, as did U.S. forces. At the same time the simple task of massive retaliation was replaced by flexible response, the first of a sequence of increasingly demanding missions. Subsequently the Soviets attained an offensive capability comparable to ours. The result is a U.S. command system that has a lower expectation of performing its assigned mission than the more primitive system that preceded it. Current trends, such as ASAT weapons, cruise missiles, and stealthy offensive forces, could replicate this syndrome.

TECHNICAL DEVELOPMENTS

Technology may either strengthen or undermine stability. Which outcome is realized depends not only on the specific technology, but also on many contextual factors, among which the political environment is obviously the most important.

Our discussion of technological trends germane to crisis stability will be very cursory; its purpose is to provide background for the arms control measures that we shall consider.

Intelligence and Early Warning

Surveillance by technical means has a broad range of purposes: assessing and targeting an adversary's forces; verifying compliance with arms control agreements; monitoring alert status during crisis; contributing to strategic warning; providing tactical warning that an attack has begun, and of ascertaining the nature and outcome of such an attack. In view of this broad range of missions, surveillance illustrates the chameleonlike character of technology. A better imaging satellite may negate ambiguous intelligence that a treaty has been violated or that attack preparations are underway, and thereby increase stability, but the same satellite might also provide otherwise unavailable data for targeting. In this instance, vulnerability and confidence are opposite sides of the same coin.

Ongoing improvements in the sensitivity and resolution of sensors, and in data processing and transmission, are stabilizing to the extent that they enhance the reliability, accuracy, promptness, and survivability of the surveillance system. Research currently supported by the SDI program should enhance U.S. capabilities for space surveillance, whether or not strategic defenses are eventually deployed. Such research can be expected to provide ground-, air- and space-based passive and active sensors of greatly enhanced sensitivity operating in the optical, infrared, and microwave portions of the electromagnetic spectrum.[1] These would contribute to more timely, accurate all-weather intelligence regarding a wide variety of military and other activities on the ground, at sea, in the atmosphere, and in space. In addition, research and development not directly connected to ballistic missile defense, and in particular in high-speed data handling and signal processing, can be expected to enhance intelligence capabilities. Obviously these trends will also improve Soviet technical intelligence capabilities.

Reductions of the infrared and radar signatures of weapon systems ("stealth") degrades the performance of sensors, and could be deleterious in crisis. Poorer confidence in attack detection, and less time to respond, increase the required speed of decision and the risk of miscalculation. On the other hand, the greater likelihood that a stealthy bomber will reach its target strengthens deterrence, and in that sense is stabilizing.

Force Modernization

Unless further limits are set by arms control, the United States can be expected to introduce thousands of new warheads[2] on sea- and air-launched cruise missiles, MX, B1, Stealth bombers, and Trident submarines.[3] How the Soviet arsenal will evolve is unclear, although there is a clear trend toward mobile ICBMs.[4] Whether these weapons will have the prompt hard-target kill capability ascribed to the silo-based SS-18 remains to be seen. Of the U.S. systems, MX and the D5 SLBM will add a very massive capability for the prompt destruction of missile silos and hardened command posts. To offset this, the Soviets can be expected to undertake any or all of the following: place a heavier reliance on prompt launch in a severe crisis, reduce their dependence on fixed command centers, or deploy new strategic weapons adapted to the evolving threat. Indeed, anticipation of fixed-silo obsolescence has already led the Soviet Union to deploy mobile ICBMs, which are likely to be emulated by the United States. Mobile ICBMs would enhance crisis stability, but they would complicate arms control because they pose some verification problems.

Among the technologies contributing to force modernization, long-range cruise missiles deserve special mention. The cruise missile is an air-breathing vehicle that flies at an extremely low altitude and therefore has a considerable ability to evade radar detection, a capability that will become more pronounced in the future when cruise missiles that exploit stealth technologies are deployed. A terrain matching guidance system gives the modern cruise missile a high accuracy that does not diminish with range, so that the nuclear-armed models have a hard-target kill capability comparable to that of ballistic missiles. The United States has deployed such cruise missiles on strategic bombers, on surface vessels and attack submarines, and as a ground-based version in Europe, although the latter should be removed by the INF Agreement. Soviet cruise missiles of comparable capabilities are to be anticipated.

Antisatellite Horizons

The U.S. air-launched "homing kill" ASAT,[5] like the Soviet ASAT first tested in 1968, are intended for low orbit interception. The same observation applies to the infrared homing interceptor tested successfully in the U.S. Army's Homing Overlay Experiment of 1984 against a dummy Minuteman warhead; this midcourse ballistic missile defense interceptor could be modified for use against satellites at altitudes comparable to those where the aforementioned ASATs operate. None of these low altitude interceptors pose a significant threat to the space-based portion of the strategic command infrastructure, which relies largely on high orbit satellites,[6] but they could provide a pathway to escalation.

Space mines, which were discussed in Chapter 6, appear to provide the only means with existing technology for prompt destruction of satellites at all altitudes. Although no test of reliable, long-term station-keeping by a small satellite seems to have been performed, space mines are a potential threat unless their testing and deployment is retarded by treaty.

If research on space-based missile defense includes tests of interception techniques against targets in space, ASAT capabilities will emerge as an inevitable byproduct.[7] Thus, directed energy systems with mirrors in GEO, such as the ground-based free electron laser, could destroy all current and planned GEO satellites long before these systems become lethal enough to perform a BMD mission. The x-ray laser, and the neutral particle-beam accelerator, could provide speed-of-light low-orbit ASAT capabilities. Also, as just mentioned, infrared homing interceptors for midcourse missile defense could serve as low-orbit ASATs.

Protection of future satellites from various ASAT threats will be discussed in connection with ASAT arms control. Suffice it to say that in an unconstrained competition between costly satellites and ASATs, the latter are likely to win, although with a concentrated effort some missions, such as communications, may be able to stay ahead of the threat.

Strategic Defense

Defense of hardened, redundant, and expendable targets appears to be technically feasible in the near term. Defense of a large set of Minuteman silos is relatively inexpensive and simple as compared to the defense of a small number of hardened command centers against a comparable threat. Defense of the retaliatory force alone would aid stability, and would not increase the first-strike threat. In the absence of negotiated restraints, however, it is likely to provoke the growth of offensive forces, especially if BMD technology could be construed to form the basis for a nationwide defense.

There is no significant body of opinion that suggests that security can be achieved by strategic defense alone. It is unclear whether the technologies under development by the Strategic Defense Initiative (SDI), or its Soviet counterpart, have a significant potential for reducing the vulnerability of key C^3I facilities beyond that which is attainable by means of mobility, covertness, and redundancy inasmuch as such technologies would also pose new threats to the space-based components of the command system.

A FRAMEWORK FOR STRATEGIC ARMS CONTROL

For many years the superpowers' strategic forces have projected a degree of mutual threat that has provoked progressively more threatening deployments. A large body of informed opinion that spans most political and national boundaries has emphasized the need to escape from this vicious circle. Nevertheless, arms control, the only visible means to that end, has not yet broken the impasse. Obviously the adversarial relationship between the two alliances is the fundamental hurdle, but there is also discord within the United States and NATO as to what would be in their own best interest.

A broad framework for strategic arms control that responds to a broad range of opinion within the Western body politic could break this impasse. Such a consensus is but one prerequisite. The other is that East and West be willing to respect the other's vital interests. Our proposals are constructed in that spirit, and it is therefore not surprising that they enjoy a considerable overlap with general features of the Strategic Arms Reductions Talks (START) between the superpowers.

Various powerful groups in the United States and among its NATO allies hold incompatible positions concerning strategic arms control. These divisions reflect different perceptions concerning the military and political role of nuclear weapons. In the short term—say the next 5 years—however, they are compatible since significantly smaller and less vulnerable strategic forces are a widely shared interim or ultimate goal. A consensus should therefore be built on that common objective, provided that no initiative is taken that would foreclose incompatible long-term objectives. We propose to burn no such bridges.

An Expanded Concept of Strategic Parity

Reductions and constraints must be sought that are seen by both sides, in their totality, as equivalent restrictions on their overall strategic capabilities; however, such equivalence does not require detailed symmetry. The destructive power of even a small number of thermonuclear weapons, the size of the existing arsenals, and each side's diversity of delivery systems together imply that *the band of acceptable strategic parity* is wide. The two strategic forces are not mirror images of each other, nor should they be expected or required to be in the future. While the band of acceptable parity would shrink somewhat were large cuts adopted, that band would remain broad enough so that these inevitable differences should not block negotiations.

Reductions

The principal objective of the reductions should be deterrent forces of reduced vulnerability. That requires a decrease in the number of accurate warheads per opposing vulnerable launcher. Ceilings on the number of accurate deliverable warheads are fundamental, therefore, and must take precedence over limits on launchers and platforms. Within such a framework the reductions of approximately 50 percent in the total number of strategic warheads, as accepted, in principle, by President Reagan and General Secretary Gorbachev should be attained during the next 5-year period.

Modernization and "De-MIRVing"

The preceding goal requires progressive "de-MIRVing" of ICBMs and SLBMs. On the other hand, both superpowers are committed to the deployment of new MIRVed missiles—MX, D5, SS-24. If reductions are to gain broad support, these commitments require the plan to permit some deployment of new MIRVed missiles. However, such modernizations must conform to the overriding requirement that the vulnerability of the resulting forces be significantly reduced. This imposes a considerable constraint on the proportion of new MIRVed missiles in the reduced force, unless the bulk of land-based forces were to become mobile, or were to be based in a much larger number of silos.

Future force modernization should concentrate on enhancing survivability. Since full-scale deployment of new MIRVed missiles on both sides would result in more vulnerable forces, expeditious movement toward single warhead ICBMs and SLBMs is important. In support thereof, the test-firing of new MIRVed missiles should be forbidden, as in the U.S. proposal presented at Moscow in 1977 and renewed in 1983. Furthermore, there should be a ban on the test-firing of missiles that are especially threatening to command: SLBMs on depressed trajectories,[8] and reentry vehicles having sufficient maneuverability to threaten mobile command posts. Experience with the SALT process demonstrates that such restrictions on test-firings can be adequately verified, although confidence in such verification would be more widely shared if telemetry signals were not encrypted.

Small Mobile Systems

The technical characteristics of the modern nuclear-armed cruise missile have already been described. Its small size and great lethality at long range create serious problems for arms control. In contrast to other nuclear delivery systems with strategic capabilities, the cruise missile is easy to conceal. Furthermore, the nuclear- and conventionally armed versions are essentially indistinguishable.

Mobile ICBMs could enhance stability because they appear to be less vulnerable than silo-based missiles. On the other hand, this advantage must be weighed against the problem of monitoring the number that has been deployed. If there are militarily significant uncertainties regarding that number, pressures to enlarge the strategic arsenals are likely to ensue.

Quite aside from the problems posed by small and mobile strategic systems for arms control, such weapons could contribute to destabilizing a crisis. As we have already emphasized, cruise missiles aboard surface ships and attack submarines involved in conventional or even prewar operations are especially worrisome in this regard.[9] Mobile long-range ballistic missiles could also introduce a volatile element in a crisis. Their geographic disposition might be changed to enhance their ability to strike a particular set of targets, or because they may have to be dispersed to protect them against barrage attack. Should the latter be necessary they would, in that important sense, resemble strategic submarines and bombers, and reduce the ability to raise the readiness of strategic forces without projecting a perception of offensive threat.

Although agreements controlling long-range cruise missiles are difficult to devise, they should be given high priority, and both sides should exercise restraint in deploying these weapons. In the case of the ALCM currently deployed on SAC bombers, verification is greatly facilitated by the fact that these aircraft (and their Soviet counterparts) form a quite small and well-defined set of platforms. For other basing modes radical cooperative measures, perhaps even more intrusive than those incorporated into the INF Treaty, may be necessary. Verification of agreements that restrict deployments of the much larger mobile ICBMs will also require cooperative verification arrangements.

Strategic Defense and Antisatellite Weapons

A clear separation between short- and long-term objectives is essential in negotiating restrictions on military space activities. Even if SDI can develop defenses that satisfy the Nitze criteria of cost-effectiveness at the margin, and invulnerability against direct attack on the defense, as well as other essential requirements, such as sound command and control,[10] it is likely to take the better part of the next decade to determine for which defensive goals these conditions can be satisfied. Arms control during that period, therefore, must meet two conditions: permit such research on strategic defense, and ensure that this research will not block the short-term reductions advocated here. Should these conditions not be met, the upshot could be enlarged offensive capabilities with no strategic defense.

These requirements could be met by modifying or supplementing the ABM Treaty to provide greater breakout protection. Possible measures toward that end could include a renewed commitment to the prohibition on nonlaboratory testing except as traditionally permitted by the Treaty, or as modified by agreement, and an expansion of the current cancellation clause from 6 months to at least 5 years. It should be noted that this modification differs from those put forward by the American and Soviet governments according to which the parties would be bound by the Treaty for a *fixed* period, say, for example, 10 years, following which deployment of defenses could begin. We believe that the requirement to give notice well in advance of any deployment would be more conducive to stability in both its strategic and political dimensions.

If SDI and its Soviet counterpart seek to develop space-based weapons, these programs are likely to produce a militarily significant ASAT capability even if they fail to produce viable BMDs. The traditional restriction on testing would impede such an ASAT development.

ARMS CONTROL TO ENCHANCE CRISIS STABILITY

We now turn to examples of arms control agreements that focus on crisis stability because they confer increased protection against surprise attack or other threatening military measures, and impede the advent of technologies that pose a special risk in crisis circumstances. Naturally, the separation between the topics to be discussed here, and those in our general framework for strategic arms control, is not unambiguous, to say the least, as was already emphasized in connection with cruise missiles. Nevertheless, the categories we are using here emphasize that not only agreements that restrict the size of deployments, but also contractual constraints on military activities, can contribute to security.

Confidence Building Measures: The Stockholm Agreement

A wide variety of military, diplomatic, and even economic policies can contribute to the strengthening or erosion of confidence between states. Thus, treaties of the SALT variety build confidence in that they give each party to the agreement a high, although not absolute, degree of assurance that the other will not spring forth with a new deployment of weapons that would jeopardize the strategic balance. The term *Confidence Building Measures* (CBMs) has a narrower definition, however:

> Unlike arms control measures, CBMs do not aim at the actual reduction of armaments or manpower. Rather, they are designed to regulate the *operations* of military forces and to provide reassurance about military *intentions*. In particular, they seek to reduce the possibility of an accidental confrontation through miscalculation or failure of communication, as well as to diminish the danger of surprise attack.[11]

Confidence Building Measures are contractual rules of behavior that regulate or constrain military operations. While these rules can be broken readily, such a breach could provide a clearer indication of hostile intent than intelligence alone could offer. As we have repeatedly emphasized, the assessment of intentions is often exceedingly difficult, even when intelligence regarding military and diplomatic activities is plentiful. For that reason, agreements between NATO and the Warsaw Pact creating CBMs can have a degree of asymmetry that favors NATO since the difficulty of promptly reaching the political consensus required for critical military decisions in a crisis is one of NATO's greatest vulnerabilities. The violation of a contractual rule—for example, the conduct during a crisis of a prohibited military exercise that could serve as a cover for an attack—should provide NATO with the impetus to reach military decisions that might not be forthcoming were such a Pact activity not legally proscribed. (It should be noted, however, that some have expressed the concern that if there are CBMs on the books, NATO would not reach such decisions *unless* CBMs are broken!)

The only relevant illustration of such a contractual commitment is provided by the Stockholm Agreement signed in September 1986.[12] The Agreement emerged from the virtually permanent negotiation process created by the Helsinki Accords, and involves not only the United States and the Soviet Union and their NATO and Warsaw Treaty Organization allies, but also all the neutral nations of Europe, such as Austria, Finland, and Sweden.

The purpose of the Stockholm Agreement is to reduce the risk that preparations for a surprise attack could be disguised as a military exercise. This familiar stratagem was used most recently by Egypt in launching its successful crossing of the Suez Canal on Yom Kippur 1973, so the Agreement does not address a hypothetical danger. In detail, the Agreement mandates prenotification of all military exercises throughout Europe—*from the Atlantic to the Urals*—involving more than 13,000 troops or 300 tanks under a single operational command. The notification period ranges from 6 weeks for exercises of from 13,000 to 40,000 troops, to 2 years for more than 75,000 troops. Prenotification must be accompanied by extensive information regarding types of units, armaments, and schedule of movements. Observers from all signatories to the Agreement must be invited to all ground-force exercises with more than 17,000 troops, or to amphibious or airborne exercises with more than 5,000. As a result the NATO allies are entitled up to 32 observers at any exercise large enough to be covered by the Agreement.

As for suspicious activities, each state is required to accept up to three localized 48-hour on-site inspections per year by any signatory on 36 hours notice. The state being inspected must provide ground and/or air transport and continuous communications to the inspectors' headquarters. The first such challenge inspection was completed in full accordance with the Agreement in September 1987 by American observers in the vicinity of Minsk.[13] There have been several subsequent challenge inspections by both sides.

The Agreement does not eliminate the danger of surprise attack, of course, although it reduces it somewhat. Important classes of military activities other than exercises that could be (and have been) used to mask surprise attacks are not covered. In particular, no advance notification is required for alert exercises of any size, although they must be open to observers 72 hours after they start. Nor are there restrictions on mobilization in place, or of a buildup of forces in garrison, or on troops ostensibly in transit (e.g., from East Germany to Afghanistan, or from Great Britain to the Middle East) that could then be used to mount an attack in Europe. Hence, the agreement may place more of a constraint on the Soviet Union's use of military exercises as a coercive tool against its satellites than on the Pact's ability to stage a surprise attack against NATO.

Despite these shortcomings, the Stockholm Agreement is a promising contribution to stability in Europe, and could be seminal departure for arms control quite generally. It has created an intrusive verification process that may offer a valuable precedent for more extensive CBMs that would restrict other military activities that could be destabilizing, and which, if complied with, would enhance confidence in a crisis that the confrontation is not about to escalate. Negotiation toward such objectives have now begun, and it is likely that they will be merged with the stalled attempt to negotiate reductions in conventional forces deployed in Europe by the two alliances (the Mutual and Balanced Force Reductions or [MBFR] negotiations).[14]

Protection of National Command Authorities

Provisions to protect the NCA as well as essential communication facilities, from a time-compressed missile attack would improve stability. Washington is highly vulnerable to attack from nearby missile submarines (SSBNs). The Soviet Union has similar, if less severe, threats to Moscow from U.S. SSBNs operating off European coasts.

These complementary concerns could be the basis for an agreement[15] to provide both capitals with a minimum warning time for attack. With current weapons systems, that could be accomplished by proscribing Soviet SSBNs in the Atlantic from a circular area centered on Washington with a radius of perhaps 1,500 statute miles, and a corresponding prohibition on U.S. and NATO SSBNs from a similar circle centered on Moscow.[16] (The INF Treaty will soon remove the Pershing II missiles from Germany, where they currently pose a prompt threat to the Soviet Union.) Were such an agreement in force, Washington would have a warning time of 15 mintues against a nuclear missile attack as compared to considerably less today. In short, this constraint on submarine operations is a very specific type of strategic CBM.

The question arises as to whether or not such an agreement is verifiable without impairing the right of vessels other than SSBNs, particularly attack submarines, to sail anywhere in international waters without notification. There appears to be widespread confidence among senior U.S. Navy officers (shared by their colleagues in the other services) that Soviet compliance with such an agreement could be adequately monitored without cooperative provisions. Whether Congress or any administration would be willing to ratify such a treaty without negotiated provisions for verification is another matter. Even if ASW techniques can detect violations with confidence, it might be difficult to establish such a finding in diplomatic fora, or in the court of public opinion, without divulging highly sensitive information concerning U.S. capabilities. For these reasons we note that cooperative technical means can be devised for verifying compliance without constraining surface vessels or submarines other than SSBNs, and which would not increase SSBN vulnerability in peace or war. The essential cooperative element in the scheme would be challenge inspections, akin in spirit to those in the Stockholm Agreement. Each side would be allowed to demand a certain number of prompt surfacings per year of SSBNs belonging to the other signatory. The surfaced submarine would use a "black box" provided by the challenger to radio an encoded signal that would allow the challenger's navigation satellites to immediately determine the position of the submarine.[17]

Antisatellite Arms Control

Before addressing the question of what protection arms control can offer to military satellites, it is essential to distinguish among various possible ASAT capabilities.[18]

There are *passive* or even transitory techniques to interfere with or disrupt the functioning of satellites, but which cause no permanent damage, such as concealment, electronic countermeasures, low-intensity laser illumination of photointelligence satellites to prevent their cameras from forming an image (dazzling), and the like. *Destructive* ASAT techniques can be divided into two categories: those for targets in LEO, and those for targets in GEO.[19] Strategic command is primarily dependent on GEO satellites, while LEO satellites have missions that are primarily important to nonstrategic forces.[20] Antisatellite weapons that can attack LEO satellites have been tested by both superpowers, and there is no technical impediment to highly capable weapon systems for that purpose. It is also important to distinguish between *dedicated* ASATs, and *residual* ASAT capabilities. The former are systems specifically designed to be ASATs; the latter just happen to have an ASAT capability, for example, an ICBM, or a manned spacecraft whose crew could approach and then destroy a satellite with a missile. The Soviet coorbital radar-homing ASAT is a dedicated ASAT, as is the U.S. air-launched homing interceptor.

Arms control for ASATs can have a variety of forms. The least ambitious would be *rules of the road,* supposedly analogous to laws that hold on the high seas in peacetime; at this time, no such constraints hold in space. A treaty could restrict the *use* of ASAT techniques, as does SALT I, which forbids interference with "national technical means of verification," such as photoreconnaissance satellites. But neither that stricture nor rules of the road would prevent the development, testing, and deployment of devices that could, at any time, be used in violation of such a treaty. In short, agreements of this sort pose no hurdle to the advent of ASATs. We have already discussed the ASAT threat to the strategic command system in Chapter 6, and the potential for escalation posed by ASAT attacks in lower-level conflicts in Chapter 9. If ASAT arms control is to enhance crisis stability, it would thus have to prevent, or at the least impede, the development and deployment of systems that could seriously damage the opponent's space-based C^3I capabilities.

Treaties cannot effectively protect satellites from passive or residual ASAT activities. Satellite hardening, redundancy and backup systems can counter such threats, as can the prospect of retaliation. The development of dedicated ASAT *systems* that pose a prompt threat to space-based commands, however, can be impeded by a treaty that can be verified with adequate confidence. Here "adequate" must be measured by comparing the treaty-constrained regime with the ASAT threat that would evolve in the absence of negotiated constraints. A treaty with that objective is advocated here. It should have the same cancellation clause as the modified ABM Treaty discussed earlier since ASAT capabilities would inevitably exist once systems that can intercept missiles in boost-phase or midcourse are deployed.

An ASAT Test Ban Treaty should forbid tests of weapons in space, or against space objects,[21] that can destroy, damage, render inoperable, or change the flight trajectory of space objects. Furthermore, to aid verification, the ban would also forbid tests of space weapons against objects in the atmosphere or on the earth's surface.[22] The test ban should apply to all altitudes to protect both LEO and GEO satellites. There are two reasons for this. First, if LEO is exempted, effective GEO ASAT techniques could be developed and tested in LEO; in particular, space mines in the short-term, and directed-energy techniques in the long-term, could evolve in this fashion. Second, attacks, and the potential for attacks, on LEO satellites in a crisis or conventional war could be an important source for escalation.

American space surveillance techniques are already very powerful and have consistently provided a basis for sound assessments and forecasts of Soviet military space activities. More sophisticated surveillance techniques, such as those being explored by SDI, will enhance those capabilities. A broad body of expert opinion holds that while some isolated illegal tests of individual components might escape detection, it would not be possible for the Soviet Union to develop clandestinely a ground-based or space-based ASAT *system* that could be expected to meet military standards of operational reliability. Nevertheless, to protect against Soviet "breakout" from an ASAT test ban, as well as various residual and passive ASAT threats, satellite protective measures would be essential. These should include hardening, redundancy, and backups, as appropriate. If there were no treaty, all these activities would have to be greatly expanded. It would then be essential to acquire intelligence concerning a broad spectrum of *allowed* Soviet ASAT activities, and means for protecting U.S. satellites against attack by deployed and thoroughly tested weapons, not to mention the necessity to develop and deploy U.S. ASATs.

NOTES

1. American Physical Society Study Group, "The Science and Technology of Directed Energy Weapons", *Reviews of Modern Physics* (1987), 59:3, Part II [cited as *APS* henceforth]; especially pp. 145–156.

2. A large portion of these will be replacements, especially in the case of strategic forces. The extent to which there would be a net expansion in the absence of new

negotiated constraints is now difficult to say in view of the Administration's stand on adherence to SALT II.

3. Here we assume that the Pershing II missiles will be removed in accordance with the recently ratified INF agreement.

4. See *Soviet Military Power 1987* (Washington: USGPO, 1987).

5. *Anti-Satellite Weapons, Countermeasures, and Arms Control,* Office of Technology, Assessment, OTA-1SC-281 (Washington: USGPO, 1985); Stares, Chapts. 2–5; Richard L. Garwin, Kurt Gottfried and Donald L Hafner, "Antisatellite Weapons," *Scientific American* (June 1984), *250*:6, 45.

6. Here we gloss over the fact that the Soviet Union uses satellites in highly elliptical orbits for early warning and communications. These could be attacked by LEO ASATs based in the southern hemisphere, but the United States has never indicated any interest in such a capability.

7. *APS,* p. 16.

8. A depressed trajectory has a lower maximum altitude than a standard (minimum energy) trajectory, and allows the missile to reach its target more quickly. It is reported that neither side has tested SLBMs on such trajectories.

9. For a fictional depiction of how conventionally armed SLCMs could (but do not) lead to escalation, see Tom Clancy, *Red Storm Rising* (New York: G. P. Putnam's Sons, 1986), p. 474 et seq.

10. See note 64, Chapter 9.

11. F. Stephen Larrabee, in *Building Security in Europe: Confidence Building Measures and the CSCE,* Rolf Berg and Adam-Daniel Rotfeld, eds. (New York: Institute for East–West Security Studies, 1986), p. 3. For discussions of CBMs, see Jonathan Alford, ed., *The Future of Arms Control: Part III—Confidence Buildup Measures* (London: IISS, 1979); Dean, Part II; Johan Jorgen Holst, "Confidence-Building Measures," *Survival* (January/February 1983), 2; and F. Stephen Larrabee and Allen Lynch, "Confidence-Building Measures and U.S.–Soviet Relation," Occasional Papers Series, No. 1 (New York: Institute for East–West Security Studies, 1986).

12. Paul Lewis, "East–West Accord Reached on a Plan to Cut Risk of War," *The New York Times,* September 22, 1986, pp. A1, 12–13. The full text of the Stockholm Agreement can be found in *Arms Control Today,* November 1986, pp. 20–24. See also James Goodby, "The Stockholm Conference: Negotiating a Cooperative Security System for Europe," Occasional Paper Series, Foreign Service Institute, U.S. Department of State, 1987; and Richard E. Darilek, "The Future of Conventional Arms Control in Europe", *Survival* (1987), *19*:1, 5.

13. Michael R. Gordon, "U.S. Praises Soviet for War Games Role," *The New York Times,* September 22, 1987, p. A3.

14. For a detailed discussion of the negotiations addressed to the military confrontation in Europe, see Dean, Part II.

15. Bracken, p. 244.

16. This would not affect the French missiles in the Midi. Since the agreement is addressed to warning time, and not to specific weapons, it would also not affect SLCMs held by NATO forces.

17. Side A would provide several "black boxes" per submarine to side B, so that the latter could disassemble a random subset to convince itself that they could not harm its submarines or provide any intelligence. The boxes would be identical except for their encryption keys, be tamper proof, and be instrumented to monitor their magnetic environment to prevent transfer to another submarine. An official of side A

would then witness the sending aboard of a specific box onto a given submarine of side B. The latter would be responsible for connecting the box to the submarine's communication system, which could be used then and there to transmit the encoded signal to A's navigation satellites to validate the proper functioning of the device.

In a challenge, side A would communicate directly to the capital of B and request the immediate surfacing of a specified SSBN. In view of the continuous contact maintained by alert SSBNs, surfacing should transpire in a period during which the vessel could only move a distance negligible to the dimension of the exclusion zone. Should side A wish to confirm that the submarine bears the correct identification number, the vessel would have to stay on the surface until A could conduct a visual inspection, say from an airplane.

The scheme therefore provides statistical assurance that SSBNs are not in the exclusion zone and that the SSBNs have not been renumbered. The purpose of the latter feature is to allow the challenger to request the surfacing of a specific submarine should intelligence indicate that a particular vessel is in the exclusion zone.

18. See note No. 5.

19. We shall not distinguish here between GEO satellites and the "semi-synchronous" Navstar Global Positioning System; for ASAT purposes that distinction is of little consequence.

20. This division is not clean-cut. Communication and navigation satellites in high orbits are used by all forces, for example.

21. In arms control treaties the term "space object" stands for an object that circumnavigates the globe above the atmosphere, and therefore excludes RVs. Thus, the Outer Space Treaty, which proscibes weapons of mass destruction from space, permits ICBMs and SLBMs. By that token the ASAT test ban proposed here would not restrict the testing of ground-based interceptors from designated test ranges against RVs, as permitted by the ABM Treaty.

22. In 1983 the Soviet Union tabled a treaty draft at the UN that contains such provisions, but its article 2.5, "Not to Test or Use Manned Spacecraft for Military, Including Antisatellite, Purposes," cannot be accepted by either side as it stands. If it were to read " . . . for Weapon, Including Antisatellite Purposes," it could at least be considered as a basis for negotiation.

12

Policy Implications—Toward Greater Stability

The forces at the disposal of the superpowers make it highly improbable that either would wittingly embark on a course that leads to nuclear war with the other. It is much more likely that they would find themselves on such a path because of a miscalculated attempt to manipulate the fear of nuclear war, or as the upshot of an altercation that did not appear to run such a risk—one that might not have even involved them the outset. We have depicted the phalanx of factors that might conspire to produce such a catastrophic chain of events. That synthesis has led us to conclusions regarding these risks, and to recommend measures—some to be taken by the United States independently, others in cooperation with the Soviet Union—that would reduce the likelihood of crisis and of ensuing escalation. We shall now summarize these findings and policy recommendations.

A CHARACTERIZATION OF CRISIS STABILITY

A net assessment of crisis stability is obviously not possible: implausible events, peculiar circumstances, and astonishing individuals have played crucial and unexpected roles in the crises of the past. Today, the risks are compounded by military forces of dazzling mobility and prodigious destructive power. Nevertheless, the facts and speculations related to crisis phenomena that we have presented do identify factors that could exacerbate or moderate a future crisis, and point to conclusions that can be stated with varying degrees of confidence. Taken together, these statements comprise our characterization of crisis stability.

In forming that characterization we do *not* judge whether diplomatic initiatives, military signals, or force of some particular kind, including the full spectrum of nuclear weapons, should or should not be used under various contingencies. Rather, the goal is to examine the implications of such actions. Moreover, we assume that there will be no profound shifts in the geopolitical setting, nor dramatic changes in the nuclear or conventional forces or doctrine of the United States and the Soviet Union and their principal alliances.

Crisis Behavior in the Past

No conflict has ever engaged nuclear-armed components,[1] and the crises between the superpowers have only involved marginal interactions between their military forces. Nevertheless, history provides some lessons that should be germane to more ominous situations.

Crisis is a no-man's land between war and peace. At either extreme the roles of diplomacy and force, and of political and military leaders, are well-defined; in principle, at least, political objectives and military strategy dominate tactics. In crisis, however, all of these relationships are in flux. Diplomacy still dominates in the pursuit of national objectives, yet there are preparations for war. Today, a conflict that does not involve the strategic forces, even if tactical nuclear weapons were already supporting conventional operations, would, in one respect, bear a resemblance to a severe pre-Hiroshima crisis because the political decision to wage "total war" would still hang in the balance.[2]

Governments of every variety have found it difficult to cope with crisis. They have often failed to anticipate crises because their adversary's political intentions frequently remain inscrutable even when intelligence about tangible indicators such as troop movements is good—as it usually is. Once a crisis breaks, existing contingency plans have rarely been appropriate to the peculiarities of the confrontation. In post-Hiroshima crises the U.S. leadership's freedom of action has often been seriously constrained by the contradictory demands of various domestic groups or of America's allies. Exceptional individuals other than the president have at times dominated American crisis decision making.[3] Beginning with the Berlin and Cuban crises during the Kennedy administration, communication technology has been sufficiently powerful to allow the apex of the U.S. government to impose a high degree of control over its forces during crises. How long such micromanagement can be maintained as the tempo, complexity, and intensity of a crisis increases cannot be predicted on the basis of this experience.

Innumerable factors can influence whether a crisis subsides or intensifies: the psychological and political context; the nature and location of the outbreak; the first response; the pace, complexity, and perceived danger of events; inexplicable actions by the adversary; whether the crisis spreads to other arenas; domestic and alliance cohesion; and such imponderables as knowledge, goals, personalities, and human error. In confronting crisis, ultimate responsibility is held by leaders who must gather information from and transmit decisions through enormous bureaucracies. In a severe or prolonged crisis, all could be suffering from fatigue and stress. And the public mood could be crucial—not only in the West.

Crisis Arenas

The geographic setting in which a crisis begins will be a critical factor in its evolution.

In Europe both alliances have tight control over their forces. Both recognize that any European conflict would be enormously destructive and would entail a high risk of nuclear escalation. On the other hand, powerful forces, both nuclear and conventional, are in close proximity; each side has important assets within easy reach of the other's forces, and a significant shift from the status quo would be perceived as a threat to vital interests. A European crisis could attain the intensity of imminent war in a matter of days. The risk to Europe's security, therefore, is high even though the probability that war will break out is small.

The NATO–Warsaw military balance is dominated by several factors: the strongest NATO member is an ocean away from the front, whereas the Soviet Union is near at hand; on the ground, the Pact enjoys superiority in forces and in strategic position, while at sea NATO has unquestioned superiority, although the growing fleet of Soviet attack submarines might cause some disruption of the transatlantic lines of supply.

The Pact's stronger conventional forces, offensive strategy, high peacetime readiness, and superior logistic position make it essential that NATO respond promptly to warning of attack if it is to realize its very considerable potential for an effective conventional defense. The widespread belief that NATO would quickly succumb to a conventional attack ignores significant factors that are difficult to quantify, such as the questionable loyalty of Soviet allies; whether the Pact could sustain an armored offensive once aircraft arrive from the United States, which should give NATO superiority above the battlefield; that the highly favorable force ratios that the Soviets appear to consider as essential for an attack hinges on whether NATO would fail to respond to strategic warning; the certainty that France would honor its commitments to NATO should Germany be invaded; and the West's economic superiority, which could only be negated by a short war confined to Europe. Despite their unquestionably strong military position in Europe, cautious Soviet planners should therefore recognize that a conventional attack on NATO would run very high risks.[4]

In contrast to Europe, the likelihood of crisis outbreak in the Middle East is high, but the risk of swift and catastrophic escalation is low. Both superpowers have commitments to states that are often at each other's throats but that they do not control, with strategically important but politically unstable nations existing in the region. On the other hand, the relatively small deployments of superpower forces, and stakes that are not as high as in Europe, give the United States and the Soviet Union more time and room for diplomacy and crisis management. Nevertheless, the reported acquistion of chemical munitions by Syria and of nuclear weapons by Israel, and the possession by several countries of delivery systems having strategic range by Middle Eastern standards, have raised the stakes considerably; they imply that a war that jeopardized the survival of states in the region could invoke global risks.

Hence, conflicts involving "small" nuclear powers, especially when accompanied by chemical warfare, may carry an even greater threat to global security than crises that begin as face-to-face confrontations between the superpowers. National and international efforts to impede nuclear proliferation should therefore be pursued with the utmost vigor.

Crises need not start on the ground. They could originate on the high seas or in space, or spread out from land into the oceans or space.

The superpowers' surface and undersea navies are in continuous contact in widely separated regions, and reconnoiter in waters where the potential adversary has very sensitive installations and activities. Such operations are not highly provocative in peacetime, but the outbreak of crisis could suddenly transform their real or perceived implications. Furthermore, the distinction between conventional and nuclear forces is murky under the sea. The oceans, therefore, have the potential for rapidly spreading and aggravating a crisis by inadvertence or by intent if either superpower's naval forces sought to threaten the other's vital interests at sea: NATO's North Atlantic sea lanes or the Soviet sanctuaries for ballistic missile submarines in the Arctic and the Sea of Okhotsk.

Satellites are increasingly important in military operations of all types. Should ASAT capabilities become available, space-based portions of command systems would lose their immunity from nonnuclear attack. In contrast to today, in a crisis that had not yet entailed the use of deadly-force techniques for interfering with military space activities may well be employed. Space would thus become a medium for exceptionally swift crisis propagation and/or escalation.

Low-Intensity Crises

The superpowers have been able to keep their direct confrontations at a low level of intensity by adhering to a tacit code of conduct: refrain from use of deadly force against the adversary or his allies; do not stampede the adversary into decisions or compel him to choose between humiliation and escalation; and refrain from spreading a crisis to another region. Even the Cuban Missile Crisis only saw marginal transgressions of this code.

This behavior pattern indicates that the prospects remain good for containing crises where both sides have modest objectives, the crisis remains localized, actions by third parties stay within reasonable bounds, and no breach of the nuclear threshold is in sight—in short, where there is a clear consensus within each government that it is really just dealing with a manageable crisis. Good prospects must not be confused with full confidence, however. Any crisis worthy of the name evokes incalculable risks, especially the possibility that its gravity is seriously miscalculated by one or both sides, or that the unexpected will cause a loss of control.

Intense Crises Short of War

Intense crises short of war are conflicts that seriously breach the tacit code, while avoiding the use of deadly force. By our definitions, of the direct confrontations between the superpowers only the Cuban Missile Crisis nearly entered this category. Such crises, therefore, lead into largely uncharted and perhaps even unnavigable seas. Statements about them are speculative, but prudence dictates that worse-than-expected outcomes deserve serious attention.

Watersheds of great military and political import would be crossed as forces are alerted in an intense crisis. American and Soviet surface and submarine fleets already interact extensively at low alert levels; were that level to rise, encounters between naval units would intensify at the same time as two-way communications with higher authorities would become restricted. While the Soviets have never held strategic alerts during a crisis, that behavior is unlikely to be maintained in an intense crisis.

In Europe, three watersheds can be anticipated. First, the transformation of command structures: the "chop" of national forces to NATO; the transition to the Warsaw Pact's wartime chain-of-command; and the activation of wartime command centers and communication networks by both sides. These would be detected by the opponent's intelligence because of changes in signal traffic that cannot be hidden. Second, the arrival of reinforcements and the call-up of reserves. Third, the dispersal of ground-based tactical nuclear weapons from peacetime storage to wartime positions. At their peacetime locations many of these weapons are high-value targets and vulnerable to conventional attack, so their dispersal could trigger conventional preemption and initiate war. That dilemma could generate dissension within NATO, as would concern that dispersal would create spontaneous or intentionally provoked panic among civilians in regions near the inter-German border.

Intense crises could involve mutual alerts that project high levels of threat and that spread geographically. An attempt to impose central control over minutiae in such large military operations would swamp national leaderships and simultaneously put the effectiveness and safety of forces at risk. In contrast to past superpower crises, many actions that could affect events would then evolve from decentralized decision making. Rising combat readiness and deepening fear that war is imminent would increase the chance that one or both of the superpowers' command systems would rashly overreact to a random event, whether violent or not, whose origin and intent is ambiguous, and which would normally be of no great consequence. In short, the likelihood of severe lapses and errors in control grows as a crisis intensifies.

Thresholds Between Conventional, Nuclear, and Strategic Conflict

The risks would grow precipitously should conventional war break out. Vulnerable command systems under direct attack would have to maintain control over thousands of tactical nuclear weapons and simultaneously ready those weapons for possible use, while the front might shift through regions where such weapons are based. Dual-purpose platforms, such as artillery and attack submarines, would be engaged in combat; at least some nuclear forces could be lost.

Military operations would quickly come under decentralized command; disruption of communications links would hamper joint consultation and decision making. The most critical decision faced by political authorities—the release of nuclear weapon employment authority—would be influenced by events and circumstances beyond their control. These are key reasons for enhancing the survivability of command systems.

NATO's policy of flexible response states a willingness to *initiate* the use of nuclear weapons. The preconditions for their employment—impending conventional defeat and alliance approval—might be met as early as several days into a conventional conflict. Maintaining alliance cohesion would weigh heavily in a decision for nuclear use, but unanimity or even consensus are not required; Great Britain or the United States, as owners of the warheads, together with the owner of the means of delivery, can make the decision.[5] SACEUR may submit nuclear requests, as can the two other major NATO commanders and any U.S. unified or specified combat commander. In a major conventional war between the superpowers, a wide variety of circumstances could therefore generate pressure for recourse to nuclear weapons.

Soviet military writings indicate a preference for a conventional blitzkrieg launched before NATO attained full combat readiness, with the prevention of nuclear use by NATO as one of its principal objectives. Should NATO appear to be on the verge of "going nuclear," the same principles of Soviet strategy could call for nuclear preemption; should NATO initiate nuclear warfare, a massive nuclear counterattack could well ensue. The interaction between these very different Soviet and NATO postures for both conventional and tactical nuclear warfare holds grave risks. In particular, an expectation that NATO may hesitate fatally could lead to hasty Soviet actions that crystalize a NATO decision and precipitate escalation.

While agreeing that current NATO policy concerning nuclear weapons is beset by a number of serious contradictions, the authors hold a spectrum of views regarding what should be done. Some believe that current policy is the only practical alternative; some that NATO should have no nuclear weapons of short range; some that NATO should only deploy nuclear weapons that do not require dispersal before use; and some that the alliance should adopt a No-First-Use policy after appropriate modifications in forces, training, and planning.

Escalation to general nuclear war probably depends, among other factors, on whether Soviet territory had suffered nuclear attacks. American analysts often distinguish between strategic and nonstrategic nuclear weapons in assessing the risk of escalation, but from a Soviet standpoint the location and type of target are probably more significant than the range of the attacking Western weapon. Great Britain and France also have many nuclear weapons that can strike into the Soviet Union. These observations raise the question of whether there is a meaningful distinction between strategic and nonstrategic nuclear conflict.

There is a widespread tendency to equate crisis stability with stability at the strategic threshold, and to then assess crisis stability by comparing the two strategic forces while ignoring their commands. Large-scale employment of strategic weapons, however, would not be under serious consideration unless there was already a major war in which tactical nuclear weapons should probably have been used. Unpredictable features of the chaos, destruction, and trauma created by that war are likely to be more critical in such decisions than a peacetime "bean count" of the strategic balance.

The Relevance and Role of Strategic Forces

The very existence of nuclear weapons has forced the superpowers to treat each other with great caution. Within a very broad band of parity, the size and composition of the strategic forces are not relevant to conflict below the strategic level. On the other hand, the readying of strategic forces could have a large impact on the course of a crisis.

The decoupling of strategic forces from lower-level conflict requires confidence on each side that both its command system and that of the adversary are sufficiently agile and robust to make preemption irrational. While the current U.S. system has serious deficiencies, in conjunction with the triad of strategic forces it meets these minimum requirements sufficiently well to deter preemption or attempts at decapitation, although it does so by relying heavily on prompt launch. Soviet command is judged to be at least as robust, although it also appears to have a considerable reliance on prompt launch. The committed U.S. command improvement program will increase the margin of safety considerably as long as high-altitude satellite capabilities are secure against prompt attack. On the other hand, even with these ongoing improvements, as well the additional measures that we shall propose, escalation to large strategic exchanges could not be contained *unless* both superpowers were to pursue a similar strategy of not attacking strategic command. Furthermore, it is questionable whether a net gain in the survivability and performance of strategic command can be expected in the face of unconstrained improvements in offensive forces, since that is likely to yield capabilities specifically designed to threaten the modernized command.

Recommendations

This analysis of crisis stability points to a number of recommendations concerning alert operations, command-and-control of nonstrategic forces, and crisis management.

Military Operations and Crisis Management. The United States, as well as other states, have often used military operations as a tool for coping with crises. In our view,

- The use of military operations, especially alerts, for political signaling can be dangerous, in a large part because such actions can be misinterpreted by the adversary. Senior military leaders have cautioned against premature or too-frequent threat of military power as a solution to diplomatic problems. In crisis, their concerns should be carefully weighed before civilian leaders resort to military means.

The centrally coordinated DEFCON/LERTCON alerting system provides flexibility for fashioning a response to provocation. Although readiness and projection of threat are not independent variables, it is possible to deemphasize the latter, especially at low alert levels. The alert posture can vary geographically, even within one theater. Strategic and nonstrategic forces need not be at the same status, and while it is much more difficult to decouple conventional from tactical nuclear forces because many delivery systems are dual-capable, there is considerable flexibility even here.[6]

It is imperative that full advantage be taken of these flexible aspects of the DEFCON alerting systems. Options are available that provide for the survival of U.S. forces while minimizing the impression that an attack is threatened. At the other end of the spectrum there are options that convey the prospect of imminent attack. Furthermore, the NATO "chop," which gives SACEUR operational command over allied forces, should be practiced in exercises.

Remote Crisis Conferencing. Improved communication links between the NCA, its advisors, and the military chain-of-command could be provided by:

- A high-quality secure teleconferencing system in the Washington area supplemented by satellite links to permit deliberations among civilian and military leaders without the inconvenience and public attention that accompany White House meetings. This system would be of special value in low-intensity crises.

A secondary purpose of this system would be to increase the contribution of advisors to the NCA during a "missile attack conference" in the event of a Soviet nuclear attack.

Tactical Command-and-Control. Enhanced command capabilities for nonstrategic forces, especially improvements in survivability, are essential, and the current U.S. program is already developing some of these. In particular, emphasis should be placed on uninterceptible communications to units that depend on covertness for survival, such as two-way encrypted radio via satellites for ground forces, and space-based or airborne blue lasers for communications to submerged attack submarines.[7] Such submarines are only required to maintain intermittent contact with today's communications, a handicap that could have serious consequences in crisis should they be in proximity of hostile naval units, or be involved in intrusive reconnaissance. In addition, covert, prepositioned command posts of modular design that could be readily placed on various mobile platforms (ships, aircraft, railcars, etc.) could be invaluable in rapidly changing situations.

The U.S. Navy's nuclear weapons are not equipped with electromechanical devices (PALs)[8] that prevent the arming of the warhead unless a coded message is received from higher authority. Given the problems associated with communications to naval units (especially attack submarines), control over weapons and assurance that they will be used when authorized is less firm than for those in other forces. This is of particular concern for the Tomahawk sea-launched nuclear-armed cruise missile. In view of its long range and high accuracy, this weapon has strategic capabilities, but it is based on surface ships and submarines that would be involved in conventional conflict. We therefore recommend that*

● Navy nuclear weapons should be equipped with modern PALs. The nuclear-armed sea-launched cruise missile should have the highest priority. The unique circumstances attending missile submarine (SSBN) operations make the SLBM a special case that might be exempted from this requirement.

---

*Paul Tomb does not concur, and records the following dissent:

PAL devices are just one method of nuclear weapons control, and were originally designed to protect weapons stored on foreign soil from unauthorized use. Locked PAL devices are justified and required on weapons stored in fixed, high-threat, overseas locations. Naval vessels are unique environments that inherently, and by several means, synergistically minimize the threat to nuclear weapons faced by those on land. The Tomahawk Land Attack Missile/Nuclear (TLAM/N) system was designed with numerous other, effective use-control means that obviate the need for locked PALs.

The navy has practiced assured, effective external use-control of deployed nuclear weapons for more than 30 years through many other measures that are periodically reviewed, improved as technology matures, and have been proved to be more than adequate. These measures include, but are not limited to, the absolute requirement for receipt of a valid order that is verified by the commanding officer and several other officers; removal, separation, and two-man control of critical components; strict control of numerous critical keys required in specific sequence to launch a weapon; precise procedures requiring the interaction of the commanding officer, numerous other officers, and the majority of the highly trained crew; electrical and mechanical interlocks in the weapons system; personnel reliability screening and monitoring; physical security measures and guard forces to prevent unauthorized access to weapons and equipment and to repel a threat from outsiders, at sea or in port.

Locked PAL devices on the navy's deployed nuclear weapons, particularly on the TLAM/N system, are not necessary. There is a fundamental and significant difference between fixed, land-based systems and the navy's operationally flexible, widely dispersed ships and submarines. Locked PALs would add unnecessary complexity and vulnerability to an already complex and proven use-control system.

Institutional Memory and Crisis Management Organizations. It is widely acknowledged that, as a body, the civilian leadership of the U.S. government suffers from endemic institutional amnesia.[9] In some respects this is an advantage over the Soviet Union, which tends to be dominated by a single clique for decades. On the other hand, in a fast-paced crisis this difference between the two governments could be a serious handicap for the United States.

Everyone knows that presidents leave Washington with libraries of "personal" documents. It is not so widely known, however, that at least several national security advisers to newly elected presidents have entered office and found virtually no files regarding critical foreign policy decisions of the outgoing administration.[10] Even the NSC, therefore, can be hobbled by a lack of institutional memory, despite the obvious fact that prompt access to the knowledge and experience gained in past crises could be critical to presidential decision making. In 1983 the Reagan administration created the Crisis Management Directorate within the NSC, which has introduced modern technology, built a new coordination center, created new data bases, and internetted computers and warning system to coordinate crisis operations between agencies. It is essential that future administrations maintain, exercise, and improve the crisis management infrastructure and data bases that have now been created.

In coping with crisis, it is important for senior decision makers to have at their immediate disposal expert current knowledge of such mundane but potentially critical details as standard operating procedures, rules of engagement, reliability of communications, ambiguities in intelligence, and so forth. This expertise is dispersed in the U.S. government at various levels of different agencies and departments. To what extent such knowledge is now readily available in the White House is not known to us, but to assure that it is a crisis support group should be a permanent component of the presidential entourage. The group should include retired senior military officers, intelligence officials, and diplomats, backed up by a small staff, and it should spend a portion of its time in the field keeping abreast of the actual operation of the various branches of the national security apparatus.[11] It would *not* be the purpose of the group to advise the president about the military, diplomatic, or political moves he might make, but to provide timely, accurate, and relevant information about the operations that these options would actually entail. Such operational details, and their potential consequences, may not be apparent to the president's principal advisers because their pressing day-to-day duties make it exceedingly difficult to acquire or maintain an adequate understanding of the complex organizations that would come into play as a crisis unfolds.

Civilian–military coordination is essential to military contingency planning. Such plans, at least implicitly, incorporate political assumptions. Civilian review, therefore, is needed if those plans are to reflect changing policy objectives. Involvement in the review process would also increase civilian policymakers' understanding of military capabilities, options, and critical operational issues. For the same reason, it is essential that military views be properly weighed by political leaders not only in coping with a crisis but before one breaks. To facilitate these interactions and to formalize the involvement of the JCS Chairman in NSC deliberations, we support the proposed revision of the 1947 National Security Act that would designate the JCS Chairman as a statutory member of the National Security Council.

Nuclear Risk Reduction Centers in Washington and Moscow were established in a U.S.–Soviet agreement signed September 15, 1987.[12] These particular centers are not intended to serve a crisis management role, but they could be a precedent for jointly staffed facilities having that purpose. As their proponents have noted,[13] the role of such centers would be very limited during intense superpower confrontations. Nevertheless, they could prove valuable both in clarifying ambiguous circumstances caused by inadvertence or accident, and during crises involving third parties.

STRATEGIC COMMAND: VULNERABILITY AND MODERNIZATION

We have stated that the strategic forces are largely irrelevant to conflicts below the strategic level provided that both sides are confident that preemption is not a rational option for either side. Whether such confidence is justified depends, in large measure, on the vulnerability of the command systems. We shall therefore summarize our assessment of U.S. command vulnerability and of the government's command modernization program, and offer suggestions for further improvements of the U.S. command system.

Command Vulnerability

The prudent opponent's assessment of the vulnerability of U.S. command, whether it be today's system or that following modernization, should be dominated by variables not under his control, and by a recognition that the command system may have crucial elements and procedures of which he has no knowledge. Many crucial variables cannot be controlled by an adversary: the U.S. alert status at the time of attack; the efficacy of response to tactical warning; prior U.S. decisions—whether to ride out, or whether to launch during the initial assault; the existence of predelegated launch authority; and the many imponderables regarding two exceedingly complex organizations confronting each other, and themselves, in totally unprecedented circumstances.

The existing U.S. command system in its peacetime posture must react to tactical warning with great alacrity if it is to avoid grave disruption from an optimally structured surprise attack involving as few as several tens of nuclear warheads. That vulnerability would be greatly reduced were the system at a reasonably high alert status, as should be the case in an intense crisis; an attack that is larger by an order of magnitude would then be required to produce an equivalent level of disruption. While such damage to the command system might prevent a *coordinated* response *following* the attack, retaliation by the large strategic forces that would survive (especially at sea) could not be prevented by any mode of attack.

When the improvement program has been completed, the unalerted command infrastructure will be roughly as resilient to direct attack as the current system is when it has been alerted. The improved system will also have a considerably greater capability for executing a prompt launch. An attack that sought to disrupt the upgraded system, when it is on alert, would require many hundreds of warheads and produce widespread collateral destruction. Furthermore, an attack focused on the alerted command system is likely to provoke the same level of counterattack, whether by means of prompt launch or in the aftermath of the initial assault, as a strike against a much larger set of targets in the United States.

This analysis of command vulnerability assumes not only that the committed program will be fully implemented, but also that the offensive threat will remain roughly constant. It assumes, therefore, that new technologies that directly threaten command, especially stealthy means of nuclear attack and high-altitude ASAT weapons, will not be deployed in significant strength.

Command improvements in themselves are unlikely to remove prompt launch from its prominent position among the United States' strategic options. Soviet strategic offensive forces are too massive and capable for that. To reduce the offensive threat to a level where the American command organization would be sufficiently sturdy to instill high confidence that a major attack could be ridden out, it would be necessary to combine command improvements with deep cuts in Soviet strategic forces, and to impose constraints on technologies that could specifically threaten vital U.S. command elements.

Modernization of Strategic Command

The U.S. program for C³I modernization is a major long-term undertaking whose principal objectives are reliable and secure communications in the face of a nuclear attack and enhanced redundancy for high-level command elements. In our view,

- The administration's committed improvement program for command, control, communications, and intelligence addresses the most vital shortcomings in the U.S. strategic posture. It should have the highest priority in the strategic budget, and be protected from deficit-reduction measures, so as to prevent any doubt about U.S. ability to control and launch strategic weapons.

We have identified a number of C³I improvements, most of which are not in the current program, but which warrant further study, including their costs and cost savings.

A Survivable Hot Line. It is essential that the superpowers be able to communicate with each other under essentially all circumstances. The existing U.S.–Soviet Hot line does not have that capability. Should strategic war break out, there might well be no means for negotiating a cease-fire because the current Hot Line is likely to collapse—it is not linked to survivable command posts, and its satellite ground terminals are neither hard nor redundant. To remove this glaring weakness in the international communications system,

- A dedicated geosynchronous satellite that is able to connect a full range of national command posts in both nations, backed up by a redundant radio network that could communicate even among disturbances due to nuclear explosions, should be deployed cooperatively by the United States and the Soviet Union.

Wartime Command and Control. The U.S. would rely heavily on airborne command posts in a severe crisis or in wartime. Their major disadvantages are limited in-flight endurance and dependence on large airfields. Short take-off and landing (STOL) aircraft as command posts would, in effect, have longer endurance because they could operate from a much larger number of fields, which would enhance their concealment and allow them to spend more time on the ground. Their communications could be routed through satellites and/or relay drone aircraft. These advantages clearly imply that the acquisition of STOL airborne command posts merits serious consideration.

In an intense crisis, stability would be strengthened by enhanced confidence in the ability to retaliate. It is therefore essential that the NCA, and its alternates, have assured capabilities to receive advice from and transmit orders to the nuclear commanders. Several steps toward furthering this end deserve consideration.

First, the means for a timely, secure missile attack conference is an urgent priority. That which is now under construction as part of the MILSTAR program would function even in the face of a nuclear attack, but an interim system suitable to a preattack environment is needed pending MILSTAR deployment.[14]

Second, pilotless aircraft could form a survivable network of radio relays linking the NCA, the NMCS, the nuclear commands, and the strategic forces, provided that high reliability can be demonstrated. Such an unmanned system could then be kept at a higher peacetime and crisis alert status than manned aircraft, and might even be continuously airborne.

Third, backup communications to submerged ballistic missile submarines could be provided by means of blue lasers based on aircraft and/or satellites.

A communication system for forces and command elements that had survived a strategic attack could provide updated intelligence and orders, communications between forces and command, and transmit assessments to a successor NCA. For that purpose:

- A Strategic Mail Box could be piggybacked at little cost on MILSTAR so as to link command elements that had survived an attack. The system would provide for automated storage and retrieval of encrypted data and messages by authorized users, and thereby link transmitters and receivers that are unable to be on station simultaneously.

The NCA must be confident that nuclear damage inflicted on key command elements and forces will be reported promptly and accurately. An integrated nuclear-damage assessment system would combine data from the satellite-based system (NDS) with that from other monitoring stations. The system should also deposit this information in the Strategic Mail Box.

It could be very difficult to move the president and his staff to a secure location in the brief interval provided by tactical warning of a missile attack. To evacuate him during an intense crisis would have political repercussions that make such a step highly unlikely. Crisis stability would be enhanced if the alternate NCA, presumably headed by the vice president, with a full support staff, were provided with an underground command center that could survive the early stages of a nuclear attack and would be readily accessible from Washington.

ARMS CONTROL AND CRISIS STABILITY

Technical and organizational improvements of the command system will enhance command performance and crisis stability only if those improvements are not overtaken by technical developments and weapon deployments that ultimately make command more vulnerable or undercut crisis stability in other ways. National security, therefore, can be strengthened by agreements that constrain military operations, deployments, and technology so as to enhance command survivability and crisis stability. Such agreements should be integrated into a general framework for strategic arms control.

A Framework for Strategic Arms Control

A diversity of views regarding the role of nuclear weapons leads powerful groups within the United States, as well as within the NATO alliance, to have incompatible long-term arms-control goals. Nevertheless, there is a broad consensus, which apparently extends to the Soviet government, that the strategic arsenals should be sharply reduced in size and vulnerability. A framework that exploits that consensus, having the following basic ingredients, should be implemented forthwith.

First, the number of strategic warheads should be reduced by approximately 50 percent in a manner that will reduce the number of accurate warheads per opposing vulnerable launcher. These cuts need not be symmetric since the superpowers' arsenals will continue to reflect long-standing differences in technology and geography, but they must result in roughly equivalent restrictions on overall strategic capabilities and leave the two sides within the broad band of strategic parity.

Second, some deployments of new MIRVed ICBMs and SLBMs (D5, MX, SS-24) can be accommodated provided they meet the overriding objective that the reduced forces be significantly less vulnerable. Future modernization, however, should concentrate on the replacement of MIRVed missiles by single-warhead missiles.

Third, long-range nuclear-armed cruise missiles have strategic capabilities, and they pose a severe verification problem. Agreements concerning them should receive high priority. Both sides should exercise independent restraint in deploying them. The survivability of mobile ICBMs enhances stability provided that the number deployed can be verified, which could be accomplished by cooperative measures.

Finally, to reinforce the movement toward greater stability,

- Test firing of new MIRVed missiles, of reentry vehicles having sufficient maneuverability to threaten mobile command posts, and of SLBMs on depressed trajectories should be banned.

The distinction between short-term goals and ultimate objectives is essential in resolving problems posed by research on ballistic missile defense. Current agreements should not preclude work toward a viable strategic defense, while on the other hand such work must not block the offensive reductions. These requirements could be met by increasing the breakout protection provided by the ABM Treaty by expanding the cancellation clause from 6 months to at least 5 years, and by a renewed commitment to the traditional restrictions on testing outside the laboratory, unless these are modified by agreement.

Confidence Building Measures

Crisis stability would be enhanced by CBMs that constrain military operations that could be used to prepare or mask an attack. The 1986 Stockholm Agreement provides a prototype for accords of this type in that it requires the Warsaw Pact and NATO to announce large military exercises well in advance, thereby making it more difficult to use such exercises as a cover for attack preparations. Verification of the agreement is aided by challenge, onsite inspections. While the Stockholm Agreement leaves other important avenues available for disguising attack preparations, it offers a promising illustration of how crisis stability can be improved without reducing or restructuring military forces.

Protection of National Command Authorities

Washington is highly vulnerable to an SLBM attack with less than 10 minutes of warning. Moscow is somewhat less threatened by missile submarines off Norway, and temporarily by the Pershing II missiles, which are to be removed under the INF Treaty. These vulnerabilities would be somewhat ameliorated were both capitals to have a minimum warning time in the event of a missile attack. To that end, we support

- An agreement that would proscribe all ballistic missiles belonging to one side, whether at sea or on land, from a circular area of perhaps 1,500 miles radius drawn about the other's capital.

A scheme for verifying such an agreement by cooperative measures has been proposed by us. These measures would not reduce the survivability of missile submarines, and they would have no impact whatsoever on other submarines or on surface ships.

Antisatellite Arms Control

Arms control can impede the development of dedicated ASATs that pose a prompt threat to a militarily significant portion of a nation's space-based C^3I system. Such capabilities would only appear with the deployment of a complex system whose reliability must be established by tests in space. Therefore we advocate:

- An ASAT Test Ban Treaty that would forbid the testing at any altitude of weapons in space, or against space objects, that can destroy, damage, render inoperable, or alter the flight trajectory of space objects.

The ban should cover all altitudes because low-orbit satellites are important to prestrategic conflict, and attacks on them could lead to escalation; furthermore, directed-energy ASATs could first be tested and developed for low-orbit targets if the ban were only applied to high altitudes. Test of weapons for space-based strategic defenses would make ASAT arms control moot, and for that reason the ASAT treaty should have the same cancellation clause as the modified ABM Treaty.

Increasingly powerful means for space surveillance are available to the United States, and would provide adequate verification of an ASAT test ban. As a hedge against violations, for protection from nondestructive ASAT techniques, and as a defense against subsidiary ASAT threats, high priority should be given to satellite protection—hardening, maneuverability, redundancy, and space-based and ground-based back-up systems. It should be recognized that in the absence of ASAT constraints satellite protection and space surveillance would have an even higher, and more costly, priority, but it is doubtful that protective measures for satellites could then cope with the ASAT threat.

*   *   *

In closing, we point to one proposition that merits support even from those who may disagree with some of our specific conclusions and recommendations:

The Executive and Congress, the media and the public, must pay more heed to aspects of national security policy that transcend the weapons themselves. In assessing military capability, or the likelihood of coping successfully with crisis, the ability of command to perform its complex tasks while under stress in a rapidly shifting scene, and even in the face of direct attack, is of paramount importance. Thus, the objective of effective command should be at the center of all facets of military planning, including its arms control dimension. The Executive and Congress should develop systematic procedures, in both classified and unclassified formats, for evaluating the impact on crisis stability of major new conventional and nuclear weapons systems, military and civilian organizational changes, alliance commitments, arms control agreements, and other national security initiatives.

NOTES

1. There is one very minor exception: the 1969 Sino-Soviet confrontation, by which time China had a number of nuclear bombs and missiles; see Chapter 10, Note 41.

2. This should not be misread to say that a conventional war would be less destructive than a "total" prenuclear war. The fire-power of today's conventional forces, and the fragility of contemporary societies, imply that a nonnuclear war in Europe would wreak far more devastation per day than did World War II.

3. General Douglas MacArthur before the Chinese intervention in Korea in 1950, and Secretary of State Henry Kissinger during the 1973 Yom Kippur Crisis.

4. We note that this is also the assessment of the International Institute of Strategic Studies: *The Military Balance 1985–1986* (London, 1985), p. 185. For discussions of the conventional balance in Europe, see Joshua M. Epstein, Kim R. Holmes, John J. Mearsheimer, and Barry R. Posen, "Policy Focus: The European Conventional Balance," *International Security* (1988), *12*:4, 152.

5. If the weapon is to be used on a target inside NATO territory, concurrence by that state would, in practice, also be required.

6. In principle, NATO could go to the highest alert level while leaving all warheads for its ground forces undispersed, and rely for nuclear readiness on dual-capable aircraft, on sea-based forces, and on missiles that can be fired from their peacetime locations. However, if that were done it would probably be impractical to subsequently bring such warheads to their means of delivery.

7. Low probability of radio interception can be provided with antennas that emit sharply focused (short wavelength) beams that are relayed via satellites such as MILSTAR, or unmanned drone aircraft (RPVs); encryption can be done by various means (e.g., digitized voice combined with spread spectrum modulation). As for laser communication to submarines, see p. 118.

8. Some depth charges on foreign soil do have PALs.

9. A recent example is provided by the Soviet "brigade" in Cuba which was "discovered" shortly after SALT II was signed; see Neustadt and May, pp. 92–96.

10. Interviews. The Six Day War of 1967 illustrates what this can lead to. In gaining Israel's withdrawal from the Sinai in 1956, President Eisenhower had apparently made

a private commitment to her should Egypt reintroduce major combat units into the peninsula. When Nasser did so in May 1967, Israel asked the Johnson administration to honor the U.S. pledge, but no record of what had actually transpired was available to the White House, which then had to rely on Eisenhower's vague recollections.

11. A similar proposal has also been made by R. James Woolsey, formerly Under Secretary of the Navy, "To Help Presidents Get Key Military Data," *The New York Times*, January 5, 1984; see also Stewart E. Eizenstat, "A Historical Memory for Presidents," *ibid.*, January 14, 1987. Note that our proposal for maintaining the expertise of the crisis support group is reminiscent of Napoleon's directed telescope (see p. 27).

12. See *Arms Control Today* (1987), *17*:8, 28.

13. William L. Ury and Richard Smoke, *Beyond the Hotline: Controlling a Nuclear Crisis* (Cambridge MA: Harvard Law School, 1984); Barry M. Blechman, editor, *Preventing Nuclear War* (Bloomington: Indiana University Press, 1985); and *Strengthening the U.S.-Soviet Communications Process to Reduce the Risks of Misunderstandings and Conflicts*, National Academy of Public Administration, Washington DC, April 1987.

14. A portion of this interim capability may now be provided on the Navy's fleet satellite communications (FLTSATCOM).

Glossary*

ABM	antiballistic missile (defense, treaty, etc.)
AFB	U.S. Air Force base
ALCM	air-launched cruise missile (carried on U.S. strategic bombers)
ANCA	Alternate NCA
ANMCC	Alternate National Military Command Center (Ft. Ritchie)
ASAT	antisatellite (weapon, treaty, etc.)
ASW	antisubmarine warfare
AWACS	Airborne Warning and Control System
BMD	ballistic missile defense
BMEWS	Ballistic Missile Early Warning System
"chop"	transfer of NATO members' forces to operational command of SACEUR
CBM	confidence building measure
CINCEUR	U.S. commander-in-chief, Europe
CINCLANT	U.S. commander-in-chief, Atlantic
CINCPAC	U.S. commander-in-chief, Pacific
CINCSAC	U.S. commander-in-chief, Strategic Air Command
CNO	U.S. chief of naval operations
COMOR	Committee on Overhead Reconnaissance (Cuban Crisis)
C³I	command, control, communications, and intelligence
DARPA	Defense Advanced Research Project Agency
DCI	director, Central Intelligence

*For full explanations see entries in index.

DEFCON	U.S. Defense condition (centrally coordinated alert posture)
DEW	directed energy weapon (lasers, etc.)
DIA	Defense Intelligence Agency
DPC	NATO's Defense Planning Committee
DSCS	Defense Satellite Communications System
Dual-Capable	any weapons system that can deliver conventional and nuclear munitions
DUCC	Deep Underground Command Center
D5	SLBM carrying 10 MIRVs to be deployed on U.S. Trident SSBNs
EAM	Emergency Action Message (e.g., an order to change alert status, to launch, to cease fire, etc.)
EHF	Extremely High Frequency radio (for line-of-sight communication)
ELF	Extremely Low Frequency radio (for communication with submerged SSBNs)
EMP	electromagnetic pulse
EOP	Emergency Operating Procedures (JCS)
ERCS	Emergency Rocket Communications System
EuCom	European Command (U.S.)
ExComm	President Kennedy's advisory group during the Cuban Missile Crisis (unofficial Executive Committee on NSC)
FLTSATCOM	Fleet Satellite Communications
FRG	Federal Republic of Germany (colloquially "West Germany")
Galosh	ground-based BMD system surrounding Moscow (also its ABM interceptor)
GEO	geosynchronous satellite orbit (a position above a fixed point on the equator at an altitude of about 22,000 miles)
G–I–N gap	Greenland–Iceland–Norway gap(s) (where passing vessels are susceptible to surveillance)
GKO	Soviet State Committee of Defense
GLCM	Ground-Launched Cruise Missile
GMCC	Ground Mobile Command Center
GPS	Global Positioning System (constellation of Navstar satellites whose radio signals allow a receiver to determine its own position and velocity with high accuracy)
GRU	Soviet Military Intelligence
GWEN	*Ground Wave Emergency Network*
HEMP	high altitude EMP
HF	High Frequency radio
ICBM	intercontinental ballistic missile

INF	Intermediate-Range Nuclear Forces
IONDS	Integrated Operation Nuclear Detonation Detection System
IR	infrared
IRBM	intermediate range ballistic missile
JCS	Joint Chiefs of Staff
JSTPS	Joint Strategic Targeting Planning Staff
LEO	low earth orbit, from hundreds to thousands of miles in altitude, in which satellites circumnavigate the globe (in about 90 minutes at lowest altitudes)
LERTCON	NATO alert condition
LF	Low Frequency radio
Looking Glass	CINCSAC's airborne command post
LOS	line-of-sight
LOW	launch-on-warning (i.e., before enemy nuclear detonations on the basis of tactical warning)
LPARs	large phased-array radars
LUA	launch-under-attack (i.e., following enemy nuclear detonations)
MBFR	Mutual and Balanced Force Reductions
MEECN	Minimum Essential Emergency Communications Network
MGT	mobile ground terminal
MHD	magnetohydrodynamic
MILSTAR	Military Strategic and Tactical Relay satellite (U.S. high altitude communication satellite, to be deployed)
Minuteman	U.S. ICBM carrying either one RV or three MIRVs
MIRV	multiple independently targeted RV
MGT	mobile ground terminal
MRBM	medium range ballistic missile
MX	U.S. ICBM carrying 10 MIRVs
NCA	U.S. National Command Authority (consisting of the president and secretary of defense, or their duly constituted successors)
NDS	Nuclear Detection System (nuclear detonation sensors aboard Navstar satellites; see GPS)
NEACP	National Emergency Airborne Command Post (pronounced "kneecap," for use by NCA and/or its alternates)
NMCC	National Military Command Center (in Pentagon)
NMCS	National Military Command System
NORAD	North American Air Defense Command
NRO	National Reconnaissance Office (responsible for satellite operations)
NSA	National Security Agency (principally responsible for SIGINT)

NSC	National Security Council. Statutory members: president, vice president, secretaries of state and defense; statutory advisers: DCI, JCS Chairman. Head of Staff: special assistant for national security affairs (colloquially national security adviser).
OAS	Organization of American States
OTH	over-the-horizon
PACCS	Post Attack Command and Control System
PAL	permissive action link (electromechanical device that prevents arming of nuclear warhead without receipt of coded message from higher authority)
PAVE PAWS	U.S. phased-array radars for early warning of SLBM attack
Pershing II	ground-mobile ballistic missile carrying one RV with terminal guidance; approximate range 1,000 miles
PVO	Soviet continental air defense forces
QRA	Quick Reaction Alert
RPV	remotely piloted vehicle (unmanned drone aircraft)
RV	reentry vehicle (ballistic missile warhead capable of withstanding atmospheric friction during reentry)
SAC	Strategic Air Command
SACEUR	Supreme Allied (NATO) Commander, Europe
SAM	Surface-to-Air Missile (for air defense)
SDI	Strategic Defense Initiative
SGEMP	System-generated EMP
SIGINT	signals intelligence
SIOP	Single Integrated Operational Plan
SLBM	submarine-launched ballistic missile
SLCM	sea-launched cruise missile
Specified Commands	SAC; Military Airlift; Aerospace, which incorporates NORAD.
SRF	Strategic Rocket Forces (Soviet)
Stavka	wartime General Headquarters of Soviet Supreme High Command
STOL	short takeoff and landing aircraft
Strategic Warning	indications that adversary is preparing forces in disposition consistent with a plan to attack
SSBN	nuclear-powered ballistic missile submarine
SSN	nuclear-powered attack submarine
SS-18	Soviet ICBM with 10 or more MIRVs
SS-20	Soviet ground-mobile theater-range (circa 3,000 miles) ballistic missile with three MIRVs
SS-24	Soviet rail-mobile ICBM with 8 to 10 MIRVs
SS-25	Soviet ground-mobile ICBM with IRV

START	Strategic Arms Reduction Talks
TACAMO	U.S. aircraft for communication to SSBNs
Tactical Warning	detection of the actual attack, before combat is joined
Tactical Nuclear Weapons	all nuclear delivery systems of less than intercontinental range, i.e., includes short-range battlefield weapons and theater-range weapons
Theater-Range	delivery systems having a range in excess of roughly 600 miles, but not intercontinental (e.g., Pershing II, SS-20, Tomahawk)
Tomahawk	U.S. cruise missile, carrying either a conventional or nuclear warhead, with range of 1,350 miles, based on land, surface ships and SSNs
TVD	Soviet Theater of Military Operations
WSAG	Washington Special Action Group (Kissinger's ExComm).
WTO	Warsaw Treaty Organization (colloquially "Pact")
UHF	Ultra-High Frequency radio
Unified Commands	Atlantic; Central (Southwest Asia & Horn of Africa, includes Rapid Deployment Force); European; Pacific; Readiness; Southern (Central and S. America, excluding Mexico); Space.
VLF	Very Low Frequency radio (for communication with submarines near the surface)
VTOL	Vertical take-off and landing aircraft

Bibliography

Abel, Elie, *The Missile Crisis* (Philadelphia: Lippincott, 1966)

Acheson, Dean, *Present at the Creation: My Years at the State Department* (New York: Norton, 1969)

Allison, Graham T., *Essence of Decision: Explaining the Cuban Missile Crisis* (Boston: Little, Brown, 1971)

Allison, Graham T., Albert Carnesale, and Joseph S. Nye, Jr., editors, *Hawks, Doves and Owls: An Agenda for Avoiding Nuclear War* (New York: Norton, 1985)

Ball, Desmond, and Jeffrey Richelson, editors, *Strategic Nuclear Targetting* (Ithaca: Cornell University Press, 1986)

Betts, Richard K., *Soldiers, Statesmen, and Cold War Crises* (Cambridge, MA: Harvard University Press, 1977)

Betts, Richard K., *Surprise Attack* (Washington: Brookings, 1982)

Betts, Richard K., *Nuclear Blackmail and Nuclear Balance* (Washington: Brookings, 1987)

Blair, Bruce G., *Strategic Command and Control* (Washington: Brookings, 1985)

Blechman, Barry M. and Stephen S. Kaplan, *Force Without War: U.S. Armed Forces as a Political Instrument* (Washington: Brookings, 1978)

Bracken, Paul, *The Command and Control of Nuclear Forces* (New Haven: Yale University Press, 1983)

Carter, Ashton B., John D. Steinbruner, and Charles A. Zraket, editors, *Managing Nuclear Operations* (Washington: Brookings, 1987); referred to throughout by *MNO*.

Collins, John M., *U.S.–Soviet Military Balance 1980–1985* (Washington: Pergamon-Brassey's, 1985)

Dean, Jonathon, *Watershed in Europe* (Lexington, Mass.: Heath and Co., 1987)

Dinerstein, Herbert S., *The Makings of a Missile Crisis* (Baltimore: Johns Hopkins University Press, 1976)

Gaddis, John L., *The Long Peace* (New York: Oxford University Press, 1987)

Garthoff, Raymond L., *Detente and Confrontation: from Nixon to Reagan* (Washington: Brookings, 1985)

Garthoff, Raymond L., *Reflections on the Cuban Missile Crisis* (Washington: Brookings; 1987)

George, Alexander L. and Richard Smoke, *Deterrence in American Foreign Policy* (New York: Columbia University Press, 1974)

Hillsman, Roger, *To Move a Nation* (New York: Doubleday, 1967)

Holloway, David, *The Soviet Union and the Arms Race* (New Haven: Yale University Press, 1984)

Horelick, Arnold and Myron Rush, *Strategic Power and Soviet Foreign Policy* (Chicago: University of Chicago Press, 1965)

Janis, Irving L., *Groupthink,* revised edition (Boston: Houghton Mifflin, 1982)

Jervis, Robert, *Perception and Misperception in International Politics* (Princeton: Princeton University Press, 1976)

Jervis, Robert, Richard Ned Lebow, and Janice Gross Stein, *Psychology and Deterrence* (Baltimore: Johns Hopkins University Press, 1985)

Joll, James, *The Origins of the First World War* (London: Longman, 1984)

Kennedy, Robert F., *Thirteen Days: A Memoir of the Cuban Missile Crisis* (New York: Norton, 1969)

Kissinger, Henry, *White House Years* (Boston: Little Brown, 1979)

Laquer, Walter, *A World of Secrets* (New York: Basic, 1985)

Larson, David L., ed. *The "Cuban Crisis" of 1962: Selected Documents and Chronology* (Boston: Houghton Mifflin, 1963)

Lebow, Richard Ned, *Between Peace and War: The Nature of International Crisis* (Baltimore: Johns Hopkins University Press, 1981)

Lebow, Richard Ned, *Nuclear Crisis Management* (Ithaca, NY: Cornell University Press, 1987)

Legge, J. Michael, *Theater Nuclear Weapons and the NATO Strategy of Flexible Response* (Santa Monica: RAND, 1983)

Long, Franklin A., Donald Hafner and Jeffrey Boutwell, editors, *Weapons in Space* (New York: Norton, 1986)

May, Ernest R., editor, *Knowing One's Enemies: Intelligence Assessments Before the Two World Wars* (Princeton: Princeton University Press, 1984)

Miller, Steven, editor, *Military Strategy and the Origins of the First World War* (Princeton: Princeton University Press, 1985)

Neustadt, Richard E. and Ernest R. May, *Thinking in Time* (New York: The Free Press, 1986)

Nixon, Richard M., *RN: The Memoirs of Richard Nixon* (New York: Grosset and Dunlop, 1978)

Paret, Peter, ed., *Makers of Modern Strategy* (Princeton: Princeton University Press, 1986)

Richelson, Jeffrey, *The US Intelligence Community* (Cambridge, MA: Ballinger, 1985)

Sorensen, Theodore, *Kennedy* (New York: Harper and Row, 1965)

Spector, Leonard S., *Going Nuclear* (Cambridge, MA: Ballinger, 1987)

Stares, Paul B., *Space and National Security* (Washington: Brookings, 1987)

Van Creveld, Martin, *Command in War* (Cambridge, MA: Harvard University Press, 1985)

Wohlstetter, Roberta, *Pearl Harbor: Warning and Decision* (Palo Alto: Stanford University Press, 1962)

About the Authors

Desmond Ball is Head and Professor in the Strategic and Defense Studies Centre at the Australian National University. He has previously held research posts at Harvard University and the International Institute of Strategic Studies, London. He has published widely on nuclear strategy and weapons, on command and control, and on national security decision making, most recently as co-editor of *Strategic Nuclear Targeting.*

Hans A. Bethe is Professor of Physics and Nuclear Studies, Emeritus, at Cornell University. A Nobel Laureate, he was director of the Theoretical Physics Division in the Manhattan Project's Los Alamos Laboratory, served on the President's Science Advisory Committee, and is a consultant to the Los Alamos and Livermore Laboratories. He has recently published several articles on strategic defense.

Bruce G. Blair is a Senior Fellow in foreign policy studies at the Brookings Institution. He was a project director at the Congressional Office of Technology Assessment and a Minuteman launch control officer. He is the author of *Strategic Command and Control: Redefining the Nuclear Threat,* which received the 1986 Edgar S. Furniss Award for Exceptional Book on National Security.

Paul Bracken is Professor of Public Policy at Yale University. A former senior staff member of the Hudson Institute for 9 years, his recent publications deal with nuclear strategy and control of security organizations. He is the author of *The Command and Control of Nuclear Forces,* and serves on the editorial boards of *Orbis, Journal of Conflict Resolution,* and *Defense Analysis.*

Ashton B. Carter is Associate Professor of Public Policy at Harvard University. After obtaining a Ph.D. in theoretical physics from Oxford University, where he was Rhodes Scholar, he worked at the Congressional Office of Technology Assessment (OTA), the Office of the Secretary of Defense, and the Massachusetts Institute of Technology. He has authored and co-edited studies on MX missile basing, ballistic missile defense, and nuclear operations, for OTA and the Brookings Institution.

Hillman Dickinson is a retired U.S. Army Lieutenant General. His last assignment was Director of Command, Control, and Communications Systems, Office of the Joint Chiefs of Staff. He previously commanded the Army Center of Command, Control and Communications, Research Development and Acquisition, served in the Defense Advanced Research Projects Agency, and commanded armored units. He is a graduate of the Army War College and holds a Ph.D. in physics from the Stevens Institute of Technology. He has published numerous articles concerning C³I, and is now an executive in private industry.

Richard L. Garwin is an IBM fellow at the Thomas J. Watson Research Center, and holds teaching and research positions at Columbia, Cornell, and Harvard Universities. He has served twice on the President's Science Advisory Committee, and on the Defense Science Board. Since the 1950s, he has been an active consultant to many branches of the U.S. government responsible for national security affairs. He has published widely on national security matters.

Kurt Gottfried is Professor of Physics and Nuclear Studies at Cornell University. He has published articles on antisatellite weapons, strategic defense, and arms control, and is a director of the Union of Concerned Scientists.

David Holloway is Professor of Political Science, and Member-in-Residence of the Center of International Security and Arms Control, at Stanford University. He is the author of *The Soviet Union and the Arms Race* and co-author of *The Reagan Strategic Defense Initiative.*

Henry W. Kendall is Professor of Physics at the Massachusetts Institute of Technology, and chairman of the Union of Concerned Scientists. He served for a decade as a consultant to the Department of Defense, and has recently published articles on ballistic missile defense and NATO's nuclear weapons policy.

Lloyd R. Leavitt, Jr., is a retired U.S. Air Force Lieutenant General. His last assignment was as Vice Commander-in-Chief, Strategic Air Command (1978–81). Before that he was Deputy Chief of Staff for Operations and Intelligence, U.S. Air Force, Europe; Deputy Director of Operations, Joint Chiefs of Staff; and held a variety of staff and command assignments. He is a graduate of the U.S. Military Academy and the National War College, and holds an M.A. in Public Administration from George Washington University. He was a Senior Vice-President of Cessna Aircraft Corp., and is now President of Qualitech Inc., in Long Beach, California, as well as a Visiting Scholar at Cornell University.

Richard Ned Lebow is Professor of Government and Director of the Peace Studies Program at Cornell University. He has previously taught strategy at the Naval and National War Colleges, and has been a scholar-in-residence at the Central Intelligence Agency. His publications include *Between War and Peace: The Nature of International Crisis, Psychology and Deterrence* (co-authored), and *Nuclear Crisis Management: A Dangerous Illusion.*

Condoleezza Rice is Associate Professor of Political Science, and Assistant Director of the Center for International Security and Arms Control, at Stanford University. She has been a Council on Foreign Relations Fellow at the Joint Chiefs of Staff, and is a consultant to The Rand Corp. and Science Applications Inc. Among her recent publications are *The Soviet Union and the Czechoslovak Army* and *The Making of Soviet Strategy.*

Peter C. Stein is Professor of Physics and Nuclear Studies at Cornell University. He has been cochair of United Campuses to Prevent Nuclear War, a campus-based organization promoting public education concerning the threat of nuclear war, and has recently served on the staff of the House Armed Services Committee.

John D. Steinbruner has been Director of Foreign Policy Studies at the Brookings Institution since 1978. Previously he was Associate Professor of Organization and Management at Yale University. He has published widely on command and control, nuclear strategy, and arms control, most recently as co-editor of the recent Brookings volume *Managing Nuclear Operations* (see bibliography).

Lucja U. Swiatkowski is Director of Soviet Studies at The National Institute for Public Policy. During 1986, she was a Guest Scholar at the Brookings Institution. She holds a Ph.D. in international relations and Soviet and East European Studies from Columbia University. From 1981 to 1985 she was a systems engineer at The MITRE Corp., where she published studies on Western and Soviet strategic C^3I.

Paul D. Tomb is a retired U.S. Navy Rear Admiral. His last assignment (1983–84) was as Deputy Director of the C^3 Directorate in the Office of the Joint Chiefs of Staff. Before that he was Vice-Director of the Joint Strategic Connectivity Staff located at SAC headquarters. Following his graduation from the U.S. Naval Academy in 1951 with a degree in electrical engineering, he served on and commanded nuclear submarines, rising to become Commander of Submarines, Mediterranean. He has also served on the staffs of the Navy Secretariat and the Chief of Naval Operations. Currently he is Deputy Director of the C^3 Systems Group at Science Applications International Corp.

Author Index

Subject Index